GOVERNANCE IN THE NEW SOUTH AFRICA

THE CHALLENGES OF GLOBALISATION

Edited by Guy Mhone and Omano Edigheji

Governance in the New South Africa: The Challenges of Globalisation

University of Cape Town Press
PO Box 24309
Lansdowne 7779

First published 2003
© 2003, University of Cape Town Press and University of the Witwatersrand

ISBN 0-191713-875

Project management: Fiona Wakelin
Copy-editing: Laurie Rose-Innes
Design and typesetting: Unwembi Communications, Cape Town
Cover design: Eugene Badenhorst
Indexing: Jan Schaafsma
Printing and binding: Paarl Print

Set in 9pt on 14 pt Stone Serif

Contents

Contributors

Patrick Bond was born in Northern Ireland and educated in the US. He is an academic and activist, based in Johannesburg since 1990, and has drafted numerous policy papers for the ANC government, but works most closely with social, environmental and labour movements. Patrick is a professor at the University of the Witwatersrand Graduate School of Public and Development Management. His books include *Unsustainable South Africa* (2002), *Fanon's Warning* (editor, 2002), *Zimbabwe's Plunge* (co-author, 2002), *Against Global Apartheid* (2001), *Cities of Gold, Townships of Coal* (2000), *Elite Transition* (2000), *An RDP Policy Audit* (co-editor, 1999) and *Uneven Zimbabwe* (1998).

Omano Edigheji is a senior researcher at the Graduate School of Public and Development Management, University of the Witwatersrand. He is a co-director of the Globalisation and Governance Project. Edigheji has extensive research experience and expertise, including as Research Co-ordinator of the National Economic Development and Labour Council (Nedlac). He is a political economist and is completing his PhD on globalisation and the political economy of South Africa at the Department of Sociology and Political Science, Norwegian University of Science and Technology, Trondheim, Norway. Edigheji has a number of publications to his name. He conducted research on issues of governance and development for organisations in and outside South Africa. In the 1990s, Edigheji was a leading human rights and pro-democracy activist in Nigeria, and was illegally detained by General Babangida's military regime in its dying days.

Nomboniso Gasa is a researcher and gender policy analyst. She is a former commissioner of the Commission for Gender Equality (CGE). In the early and mid-1990s, she worked for the ANC Commission on the Emancipation of Women and was part of the policy and constitutional debates on gender equality. Gasa has worked in Nigeria on constitutionalism, democracy and governance, and developed the Nigeria Programme for the International Institute for Democracy and Electoral Assistance. She has written extensively and has published academic, creative and journalistic pieces on women's status, gender equality and masculinity. In her current research, she interrogates the meanings of manhood in Xhosa traditional society and the implications for women and equality. Gasa is a poet and has a novel in preparation.

Thulani Guliwe is an independent researcher and a student at the Graduate School of Public and Development Management. He studied social policy at the University of Durban-Westville, and has worked on rural water projects in KwaZulu-Natal. His interests include neo-liberal processes in global and local settings.

Adam Habib is Director of the Centre for Civil Society (CCS), a professor at the School of

Development Studies, University of Natal, and a part-time research director at the Human Sciences Research Council (HSRC). He serves on the boards of directors and/or advisory boards of the International Society for Third Sector Research (ISTR), the Centre for Public Participation (CPP), Thusanang (Southern African Non-Governmental Organisation Network, Sangonet), and the Alternative Information Development Centre (AIDC) in Cape Town. Adam has also served on the Council of the University of Durban-Westville. He has extensive academic experience, having taught at both graduate and undergraduate levels, and having supervised both Masters and Doctoral students. He has published extensively, with over 40 edited books, chapters, and national and international journal articles in the areas of democratic transition, political economy, institutional transformation, higher education reform and state-civil society relations. Adam also co-edits the well-known South African social science journal, *Transformation*, and the political science journal, *Politikon*. He regularly contributes opinion editorials and is approached for commentary on political issues by both the print and broadcast media in the country.

Ebrahim-Khalil Hassen is the head of public-sector research at the National Labour and Economic Development Institute (Naledi). This think-tank is the key informer of trade union policy in South Africa and is highly influential in determining labour's positions. The public-sector programme runs a research project for Cosatu, the South African Council of Churches and the South African NGO Coalition on public expenditure, to influence government budget decisions. Its research has influenced the restructuring of Spoornet and it has managed similar research on Eskom and Telkom. The unit is expanding into other areas, including service delivery. Between 1996 and 1998, Hassen worked for the Gauteng provincial government. He is a graduate of the University of the Witwatersrand.

Hermien Kotzé is Research Manager of the Centre for Civil Society (CCS) at the University of Natal, where she runs a research grant programme and does research and post-graduate teaching. She holds a Masters degree from the London School of Economics and has extensive experience in the field of development and civil society, both at tertiary education level and in the NGO sector. During the 1990s she held a number of senior management positions in NGOs, more particularly at the Institute for Democracy in South Africa (Idasa). Her experience in NGOs ranges from peace facilitation to managing a development organisation's projects and policy research on poverty and development issues. She has published a number of opinion pieces and chapters in books on these topics.

Kirsty McLean began her university career studying music with a BMus at the University of the Witwatersrand from 1992 to 1995. After performing and teaching for a number of years, she returned to the university to complete her LLB in 2001. In 2002, McLean worked as a legal researcher for Justice Kate O'Regan at the South African Constitutional Court and as a part-time lecturer in law at the School of Law, University of the Witwatersrand. She intends to undertake a PhD in the enforcement of socio-economic rights.

Anne Mc Lennan is a senior lecturer and Assistant Director: Academic Affairs at the Graduate School of Public and Development Management, University of the Witwatersrand. Her doctoral thesis, entitled *Education Governance and Management in South Africa*, was read at the University of Liverpool. She received a Master of Education with distinction from the University of the Witwatersrand in March 1992, where she had also obtained her BA and Honours in Political Studies. Before joining the "P&DM" as research co-ordinator and lecturer in 1992, Anne was employed as an education policy researcher at the Education Policy Unit (Edupol). In addition to her academic work, Anne is involved in management development initiatives and policy work at national and provincial levels. Anne has published in the areas of gender, public service change, education management, development and change and course development. She has co-edited a book with Barry Munslow and Patrick FitzGerald entitled *Managing Sustainable Development in South Africa*.

Guy Mhone is a professor of Public and Development Management at the University of the Witwatersrand. He was previously with the South African Department of Labour, the International Labour Office and the Sapes Trust, as well as having taught at the State University of New York, the New School, Howard University and the University of Zimbabwe. He is trained as an economist and has written and published on development and labour market issues in Africa, Southern Africa and individual countries in the sub-region. He serves on a number of boards of research organisations, including the Council for the Development of Social Science Research in Africa (Codesria).

Thomas Mathukhu Mogale is a senior lecturer at the University of the Witwatersrand's Graduate School of Public and Development Management. His undergraduate studies were completed at the University of the North. He obtained his MSc in politics at the University of London's Graduate School of Oriental and African Studies, and then a PhD at the University of Pittsburgh. Thomas lectures courses on development management and local governance in the Masters programme at the School of Public and Development Management. He has undertaken several studies on local governance, planning and economic development, rural development planning and poverty reduction, SMMEs and the social impact of micro-finance on livelihoods in rural provinces in South Africa.

Preface and Acknowledgements

This book is a product of a research project entitled "Globalisation and the Challenges of Governance in Post-Apartheid South Africa".

The idea for the research arose out of a number of extended conversations we had in 1999 about the likely impact of globalisation on governance, democratisation and development in Africa. These conversations occurred at a time when African countries, including South Africa, were under both internal and external pressures to liberalise their economies and at the same time promote democratic governance as the solution to their political and economic problems. Economic liberalisation and democratic governance were seen by their proponents as the basis for global competitiveness and equitable development. Following these conversations, we decided to carry out a research project that focused on South Africa. This choice was informed by the fact that following the 1994 non-racial multiparty elections, the democratic government in South Africa was confronted with the need to develop effective governance mechanisms and structures, within and outside the state, that would be effective, efficient, responsive, representative, participatory, transparent and accountable. These were seen as necessary conditions for the state to be able to meet its developmental challenges of promoting social equity, eradicating poverty, creating jobs and increasing access to basic services, especially to the previously disadvantaged communities, while at the same time growing the economy and ensuring its global competitiveness.

The government has set up mechanisms towards the realisation of democratic governance, which have entailed the decentralisation of powers between the three spheres of government, namely, the national, provincial and local levels, all of which are distinctive, interdependent and interrelated. Furthermore, a strategic priority for the democratic government has been the need to promote participatory policy making by involving trade unions, business and civil society in the policy process. These developments, however, coincided with the globalisation of economic, political and socio-cultural activities, with profound implications for democratic governance and the promotion of equitable growth and development across the globe, including South Africa. Given its quest for democratic governance, reintegration into the global economy, economic growth and sustainable human development, South Africa provides an appropriate case-study to examine the feasibility or otherwise of achieving these objectives in the era of globalisation. We are also interested in the South African case because we believed that its successful political and economic transformation would have positive ramifications for the rest of the African continent.

Against this background, a research project was proposed, which was subsequently funded by the Ford Foundation. The research project was exploratory and was undertaken to assess the implications of globalisation on the nature, capacity, character and scope of democratic governance and the pursuit of development in the post-apartheid period. A central *problematique* of the research relates to the challenges of globalisation on governance and its impact on equitable development in South Africa. The research had three broad aims:

- to examine the challenges of globalisation, both opportunities and constraints, on governance and development;
- to provide research outputs that will assist policy makers in government, business, trade unions and civil society to enhance their governance capacity; and
- to promote critical participation and dialogue between academics and policy makers on the issues of globalisation, governance and development in South Africa.

After the funding was secured, researchers from different academic disciplines were invited to participate in the project, with the aim of developing deeper and broader insights into the research *problematique* while ensuring interdisciplinarity in our approach. We started by holding a methodology workshop for all the researchers. This was followed by the actual research and the writing of the various chapters, on completion of which a workshop was held for academics and policy makers where all the papers were presented. This book is a product of this research.

We owe a number of people and institutions gratitude and appreciation. To begin with, we would like to express special thanks to all the researchers whose participation and co-operation contributed to the successful completion of the project. We are especially thankful to the Research Assistants, Thulani Guliwe, Ronnet Ravhura, Maputle Kgasago and Jimmy Mawelela for their able assistance.

We are grateful to the participants of the workshop, including the Acting Vice Chancellor of the University of the Witwatersrand, Professor Loyiso Nongxa, and the Minister of Public Service and Administration, Ms Geraldine Fraser-Moleketi for their critical and constructive inputs, which enabled all the researchers to sharpen their analysis and revise their respective chapters. The debates were greatly enhanced and enlivened by the penetrating comments and participation of Gillian Hart, Shedrack Gutto, William Mervin Gumede, Devan Pillay, Steven Friedman, Moeletsi Mbeki, Chris Lansberg, Michael Sachs, Godfrey Mokate, Sanusha Naidu, Gayleatha Brown, Alison Gilwald, Thembeka Mufamadi, Peter Draper, Hanlie Van Dyk-Robertson, Musa Abutudu, Nico Cloete, Halima Mahomed, Ivor Chipkin, Paula Nimpuno, Korwa Adar, Tholakele Khumalo, Eddie Webster, Shireen Hassim, Raymond Suttner, Mohamed Motala, Margarethe Mostert,

Horald Motshwane, Doreen Musson, Paul Graham and Herbert Vilakazi. Furthermore, we are particularly indebted to all the anonymous reviewers of the various chapters for their insightful and constructive comments.

We are extremely grateful to the Ford Foundation for its generous funding of the research project, which enabled us to develop our ideas more fully. Special thanks are due to John Nkomo for encouraging us to embark on the project and to Gary Hawes for his patient and continuing support.

Also, special thanks are due to the Graduate School of Public and Development Management of the University of the Witwatersrand for providing us with administrative support and the intellectual environment to undertake the project.

On a more personal note, we owe our deepest gratitude to our partners, Yvonne Mhone and Sharon Edigheji, for all their emotional and intellectual support in the course of the research.

Guy Mhone and Omano Edigheji

Graduate School of Public and Development Management
University of the Witwatersrand
South Africa

July 2003

Dedication

Millions of ordinary South Africans struggled ... over decades, to improve their lives, to restore peace, and to bring about a more just society.

... Only a comprehensive approach to harnessing the resources of our country can reverse the crisis created by apartheid. Only an all-round effort to harness the life experience, skills, energies and aspirations of the people can lay the basis for a new South Africa.

... No democracy can survive and flourish if the mass of our people remain in poverty, without land, without tangible prospects for a better life. Attacking poverty and deprivation must therefore be the first priority of a democratic government.

... Above all, the people affected must participate in decision-making. Democratisation must begin to transform both the state and civil society. Democracy is not confined to periodic elections. It is, rather, an active process enabling everyone to contribute to the reconstruction and development.

... We must not perpetuate the separation of our society into a "first world" and a "third world" – another way of preserving apartheid. We must not confine growth strategies to the former, while doing patchwork and piecemeal development in the latter, waiting for trickle-down development.

The Reconstruction and Development Programme, 1994

1

Globalisation and the Challenges of Governance in the New South Africa: Introduction

Guy Mhone and Omano Edigheji

Introduction

The demise of apartheid and advent of democratisation in South Africa coincided with a number of critical global developments, namely, the ascendancy of globalisation and economic liberalism based on market fundamentalism, and the emergence of the "third wave" of democratisation encompassing countries of the former socialist bloc and spreading to a number of developing countries in Africa, Asia and Latin America. This conjuncture also coincided with an undercurrent of increasing dissatisfaction with the emerging global order and its associated market fundamentalism and negative consequences for equitable development, governance and environmental sustainability. It coincided, too, with increasing interest (propelled by the revival of institutional analysis) in the lessons to be learned from the East Asian experience with respect to the role of the state in promoting development (Amsden, 1989; Evans 1995; Wade 1990).

This conjuncture has particular import for a country like South Africa, given its history and enduring socio-economic legacy of inequalities with respect to wealth and income distribution, and access to employment and income generating opportunities, social services and economic infrastructure, whereby the majority Black and predominantly African population has been disadvantaged and the White population has been the privileged minority. Thus, South Africa is confronted with the major challenges of attempting to promote democratisation, good governance and sustainable human development in the context of gross domestic socio-economic inequalities and a history of past conflict, and in the context of an increasingly integrated global order driven by market fundamentalism, albeit one that is being challenged from a number of quarters.

Within the above context, democratic South Africa desires and is expected by domestic constituencies and various external parties to develop effective governance mechanisms – institutions (rules) and organisations – to make its economy globally competitive while simultaneously improving the standard of living of all South Africans, especially the previously disadvantaged communities. The need for the latter is especially compelling, because there is the expectation by the Black population that democracy will result in the improvement of their material conditions through expanded services and improved service delivery and increased employment and income generating opportunities.

Towards the realisation of these objectives, and in the context of a number of other social, economic, and sectoral policies, new governance mechanisms, which include the restructuring of the public sector, and an emphasis on the participation of key social actors – business (private sector), labour and other civil society organisations (CSOs) – in the policy process, are being pursued by the democratic government. Similarly, there are constitutionally enshrined institutions that act as a check on state power. These developments coincide with the emergence of globalisation. Global processes such as international trade, foreign direct investment, portfolio investment and financial flows, the activities of trans-national corporations (TNCs) and multilateral organisations like the World Trade Organisation (WTO), the International Monetary Fund (IMF) and the World Bank are influencing governance in South Africa, as they do in other parts of the world. To a large degree, these processes and actors exert pressure on the state to liberalise and deregulate the economy, as well as to privatise public enterprises. Thus, the nature of socio-economic policies is substantially influenced by globalisation processes that significantly reduce the scope for government intervention. However, the ability of the South African government to meet its democratic commitments to the people – by, for instance, expanding job and income generating opportunities, providing expanded and improved basic services, and generally ensuring an expanding and inclusive globally competitive economy – and to meaningfully engage with the globalisation process also very much depends on the governance capacity within and between the state and society, albeit within constraints and possibilities imposed by both the domestic and external environments.

This book is a compilation of research papers that address the overall challenges and tensions that confront South Africa in its quest for democratisation and good governance, and the promotion of equitable growth and development, in the context of domestic and external pressures to adhere to economic liberalism and the imperatives of globalisation. This *problematique* or nexus of challenges is not unique to South Africa. There is an extensive literature that discusses: the prerequisites for consolidating democracy in the context of the current global order (Huntington, 1991; Przerwoski, 1991); the requirements of a developmental state that is also compatible with democratic forms of governance (Evans,

1995, 1996; Leftwitch, 1996; Weiss, 1998; Sklar, 1996; Robinson and White, 1998); the degree to which the quest for democratic governance and development may be compatible with economic liberalism and market fundamentalism (Przerwoski, 1991); and the political economy of the relations between the state and its various tiers or spheres, between the state and civil society and between the social partners (government, labour and employer organisations) and the manner in which each one of these is constituted in relation to the tasks of democratisation and the promotion of development, implying inclusive, broad-based and equitable economic growth (Manor, 1998). This book attempts to bring the themes arising from the literature to bear on the South African situation. The research upon which the book is based relied primarily on secondary material, coupled with interviews in some of the contributions, with the aim of tabling the issues for further debate and research with respect to the South African situation.

It is necessary at this stage to give an indication of our general understanding of the key concepts that are the basis of engagement in this book, even if these concepts are discussed further in subsequent chapters, especially Chapters 2 and 3. The aim here is to give a working definition of the concepts without necessarily discussing the various contending views related to them, even if these are indicated to some degree in this introduction.

The concept of *democratisation* is understood to entail two aspects: a formal aspect, which relates to the need for representative forms of government with periodic elections based on universal adult suffrage and other related aspects of what is normally understood to be representative democracy, underpinned by constitutionally and legally entrenched protection of universal human rights and freedoms; and what may be referred to as the substantive aspect, which refers to the need to ensure that the citizenry has access to socio-economic entitlements such as key assets, income generating and employment opportunities, and basic services such as housing, water, education, health, sanitation, safety and security. The assumption underlying the various contributions in this book is that the consolidation of democracy, that is, entrenching democratic governance, should entail the need to ensure that both formal and substantive aspects of democracy are promoted.

The concept of *governance* is understood to refer to the manner in which the apparatus of the state is constituted, how it executes its mandate and its relationship to society, in general, and to particular constituencies such as the private sector, civil society, non-governmental organisations and community organisations, and how it fulfils the substantive aspects of democracy as defined above. Hence, good governance may be understood to have at least three aspects: first, the need for a rule-based, open, transparent, efficient and accountable government; second, the need for the government to undertake its task in a manner that is participatory and consultative and that generally lives up to the democratic precepts of formal democracy; and, third, the need for the government or the state to ensure that substantive aspects of democracy are achieved, which would be compatible with the need to attain sustainable human development in the long term. Thus, good governance refers both to the overall environment that is deemed conducive to all three outcomes, and to the degree to which each of the outcomes is formalised and made routine in the everyday affairs of the government and state.

The notion of *development* is understood to refer to the various aspects generally subsumed under the goal of sustainable human development. This encompasses the need to promote economic growth in an inclusive manner, such that the majority of the labour force is involved in contributing to economic growth, and the majority of the population shares in its fruits without compromising the needs of future generations to enjoy similar or better standards of living. Thus, development, as it is generally accepted, has economic, social, human and environmental dimensions, all of which need to be promoted in a mutually sustainable manner. For developing economies, the promotion of sustainable human development, or development in short, necessarily entails structural transformation of the domestic socio-economic environment such that underdevelopment and its associated economic, social, human and environmental maladies are progressively eliminated, at the same time that the country's position and role in the international economy are also redefined to sustain the development outcome. Thus, development, or sustainable human development, refers to growth with equity and environmental sustainability.

The term *globalisation* is understood to refer to the growth and expansion of various international flows, such as those related to goods and services, finance, information, individuals, technology and capital goods, in a manner that considerably limits the ability of individual nation-states, or current multilateral and bilateral bodies, to control or regulate them adequately. As noted by Hirst and Thompson (1996:263), for instance:

> There is no doubt that the salience and role of nation-states have changed markedly since the Keynesian era. States are less autonomous, they have less exclusive control over the economic and social processes within their territories, and they are less able to maintain national distinctiveness and cultural homogeneity.

Globalisation is understood to be a phenomenon that is primarily driven by the imperatives of major multinational corporations and their home governments, with various multilateral and bilateral agencies as their intermediaries and facilitators. The phenomenon is one that has its structural manifestations and underpinnings in market-driven economic processes and market fundamentalism. These processes are rationalised through the dogma of economic liberalisation, as represented by what has been referred to as the Washington Consensus, or neo-liberalism, in some circles. In Africa, and many developing countries elsewhere, this aspect has been manifested in the adoption of structural adjustment and stabilisation programmes. A major feature of globalisation is that it has unequal benefits, which tend to be concentrated in countries that are already better off, while the negative consequences tend to be concentrated among developing countries that find such outcomes relatively unmanageable. Thus, Castells (1998) observes that globalisation represents:

> a dramatic leap forward in productive forces and economic growth. Yet, it also displays its exclusionary logic as millions of people and large areas of the planet are being excluded from the benefits, ... both in the developed and developing worlds.

In a similar vein, the founding document of the New Partnership for Africa's Development (Nepad, 2001:7) notes that:

> Globalisation has increased the ability of the strong to advance their interests to the detriment of the weak, ... It has limited the space for developing countries to control their own development, as the system makes no provision for compensating the weak. The conditions of those marginalised in this process have worsened in real terms. A fissure between inclusion and exclusion has emerged within and among countries.

It should be noted, nonetheless, that the process of globalisation is generating oppositional forces from below, intent on controlling, reversing or modifying this process to the benefit of humankind.

The above concepts and their associated *problematique* are of particular relevance to South Africa. This is a country that has emerged from one of the most oppressive and exploitative regimes in modern history in which racial, class and gender oppression were consciously intertwined to underpin a system of domination and subjugation that kept the majority Black and predominantly African population in relative poverty and destitution, while it systematically empowered the White minority economically, socially and politically. Thus, the previous system was patently undemocratic, reflecting what in current terminology would be referred to as bad governance, especially from the point of view of the Black and African population. In addition, while the system managed to achieve a fairly high degree of development for the minority White population, the Black majority remained relatively impoverished with a high incidence of unemployment, poverty and attendant social and health maladies. This system was challenged from within and without, resulting in its collapse and the emergence of a new dispensation based on democratic and developmental precepts.

The new South Africa has one of the most progressive and enlightened constitutions, which has been buttressed by complementary legislation to lay the ground for formal democracy in unequivocal terms. It is a country that has also committed itself to good governance through various initiatives that encompass the establishment of consultative and participatory statutory bodies such as the National Economic Development and Labour Council (Nedlac) and the Gender and Youth Commissions. It has gone further to ensure that independent structures are in place to monitor relations between the state and the polity through such bodies as the Human Rights Commission and the Public Protector. Accordingly, the apparatus of the state has been transformed to ensure that it has the potential and capability to live up to good governance as reflected, for instance, in the *Batho Pele*, the public sector restructuring that such governance has entailed to facilitate its realisation. Thus, South Africa is committed not only to formal democracy, but also to good governance in both its narrow and broad dimensions.

The new South Africa is also committed to substantive democracy and sustainable human development. With the Reconstruction and Development Programme and the policies, programmes and projects emanating from it that are being implemented, the government has insisted on the need to progressively reduce the various economic, social, health and human development deficits inherited from the apartheid era, which continue to haunt the polity. It has positioned itself as a developmental state committed to fast-tracking economic growth, social delivery, employment promotion, poverty reduction and general social upliftment, by ensuring that an economy grows and develops that is competitive, inclusive of the historically excluded and marginalised, and environmentally sustainable. While accepting the imperatives of globalisation and the market, as reflected in the adoption of the Growth, Employment and Redistribution macroeconomic management policy framework, it has resolutely articulated the need for the state to proactively steer the economy toward the outcome of sustainable human development for the majority of its populace. The African National Congress (ANC) government and the country cannot be faulted with respect to a commitment to democracy, development and good governance. It is of interest, nonetheless, to assess the degree to which the objectives of development, democratisation and good governance can be achieved in the current global environment, within an economic policy framework informed by the Washington Consensus as the overriding paradigm, and given the nature of existing social relations and configurations within society, in general, and civil society, in particular, and between these two and the state.

As noted, this book attempts to assess the implications of globalisation and its associated market fundamentalism for the pursuit of democracy and development through good governance. Accordingly, the book addresses the following themes:

(a) The relationship between the quests for democratisation, good governance and promotion of equitable growth and development and the reliance on market fundamentalism and economic liberalism as the dominant and overriding paradigm within which economic and social policies are formulated and implemented.

(b) The implications of tensions and/or synergies arising from (a) for relations between the state and society in the quest for formalising and institutionalising democratic forms of governance.

(c) The implications of the tensions and/or synergies arising from (a) for the relations between civil society and the state, for the manner in which civil society may be constituted and for the ability of the state to promote democratisation, good governance and development in the context of economic liberalism.

(d) The implications of the quest for decentralisation for the promotion of democracy, good governance and development in the context of economic liberalism.

This book considers the above issues on three levels. At one level, the contributions interrogate the various themes deductively, in order to assess the compatibility or non-compatibility of the quest for development, democratisation and good governance with the pursuit of integration into the global economy based on economic liberalisation of the economy and the pursuit of various policies predicated on the efficacy of the market as the fundamental mechanism for allocating resources and promoting development. At this level, the issue is to assess whether, in the current conjuncture, the objectives of democracy, good governance and development are inherently compatible with the imperatives of globalisation and market fundamentalism. The issue posed at the first level is the preoccupation of many of the contributions in the book, and claims made can be assessed on their analytical merits.

At the second level, the contributions pose a purely positivistic concern, amenable to subsequent empirical testing or verification, as to what the consequences of the current configuration of policies and practices entail for the pursuit of democracy, good governance and sustainable human development. At this level, one takes the claims of the government at face value and merely investigates what their possible outcomes have been so far and what they are likely to be in the foreseeable future. This is an empirical issue for which this book has not summoned enough data to make a compelling case for any conclusions reached, and is one that would need a more detailed follow-up study.

The third level is purely normative and is premised on a simple desire to have the plight of millions resolved, based on the need to promote and attain sustainable human development, along the lines of the various millennium goals that are being proposed internationally. Of course, it is recognised that good intentions are not enough, in themselves, to inform on the specific nature of the policies needed to achieve the goals; but it is necessary to restate them as a basis for policy debate and the search for alternative ways of achieving the goals, in order to avoid any tendencies toward complacency or, indeed, intransigence as policy makers withdraw into their comfort zones.

The structure of the book

The book is divided into three thematic parts: Part 1 on economic liberalisation and the quest for development and co-operative governance; Part 2 on decentralisation and development; and Part 3 on the state and civil society. In addition to these thematic parts, Part 4 considers democratic governance and developmentalism.

Part 1 problematises the overall issue of the relationship between the pursuit of the objectives of development, democratisation and good governance and the perceived need to align the country's economy with global imperatives through the adoption and implementation of policy measures primarily guided by market fundamentals and economic liberalisation. This section also addresses the nature of state-society relations in the context of globalisation and policy developments predicated on market imperatives.

In Chapter 2, Guy Mhone addresses the relationship between democratisation, economic liberalisation and the quest for development in South Africa. The chapter begins by reviewing the literature pertaining to the key concepts of development, globalisation, democratisation and governance, and then proceeds to discuss the potential tensions between the need to promote sustainable human development and both formal and substantive democracy and the pursuit of neo-liberal policies as the instrument for achieving these goals, especially in the context of a developing country like South Africa, which has been bequeathed high levels of inequality, unemployment and poverty. The chapter attempts to demonstrate the foregoing tension deductively, but also proceeds to contend that current developments in South Africa are such that the objectives of sustainable human development and democracy are likely to be compromised, unless the policy paradigm is heavily skewed toward proactive developmental measures rather than the need to accommodate global and market imperatives *per se*.

In Chapter 3, Omano Edigheji examines state-society relations in post-apartheid South Africa, considering the National Economic Development and Labour Council (Nedlac) and how the government has adopted some major policies without recourse to the council. The chapter shows the tensions and contradictions between reforms based on an ideology of market triumphalism and co-operative governance, which are often overlooked by proponents of consultative and participatory processes across the political spectrum. Some of these market-driven reforms lacked popular support, as the government bypassed participatory structures and consultative processes to impose such policies on society, which in turn undermines the trust, reciprocity and co-operation that are necessary if consultative and participatory processes and structures are to succeed. The writer shows that the outcome of participatory processes is not given – at times it can enhance development and democracy, and at other times it can undermine development and democracy, including entrenching the interests and dominance of privileged groups in society to the detriment of the poor and the marginalised. Edigheji proposes what he calls "a different kind of politics" as an alternative to "the god of the market and its values of commodification, individualisation and monetisation", in order to ensure democratic governance and sustainable and equitable development.

Ebrahim-Khalil Hassen, in Chapter 4, focuses on state-society relations in the South African public service, using the bargaining council, the Public Service Co-ordinating Council (PSCBC) and collective bargaining between the public sector unions and the government as the focus of the analysis. The writer discusses the evolution of state-society relations in the public service in terms of three phases. He discusses how international trends and global discourses of new managerialism, located in the neo-liberal framework, have influenced the restructuring of the public service in the democratic dispensation. He proceeds to explore the implications of this approach to public sector reforms for governance in the sector, in particular, and democratic governance, in general, as well as for the capacity of the state to provide basic services to the population in a way that is efficient, effective and equitable. Hassen concludes that the ascendancy of new managerialism in the South African public service has the tendency to consolidate the power of senior state bureaucrats over the content and nature of the reform process, with attendant negative consequences on democratic governance. He concludes, further, that there is a need to redefine the relationship between the government and citizens, who are consequently conceived of as clients and consumers, rather than as the electorate from whom the government derives its mandate and to whom it must be accountable.

Part 2 addresses issues related to decentralisation and development. The chapters in this section investigate the nature and impact of intergovernmental relations, intergovernmental fiscal relations and the need for service delivery and citizens' participation in governance and the pursuit of development, and how these are impacted upon by economic liberalisation, deregulation and privatisation of the provision of basic services.

In Chapter 5, Kirsty McLean examines housing delivery in the context of co-operative government in post-1994 South Africa. Writing from a legal perspective, McLean reviews and interprets legal provisions, policy documents and court judgments related to housing provision. Against this background, she discusses the practices of co-operative government in the housing sector and how they differ from the legislative and constitutional model of co-operative governance. Further, McLean notes the various factors that have shaped South African housing policy, and identifies one area of major concern in South African housing policy, which relates to the need to give certainty to the market, an approach that has been hailed by its proponents as a necessary condition for global competitiveness. The writer demonstrates how the decentralisation of housing has resulted in role confusion and tensions and the consequent competition between the different spheres of government, thereby raising the potential of the different spheres developing divergent policies. This is seen to lead to conflicts that impact negatively on effective housing delivery. McLean observes that provincial governments are abdicating their responsibility for housing delivery to local governments, in the face of which local governments are taking up the responsibility for housing delivery, for which they have no legislative mandate – this is what the writer calls the "unfunded mandate" of local government coupled with a lack of institutional capacity for housing delivery. While acknowledging the merits of co-operative government, which she notes is still in its formative stages, the writer observes that even when the specific roles and duties of the different spheres become clearer, more concrete tensions will still emerge.

In Chapter 6, Anne Mc Lennan explores the relationship between globalisation, governance and development in the South African education sector by tracking the process and implications of decentralisation. The writer examines in detail the resultant tensions and contradictions flowing from the influence of globalisation on governance in the post-apartheid education system. Mc Lennan points out that post-apartheid education governance has been shaped by global conditions and local contexts, with their contradictory effects on education governance and development. The writer shows that decentralisation of education, with its emphasis on partnership and the sharing of responsibility, has tended to privatise the cost of education by passing costs to local communities, which, in turn, reinforces racial inequalities in the system, as the privileged White communities (and the small Black élite) who are able to afford the fees take advantage of the decentralisation process. Thus, according to Mc Lennan, there is nothing inherent in decentralisation that would necessarily improve the interactions between stakeholders, nor is it given that it would lead to equitable development, as the South African education system seems to illustrate.

The contribution by Thomas Mogale, in Chapter 7, examines the relationship between developmental local governance and decentralised service delivery. It explores the implications of current policies aimed at promoting local economic development and poverty reduction in the context of the current thrust of decentralisation in South Africa, which aims to locate developmental initiatives within local authorities while also encouraging consultative and participatory approaches to policy making and implementation. Mogale discusses the various tensions arising partly from the nature of the formal dispensations that underpin the mandates of the three spheres of government; partly from the packages of policies that are being promoted as vehicles for local development and poverty reduction, especially in so far as they are constrained by macroeconomic parameters and the need to conform to market-driven modalities; partly from the nature of the fiscal allocations between the three spheres of government; and partly from the shortcomings of the current participatory and consultative mechanisms and processes at the local level. Mogale concludes that the main challenge for developmental local government in South Africa is the need to ensure that current decentralisation efforts are associated with deliberate efforts to mobilise and strengthen civil society structures, processes and institutions at lower levels, in a manner that enhances the capabilities of local structures to interact with higher spheres of government in a mutually reinforcing virtuous cycle of developmental outcomes.

Part 3 addresses the state of civil society in the democratic dispensation with respect to its nature, role and limitations in socio-economic transformation and participatory democracy, given the imperatives of globalisation and the current approach to economic management and the resulting configuration of social and economic policies and programmes in South Africa.

The contribution by Adam Habib and Hermien Kotzé, in Chapter 8, addresses the nature of civil society and its relationship to governance and development in South Africa in the context of globalisation. The chapter explores the nature of civil society from what the authors call a "systemic perspective", which examines structural variables such as the socio-economic environment, the political system and the prevailing flow of resources to the third sector, comprising civil society and non-governmental bodies. The writers seek to understand the dynamics of how the sector is being systemically constituted and reconstituted by various factors, how it is positioned in space between the state and the private sector, and how it engages with both in the quest for democratisation and sustainable human development. They utilise this approach to explore the manner in which the apartheid environment influenced the nature and role of civil society at the time and what it bequeathed to the post-apartheid period, characterised by a democratic dispensation and a government committed to pursuing democratic and development ideals. The chapter explores the impact of international factors on the nature and evolution of civil society, and especially the impact of neo-liberalism and globalisation, in their generality and with respect to the South African situation. The chapter notes that while the new dispensation can be said to have normalised South African society, it has done so in the context of embracing a neo-liberal agenda, which continues to exacerbate problems of poverty and marginalisation. Within this context, civil society is seen to be reconstituting itself as a result of various internal and external pressures that are occurring simultaneously. Habib and Kotzé argue that the challenge for civil society is to ensure that there is continuous and vigorous engagement with the state, in order to pressure for necessary changes in the systemic environment, in the nature of policies pursued, and in the nature of the flows to civil society, such that the objectives of democratisation, good governance and sustainable human development are realised in the long term.

In Chapter 9, Nomboniso Gasa discusses the quest for gender equality in South Africa in the context of globalisation. The writer examines women's struggles for equality from both a historical and contemporary perspective, with a view to identifying the lessons in order to inform on future strategies and policies. Gasa locates the *problematique* of women's disempowerment in the triple forms of oppression and exploitation inherited from the past, namely those of gender, class and race. She proceeds to discuss the various ways in which women have attempted to deal with the triple legacy at the individual, family, community and organisational levels, and what the implications of the dramatic changes and transformations that have taken place since the democratic dispensation have been, both in terms of the ability of women to liberate and empower themselves and in terms of continuities of disadvantage from the past. The writer attempts to demonstrate the fluidity and nuances of women's struggles, and the complexity of the issues that arise in attempting to conceptualise such struggles in each historical epoch as constituting a women's movement in South Africa, while the overall and gender-specific struggle unfolded and evolved. In the process, Gasa reviews the various constitutional, legal, institutional and organisational mechanisms that have been put into place to promote the interests of women, and discusses why they appear to have an ambiguous and indeterminate impact, in spite of the honourable intentions behind them. The writer, nonetheless, concludes that major gains have been made by women since the advent of democratic rule and governance, and that while the conventional and inherited women's organisations are repositioning and regrouping themselves, new ones are emerging that are beginning to change the landscape of the women's movement. She concludes that the ability of women to enhance their own interests in the long term, while contributing to the broader agenda of political, economic, and social reconstruction, will depend on the manner in which both old and new organisations reconfigure and align to form a viable women's movement.

In Chapter 10, Patrick Bond and Thulani Guliwe present an account of South African civil society advocacy and work in relation to sustainable human development, and their link to issues of globalisation and governance. The authors proceed along the lines pursued by other writers in this book by discussing the tensions between state and civil society (often leading to open confrontation) and within civil society over policies based on market fundamentalism. They identify the emergence of "progressive" civil society organisations (CSOs) that are challenging the state's adoption and implementation of such policies with some positive results. Although the writers see hope in this progressive movement (through local mobilisation and advocacy, as well as regional, continental and global networks), they caution CSOs to be vigilant to avoid being co-opted by "green business", which has appropriated the terminology of sustainable development in its discourse in the service of capital accumulation. As an alternative, Bond and Guliwe propose a hybrid of the red-green alliance and networks – ecosocialism – whose discourse and practical politics must be rights-based, linking the capitalist mode of production with the environmental crisis, and founded on popular mobilisation.

In Part 4, Chapter 11, Guy Mhone and Omano Edigheji bring together all the major themes explored in the book and the emerging governance and development modes in the new South Africa. The authors propose an alternative developemental path that is conducive to the achievement of democratic governance and sustainable development in South Africa.

Conclusion

On a general level, the contributions in this book lead to one major, inescapable conclusion, arrived at both deductively and through formal analysis of current developments. This is that the prospects for consolidating democracy and promoting good governance and sustainable human development in a manner that can undo the legacies of the past and redefine a new chapter for the South African polity, economy and society are being compromised by reliance on economic liberalism and market fundamentalism as the primary vehicles for effecting these objectives, in spite of the well-intentioned development-related initiatives currently being pursued. Some of the common issues that arise from the contributions in this respect are the following.

There is the tendency for privatisation and economic restructuring of service delivery to shift the burden of social provisioning to individuals, households and communities whose capacities, already compromised by unemployment, low incomes, poverty and the HIV/Aids pandemic, are being taxed to the limit by these new responsibilities.

There is the tendency for the new paradigms of public management and service delivery, informed by the imperatives of globalisation and the doctrine of the market, to overly technocratise and bureaucratise policy formulation, implementation, monitoring and evaluation, to the extent that both good governance, in the broader sense, and political involvement are being compromised. Cerny (1996:133) observes, more generally, that:

> the state is promoting the commodification or marketisation of its own activities and structures ... in effect it's the transformation of the mix of goods from public-dominated into private-dominated which in turn transforms the state from a primarily hierarchical, decommodifying agent into a primarily market-based, commodifying agent.

There is the tendency for market-driven modalities and policies, together with integration into the global arena in the absence of proactive and bold developmental measures for socio-economic transformation, to not only fail to resolve legacies of inequality and destitution based on race, gender and class, but also to reinforce and perpetuate these same legacies.

There is the tendency for current developments to result in the realignment of economic, social and political forces across the whole spectrum.

The above findings are not unique to South Africa, as the following comment by Cerny (1996:130) illustrates:

> Thus globalization entails the undermining of the public character of public goods and of the specific character of assets, i.e. the privatisation and marketisation of economic and political structures. States are pulled between structural pressures and organizational levels they cannot control. Economic globalization contributes not so much to the supersession of the state by a homogenous global order as to the splintering of the existing political order. Indeed, globalization leads to a growing disjuncture between the democratic, constitutional and social aspirations of people – which are still shaped by and understood through the frame of the territorial state – on the one hand, and the dissipating possibilities of genuine and effective collective action through constitutional processes on the other. Certain possibilities for collective action through regimes may increase, but these operate at least one removed from democratic or constitutional control and accountability; they are also vulnerable to being undermined by the anarchic nature of the international system.

As noted earlier, the writers of this book are motivated by at least three considerations in addressing the issues at stake. One is the genuine intellectual task of wanting to understand what is currently going on and, by the same token, proposing alternative interpretations of the implications of the interface of globalisation, economic liberalism and the quest for good governance, democratisation and sustainable human development. Another concerns the need to attempt to assess the implications of current developments arising from the package of economic and social policies that are being pursued by the government, especially given the context of globalisation. Finally, the writers are motivated by a normative interest in promoting genuine democratisation and equitable development based on inclusiveness and empowerment in the economic, social and political spheres within the country and at the global level. A future research agenda needs to explore further the analytical and empirical issues posed and should give greater attention to policy alternatives for consolidating democratic governance and promoting equitable growth and development

The writers recognise that South Africa is placed in a unique situation, given its developmental and political potential domestically, regionally, continentally and internationally. More importantly, the emergence of a democratic South Africa, stripped of the vestiges of racism and exploitation, is a beacon of hope for Africa. It is, therefore, imperative that South Africa not only learn from the lessons of other African countries that have gone along a similar path, but that in doing so it is able to chart a new path for itself and the continent.

References

Amsden, A. (1989) *Asia's Next Giant: South Korea and Late Industrialization.* New York: Oxford University Press.

Cerny, P. G. (1996) "What Next for the State?" In Kofman, E. & Youngs, G. (eds) *Globalisation: Theory and Practice.* London: Pinter.

Castells, M. (1998) *End of Millennium.* Volume III. Oxford: Blackwell Publishers.

Evans, P. (1995) *Embedded Autonomy: States and Industrial Transformation.* New Jersey: Princeton University Press.

Evans, P. (1996) *State-Society Synergy: Government and Social Capital in Development.* Berkeley: University of California at Berkeley.

Hadenius, A. (1991) *Democracy and Development.* Cambridge: Cambridge University Press.

Hirst, P. & Thompson, G. (1996) *Globalisation in Question.* Second edition. Cambridge: Polity Press.

Huntington, S. P. (1991) *The Third Wave.* Norman: University of Oklahoma Press.

Leftwitch, A. (1996) *Democracy and Development: Theory and Practice.* Cambridge: Polity Press.

Manor, J. (1998) "Democratisation and the Developmental State: The Search for Balance." In Robinson, M. & White, G. *The Democratic Developmental State: Politics and Institutional Design.* New York: Oxford University Press.

Przerwoski, A. (1991) *Democracy and the Market: Political Reform and Economic Reforms in Eastern Europe and Latin America.* Cambridge: Cambridge University Press.

Robinson, M. & White, G. (1998) *The Democratic Developmental State: Politics and Institutional Design.* New York: Oxford University Press.

Sklar, R. L. (1996) "Towards a Theory of Developmental Democracy." In Leftwitch, A. *Democracy and Development: Theory and Practice.* Cambridge: Polity Press.

Wade, R. (1990) *Governing the Market.* New Jersey: Princeton University Press.

Weiss, L. (1998) *The Myth of the Powerless State: Governing the Global Economy.* Cambridge: Polity Press.

Part One

Economic Liberalisation, Democratisation, Co-operative Governance and Development

2 Democratisation, Economic Liberalisation and the Quest for Sustainable Development in South Africa

Guy Mhone

Introduction

South Africa is approaching its tenth anniversary of democratic majority rule; hence, it is not surprising that there is increasing interest in assessing what the country has achieved so far and in attempting to gauge where the country might be destined in the future. In the light of the legacy of apartheid, which uniquely characterised South Africa for about five decades of white minority rule and domination, it is generally accepted worldwide that the transition to democratic rule was indeed miraculous, especially in that no major social and political convulsions occurred in the process. However, given the antagonism that characterised the pre-democracy period and the nature of the aspirations and demands that guided the fight for liberation among the majority of the excluded, oppressed and marginalised Black population, it is of interest to assess the degree to which the democratic dispensation can be seen to have met the objectives of the previously oppressed Black majority, or can indeed be seen to be meeting the chief objectives of the organisation (the African National Congress) that most effectively articulated the demands of the majority and that ushered in the new democratic era.

More generally, the question arises as to the degree to which the new democratic dispensation and the economic and social policies emanating from it can be consolidated and made sustainable in the long term. This is a question that many analysts have begun to ask and address through various writings, and which this chapter seeks to shed further light on. South Africa is a country that is accepted as having made the transition to democracy, and one whose government has embarked upon a decidedly neo-liberal economic policy platform on the basis of which it hopes to promote the much-desired objective of sustainable human development in South Africa. More specifically, this chapter seeks to interrogate the relationship between formal democratisation, the pursuit of neo-liberal economic policies and the quest for sustainable human development in South Africa in the context of globalisation and calls for good governance. It seeks to explore the nature of the synergies, contradictions and tensions among all of the foregoing objectives. In particular, the chapter attempts to demonstrate that in a country like South Africa, with fundamental structural socio-economic inequalities, the conventional understanding of democracy as currently pursued in South Africa, coupled with economic liberalism as the dominant approach to economic and social policy, while compatible with global and other external imperatives, is at odds with the need to promote sustainable human development and good governance, and hence is ultimately detrimental to the consolidation of both formal (procedural and representative) and substantive (or emancipatory) democracy in the long run.

In his inaugural address to the Joint Sitting of Parliament, Mr Mandela, the first president of a democratically elected government of South Africa, expressed the vision of the new government as follows:

> My government's commitment to create a people-centered society of liberty binds us to the pursuit of the goals of freedom from want, freedom from hunger, freedom from deprivation, freedom from ignorance, freedom from suppression and freedom from fear. These freedoms are fundamental to the guarantee of human dignity. They will therefore constitute part of the centrepiece of what this Government will seek to achieve, the focal point on which our attention will be continuously focused. The things we have said constitute the true meaning, justification and purpose of the Reconstruction and Development Programme (RDP), without which it would lose all legitimacy. (Preface to the RDP White Paper, 1994)

Indeed, the new democratic dispensation has been built on a solid constitutional foundation, which most observers agree is one of the most enlightened in the world. The Constitution of South Africa provides for a broadly representative constitutional democracy with adult suffrage, protection of individual rights as enshrined in a Bill of Rights, and emphasis on public participation and consultative processes of policy making. Among the rights enshrined in the Bill of Rights are the following: the right to life, equality and human dignity; the right to freedom and security of the person; the right not to be subjected to servitude or forced labour; the right to privacy, freedom of religion, belief, opinion and expression; the right to freedom of association, assembly, demonstration, picketing and petitioning; the right to freedom of movement and residence, trade, occupation and profession; the right to fair labour practices and to strike; the right to a safe and healthy environment; the right to property; and the right to socio-economic benefits such as health care, food, water and social security, whereby "the state must take reasonable legislative measures within its available resources, to achieve the progressive realisation of each of these rights" (Constitution, 1996). The Constitution also guarantees equality on the basis of race and gender. In other words, the Constitution provides for both formal democracy, as generally understood and accepted, and for the possibility of realising what may be called emancipatory or substantive democracy, implying the need to ensure the participation of the common person as well as to meet the basic needs of the populace.

As the democratic dispensation was approaching, the African National Congress (ANC) embarked upon an extensive consultative process that resulted in the formulation of the Reconstruction and Development Programme (RDP) as the major guiding policy document of the movement and the imminent new government. This initial document was later formally issued as a government White Paper immediately after the ANC assumed state power. The White Paper describes the RDP as "an integrated, coherent socio-economic policy framework. It seeks to mobilize all our people and our country's resources toward the final eradication of the results of apartheid and the building of a democratic, non-racial and non-sexist future. It represents a vision for the fundamental transformation of South Africa." (RDP White Paper, 1994)

The White Paper went on to outline the six basic principles of the RDP:

1. The need to pursue an integrated and sustainable programme, since the legacy of apartheid "cannot be overcome with piecemeal, uncoordinated policies. The RDP brings together strategies to harness all our resources in a coherent and purposeful effort that can be sustained into the future. These strategies will be implemented at national, provincial and local level by government, parastatals, business and organizations within civil society all working within the framework of the RDP. All levels of government must pay attention to affordability given our commitment to fiscal discipline and to achievable goals."

2. The RDP must be a people-driven process: "Our people, with their aspirations and collective determination, are our most important resource. The RDP is focused on people's immediate needs and it relies, in turn, on their energies. Irrespective of race or sex, or whether they are rural or urban, rich or poor, the people of South Africa must together shape their own future. Development is not about delivery of goods to a passive citizenry. It is about active involvement and growing empowerment."

3. There must be peace and security for all.

4. The above will facilitate nation building: "We are a single country, with a single economy, functioning within a constitutional framework that establishes provincial and local powers, respect for protection of minorities, and a process to accommodate

those wishing to retain their cultural identity. It is on the basis of our unity in diversity that we will consolidate our national sovereignty."

5. "[N]ation-building links reconstruction and development. The RDP is based on the notion that reconstruction and development are parts of an integrated process. The RDP integrates growth, development, reconstruction, redistribution and reconciliation into a unified programme."

6. All of the foregoing will depend on the need for "thorough-going democratisation of South Africa. Minority control and privilege in every aspect of our society are the main obstruction to developing an integrated programme which will unleash all the resources of our country and fundamentally change the way that policy is made and implemented."

The RDP White Paper proceeded to outline the five main programmes originally stated in the RDP base document, the original ANC policy statement, as the following:

- meeting basic needs;
- developing human resources;
- building the economy;
- democratising the state and society; and
- implementing the RDP.

It is clear from the above that the key areas of focus of the RDP were the need to consolidate democratisation and the need to promote sustainable human development, and that the two are interlinked since "if we do not succeed in democratising the State and Society, the resources and potential of our country and people will not be available for a coherent programme of reconstruction and development. In linking democracy, development and a people-centered approach to government, we are paving the way for a new democratic order" (RDP White Paper, 1994). The RDP then was seen as a "vision for the fundamental transformation in our society". Through the RDP, it can be inferred that the new government was intent on pursuing the following objectives: formal and substantive democracy; a pluralistic and participatory form of governance; and a developmentalist agenda. These objectives will be discussed further below.

In the course of commenting on the need to be conscious of the dangers and opportunities associated with the new globalised international environment, and the need to reintegrate South Africa as an active player in the regional economy and to promote regional development, the RDP White Paper makes an interesting observation about an eventuality that had occurred elsewhere but was soon to haunt it. It comments as follows:

> The pressures of the world economy and the operations of international organizations such as the International Monetary Fund (IMF), World Bank and GATT, affect our neighbours and South

Africa in different ways. In the case of our neighbours they were pressured into implementing programmes with adverse effects on employment and standards of living. It is essential that we combine to develop an effective growth and development strategy for all Southern African countries. (RDP White Paper, 1994)

Thus, the RDP White Paper was cognisant of the negative impact of structural adjustment and stabilisation programmes in the rest of southern Africa, and was aware of the need to formulate a growth and development strategy as an alternative. The government did proceed to implement the RDP, first, by ensuring that there was a co-ordinating ministry attached to the Office of the President and that the various programmes were assigned to line ministries and departments for execution. The government also embarked on a low-key process of formulating a growth and development strategy, which galvanised both national and provincial levels of government in the exercise. Two years later, the RDP Ministry was disbanded and the growth and development process was in limbo as the government announced the new macroeconomic policy framework in the name of the Growth, Employment and Redistribution (GEAR) policy framework document (Department of Finance, 1996).

This policy document, which was voluntarily embarked upon by the government with the encouragement and support of the International Monetary Fund (IMF) and World Bank, who were periodically consulted in its preparation, was very much a structural adjustment and stabilisation prógramme of South Africa's own making. The government gave as its rationale for adopting the framework the changing international economic environment, especially the need to insulate South Africa from the Asian economic and financial crisis and other similar crises that might occur among emerging markets in the future. Implicit in adopting GEAR was the contention that the government needed such a policy statement as a way of not only allaying the concerns and fears of foreign and domestic investors, but of actually attracting such investors as well. The document cites the implications of the depreciation of the rand, which had just occurred, as presenting both a threat and an opportunity, hence "an uncoordinated response, embroiled in conflict, will cause further crisis and contraction. Linked to an integrated economic strategy, on the other hand, it provides a springboard for enhanced economic activity" (Department of Finance, 1996:1). The foregoing statement was meant, in part, to suggest that current global and domestic circumstances demanded drastic measures to be put in place and, in part, to indicate that the government would not tolerate unnecessary debate over the new policy.

GEAR begins by noting that, as the next century approached, South Africa would seek to achieve the following:

- a competitive, fast-growing economy, which creates sufficient jobs for all work seekers;
- a redistribution of income and opportunities in favour of the poor;
- a society in which sound health, education and other services are available to all; and
- an environment in which hopes are secure and workplaces are productive.

The GEAR policy framework was seen as "a strategy for rebuilding and restructuring the economy … in keeping with the goals of the Reconstruction and Development Programme". It further claimed that "in the context of this integrated economic strategy, we can successfully confront the related challenges of meeting basic needs, developing human resources, increasing participation in the democratic institutions of civil society and implementing the RDP" (Department of Finance, 1996:1). The document notes that while considerable progress had been made in repositioning the economy, re-establishing growth in Gross Domestic Product (GDP) that was in excess of growth in population, lowering rates of inflation, opening up the economy and securing new markets, restructuring the public sector and reforming the civil service, and establishing a policy framework for delivery of social services, much more needed to be done. In particular, it was noted that the growth achieved thus far was not enough to address the high levels of unemployment that were in existence, did not generate enough resources to address the deficit in social services, and yielded "insufficient progress toward an equitable distribution of income and wealth".

The core elements of the integrated strategy were stipulated as the following:

- a renewed focus on budget reform to strengthen the redistributive thrust of expenditure;
- a faster deficit-reduction to contain debt service obligations, counter inflation and free resources for investment;
- an exchange-rate policy to keep the real effective rate stable at a competitive level;
- consistent monetary policy to prevent a resurgence of inflation;
- a further step in the gradual relaxation of exchange controls;
- a reduction in tariffs to contain input prices, facilitate industrial restructuring, compensating partially for the exchange-rate depreciation;
- tax incentives to stimulate new investment in competitive and labour-absorbing projects;
- speeding up the restructuring of state assets to optimise investment resources;
- an appropriately structured flexibility within the collective bargaining system;
- an expansion of trade and investment flows in southern Africa; and
- a commitment to the implementation of stable and co-ordinated policies.

The above approach was expected to attain "a growth rate of 6% per annum and job creation of 400,000 per annum by the year 2000". Essentially, GEAR was a conventional structural adjustment and stabilisation programme, along the lines advocated by the Bretton Woods institutions and implemented in a number of African and Latin American countries in the 1980s and mid-1990s.

Within the above parameters, various measures mooted in the RDP were also to be pursued, especially with respect to industrial policy, delivery of social services, human resource development, crime prevention, local economic development and infrastructure development. The message of GEAR was however clear, and this was that the market would be the paramount vehicle for allocating resources and that macroeconomic fundamentals would be pursued resolutely and not tampered with in achieving this goal. As the framework document's name implies, the pursuit of growth was primary and seen as the vehicle for promoting employment and achieving the much-needed redistribution. This departed from the simultaneous approach to growth and development, with redistribution as a key aspect of both processes, implied by the RDP.

While the government has continued to insist that GEAR merely represented the clarification of an obvious omission in the RDP, namely the absence of an explicit macroeconomic framework, and that as such it was a continuation of the RDP, many have seen in GEAR an explicit break with the RDP, with the government shifting toward the Washington Consensus characteristic of structural adjustment and stabilisation programmes associated with the Bretton Woods institutions. In adopting GEAR, the government was predicating growth and development on the inherited formal economy as the engine, through demand contraction, price correction and realignment, increased foreign and domestic investment and increased exports. The government would focus on regulation and providing an enabling environment, enhancing administrative, revenue extraction, policy making and implementation capacities. Henceforth, social and developmental policies would be undertaken within the context of the above parameters, thereby implying a greater concern for affordability, cost recovery and financial sustainability in the provision of social services and economic infrastructure.

The government insists it has not changed policies, but has merely adapted to changing domestic and global circumstances; however, within the ANC alliance itself and among many non-governmental organisations and expert observers on the right and the left there is consensus that, with the adoption of GEAR, the government has made a major paradigm and policy shift to the right. This has been well recognised by proponents of the status quo, who have applauded the government's shift, but who continue to lament its lack of resolve to implement the GEAR ethos much more comprehensively and resolutely, especially with respect to labour market polices that are seen to be relatively rigid. The shift has been lamented by the left, who see in it the government's capitulation to the neo-liberal paradigm. This chapter does not so much seek to assess how and why the government adopted GEAR, nor does it seek to assess the viability of GEAR as a policy that would achieve its stated objectives; rather, the chapter seeks to assess whether (a) insertion into the global economy (through outward orientation, and economic liberalisation) as demanded by market fundamentalists, (b) consolidation of democracy and good governance, and (c) the pursuit of developmentalism as mooted in the RDP are mutually compatible goals and objectives.

The problem

At the moment, the dispute over GEAR threatens to disrupt the alliance of the dominant ruling party, the ANC, with its main partners, the Congress of South African Trade Unions (Cosatu) and the South African Communist Party (SACP), which vehemently disagree with the ANC over the shift toward economic liberalism. Major groups within the status quo, primarily consisting of the main opposition party, the Democratic Party, and major business and professional organisations, have persistently commended the government on its new stance and have urged it not to cave in to what they refer to as "populist" pressures, such as those emanating from trade unions and non-governmental organisations. The government continues to contend that it has not deviated from its original policies, and continues to resort to RDP and, at times, radical or progressive rhetoric to insist that it is still committed to a people-centred democracy and sustainable human development as envisioned in the RDP.

Thus, the nature of the debate over the government's current policy stance is rather blurred by the different interpretations imputed to it by itself, its critics and its supporters. Rather than attempt to discuss the relative merits of these three positions, this chapter will proceed by taking the government's claims at face value, and will then assess whether the pursuit of economic liberalism, as implied by the adoption of GEAR, is facilitative of both the consolidation of democracy and the promotion of sustainable human development. In other words, the chapter asks whether, given South Africa's socio-economic legacy and prevailing economic circumstances, economic liberalisation as demanded by global forces and some domestic constituencies, democratisation (both formal and substantive) and developmentalism are compatible goals or processes as currently being pursued by the government. This chapter, therefore, proceeds on the following assumptions about the government's perception of its own approach to policy:

● the government is convinced that the best approach to economic policy management is through liberalisation and outward orientation, under the assumption that this is the most effective way to maximise the benefits of globalisation and to attain sustainable human development in South Africa;

● the government is convinced that it has established a basis for both formal democracy and substantive democracy, so that democracy is likely to be consolidated in the long term; and

● the government is developmental in its approach to democracy, governance and economic and social policy.

The chapter seeks to assess whether the forgoing assumptions are tenable and compatible in the context the current situation in South Africa, with all its historical socio-economic legacies. The nature of the problem at hand is best appreciated by first considering, albeit briefly, some general observations about the major objectives at stake, namely: the nature and meaning of *globalisation and economic liberalisation* and their implications for the pursuit of development; the nature and meaning of *democracy and democratisation* during what Huntington has referred to as the "third wave"; the nature and meaning of *governance*; and the nature and meaning of *developmentalism or a developmental state*. At the general level, it will be argued that the foregoing objectives are not mutually compatible for latecomers to the development scene. At the specific level, as related to the South African situation, it will be contended that the insistence that the objectives are compatible merely obfuscates the issues at stake, and works to the benefit of the status quo, that is the historically privileged groups in the country and external interests, and that, by the same token, it works against the interests of historically disadvantaged groups, Black people in general and Africans in particular, who constitute the majority.

Globalisation and economic liberalisation

Current discussions attempt to make a distinction between internationalisation and globalisation. The former has been a phenomenon for centuries and is associated with the movement of goods and services, people, finance and information across borders, as a consequence of a number of possible vehicles such as trade and exchange, wars and conquest, voluntary and forced migration and so on. During the era of internationalisation, nation-states still remained the dominant arbiters of the resulting internationalisation, even if the actual agents in the process were private entities or individuals. The regulatory and institutional environment within which internationalisation has taken place has primarily been determined by nation-states or governments or their delegated international bodies.

The concept of globalisation is seen as a relatively more recent phenomenon. While analysts may differ as to its extent, there is general agreement that some international exchanges or movements represent something more than internationalisation, especially since the nation-state is unable to control the rapidity or intensity at which such transactions occur, so that they appear to be independent of any one entity. This has been made possible by a number of advances of a technological, political, economic and sociological nature.

Lubbers and Koorevaar (1999) describe the advent of globalisation as follows:

> Due to technological innovation, especially ICT and in miniaturization and dematerialization of products, it has become easier to travel, trade, produce, consume, communicate and entertain across borders, worldwide. We have seen an outburst in communication and mobility.
>
> National economies become integrated in the world trade and finance markets, foreign direct investments are easier to make, monitor and withdraw when deemed necessary. Most countries try to gain from this internationalisation of the economy by opening borders for international finance and transactions. The integration of national economies and markets into a world market goes hand in hand with the spectacular rise and strengthening in neo-liberal ideology.

They note that these developments have gone hand in hand with the entry into the global order of the newly industrialising countries of South East Asia, the collapse of the Soviet Bloc and relative demise of socialism as an option, all of which have led to the "triumphalism" of the "market and democracy". Thus, the World Bank (1995:1) has noted:

> These are revolutionary times in the global economy. The embrace of market-based development by many developing and former centrally planned economies, the opening of international markets and great advances in the ease with which goods, capital, and ideas flow around the world are bringing new opportunities, as well as risks to billions of people.

Globalisation has been associated with increased integration, prosperity, democracy and development. Thus, the World Bank (1995) observes how globalisation benefits workers:

> Fears that increased international trade and investment and less state intervention will hurt employment are mainly without basis. Workers have made great advances in many countries, especially those that have embraced these global trends, effectively engaging in international markets and avoiding excessive state intervention. … [P]roblems of low incomes and poor working conditions, and insecurity affecting many of the world's workers can be effectively tackled in ways that reduce poverty and regional inequality. But to do so will require sound domestic policy and a supportive international environment. This means governments must:
>
> ● Pursue, market based growth paths that generate rapid growth in demand for labour, expansion in skills of the workforce and increasing productivity.
>
> ● Take advantage of new opportunities at the international level, by opening up to trade and attracting capital – but manage dislocation that international change sometimes brings.

At least three points need to be stressed with respect to globalisation along the lines advocated above by the World Bank and others. First, the benefits of globalisation are associated with increased reliance on market forces and, by extension, on increased democratisation, generally understood to mean procedural and representative democracy but accompanied by a strong and explicit legal and regulatory regime protecting the property rights of both domestic and foreign investors.

Second, supporters of the globalisation process also acknowledge that globalisation is accompanied by threats and penalties if individual countries violate its requirements, or attempt to opt out of it or "de-link" from the global economy. Some of these penalties are negative in nature, reflected in the drying up of foreign investment and aid resources, for instance. Others are proactively implemented by the major international agencies that supervise various aspects of the current global order, such as the World Bank, the IMF, the World Trade Organisation (WTO) and the various groupings of major developed countries like the Group of Eight and the World Economic Forum.

Third, the phenomenon itself has emerged as an extension of the activities of multinational corporations in their pursuit of profit, so that it is not only a de facto situation for many countries (other than those that continue to stay out of it, such as Cuba), but it is also such that the global rules to govern the phenomenon are being considered after the fact, and mostly by way of rationalising and legitimising what is already taking place. Thus, both the phenomenon and the emerging rules of globalisation tend be of benefit to the multinational corporations themselves, first and foremost, and only secondarily of benefit to the developed countries. It is in recognition of this third aspect that Castells (1998:337) argues that a dynamic global economy has emerged, in which:

> Networks of capital, labour, information, and markets link up, through technology, valuable functions, people, and localities around the world, while switching off from their networks those populations and territories deprived of value and interest for the dynamics of global capitalism.

There are, of course, views critical of globalisation. The concept and process of globalisation raise concerns very similar to those that relate to the other notions discussed below. There are those who question whether globalisation has indeed occurred as a process qualitatively different from other processes associated with internationalisation. Thus, Hirst and Thompson (2000:2) note that the concept, as "conceived by the more extreme globalizers, is largely a myth". There are those who contend that globalisation requires taming, given that it has run far ahead of the ability of global society to develop appropriate legal and regulatory regimes and modes of governance to manage the phenomenon (Soros, 1998). There are those who criticise globalists for ignoring the fact that the market, at both global and national levels, cannot provide all the answers for desired resource allocation and utilisation. There are those who insist that the global order is a fundamentally unequal one in which a few players (in terms of both developed countries and multinational corporations) benefit, while a large proportion of the world population is simultaneously marginalised as it is incorporated into the global order (Castells, 1998). The uneven manner in which globalisation and market orientation are promoted is cited with respect to how labour mobility is controlled and how subsidies and trade barriers are strategically deployed by developed countries to protect and promote their own local secondary and primary industries, while through various multilateral and bilateral organisations, developing economies are pressurised to engage in wholesale liberalisation. Finally, there are those who challenge the empirical evidence summoned in support of the presumed benefits resulting from integration into the global economy; in particular, the World Bank's interpretation of the East Asian experience, which attributed the rapid success of these countries to their outward and market orientation. Critics have adequately demonstrated the strategic role played by the state in East Asian countries and its handin-glove relationship with the private sector in steering the market and transforming their economies. Indeed, the major obfuscation or mystification promoted by globalists is the insistence that there are natural laws that govern the operation of globalisation, which, if ignored, have serious consequences. Of this view, Schroyer (1975:25) comments:

> The "post-industrial society" image of contemporary society is treated as flawed and ideological to the extent to which it permits historical domination to appear as a natural process. In so far as contemporary science uncritically promotes this image, it becomes not only, in Marxist terms, a factor of production, but also an ideological relation of production. In a new guise, this technocratic celebration of instrumental progress perpetuates the grim determinism of an earlier industrial ideology. Whereas the first industrial societies understood their development in terms of the "economic necessities" of the market, today we conceive our shackles of "development" as linked to the internal "needs" of the industrial system. In the earlier market-ideology, history was reduced to the necessity of natural law: in the current image of "post industrial" society the internal dynamic of social change has been elevated to the status of cybernetic process. Both social images imply that chances for human liberation are related to the capacity of man to adapt to an external imposed "natural" necessity.

Over the past two decades, at the behest and under the tutelage of the Bretton Woods institutions, African countries have been seriously experimenting with integration into the global economy by reorienting their economies outwardly and reasserting the primacy of the role of the market, all to little avail. Indeed, since the demise of the Soviet Bloc, there have been very few countries that can be said to have benefited from globalisation in a qualitatively unequivocal manner, other than those that were already successful (the developed economies and the East Asian economies). The most that can be said about many of the developing countries is perhaps that matters could have been worse in the absence of resorting to economic reforms and integration into the global economy. Nonetheless, it is clear that the benefits of globalisation have been highly unequal and highly marginalising for the poorer countries, especially those in Africa. The fundamental problem that remains with the process of globalisation is that it is inherently predicated on unequal centre-periphery relationships, which extend into the heartland of developing nations and in which global processes are linked to internal centre-periphery relationships between classes and formal and non-formal sectors. Thus, for latecomers that uncritically embrace neo-liberalism and globalisation, the simultaneous processes of incorporation and marginalisation that occur at the global level are reproduced internally at the national level, as well, in the form of increased unemployment, underemployment and impoverishment for the majority, while the presumed benefits of economic reform and globalisation only accrue to a few within the developing country and to those in developed countries.

Schroyer (1975:172) suggests the need to consolidate and reinforce critical theory as a basis for arriving at different interpretations of reality and for proposing alternatives:

> Because science and technology are now a major mode of ideological mystification of power relations, critical theory must extend to the community of those who are its living embodiment. It must restore to scientists the actual relation between science and society and expose the deepening contradictions of the scientific ideology and the objective containment of science for the purpose of extending exploitation and domination throughout the world. Development of critical social theory within the scientific community can contribute to the creation of alternative programs for research and development. In this way, knowledge can be generated that relates to the needs of peoples who are trying to build social community, resist cultural manipulation, facilitate decentralization movements, and in general contribute to the actualisation of human needs that are otherwise ignored. By reorienting the scientific community, at least a significant sector of it, critical theory can become a material force for change by counteracting the current drift of science toward the formation and implementation of state policy.

When the above criticisms and the unspectacular performance of the developing economies that have adopted Bretton Woods-type economic reforms in the hope of benefiting from globalisation are taken together, it can be contended that under current circumstances there is very little evidence that globalisation can yield the claimed benefits to developing economies that opt to incorporate themselves into it, without a developmental approach to economic management guided by a proactive state. Therefore, by predicating its hopes on economic liberalisation and outward orientation, while having an ambiguous development programme and indeed one that is constrained by the very policy framework that has been adopted in the form of GEAR, it can be expected that South Africa is unlikely to succeed in resuscitating its economy. More pertinently, it can be advanced that since, for recent entrants into the global arena, globalisation has had the effect of marginalising both countries and entities (and the poorer sections of these countries' populations, who constitute the majority in many cases), the current macroeconomic stance is likely to exacerbate rather than resolve the economic and social deficit experienced by the historically disadvantaged portions of the population, even if minorities among them benefit as a consequence. Under such circumstances, in the absence of an internal strategy of transformation, integration into the global economy is likely to compromise the attainment of both substantive democracy and sustainable development.

Democratisation

With respect to democratisation, we proceed by appealing to Huntington's (1991) analysis of the nature of the third democratic wave, with the aim of arriving at a hypothesis that would inform on how democracies become consolidated. Given that Huntington suggests that one of the major difficulties in consolidating democracies is the ability to address issues of inequality, poverty and underdevelopment, we will then proceed to consider problems posed by economic liberalisation for democratisation and the attainment of sustainable human development.

Huntington begins by noting that democracy can be defined with respect to sources of government authority, purposes served by government and procedures for constituting government. The first two elements of this definition of democracy tend to emphasise what is commonly referred to as "the will of the people" as the source of authority, and pursuit of "the common good" as the main purpose of government. Huntington argues that such approaches, while legitimate, are open to too many qualifications and are difficult to operationalise for the empirical analysis of different variations of democratic systems and their development over time. He suggests, instead, the need to apply a procedural definition along the lines advanced by Schumpeter in *Capitalism, Socialism and Democracy*, where a political system is defined to be democratic when:

> Its most powerful collective decision makers are selected through fair, honest, and periodic elections in which all the adult population is eligible to vote. So defined, democracy involves the two dimensions – contestation and participation ... It also implies the existence of those civil and political freedoms to speak, publish, assemble, and organize that are necessary to political debate and the conduct of electoral campaigns. (Huntington, 1991:7)

Huntington warns that this procedural definition does not answer all the concerns normally raised about the essence of democracy, some of which are currently being posed with respect to the conduct of the current government in South Africa. He points out additional qualifications to the definition. First, he notes that:

> the conduct of elections is a minimal definition since many would add the need for "true democracy" or what some have referred to as substantive democracy to mean "liberte, egalite fraternite", effective citizen control over policy, responsible government, honesty and openness in politics, informed and rational deliberation, equal participation, and various other civic virtues. (Huntington, 1991:9)

Not only does South Africa live up to the minimalist procedural definition cited above as provided for in the Constitution and actual practices to date, and not only does the Constitution prescribe the purposes to be fulfilled by the government such as the meeting of basic needs, but the RDP and various subsequent policy documents have also insisted on the need for the government to live up to substantive notions of democracy rooted in the "will of the people" and the "common good". Thus, for instance, the RDP notes:

> Democracy for ordinary citizens must not end with formal rights and periodic one-person one-vote elections. Without undermining the authority and responsibilities of elected representative bodies (Parliament, provincial legislatures, local government) the democratic order we envisage must foster a wide range of institutions of participatory democracy in partnership with civil society on the basis of informed and empowered citizens and facilitative direct democracy ... social movements and CBOs are a major asset in the effort to democratise and develop society. (quoted in De Villiers, 2001:23)

Thus, while it may be accepted that the transition to formal democracy has been achieved, the government can still be assessed on the basis of the degree to which it has been able to been promote substantive democracy in the manner envisioned in the RDP base document. As will be seen, a number of observers have insisted that not only did the government adopt GEAR in a non-consultative and non-participatory manner, that is unilaterally, but also, since the adoption of GEAR, it has tended to drive a number of economic policies unilaterally as well.

One proposition that needs to be explored concerns the manner in which good governance has been promoted through ensuring the participation and consultation of citizens beyond mere claims to that effect by incumbents in power. This is an important consideration in the context of South Africa, since one sure way of ensuring that the interests of those who have been historically disadvantaged, who constitute the majority, are taken on board and translated into actual policies is through ensuring their participation and consultation in policy making.

A second qualification raised by Huntington is that the procedural definition does not imply that the elected officials will always exercise real power without being influenced by parochial interests. Again, this is an issue of relevance in the South African context, since the current shift in policy is attributed to the dominance of a combination of élite, emerging Black capitalist and status quo business and professional interests, some of which have been the historical beneficiaries of the pre-democracy apartheid dispensation, and others of which are beneficiaries of recent policy developments arising from the democratic dispensation.

Thirdly, Huntington points out the need to distinguish between the nature of a democratic regime and the factors that account for its stability. The latter may be unrelated to the democratic nature of the regime *per se* and may also influence the degree to which democracy may be consolidated. One such factor is the degree of economic development and, in particular, the nature of the poverty obtaining. This is an important consideration in the context of South Africa, and one to which we will return.

A fourth concern arising from Huntington's review of international experiences in the third wave relates to the fact that successful transitions to democracy often entail compromises between the victors and the defeated or exiting incumbents. Such compromises, by their nature, imply that the victors cannot get everything that they fought for prior to the transition and that they may have to tone down some of their initial demands and also give some assurances and guarantees to the defeated in order to secure their participation in the new dispensation. South Africa made its transition through a negotiated settlement that lives up to this scenario. Indeed, some have noted that the negotiated character of the settlement has severely affected the nature of governance and the ability of the new government to pursue the original mandate of the movement and the fight for democratisation. In this respect, it has been argued that the very nature of procedural democracy has worked to the benefit of the previously advantaged groups and, in the process, has compromised the participatory and consultative forms of governance that had been emphasised in the original RDP document.

Thus, for some, the anticipated "people's democracy" has degenerated into a "bourgeois democracy", in which the interests of the privileged are dominant. Perhaps the issue is rather the degree to which the initial project driving it has been compromised in favour of a new project that may serve different interests from those that were the rationale for democratisation. Currently, apart from the formation of the National Development and Labour Council (Nedlac), which is the statutory consultative body with major influence on labour (and, to a degree, social policy), consultation and participation of the people have been rather ad hoc and perfunctory in nature, and primarily promoted through exhortations for communities to engage in self-help initiatives.

While Huntington believes that whether or not a government has lived up to its purpose is not the necessary or true test of democracy, but rather that it is necessary to stick to the procedural criteria, he also admits that the ability of a government to live up to its presumed purpose is an important consideration for the consolidation of democracy. Many staunch supporters of the idea that procedural democracy is the essence of democracy would insist that once some purpose is identified as a project to be pursued by the government, democracy is by that very same token compromised. Nonetheless, it is useful to apply this aspect as one additional assessment criterion, since the government itself insists that it should be judged by its ability to meet the aspirations of the people. GEAR was adopted in the absence of consultation and an explicit mandate from the people or key constituencies other than business, but it is claimed by the government that GEAR is in the long-term interests of the historically disadvantaged majority. Thus, even if it is accepted that the procedural criteria for democracy have been met, the question still arises as to whether GEAR is the right approach to addressing the needs of the majority, or whether it is a capitulation to dominant minority interests representing the old status quo and the new élite drawn from the historically disadvantaged groups; or indeed whether it merely reflects the policy confusion and indeterminacy of a transitional democratic regime, as various class interests assert themselves on the government thereby producing a smorgasbord effect in policy formulation. This latter aspect is interesting, given the recent position articulated by the ANC in strategy and tactics documents presented at their recent Congress, in which they insist that they are neither neo-liberal nor ultra leftist:

> The ANC is a national liberation movement, which places the interests of the poor and the role of the working class at the centre of theory and practice. It is a discipline of the left, organised to conduct the struggle in pursuit of the interests of the poor. (quoted in *Business Day*, December 19, 2002)

Here again we cite Schroyer (1975:240), who comments:

> To the extent, then, that the existing process of political consensus formation has internal to it restrictive mechanisms which constrain the types of needs that can be represented and responded to, we must recognize that the social controls which protect the system priorities are inherent in the political institutions themselves. The interests of the corporate capitalists sector are not like other interests – their reproduction defines the common system's interest, which the political process strives to maintain in a dynamic equilibrium. Consensus formation proceeds, therefore, within a framework that is essentially one of preventive crisis management for corporate capitalism, to this extent, narrows the nature of political debate to the technical problems of systems maintenance.

Hence, it is of interest that the ANC articulates a leftist stance at the same time that it also adheres to a policy framework that essentially is a "systems maintenance" policy regime for domestic and international capitalist interests, with marginal benefits for the poor who are stated to be the main *raison d'être* of the party.

Other analysts insist, in support of Huntington, that the consolidation of democracy in the final analysis should depend on the degree to which all parties agree to live by democratic rules and procedures, and that democracies built on pacts will only last as long as the conditions leading to the pacts obtain. Once these conditions have dissipated, the chances are that democracy will collapse. Przeworski (1991:26) observes that:

> Democracy is consolidated when it becomes self-reinforcing, that is, when all the relevant political forces find it best to continue to submit their interests and values to the uncertain interplay of the intuition. Complying with the current outcome, even if it is a defeat, and directing all actions within the institutional framework is better for the relevant political forces than trying to subvert democracy. To put it somewhat technically, democracy is consolidated when compliance – acting within the institutional framework – constitutes the equilibrium of the decentralized strategies of all the relevant political forces.

A number of issues that are pertinent to the South African situation arise form the above discussion. It is well known that the transition to democracy was based on a pact, generally referred to as reconciliation, and understood to have entailed protection of minority political, social, cultural and economic interests. Thus, the first question that arises concerns how tenable such a pact can be, given the social and economic deficits that have to be addressed in the context of South Africa. In this respect, the experience of Zimbabwe is illustrative, since it also made its transition through a pact, which had the effect of making the government postpone a number of critical decisions that should have been made to promote equitable development. The second concern relates to the rules that all are required to abide by in order to make democracy sustainable. If the rules are biased in favour of maintaining the status quo, as current rules and laws in South Africa are, what is it that would induce those outside of the status quo, who do not benefit from the status quo, to comply with such laws in the long term, especially if the benefits of doing so are seen to be slow in being realised? This surely cannot be solely their faith and patience in waiting for long-term outcomes. Of course, the key issues relate to what factors actually facilitate such an outcome and how one incorporates actors who are not part of organised political groups, since instability may arise even when there is general agreement among formal political forces to abide by the rules. These concerns lead us to the notion of governance.

Governance

The issue of governance arises at both national and global levels. Mayntz (1998) notes that the original meaning of the term "governance" entailed the notion of a government's ability to steer with the aim of shaping the nature of socio-economic structures and process, generally as an element of one form of planning or another. The term has assumed new, recent meanings, among which are (a) the co-operative, inclusive and consultative forms of interaction between the state and non-state actors, and (b) the different modes of co-ordinating individual actions, or basic forms of social order such as clans, associations and networks. Mayntz (1998) notes that this latter understanding of governance, arising from Williamson's analysis of transaction-cost economics, appears to be the more general form of the term within which the other two versions (steering and co-operative) may be located as subtypes. Of relevance to us is the concern over what forms of governance facilitate consolidation of democracy and developmentalism at the national level and what forms of governance are needed at the global level.

At the national level, some characteristics of good governance are the following, as summarised by Edigheji (2002):

- the need for the state to be relatively autonomous from the interests of particular groups;
- the need for strong civil society, which is able to articulate and promote the interests of the members of their respective groups;
- the need for devolution of power through decentralisation to facilitate a greater responsiveness to local needs;
- the need for embeddedness, whereby there are formal and institutionalised ways in which the interests of various groups are synergised within the state;
- the need for institutionalised procedures and processes for accountability;
- the need for a strong and adaptable bureaucracy that is able to accomplish its administrative, management, implementation and monitoring tasks efficiently and effectively; and
- the need for the primacy of the rule of law.

In the light of the foregoing, there has been much discussion about what suits particular societies in terms of state-society relationships, and how they could be institutionalised for purposes of enhancing governance, democratisation and development. Nonetheless, the notion of governance, like those of globalisation and democracy or democratisation, is a rather fuzzy and superficial one, unless it addresses the core concern of unequal power and how this can be accommodated in the actual practice of governance. As it stands at the moment, the notion is generally utilised uncritically under the assumption that governance can be appended to procedural and representative democracy to enhance the consolidation of democracy and to promote development.

The fundamental question concerns whether good governance structures precede the formulation of the parameters of political debate and the definition of the rules of the game, or whether they follow these once they have been determined by a parochial and top-down process. This is easier to appreciate at the global level. Currently, for some organisations and global transactions, the rules have already been set by the major players, primarily consisting of the developed countries and their erstwhile corporate interests, and are reflected in the statutes and rules of the IMF with respect to international finance, the World Bank with respect to development-related transactions, and the WTO with respect to trade-related matters. A discussion about forms of governance that need to be appended to these bodies will of necessity have to take the fundamental rules and essential nature of these bodies as given. There is very little chance that a new form of governance will be allowed to evolve that would drastically redefine the nature of these bodies and the rules governing them. It would, however, be desirable for a governance structure to be established that is adequately representative of all concerned parties, and that is also equitable on the basis of how the rules governing the respective organisations and their related international transactions are determined.

At the national level, the search for good governance is caught between tokenism and the buying off of constituents, while its relationship to procedural democracy remains ambiguous as well. This is a major problem in countries lacking homogeneity politically, socially and economically, and especially in countries such as South Africa where fragmentation along these lines is quite pronounced both vertically and horizontally. With the establishment of Nedlac, the devolution of development and delivery initiatives to the local level, and the *Batho Pele* (People First) initiative for service delivery, the South African government has taken major strides toward good governance. However, these efforts still remain relatively disarticulated and rather removed from some areas of policy making that would substantively redefine the overall purpose of government, especially with respect to issues of redistribution and promotion of development.

We can expect, therefore, a fairly muted and ambiguous form of governance in a country such as South Africa, for at least two reasons. The first is because the government claims that it has made a policy shift based primarily on a procedural mandate on the basis of which it adopted GEAR without much public discussion or consultation. Secondly, in spite of its enlightened form of procedural democracy, the government has yet to be able to define an all-embracing form of governance that can reflect the diversity of interests in the country, and the need for all such interests to have a say in major policy issues, especially regarding the choice of an economic policy paradigm and the rate and pace at which redistribution of assets can be accomplished on the basis of both welfare and development grounds. In his insistence on the primacy of politics in the pursuit and promotion of democratic governance and democratic development, Leftwitch (1996) observes as follows:

> I start from the assumption that human societies are characterised by diversity of interests, preferences, values and ideas. Each of these directly or indirectly involves the use of resources, or ways of doing things with resources, which individuals or groups seek to protect. In general, also, people prefer to get their way. But they also have to live together and cooperate if they are to prosper, and so constant war and outright victory in dispute is not a viable long-term solution to the problem of diversity of interests, though it often happens. With one possible exception, the human species is the only one to have evolved a set of conscious processes for trying to sort out or resolve these differences. These processes are what I call politics, which may be defined to mean, all the activities, cooperation and negotiation involved in the use, production and distribution of resources, whether material or ideal, whether at local, national or international levels, or whether in the public or private domains. And of course achieving cooperation and negotiation has always been much harder to attain where the differences have been sharp and hence less compatible.

Developmentalism

In the case of South Africa, the issue of purpose is linked to the need to transform the economy in order to make it more inclusive of the previously excluded majority and to ensure the provision of basic needs and appropriate social safety nets. This, indeed, is the development problem that the government has to grapple with and which, in the eyes of the historically disadvantaged majority, is the very reason for government. In his review of the development of democracy, one major conclusion Huntington (1991) arrives at is the fact that the consolidation of democracy requires the realisation of inclusive growth and development, which is the general understanding of what sustainable human development means. Huntington shows that while the major first and second wave democracies embarked on market-led growth and development, more or less at the same time as they embarked upon democratisation through major social and political convulsions, third wave democratic change has been associated with an initial disjuncture between the emergence of democracy and inclusive growth, each of which has preceded or followed the other depending on the context. He argues that among the third-wave countries the sustainability and consolidation of democracy has very much depended on the ability of the government to initiate and sustain broad-based growth and development.

Developmentalism can be understood to refer to a conscious, strategic stance taken by government to promote accelerated economic growth, structural transformation, social development and the repositioning of the economy in the international division of labour by consciously influencing the performance of the market. The nature of the developmental stance can range from mild planning, with the market as the main player, to mandatory planning and socialism at the other extreme, or some form of mixed economy in between. Since the beginning of the 1990s, following the demise of the socialist bloc and the recognition of the success of the East Asian Tigers in their exploitation of both domestic and international market forces through state involvement, the focus of developmentalism has been on the potential for development that could be accomplished through proactive state initiatives in collaboration with private sector actors within a domestic and global market environment. The 1990s have also seen the preoccupation with democratisation as a global concern, and the recognition that many of the East Asian success stories were realised under fairly undemocratic regimes, which would be unacceptable under present circumstances. Thus, in the 1990s, the focus of scholars turned to the potential for promoting developmental democracy, which referred to the need to promote development under democratic and market-based conditions.

Sklar (in Leftwitch, 1996) comments that:

> There are no iron laws of appropriate ideology for either social classes or the functional estates of society. Everywhere, mixed ideologies, like mixed economies, are required to cope with the challenges of our time. A developmental democracy would combine a reasonable measure of social justice, defined as fairness in the distribution of wealth, with economic and political freedom, neither of which has been secure in the midst of deprivation, misery and poverty.

White (in Robinson & White, 1998), in his essay entitled "Constructing a Democratic Developmental State", summarises the different views on the relationship between democracy and development as follows. He identifies, first, an optimistic view, associated with Western donor agencies, whereby liberal democracy is seen to act as a powerful stimulus to societal progress in that it provides a market environment conducive to development. He notes that this view is not adequately supported statistically and that the maintenance of minimal democratic institutional forms is compatible with a pattern of élite-dominated growth that is socially discriminatory, exclusive and politically disempowering. As a second view, he identifies that which insists that while democracy may be a valuable long-term goal it may not be compatible with the need to accelerate economic growth and development in the medium term. White points out that the case for authoritarianism as an instrument for promoting development is weakened once it is recognised that there are many authoritarian states that have mired their countries in poverty, even if a few like the East Asian Tigers can be said to have utilised such regimes in a developmentally successful way. He identifies as a third school one which claims that democratic regimes are not legitimised by their performance but by their procedures. He rightly points out that this argument is sustainable in many least-developed economies, as adequately demonstrated by a number of African countries, where failure to perform or deliver has resulted in unstable democracies. He identifies as a fourth view that which focuses on good governance and state capacity as the major determinants of the developmental performance of a developing country, be it democratic or authoritarian. White notes that the prospect of good governance is questionable in an authoritarian state, and that a good capacity *per se* may not be enough to result in developmentalism as, again, some African states have shown.

White suggests that it is possible to identify requirements for a successful developmental state, which may need to be located within democratic parameters. He identifies the following as main features:

- the need for the élites to have relative autonomy so that they can pursue and implement developmental programmes resolutely (but this should entail consensual autonomy);
- the need for the autonomy to be pursued within the context of embeddedness, whereby "states are part of broader alliances with key social groups which are themselves the stimulus to socio-economic change";
- the need for institutional coherence;
- the need for authoritative penetration, whereby "state institutions are able to extend their regulative and extractive capacities on a consensual basis"; and
- the need for inclusive embeddedness, whereby the élites are made accountable to a much broader range of constituents.

White (in Robinson & White, 1998:31) notes that:

> this political and institutional model of a democratic developmental state should be seen as merely one alternative among a wide range of political economies of democracy with differing levels of state autonomy, institutional coherence, and authoritative penetration and varying ranges of accountability and embeddedness.

He notes, further, that all this depends on the nature of the socio-economic system, civil society, political society, state institutions and the international environment. The requirements stipulated, while informative, might make one wonder as to the feasibility of a democratic developmental state. Also, the list of requirements appears to be more an *ex post facto* explanation and rationalisation of what has transpired elsewhere, rather than a deductively compelling outcome of rational analysis. In any case, the criteria provide a useful checklist that needs to be interrogated in examining the potential, strengths and weaknesses of executing the developmental agenda in any country where the state claims to be developmental, such as in South Africa.

While many of the discussions about the relationship between democracy and development tend to be normative, some analysts have tried to test the statistical relationship between the two objectives (to little avail, however). Hadenius (1991) attempted a number of statistical exercises to tease out the relationship and, primarily, found a weak relationship for which the direction of causality was difficult to identify. Erosson and Lane (in Leftwitch, 1996) tried a similar exercise, and also found weak relationships. Perhaps the conclusion that can be made is that democracy does not impede development, and that it is preferred normatively that development be pursued democratically. The ambiguity of the results may hint at a major problem with the pursuit of development, broadly defined to mean inclusive development, which uplifts the standard of living of the majority of the people.

The problem, as many observers have noted, is that in order to precipitate a developmental momentum redistributive measures are needed, which may not be easily compatible with current definitions of democracy, especially when its procedural or bourgeois form is assumed. Essentially, in countries with grave inequalities, the initiation of development may require tampering with the property rights of privileged individuals or groups, unless these individuals or groups agree to such measures in their own long-term interests or in recognition of the positive outcome that would result in the long term. Hence the need for such pacts to be built into the democratic agenda right from the beginning of the transition to democracy. Again, the case of Zimbabwe provides a good lesson for South Africa. In Zimbabwe, not only did the state eventually resort to undemocratic means because of prior constraints placed on the manner in which land could be distributed, which were built into the transition pact in 1980, but also it was only when the privileged white farmers were pushed into a corner that they began to propose innovative ways in which land could be shared with the majority African population.

The problem in South Africa

The development problem raises at least two issues in the context of the sustainability of democracy. Currently, the South African government has adopted GEAR as the major basis for economic reforms, and in doing so it is confronted with a political problem and an economic one. The political problem relates to the degree to which the government can continue to rely on the support of its major constituencies and other allies outside the alliance in pursuing the adopted economic reforms. Dissatisfaction is emerging among the alliance partners and among the traditional constituencies of the dominant party. The economic problem concerns the degree to which the economic reforms can begin to deliver in terms of achieving the goal of sustainable human development, especially to the benefit of the majority of the historically disadvantaged constituency. Both considerations combine to influence the degree of confidence that the majority of the people have in the economic reforms and in the ability of the government to deliver on its promises. As Przerwoski (1991:168) observes:

> Confidence does play a crucial role in shaping popular reactions. People's evaluation of their future streams of consumption depends on how certain they feel their consumption will in fact increase as a result of present sacrifices. They are willing to suffer in the short run if they believe in the long run. This confidence is to a large extent endogenous. The reason is that people do not know how costly and how long the transition will be. Structural transformations of the economy are a plunge into opaque waters: The people do not know where the bottom is and how long they will have to hold their breath. All they know is what they were told would happen and what is happening: whether they are still plunging or already emerging, whether things have turned around … Confidence is a stock: It can be depleted and it can be accumulated. It can be eroded in two ways: by erroneous forecasts and by vacillations.

In the case of GEAR, the forecasts on the real side (output and employment growth) have been erroneous, being well below the announced targets, and the government has decided not to vacillate, or be seen to be doing so, by sticking to its announced programme. Meanwhile, time is moving on in the absence of demonstrable real results from the economic reforms. The issue, then, is not so much one of patriotism or the lack of it, if one asks what the consequences of this outcome are for the future of democracy in South Africa. This is a question that is in the interests of both the people and the government of South Africa, if subsequent political disasters are to be avoided.

Przerwoski (1991:189) concurs with Huntington that democratisation in relatively poor countries like South Africa is a particularly onerous task. He observes that, in order to be consolidated:

> democratic institutions must at the same time protect all major interests and generate economic results … The durability of the new democracies will depend, however, not only on their structure and the ideology of major political forces, but to a large extent on their economic performance. Profound economic reforms must be undertaken if there is to be any hope that the deterioration in living conditions experienced by many nascent democratic will ever cease.

The danger is that when results become elusive and the confidence among groups begins to wane, the temptation to move toward authoritarianism becomes great; as the economy of the country declines, "the technocratic style of policy making, and the ineffectiveness of the representative institutions undermine the popular support for democracy" (Przerwoski, 1991:190).

However, as noted by Bratton and Van de Walle (1997:240):

Democratic governments rarely rely for legitimacy on economic performance to the same extent as authoritarian governments do, but they too must improve the material conditions on their watch. In a consolidated democracy, economic grievances are expressed through the ballot box and can lead to the replacement of one elected government by another; in non-consolidated democracy, however, the penalty for poor performance may well signal the end of democratic rule itself and return to authoritarianism ... As anywhere elected governments enjoy an initial honeymoon during which they are not held responsible for economic conditions. Soon enough, however, populations forget previous hardships and come to associate their own well-being with the current government's policies and actions.

On the basis of a review of recent experiences in Africa, the authors conclude that the "condition of the economy thus typically poses a daunting challenge for Africa's fledgling democracies". Przerwoski (1991) and Huntington (1991) share this view.

The adoption of economic reforms aimed at liberalisation and outward orientation of the economy along the lines of GEAR have profound implications for both the substantive content of democracy and the pursuit of the development project. Some observers note that the process of economic reform tends to lead to the realignment of government and various interest groups. It results in the strengthening of the executive branch, and a reliance on technocrats, while power in government also shifts to ministries of finance. The isolation of economic advisors increases while the role of technocrats increases. The politician's dilemma is seen to be the need to contain parochial and clientelist policies, and redistribution policies, by empowering distanced agents to make recommendations; hence, the reliance on technocrats, seemingly under the assumption that they are best suited to maximise long-term social rather than private interests. Unfortunately, this ignores the fact that, even under such circumstances, the policy environment favours owners of capital, and the procedural form of democracy actually facilitates their interests. Owners of capital would tend to be very supportive of such changes, as long as they have avenues of influencing government policies. In the final analysis, it is the masses of the people whose interests are compromised in the name of anticipated long-term gains.

Whatever the speculations about the relationship between the pursuit of economic reforms and the consolidation of nascent democracies, the issues at stake are quite straightforward in terms of their long-term implications for stability and viability of governments. First, in countries that are impoverished or that are characterised by gross inequities, such as those in South Africa, with one group very well provided for as a consequence of past policies promoted by a biased and discriminatory state while the other group is very poor, it is necessary to ask whether GEAR-type economic reforms can provide an adequate overarching framework within which to pursue a development agenda. This issue can be explored theoretically and with respect to actual outcomes of economic reforms in South Africa.

Since there is enough evidence to show that the economic reforms are not yielding much on the real front, the second issue concerns the degree to which the negative consequences of the declining economic conditions and living standards among the government's main constituency may be leading to disillusionment, and thus to what degree such disillusionment might pose a threat to the consolidation of democracy.

The third issue concerns what options would be available in attempting to maintain, promote and consolidate sustainable human development through a combination of the economic and social upliftment of the majority and democratisation, so as to avoid instability that might reverse the democratic gains that have been made so far.

In the light of the above issues, the following propositions may be advanced:

1. While procedural provisions and practices are the *sine qua non* of democracy, as currently understood by many in the West, they are not enough to accommodate and facilitate the needs of the poor, marginalised and previously excluded majority in South Africa, given that this country has inherited structural forms of exclusion and marginalisation that continue to operate, often reinforced by market forces. The contention here is that substantive forms of consultation and participation are needed to supplement procedural provisions and practices. In particular, there have to be institutionalised ways in which previously disadvantaged groups can directly influence policy, to ensure that the government lives up to the purpose for which it was elected (that is, by ensuring that the "common good" and the "will of the people" are largely guaranteed).

2. It will be argued that the structural legacies of exclusion and marginalisation in South Africa and the consequent inequities these imply are such that a policy approach predicated on a paradigm that requires developmental measures to be subordinated to the primacy of macroeconomic fundamentals and restructuring policies, such as those of GEAR, is not likely to succeed in promoting sustainable human development; it is more likely to pose insurmountable problems in the medium to long term for the consolidation of democracy, the procedural gains notwithstanding.

3. In the light of the above, it will be argued that the problem is such that it demands a revisiting of the nature and meaning of democracy, and the need to subordinate macroeconomic policies to a proactive development programme, which should have primacy in policy making.

The above propositions tally with the sentiments expressed by various critics of the present transition, especially with respect to the adoption of GEAR as the dominant policy regime. Thus, Marais (1998:5) has observed that:

> Left unchecked the defining trends of the transition seem destined to shape a revised definition of society, with the current order stabilized around at best 30% of the population. For the

rest (overwhelmingly young, female, and African) the best hope will have some trickle-down from a 'modernized" and 'normalized' new South Africa. This raises not only moral but political dilemmas, not least of which is the danger that the incumbent elites come to view the excluded majority as a threat to newly acquired privilege and power, thereby introducing the spectre of a new bout of authoritarianism in response to social instability.

Similarly, Bond (2000:8) has commented that:

> Being quite close to key decision-makers, both political and bureaucratic, has given me the conviction that a through-going democratic transition beyond what elite South Africa offers is not only a matter of understanding the objective preconditions – which now, at the moment of neo-liberalism's global gaffes, are ripe indeed – but subjectively a matter of political will. Rebuilding the mass democratic movements to articulate a programme for a society and economy beyond what decaying capitalism has on offer, is thus now more urgent than ever.

From a different perspective altogether, Giliomee and Simkins (1999:44) arrive at a similar conclusion by analysing the prospects of the dominant party consolidating itself and, thereby, also consolidating democracy:

> Several variables affect the adaptive capacity of the dominant party and its ability to deepen the democratic system over which it presides. Broad-based economic development, which narrows inequalities and improves per capita income is undoubtedly most desirable for movement in the direction of liberal democracy with a competitive party system. It is no coincidence that the prospects for democracy are best in Taiwan where inequalities between the top and lowest quintiles were the narrowest in the industrializing world when it embarked on democratisation. By contrast, Mexico and South Africa show the greatest inequality among the countries for which data are available and the prospects for a stable and lasting liberal democracy are uncertain. The ANC is also a racially based party and the greatest test will be how, in conditions of low economic growth, the party will handle white-black inequalities.

The economic limits to GEAR

GEAR may be an appropriate strategy to stabilise the domestic economy and integrate the formal and dynamic part of it into the global economy. It does not suffice as a growth and development strategy. It might be claimed that not enough time has been allowed for the restructuring envisioned by GEAR to take place, which would result in a virtuous cycle of growth and development, and that in any case the government has some developmental measures in place and is continuously refining its implementation policies to better impact on growth and development. Such claims are predicated on the assumption that the market can undo the structural constraints inherited from the past, and that the developmental initiatives in place are coherent enough and of sufficient critical mass to kick-start an inclusive growth path toward sustainable development. These claims are not sustainable under current circumstances.

Democratic South Africa inherited an economy that was dominated by an enclave formal sector, which acted as the engine of growth based on past protectionist and discriminatory policies, and which while utilising part of the majority population as its labour force also excluded and marginalised it. This was institutionalised through apartheid. The consequences of an interventionist and protectionist state combined with formal discrimination are many and complex.

The overall problem confronting the economy, and on the basis of which the development problem rests, relates to the fact that a significant proportion of the labour force is marginalised and under-utilised, because of the historical reasons of discrimination and the very manner in which settler capitalism developed. This residue of underemployed labour acts as a damper on growth and development by constraining the ability of the economy to precipitate an endogenous, virtuous cycle, founded on the broad-based participation of the majority in productive activities, which should lead to increased internal demand, and the generation of increased domestic savings as a basis for mobilising internal resources, which should fuel growth and development. By the very same token, the economy is disarticulated in a manner that marginalises and excludes a large segment of the labour force while exploiting it as a basis for the dynamism of the formal economy.

The disarticulation of the economy is manifested in a number of eventualities, which underpin the coexistence of a low-income equilibrium trap of underdevelopment in particular sectors, such as the rural and informal sectors, with a relatively dynamic, but enclave, formal sector.

First, there are distributive inequalities, which act as a constraint on one segment of the population but act as a facilitator of economic participation on another part of the population. These relate to unequal access to physical and financial resources, land, human capital and social capital. These endowments have historically been biased in favour of the White population, which constitutes about 13% of the population but controls the majority of these assets, and against the Black, in particular the African, population. This inequality conditions chances of economic participation and success not only in a static manner, but also a dynamic manner, since the benefits accruing from ownership of productive assets tend to be self-reinforcing and cumulative over time. The performance of the market merely facilitates the reproduction of existing inequalities in access to assets. It should be noted here that, while there can be marginal changes in resource endowments, with previously excluded groups making inroads into existing ownership structures or actually adding to an existing stock of overall assets, the broad parameters of the distribution of assets are not easily changed through market activity. In addition, it should be noted that the initial distribution of endowments was not itself based on market principles. The unequal distribution of assets implied unequal abilities to participate in the market, and unequal benefits from participating in market activities.

Second, there are allocative inefficiencies resulting from the discriminatory allocation of labour, land, government expenditures on infrastructure and incentives structures. There is a tendency for over-consumption and under-utilisation of such assets among the privileged groups, and under-consumption and under-utilisation among the disadvantaged. Generally, these have resulted in relatively capital-intensive forms of production and a bias toward relatively large-scale forms of enterprise. Thus, employment elasticities with respect to output and investment tend to be low, while the allocation of investments is biased toward those activities for which effective demand is increasing and for which returns are high. Such activities may not necessarily be the ones with high employment multipliers and broad developmental spill-over effects in the economy. Within this context, the allocation and utilisation of labour in South Africa represents a major misallocation of resources, because of the manner in which the labour force is segmented on the basis of race and gender, and the manner in which access to education and training was manipulated to reproduce a particular type of labour-force composition that fitted into a discriminatory demand structure of labour utilisation. Consequently, there is an oversupply of lower level (secondary) labour, while there is a shortage of higher level (primary) labour. Meanwhile, the economy's demand for labour is shifting from reliance on lower skilled labour to reliance on relatively skilled labour, which the economy is unable to supply in adequate numbers, because of past biases in education and training.

Third, there are microeconomic constraints that relate to the fact that many firms have historically under-performed, because of the protective environment that nurtured them, and even if they are now forced to restructure and operate more efficiently such restructuring presents major hurdles. Small, micro and medium enterprises (SMMEs), which should be the vehicle for broadening the economy, have not only been constrained by inadequate access to capital and other related resources, but have also been penalised by a non-conducive policy environment biased against them in favour of large-scale firms, and by the under-development of value chains, particularly in rural areas. All these consequences imply that SMMEs cannot uplift themselves by their bootstraps and take advantage of a supposedly conducive market environment that easily, without any additional support or incentives.

Fourth, spatial patterns arising from apartheid zoning regulations have increased transaction costs for many rural and township residents, while militating against clustering and exploitation of economies of agglomeration among the historically disadvantaged. The increased transaction costs act as a major constraint on economic participation. The spatial legacies in South Africa are biased against rural development in former homelands and in favour of concentrating economic activities in the major centres that have already developed. An inclusive growth path would demand dispersion of growth points, such that smaller and medium-sized agglomerations begin to create a basis for the development of SMMEs and rural non-farming activities.

Finally, there are dynamic consequences of the economic enclave legacy, which entail a low-income equilibrium trap whereby the presence of a large under-utilised labour force implies low effective internal demand that, in turn, leads to excess capacity in some enterprises and sectors. The low levels of internal demand also imply inadequate incomes and inadequate internal savings and resources for investment. Thus, the economy is forced to rely on external demand, in the form of exports to shore up demand, and on external savings and investment for resource mobilisation. In addition, given that a large segment of the population does not contribute to production, and government revenues have not satisfied social needs (many of which are a result of past injustices), the state is confronted with increasing social demands while its capacity to meet them is limited.

GEAR is predicated on creating an enabling environment for the market to restructure the economy through the vertical and lateral expansion of the formal part of the economy, as increased formal domestic and foreign investments drive growth; and as SMMEs benefit from the growth in the large-scale formal economy through trickle-down effects and exploitation of the new market environment; and while the non-formal sectors and the formal sector integrate, as the latter transforms the former. Within this context, the government is expected to play an enabling role by providing a good macroeconomic environment, and by nudging the economic players through provision of infrastructure and incentives and an appropriate regulatory environment. Also within this context, in order to facilitate restructuring and to boost investor confidence, the government is expected to continue with privatisation and realignment of the public sector. Furthermore, the government has also committed itself to developmental microeconomic initiatives such as development corridors, a new manufacturing strategy, a skills-development strategy, local economic development, municipal infrastructure programmes and other similar measures. But these measures have been marginal to the major stance taken, implying that the market should do the main job of restructuring the economy. In addition, the various developmental measures have not had the scale and critical mass to appreciably begin to make a difference to the structure of the economy, especially with respect to its inclusiveness. Indeed, any measures that have been seen to be too interventionist have been met with an immediate reaction from investors, who have objected to them through the stock market and by voicing their dissatisfaction in the media. This has been the case particularly with Black Economic Empowerment initiatives such as the Mining Charter.

It is on the basis of the foregoing assumptions that GEAR projected a growth rate of about 6%, which would begin to eat away at the backlog of under-utilised labour in the economy. However, the economy has been unable to break through the 3% annual growth rate in gross domestic product, while unemployment and poverty levels have been increasing. The claim being made here is that, in the absence of bold measures to address the structural distortion discussed above, the economy will be caught in low equilibrium trap of low employment levels, low levels of internal savings, consumer demand, skills, and internal investment, primarily because structural factors prevent a significant majority of the labour force from engaging in productive economic activities. Indeed, the contractionary consequences of the economic reforms have been greater than their stimulative effects on the economy.

"Real"-economy consequences of GEAR

Whatever its justification on theoretical grounds, GEAR has not been able to result in an appreciable improvement in the real economy. One might argue that matters could have been worse in the absence of GEAR-type measures, given the turmoil in world markets since the democratic dispensation. It could also be claimed that external factors have constrained the efficacy of GEAR. It is, nonetheless, true that the government has not had a bold approach to development, so the consequences of a proactive and grand state-led strategy of transformation are also not known.

Regardless, the issue is that the marginal changes anticipated by GEAR have not materialised on the real economy side, and the major structural inequities inherited from the apartheid era have either worsened or not changed much at all. Interestingly, also, recent evidence suggests that income inequalities among Africans are increasing.

The indications so far are that there is unlikely to be a major challenge to the democratic dispensation soon. While there are sporadic instances of protest, particularly among the very poor in informal settlements and among some landless rural folk, these have been relatively uneventful and within what would be permissible in a democratic dispensation. It is also clear that the government is making an honest effort to improve service delivery with respect to expanding access to water, health, education, electricity and housing, and that there is interest in providing a comprehensive social safety net as well. The major concern, however, remains the fact that unemployment, poverty and socio-economic inequalities, with their associated social pathologies such as high levels of crime, abuse of women and children, social dislocation, and now the impact of HIV/Aids, continue to beleaguer the South African polity. When socio-economic maladies afflict a large proportion of the population, and persist unabated, they do not only represent a development problem, rather than a mere growth problem, but they also pose a risk to the maintenance and consolidation of a democratic dispensation. Below, we give some illustrations of the inadequacy of the incremental or marginal changes in key real-side economic aggregates and of some indicators of the enormity and gravity of the deteriorating socio-economic situation for the majority of the population, who are the presumed beneficiaries of the new democratic dispensation.

Trends in major economic aggregates

Macroeconomic fundamentals

The government has achieved major successes in stabilising the economy in the process of integrating and repositioning it in the regional and global economies. Through tight monetary and fiscal policies, the rate of inflation has been brought down considerably from its the double-digit levels of the pre-1994 period. Between 1994 and 1997 the consumer and production price index was between 8% and 10% and declined progressively thereafter to below 6% in 2000 and 2001, although it began to increase again in 2002. The decline and relative stabilisation of inflation has been due to tight monetary policy reflected in high interest rates, with the repo rate hovering above 10% (even if it had declined from its relatively high levels of the pre-1994 period, when it was above 15%), and due to the drastic reduction in the government deficit from about R25 billion in 1994 to under R20 billion five years later.

However, the liberalisation and opening up of the economy has also resulted in the depreciation of the rand against the currencies of major trading partners, which has put pressure on prices as well. The rand plummeted in value from about R3.50 per US$ in 1994 to an average of more than R10.00 per US$ during the first two years of this century, although it is currently firming up and, at the time of writing, has gone below R8.00 to the US$.

External influences and considerations appear to be the primary determinants of macroeconomic policy in South Africa, while internal considerations of restructuring and development remain secondary, in that they have to be accommodated within the broader externally pitched macroeconomic policy regime. Put differently, the government believes that by stabilising the economy through tight fiscal and monetary policy, coupled with liberalisation of the trade regime and domestic markets, it is creating an environment conducive to growth and development. Thus, the various developmental measures currently being promoted are being undertaken within the constraints and parameters of stabilisation policies. The question that arises is whether this approach allows for an adequate developmental critical minimum effort or "big push" to address the task at hand. Developments on the real side of the economy suggest otherwise.

Trends in economic growth

When the democratic dispensation came into place, GDP had been declining progressively from the 1980s onwards. In 1995, the average rate of growth in GDP was below 2%. It increased dramatically in 1996, averaging more than 4%, but declined again until 1998, when it fell below 2%. It has been increasing since 1999 but still remains lacklustre at between 3% and 4%. GEAR had predicted a growth rate that would have been approaching 6% by the end of the twentieth century. When the growth rate in GDP hovers around 3%, it is barely above the growth in population, which is slightly above 2%, hence per capita incomes are only marginally increasing (South African Quarterly Bulletin, 1994–2001).This is a major problem in a country with such a backlog of socio-economic needs, especially when the resulting growth, even though minimal, is not equally shared.

Trends in employment and unemployment

The low rates of GDP growth have been reflected in low rates of employment expansion in the formal economy. Although it is estimated that more than a million jobs were created over the first five years of democratic rule, most of these jobs were in the non-formal sectors and many of them represented atypical forms of employment. Nonetheless, the rate of job creation or labour absorption has been so low that unemployment has been increasing. In 1998, the Industrial Development Corporation (IDC) commented as follows with respect to their scenarios on employment:

> The BASELINE scenario is characterized by marginal employment, with the bulk of additional job opportunities arising from the services sector. The HIGH scenario, on the other hand, witnesses acceleration in manufacturing employment growth. The economy is expected to become more capital intensive. In most sectors: the capital-to-labour ratio is set to rise; capital productivity should decline; and labour productivity may improve. This reflects a pattern of industrialization that is more typical of a developed, rather than a developing economy. (IDC, 1998)

Statistics South Africa (2001) reported that the number of people employed in both formal and informal sectors increased from 9.6 million in 1995 to about 10.4 million in

1999, while the number of unemployed, by the official (strict) definition, increased from 1.8 million in 1995 to about 3.2 million in 1999. While some sectors have been expanding employment, as a result of the restructuring taking place, many more have been shedding labour, so the net increases in formal sector employment have been low. Under such circumstances, with the population increasing, unemployment has grown at an alarming rate. By 1999, the overall unemployment rate, by the strict definition, was 23.2% (while by the expanded definition it was 36.2%) and has been increasing since then. The unemployment rates differ by gender, race and location. Thus, in 1999 the unemployment rates (expanded in brackets) were: 20% (30%) for males and 28% (43%) for females; 29% (44%) for Africans, 15% (24%) for Coloureds, 16% (20%) for Indians and 5% (7%) for Whites; and 18% (26%) for males in urban areas, 23% (37%) for males in non-urban areas, 26% (38%) for females in urban areas and 32% (53%) for females in non-urban areas.

When the high rates in unemployment are combined with the numbers of those who are underemployed in the rural and urban non-formal sectors, it is obvious that the proportion of the labour force that is either unutilised or under-utilised is quite high; and this is one way of appreciating the nature of the development task that still confronts South Africa. It has to be reiterated that with current rates of economic growth well under 6%, each year results in a net addition to this pool of under-utilised resources. Apart from the welfare and growth implications of this labour reserve, there may be a major threat to the sustainability of the democratic process if measures are not put in place to address the problem of unemployment and underemployment.

Pervasive and persistent poverty

Figure 2.1 shows that levels of poverty are quite high and increasing. This poverty is underpinned by inadequate employment opportunities, low levels of education and inadequate access to economic assets. The incidence of poverty is further compounded by the increase in the incidence of HIV/Aids and by the privatisation or restructuring of social services such as health, water, electricity, education and housing provision. A participatory poverty assessment (May *et al.*, 1998) confirmed that:

● there is a wide array of distortions, which characterise most markets in South Africa, that are as much a result of dispossession and restriction as of subsidies and privilege;
● the abuse of children in all forms is pervasive;
● seasonal changes increase stress placed on the poor;
● men have become marginalised through unemployment, social institutions and the absence of alternative opportunities and, as a result, can be an economic and physical threat to women and children;

Figure 2.1: Poverty incidence by province

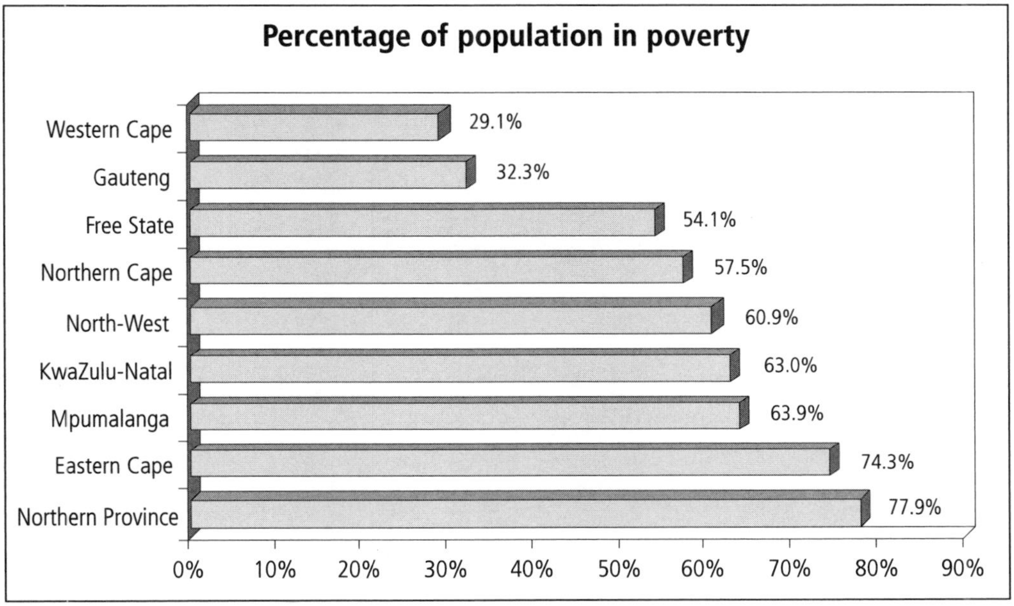

Percentage of population in poverty

Province	Percentage
Western Cape	29.1%
Gauteng	32.3%
Free State	54.1%
Northern Cape	57.5%
North-West	60.9%
KwaZulu-Natal	63.0%
Mpumalanga	63.9%
Eastern Cape	74.3%
Northern Province	77.9%

Source: Whiteford & Van Seventer (1999), reproduced in Department of Social Development (2002)

- local government and local community structures are fragmented and in disarray; and
- disasters, including violence and crime, play a devastating role by stripping the poor of their hard-won assets.

The poverty assessment concludes that despite hardships confronting the poor, they have shown a high degree of resilience and represent an enormous resource for growth and development that can only be realised once the constraints that block their participation in the economy are removed.

Employees per household

Figure 2.2 shows that households in the lower-income deciles tend to have fewer workers than those in the higher-level deciles. This is another way of illustrating how income and asset differentials get reproduced over time, since the poorer households tend to have lesser incomes for both consumption and savings, while the households at higher-income deciles tend to have greater access to income sources and, therefore, have a greater ability for consumption and savings.

The increased differentiation in incomes is illustrated by Figure 2.3 below, which shows that the largest increases in income have occurred among the richest 20% of Blacks, while

Figure 2.2: Employment per household by income decile

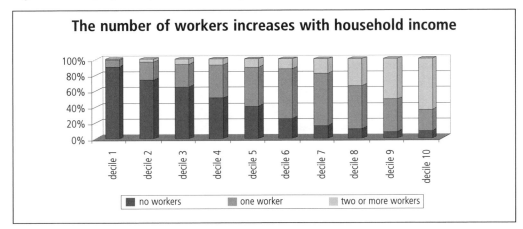

Source: Department of Social Development (2002)

incomes have declined among Whites generally. Thus, it can be accepted that redistribution has been taking place over the years but that this redistribution has also resulted in differentiation among Blacks, whereby the poorer groups have tended to become even poorer. This is an outcome that goes against the objective of promoting sustainable development, in terms of which growth is supposed to impact positively on the poorest groups in the society.

Household income by race

Figure 2.3 shows growth of household income by race. The data hints at an increasing differentiation among Blacks, in that the incomes of the upper quintiles are increasing and those at the bottom end are declining. Further, it shows that the gap between Whites and Blacks is narrowing, in part through increases in the incomes of upper-level Blacks and in part because of declining incomes among Whites. This has important implications for the politics related to the thrust of economic policy and democracy. It can be speculated that the fact that there are differential gains among Blacks from the current economic environment and policy regime might imply that the Black constituency is becoming relatively fragmented and differentiated, with attendant implications for the political economy of democratisation and the contestation of the direction of economic policy.

Income distribution

Table 2.1 shows the income shares by race over the period 1970 to 1996. The table shows that by 1996, Whites, who accounted for about 13% of the population, received about

Figure 2.3: Growth of household income by race (1991–1996)

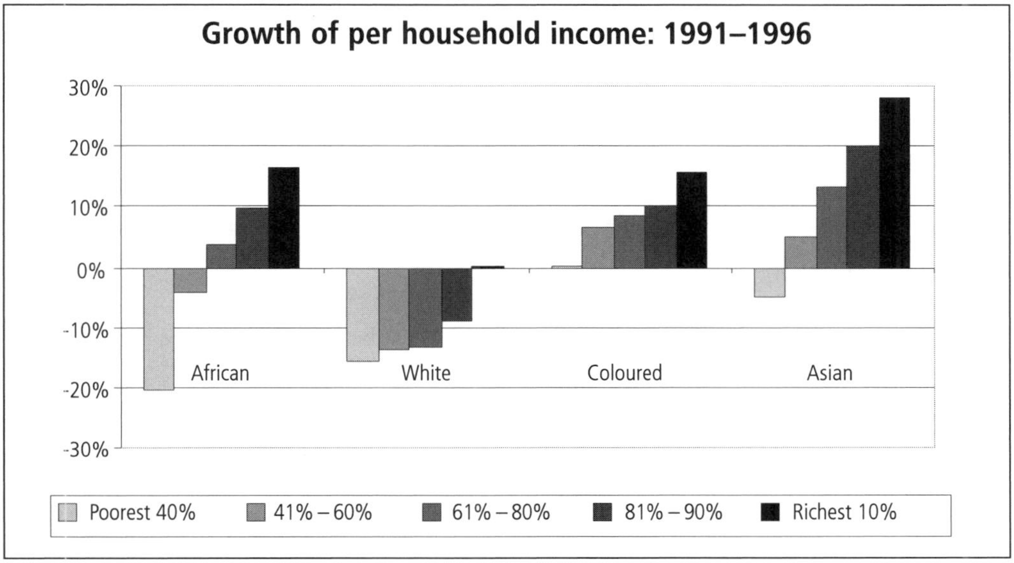

Source: Whiteford and van Seventer (1999:ii), reproduced in Department of Social Development (2002)

Table 2.1: Racial income and population shares (1970–1996)

	Share of total income				Share of population			
	1970	1980	1991	1996	1970	1980	1991	1996
African	19.8%	24.9%	29.9%	35.7%	70.7%	72.4%	75.2%	76.2%
White	71.2%	65.0%	59.5%	51.9%	17.0%	15.5%	13.5%	12.6%
Coloured	6.7%	7.2%	6.8%	7.9%	9.4%	9.3%	8.7%	8.6%
Asian	2.4%	3.0%	3.8%	4.5%	2.9%	2.8%	2.6%	2.6%
Total	100%	100%	100%	100%	100%	100%	100%	100%

Sources: 1970 and 1980 data from McGrath (1983), 1991 data from Whiteford and McGrath (1994), 1970 and 1980 population data estimated from Sadie (1993), as presented in Department of Social Development (2002)

Note: totals may not add up to 100% due to rounding

52% of the total income. The shares are highly unequal in spite of the declining White share of income and the increasing African share of income over the years. The increased share of income among Africans has been accompanied by increasing differentiation among Africans, with the growth of an African élite, which may account for some of the increased support for GEAR-type measures among some African professionals and entrepreneurs. More recent data confirms the above trends.

The following tables illustrate that the situation has not changed much. Table 2.2 shows the disproportionate nature of the income shares on the basis of race for each income group. As can be seen, the unequal nature of the composition of income shares has not changed much between 1996 and 2000, with Blacks and Africans, in particular, accounting for smaller shares of the upper-income brackets and bigger shares of the lower-income brackets, with the reverse applying for Whites.

Table 2.2: Total personal income by population group and income group, 1996 and 2000 (current prices)

	Year	Indians Rm	%	Africans Rm	%	Coloureds Rm	%	Whites Rm	%	Total
Low										
Up to R6 000 pa	1996	431	1.6	22 979	83.6	2 668	9.7	1 393	5.1	27 471
Up to R7 710 pa	2000	568	1.5	32 122	84.2	3 498	9.4	1 870	4.9	38 058
Low-middle										
R6 001–R30 000	1996	6 153	4.5	88 147	64.8	16 019	11.8	25 780	18.9	136 091
R7 711–R38 550	2000	8 599	4.4	129 528	66.2	22 682	11.7	34 603	17.7	195 412
Middle										
R30 001–R72 000	1996	8 856	5.7	72 341	32.7	12 158	7.8	113 356	53.9	156 661
R38 551–R92 520	2000	11 995	5.6	51 197	33.0	17 206	8.0	84 4505	2.7	214 898
High-middle										
R72 001–R192 000	1996	4 738	4.4	15 019	13.8	3 350	3.1	85 605	78.7	108 712
R92 521–R246 720	2000	7 356	4.8	25 892	16.9	5 034	3.3	114 905	75.0	153 187
High										
R192 001+	1996	1 718	3.3	6 489	12.4	1 072	2.0	43 031	82.3	52 310
R246 721+	2000	2 778	3.5	17 740	22.0	2 045	2.1	57 758	71.9	80 321
Total	1996	21 896	4.5	183 831	38.1	35 267	7.3	240 259	49.9	481 254
	2000	31 296	4.6	277 623	40.7	50 465	7.4	322 492	47.3	681 876

Source: Bureau of Market Research (2000)

Note: At 1996 prices, low income refers to: individual income up to R6 000 per annum, low-middle (R6 001–R30 000 per annum), middle (R30 001–R72 000 per annum), high-middle (R72 001–R192 000 per annum), and high (R192 001+ per annum). This translated to approximately the following income groups for 2000: low (up to R7 710 per annum), low-middle (R7 711–R38 550 per annum), middle (R38 551–R92 520 per annum), high-middle (R92 521–R246 720 per annum) and high (R246 721+ per annum).

Table 2.3: Personal income per capita by racial group, 1960–2000 (constant 2000 prices), and Indian, African and Coloured income as a percentage of White income per capita

Year	Indian		African		Coloured		White	Total
	Personal income R	As a % of White income per capita	Personal income R	As a % of White income per capita	Personal income R	As a % of White income per capita	Personal income R	Personal income R
1960	6 159	17.5	2 874	8.2	5 236	14.9	35 328	8 986
1970	10 084	20.4	3 854	7.8	7 714	15.6	49 455	12 157
1980	15 786	29.7	5 425	10.2	10 413	19.6	53 193	13 584
1990	21 039	33.9	6 405	10.3	12 049	19.4	62 072	14 665
1994	23 468	40.7	6 680	11.6	11 951	20.7	57 675	13 983
2000	28 377	46.0	8 022	13.0	13 420	21.8	61 637	15 253

Source: Bureau of Market Research (2000)

Table 2.3 shows that while some gains have been made in that the per capita incomes of Blacks have been increasing absolutely and as a percentage of the per capita incomes of Whites, the income disparities are still quite huge, and that between 1994 and 2000 the gains made by Blacks were relatively marginal.

Table 2.4: Total personal income by population group, 1960–2000 (current prices)

	Indian	African	Coloured	White	Total
1960 Rm	91	1 037	241	3 248	4 409
%	2.0	22.5	5.2	70.4	100
1970 Rm	258	2 422	645	7 483	
%	2.4	22.4	6.0	69.2	100
1980 Rm	1 392	12 361	3 030	25 943	42 726
%	3.3	28.9	7.1	60.7	100
1990 Rm	8 706	77 266	16 509	131 716	236 196
%	3.7	33	7	56.2	100
1994 Rm x	16 115	138 325	27 383	197 165	378 988
%	4.3	36.5	7.2	52	100
2000 Rm	31 296	277 623	50 465	322 492	681 876
%	4.6	40.7	7.4	47.3	100

Source: Bureau of Market Research (2000)

Table 2.4 shows that the proportional shares of income on the basis of race are narrowing significantly as Blacks move into previously excluded forms of employment and economic activity. It should be noted, however, that within this context income differentials within the Black community are increasing, with the poorer majority accounting for a smaller share. The table, nonetheless, shows the grave nature of inequalities in that Whites, who account for about 13% of the population, accounted for 47% of incomes in 2000, while Africans, who account for about 76% of the population, accounted for only 41% of total income in 2000. Figure 2.4 shows the income shares of each racial group in each decile range.

Figure 2.4: Income deciles by racial/population group, 1993.

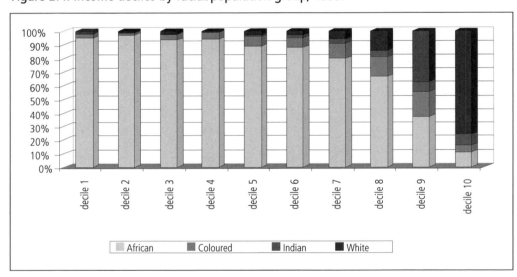

Source: Department of Social Development (2002)

Composition of Household Income

Figure 2.5 shows that transfers account for a greater part of the income of the lowest three deciles, while wage income, followed by self-employment and capital income, accounts for the greater part of the income of the higher deciles, thereby underscoring the importance of employment as a direct and indirect (through remittances) source of livelihood. When this aspect is linked to the data on employment and unemployment discussed above, it is clear that poverty is underpinned by the inadequacy of employment and income generating opportunities, again underscoring the nature of the development problem that confronts South Africa.

Figure 2.5: Composition of household income by decile and source

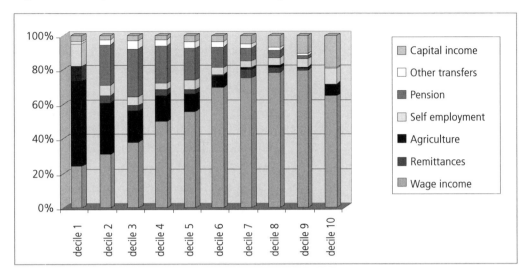

Source: Department of Social Development (2002)

Notes: Wage income includes regular wages (after tax), casual wages and the value of employer subsidies of transport, food and housing; remittances include the value of remittances in money and in kind; agriculture includes the value of agricultural production whether consumed or sold; self-employment comprises the profits earned from self-employment; pension comprises government old-age pensions; other transfers comprise other public transfers; capital income includes income from capital, actual and imputed rent on land and property, interest on financial assets and income from contributory pension schemes. n = 8567.

● The top five deciles were heavily dependent on wages from regular employment. The top, or 10th, decile supplemented wage income (64.5%) with small but significant incomes from agriculture (6.8%), self-employment (6.7%) and income from capital (12.1%).

● Government old-age pensions were of minimal importance to the top decile (at less than 1.0%). The lower, poorer deciles relied more heavily on remittances and old-age pensions.

● Income from agricultural production was of little importance, except to the top decile (which included high-income, capitalist farmers) and the bottom decile (where the incomes were so low that even R8 per month from smallholdings was an important contribution to the decile's income).

● Public transfer payments other than old-age pensions were of little importance.

Access to services

The government's best performance has been in the delivery of services. This is a key area, since it is the basis on which the public and, in particular, the historically disadvantaged majority is likely to lay primary emphasis, second perhaps to employment, in assessing government performance and the success of the new dispensation. Based on findings of the October Household Surveys from 1995 to 1999, Statistics South Africa (2001) reports as follows.

Housing: Between 1995 and 1999, the proportion of households living in formal dwellings increased from 66% to 70%, while those living in informal dwellings also increased from about 8% in 1995 to 12% in 1999. There was a decrease in the proportion living in traditional dwellings, from 15% in 1995 to 11% in 1999. Progress is still being made on the housing front, but the backlog far outruns the construction and delivery of housing.

Water: This is an area that has received much publicity from the government and in which there has been some progress, with about 83% of households having access to water in 1999 compared to 79% in 1995. Not only is the increase rather small, however, but the proportion of those resorting to non-piped sources of water remained constant, "possibly indicating that improved access to clean water had not significantly affected previously disadvantaged households living in deep rural areas" (Statistics South Africa, 2001:4).

Electricity: There was a gradual increase in households using electricity for lighting, from 64% in 1995 to 70% in 1999, with a gradual decrease in the percentage using paraffin and candles. The proportion of those using electricity for cooking remained constant over the period, at slightly more than 50%, which "may be due, in part, to costs for electricity and appliances", as demonstrated by the fact that the proportion using paraffin for cooking increased over the period (Statistics South Africa, 2001:4).

Healthcare: Public health facilities were the most commonly utilised health facilities over the period, but the proportion of households using such facilities remained relatively constant, at 68% in 1995 and 69% in 1999.

Refuse removal: There was no marked change in this category, with 55% of the households having access to this service over the period.

Sanitation: There was a slight decrease in the proportion of households with access to flush or chemical toilets, from 57% in 1995 to 56% in 1999. At the same time, there was a slight increase, from 8% to 11%, in the proportion of households using informal facilities such as a river, stream or bush (Statistics South Africa, 2001:4).

Telephones: The proportion of households with mobile or home telephones increased from 29% to 35%.

Education: About 94% of children between the ages of seven and 15 are able to attend school at the moment in South Africa; however, "actual education attainment among school-goers (as well as adults) tends to be rather low. Children seem to be struggling to complete both primary and secondary school. Relatively few people attend tertiary school" (Statistics South Africa, 2001:2). About 16% of those who were 16 years and older could not read in at least one language. Attendance at non-school educational institutions tended to be low over the period.

From the above, a number of points may be stressed. Given that this is a key area of government focus, it is surprising that the gains made over the period tend to be marginal in nature and that in some of the areas access is relatively low. While it is true that service delivery has continued into the new century, it is also true that in almost all the areas delivery and pricing regimes are being restructured to accommodate efficiency criteria guided by GEAR, so that, increasingly, equity considerations are being compromised. Thus, with increasing inflation and tariffs being instituted for most services, one can expect further constraints being imposed on access to services such as water, electricity, telephones, housing, healthcare and education. Another point is that the data presented above are in aggregate, so that if access to services by historically disadvantaged groups were to be considered separately the picture would be quite disappointing. It may be noted, too, that services are plagued by service-delivery bottlenecks from within the government, itself, in spite of its *Batho Pele* motto, so that governance issues loom large in this area as well. Finally, when an expanding population, increased migration and the consequences and care needs of the HIV/Aids epidemic are all taken into account, it is clear that the government has a huge task on its hands and that the constraints imposed by GEAR on service delivery become even more questionable from the equity point of view.

Trends in political attitudes and perceptions

Most polls have shown a progressive decline in people's support for the government. *Business Day* (29 July 2002) recently carried an article, entitled "Poll findings represent a sharp warning to government", based on a Nielsen Poll that summarised the state of political perceptions in the country. In this poll, nearly 40% gave the ANC a poor to very poor rating, while just under 30% gave the ANC a good to very good rating for performance. Of interest was the fact that high-income earners tended to give the government a high rating for performance, while the normal constituency of the ANC, the poor, gave the government a very low rating for performance. Recent polls also seem to suggest that the euphoria that greeted the new government in 1994 when Mandela was the president has faded away among the poor, but that the approval ratings from middle and high income groups has increased. The writer of the article observes that "today's poor ratings of government performance by the worse off suggest that the ANC's bedrock constituency is losing faith", and that:

> Mbeki and the ANC's increasingly favourable reception by white English-speaking and Afrikaans-speaking respondents suggests the traditional supporters of the Democratic Party and New National Party are more sympathetic than they used to be. This is cold comfort for the ANC, as its long-term prospects in government depend not on the minorities, but on the approval and loyalty of black urban voters whose opinions are predominant in this survey.

A prior poll undertaken by SABC/Markinor (February 2001) confirms these more recent results. This particular poll gave as its highlights the following findings:

- the evaluations of the performance of the president and deputy president were "rather lukewarm";
- the areas of basic service delivery are areas of relative strength for the government in the perceptions of the public;
- only about one third of the potential voters perceive the performance regarding fighting corruption, appointing the right people to key positions and the maintenance of transparency and accountability to be "very" or "fairly" good;
- the government's handling of issues around unemployment is unsatisfactory, and job creation is seen as a high priority; and
- access to land and the HIV/Aids pandemic demand attention.

While these polls do not represent scientific proof of declining ratings of the government, they do point to a general trend, which is that support for the government has been declining among the traditional constituency of the ANC and that beneficiaries of the status quo appear to giving the government increased support as it steadfastly sticks to its GEAR policies. Recent events have tended to show that the government is also increasingly moving its stance to the right. It remains intransigent over increased social expenditures on health (for example, the provision of anti-retroviral drugs for pregnant mothers-to-be), and has become quite sensitive over any suggestion that it is hurting investor confidence (as with the proposed mining bill that recommends greater and bolder black-empowerment policies in this sector). The government is increasingly demonstrating its resoluteness to fight so-called populist pressures and to placate status quo interests in the hope of impressing investors, foreign and domestic.

Conclusion: Beyond GEAR

A lesson from recent experiences of newly industrialising countries is that an inclusive development path can only be precipitated by undertaking a major policy intervention that redistributes assets and undoes major allocative, technical and microeconomic constraints, so as to kick-start a virtuous cycle of growth and development that is endogenously driven, and complemented by external factors such as exports and foreign investment.

The ability of the majority to benefit from formal-sector growth, when this occurs, is limited by low employment elasticities and low poverty-reducing growth elasticities, by lack of linkages of the majority to internal and external growth sectors, and by the underdevelopment of value chains and value channels among the excluded and marginalised, especially in the non-formal sectors. Overall, economies are characterised by inherited, enclave, formal economic structures, which are relatively disarticulated from the non-formal sectors and which display manifest allocative inefficiencies, microeconomic distortions and distributive inequities with respect to access to land, financial capital, technology and social capital. Many of the foregoing are perpetuated and reinforced by policy biases that see inherited formal structures as the "goose that lays the golden egg" and, hence, which need to be pampered and protected. In the process, and as a consequence of the exclusion of the majority from productive activities, this acts as a dead-weight on the economy, with major economic, social, and environmental consequences, which constrain the attainment of sustainable human development. Indeed, the reverse paradigm requires that the majority of the labour force, which is currently outside of the formal sector, be seen as the "goose that *should* lay the golden egg".

Hence, the main objectives of sustainable development should be the promotion of inclusive growth and development, social equity and social security, and environmental sustainability. The pursuit of international competitiveness needs to be undertaken with the foregoing as joint and mutually reinforcing pursuits. Thus, employment promotion ceases to be a residual or an appendage, but is the essence of precipitating an inclusive growth path toward sustainable development. The development strategy that emerges from such an approach is one in which the growth momentum is located internally by broadening the economic base through increased employment and income generating opportunities that are accessible to, and that absorb, the historically excluded and marginalised portions of the labour force, which normally eke out survival in urban and rural non-formal sectors. The external environment, outward orientation with respect to promoting international trade and attracting foreign investment, donor aid and technology should be seen as supplementary propellers of growth. The internal momentum has to be based on the ability of an inclusive growth path to promote mutually interacting dynamics of supply, arising from the productive participation of the majority, which yields its own demand for goods and services, while also precipitating savings generation and investment resources internally, and enhancing the capacity of individuals, households and the state to provide for social welfare needs.

The idea is to kick-start a process of *primary accumulation* based on the interaction of broadening economic participation and the generation of various linkages throughout the economy. For this to result in a virtuous cycle, it is necessary that there be *critical minimum effort* of joint or complementary interventions (across value chains, value channels, economic infrastructure, asset redistribution, etc.) that can trigger the process of inclusive growth in a given locality, region or country, and that can give the process the impetus it needs for an internal momentum to be generated, such that qualitative and quantitative changes begin to occur in all aspects of the economy. Generally, interventions below this critical minimum effort will falter. Not only does inclusive growth provide a sustainable basis for self-support, thereby reducing the social-security demands on the state, but it also enhances the capacity of the state to provide for emerging social needs as the economy develops. In addition, inclusive growth provides the wherewithal to economise on the use of natural resources, thereby contributing to environmental sustainability as well.

The model of growth that emerges requires paying appropriate attention to the interaction of primary, secondary and tertiary sectors, the development of value chains and value channels such as production and management and marketing capabilities, and the provision of social and economic infrastructure in a way that deepens and expands the range of productive economic activities and their ability to absorb the majority of the labour force. The aim is to precipitate a virtuous circle of dynamic interactions between the formal and non-formal sectors, and within each of these sectors, with a view to transforming the latter.

For such a paradigm, which places the majority of the people at its centre, to prove sustainable and implementable there is a need for it to be rooted in participatory and consultative approaches to policy making and implementation, while also living up to some of the earlier-stipulated requirements for a developmental state. Hence, resources and activities to be promoted have to be prioritised such that they address the immediate and long-term needs of the excluded, marginalised and impoverished, and in the process the people have to hold the state accountable to them. It is through such consultation and participation that the hidden and under-utilised resources (human, financial and social capital, and indigenous knowledge systems) of the people in the non-formal sectors can be unleashed to more efficiently contribute to their own and their country's development.

Finally, a people-rooted and people-driven approach to employment promotion and inclusive growth necessitates that developmental initiatives be pursued in an integrated and mutually supportive manner. Thus, not only should the economic, social and environmental policies of the government be comprehensive, integrated and mutually reinforcing, but the initiatives of bilateral and multilateral donors and organisations should be pursued in a manner that complements the overall approach. This requires a proactive state that is able to redefine and implement the development vision and strategy, conscious of the relative strengths of various actors in a mixed economy. More generally, the state and society first need to define a pact that allows redistributive and proactive measures as acceptable forms of intervention within a democratic dispensation; the state and society then need to agree to implement as many as possible of the requirements identified by White (see p.40 above) to institutionalise a developmental state.

The import of the analysis in this chapter is as follows. The South African socio-economic environment is fundamentally one in which legacies of past oppression and inequality still obtain, and such liberal democracy and its accompanying economic liberalisation merely entrench the interests of the historically advantaged and the new élite drawn from among the historically disadvantaged. Thus, the current environment compromises both substantive democracy and developmental objectives, and under such circumstances it is questionable whether democracy can be consolidated. Indeed, the situation should be cause for concern from the point of view of equity and from the point of view of safeguarding the interests of democracy in both its procedural and substantive forms.

We began by stating the problem confronting South Africa in its desire to democratise and, at the same time, attempt to promote sustainable development. The above discussion suggests that South Africa has succeeded in making the transition from an oppressive non-democratic system to a democratic one through institutionalisation of procedures and constitutional provisions that have become the basis for regular democratic practices. The analysis also shows that, while committed to development, the government has been far less successful in promoting sustainable human development by precipitating an inclusive growth path, which would broaden the economic base to the benefit of the historically disadvantaged groups, primarily in a positive sum outcome of growth and development. With the adoption of GEAR as the lynchpin policy paradigm, the government appears to have placed itself in a quandary. This may reflect a realignment of class dominance within the ruling party, implying a shift of influence in favour of an emerging middle- and upper-class élite of professionals, entrepreneurs and middleclass workers, whose interests may be seen to harmonise more with those of the status quo White population and those of influential external bodies, among which the IMF and the World Bank stand out.

It has been shown that GEAR is not adequate to address the major economic and social legacies inherited from the past and is not able to promote sustainable human development. While procedural democracy and economic liberalisation as represented by GEAR appear compatible, in that the status quo can find solace in and is supportive of both, it is questionable as to whether this mix provides a basis for the consolidation of democracy and the promotion of sustainable human development in the medium to long term. If sustainable human development is to remain a primary goal of government then the nature of democracy has to be deepened beyond procedural formalities toward substantive realities rooted in a combination of formal, participatory and consultative structures that adequately represent the disadvantaged, with the adoption of a development-oriented stance and an economic policy paradigm that places the interests of the majority at the fore.

This would require the centre of influence to shift in favour of the poor and underprivileged, or that a splinter party that accommodates such interests emerges to pursue and promote the developmental project. In the absence of such an outcome, it is likely that the hard-won gains of procedural democracy are likely to be dissipated on the altar of narrow interests. This is partly a normative issue, which needs to be addressed on these very same grounds; but it is also a positivist prediction, which hypothesises that the current status quo is not likely to be sustainable in the long term if issues of substantive democracy and development are not addressed boldly.

References

Ademolekun, L. (1999) *Public Administration in Africa*. Oxford: Westview Press.

African National Congress (1994) *Reconstruction and Development Programme*. Johannesburg.

Bond, P. (2000) *Elite Transition*. London/Durban: Pluto Press/University of Natal Press.

Bratton, M. & Van de Walle, N. (1997) *Democratic Experiments in Africa: Regime Transition in Comparative Perspective*. Cambridge: Cambridge University Press.

Bureau of Market Research (2000) "Personal Disposable Income in South Africa by Population Group, Income Group and District." Research No. 282, University of South Africa, Pretoria.

BusinessMap (1999) *South Africa Performance Rating*. Johannesburg, August.

Castells, M. (1998) *End of Millennium*. Volume III. Oxford: Blackwell Publishers.

De Villiers, S. (2001) *A People's Government: The People's Voice*. Cape Town: Parliamentary Support Programme.

Department of Finance (1996) *Growth, Employment and Redistribution: A Macro-Economic Strategy*. Pretoria.

Department of Social Development (2002) *Transforming the Present – Protecting the Future. Report of Committee of Inquiry into a Comprehensive System of Social Security for South Africa*. Pretoria.

Department of Welfare (1996/1997) *Social Welfare in South Africa*. Pretoria.

DPMN Bulletin (1999) "Institutionalisation of the Development and Democratisation Processes: The African Perspective", Vol. VI, No. 1.

DPMN Bulletin (1999) "The State and Civil Society: Partners or Adversaries", Vol. IV, No. 3.

Edigheji, O. (2002) "Globalisation and Governance: Towards a Conceptual Framework." Mimeo, Graduate School of Public and Development Management, University of the Witwatersrand, Johannesburg.

Gallup International Association (2001) *Global End of Year Poll.*

Geoffrey, N. M. (1999) "From Miracle to Mirage: The ANC's Economic Policy Shift form MERG to GEAR." Unpublished Master of Arts Thesis, University of the Witwatersrand, Johannesburg.

Giddens, A. & Held, D. (1983) *Classes, Power, and Conflict: Classical and Contemporary Debates.* London: Macmillan Press.

Giliomee, H. & Simkins, C. (1999) *The Awkward Embrace: One Party – Domination and Democracy.* Cape Town: Tafelberg Publishers.

Government of South Africa (1994) *RDP White Paper.* Pretoria.

Grindle, M. S. & Thomas, J. W. (1991) *Public Choices and Policy Change.* Baltimore: Johns Hopkins.

Hadenius, A. (1991) *Democracy and Development.* Cambridge: Cambridge University Press.

Held, D., McGrew, A., Goldbatt, D. & Perraton, J. (1999) *Global Transformations: Politics, Economics and Culture.* London: Polity Press.

Hirst, P. & Thompson, G. (2000) *Globalisation in Question.* Cambridge: Polity Press.

Hunter, D., Bailey, A., & Taylor, B. (1997). *Cooperacy.* Johannesburg: Zebra.

Huntington, S. P. (1991) *The Third Wave.* Norman: University of Oklahoma Press.

Industrial Development Corporation (1998) *Trade for Growth: Overview of South African Trade and Industrial performance.* Johannesburg, May.

Industrial Development Corporation (1998) "Measures and Policies Impacting on South African Industry", IDC Information Series No. 6.

Industrial Development Corporation (1998) "Sectoral Challenges of High Growth", Sectoral Series, SS4.

Industrial Development Corporation (1998) *Sectoral Prospects: Growth Guidelines for 80 South African Industries, 1997 to 2001.*

Industrial Development Corporation (1998) "Industrial Development Series, Selected Trade Trends: 1998", IDC Information Series.

Industrial Development Corporation (1997) "The Impact on the South African Economy of Accelerated Trade Liberalization in the Context of Currency Depreciation", IDC Information Series, IS2.

Industrial Development Corporation (1996) "Foreign Direct Investment into South Africa", IDC Information Series.

Koebler, T. (1999). "Globalisation and Democratisation: The Prospects for Social Democracy in South Africa", *Politikon.* Vol. 26, No. 2, pp. 259–268.

Leftwitch, A. (1996) *Democracy and Development: Theory and Practice.* Cambridge: Polity Press.

Lodge, T. (2002) "Poll Findings Represent a Sharp Warning to Government", *Business Day,* 29 July.

Lodge, T. (2002) "Image of ANC is Still Negative – Survey", Business Day, 29 July.

Lubbers, R. F. M. & Koorevaar, J. G. (1999) "Governance in an Era of Globalisation." Paper presented at the Club of Rome Annual Meeting. Vienna, 26–27 November.

Marais, H. (1998) *South Africa: Limits to Change: The Political Economy of Transition.* London/Cape Town: Zed Books/University of Cape Town Press.

Marx, K. (1984) *The Eighteenth Brumaire of Louis Bonaparte.* London: Lawrence and Wishart.

May, J. (1998) *Poverty and Inequality in South Africa.* Pretoria: Government of South Africa.

May, J. with Atwood, H., Ewang, P., Lund, F., Norton, A. & Wenzental, W. (1998) *Experiences and Perceptions of Poverty in South Africa.* Durban: Praxis Publishing.

Mamdani, M. (1996) *Citizen and Subject.* Kampala: Fountain Publishers.

Mayntz, R. (1998) "New Challenges of Governance Theory." European University Institute, Jean Monnet Chair Paper, RSC No. 98/50.

Meir, G. M. (1991) *Politics and Policy Making in Developing Countries*. San Francisco: JCS Press.

Meth, C. (2001) "Social Exclusion and Social Protection." Background Paper for the Committee for a Comprehensive Social Security System in South Africa. Pretoria: Department of Social Development.

Mhone, G. C. Z. (2000) "Enclavity and Constrained Labour Absorption in Southern African Economies." Discussion Paper, ILO/SMAT. Harare: United Nations Research Institute for Social Development.

Nzongola-ntalaja, G. & Lee, M. C. (1997) *The State and Democracy in Africa*. Asmara, Eritrea: Africa World Press.

Poswell, L. (2002) *The Post-Apartheid South African Labour Market: A Status Report*. Cape Town: Development Research Unit, University of Cape Town.

Przerwoski, A. (1991) D*emocracy and the Market: Political Reform and Economic Reforms in Eastern Europe and Latin America*. Cambridge: Cambridge University Press.

RDP (1996) *Key Indicators of Poverty in South Africa*. Pretoria.

Robinson, M. & White G. (1998) The *Democratic Developmental State*. Oxford: Oxford University Press.

Rosen, M. & Wolff, J. (1999) *Political Thought*. Oxford: Oxford University Press.

Schroyer, T. (1975) *The Critique of Domination*. Boston: Beacon Press.

Soros, G. (1998) *The Crisis of Global Capitalism*. London: Little, Brown and Company.

South African Institute of Race Relations *Race Relations Survey*. Various years from 1994/95 to 2000. Johannesburg.

South African Quarterly Bulletin (1994—2001) Various issues.

South African Reserve Bank (2000) *Quarterly Bulletin*. Pretoria. June.

Statistics South Africa (1998) *Women and Men in South Africa*. Pretoria.

Statistics South Africa (1998) *Unemployment and Employment in South Africa*. Pretoria.

Statistics South Africa (2000) *Measuring Poverty*. Pretoria.

Statistics South Africa (2001) *South Africa in Transition: Selected Findings from the October Household Survey of 1999 and Changes that have Occurred between 1995 and 1999*. Pretoria.

Statistics South Africa (2002) *Women and Men in South Africa: Five Years On ...* Pretoria.

Statistics South Africa (2002) *Labour Force Survey: September 2001*. Pretoria.

UNDP (2000) *South Africa: Transformation for Human Development*. Pretoria.

UNRISD (1995) *States of Disarray: The Social Effects of Globalisation*. Geneva.

UNRISD (2000) *Taking Responsibility for Social Development*. Geneva.

Van Niekerk, D., Van der Waldt, G. & Jonker, A. (2001) *Governance, Politics and Policy in South Africa*. Cape Town: Oxford University Press.

Vizey, J. (1971) *Revolution of our Time: Social Democracy*. New York: Praeger Publishers.

Wolff, R. B., Moore, B. & Marcuse, H. (1965) *A Critique of Pure Tolerance*. Boston: Beacon Press.

World Bank (1995) *World Development Report: Workers in an Integrating World*. New York: Oxford University Press.

3

State-society Relations in Post-apartheid South Africa: The Challenges of Globalisation on Co-operative Governance[1]

Omano Edigheji

Introduction

The most fundamental and dramatic political transformation in Africa in the last decade of the twentieth century was the dismantling of apartheid and the introduction of non-racial, multiparty democracy in South Africa in 1994. The democratic government inherited an economy in decline. By 1994, South Africa had experienced a two-decade-long economic stagnation reflected in the rate of decline of the Gross Domestic Product (GDP) from about 5.5% in the 1960s to about 1.2% in the 1980s, a negative growth rate of -0.2% by 1993 (South African Reserve Bank, 2000), a decline in real investment, high inflation and severe fiscal difficulties. At the same time, South Africa became one of the least egalitarian countries in the world (ranking second only to Brazil), as apartheid policies skewed the distribution of income and wealth along geographical and racial lines. Consequently, 17 million people, mostly Blacks, lived below the poverty line without access to basic social and physical services; 11 million of these lived in rural areas (African National Congress, 1994). Unemployment stood at about 45% during this period. Furthermore, the apartheid regime was authoritarian, repressive, unaccountable and non-transparent. As a result, the majority Black population was excluded from the governance process. South Africa was, therefore, a country divided along racial lines – participation in decision-making processes and their benefits were defined in racial terms.

Thus, the major challenge that confronted the new government was to reverse the apartheid inheritance by promoting co-operative governance and a *shared growth*, that is, an economic growth that benefits all South Africans irrespective of race and gender. Concurrently, the new government began to initiate policies of outward orientation and domestic economic liberalisation as solutions to the socio-economic malaise. This policy orientation was codified in the Growth, Employment and Redistribution (GEAR) document, on the grounds of integrating into the global economy – globalisation made us to do it, argued the state. The argument is that for South Africa to compete in the global economy, attract foreign investment and create jobs, there is an urgent need to liberalise the economy (i.e. the reduction of subsidies, privatisation and commercialisation of state-owned enterprises, fiscal restraints and an uncritical acceptance of a minimalist state).

The new policy direction, as exemplified by the Reconstruction and Development Programme (RDP), initially redefined the role of government and state-society relations with a new emphasis on co-operative governance as a mechanism for involving other socio-economic actors – business and trade unions, and to a varying degree, broader civil society – in transforming the national economy. Consequently, there have been legislative and institutional reforms favourable to co-operative governance, in contrast to the period of apartheid, autocratic government and unilateralism by management and the state.

Unlike the apartheid governance system that catered for the interests of the White minority, the governance system in the new dispensation would have to cater for the needs of all South Africans. In its electoral manifesto, the ANC set the scene for future policy. Accordingly, it pledged to promote representative and participatory democracy. This entailed the restructuring of state institutions to make them "efficient, effective, responsive, transparent and accountable" (ANC, 1994:120). Co-operative governance would mean fostering a constructive relationship between civil society, trade unions and the democratic government. This would involve the establishment of participatory structures to promote consultation to enable civil society to take part in decision-making and implementation. Policy formulation and implementation would be a *people-driven process*. As the ANC (1994:5) argued: "Our people, with their aspirations and collective determination are our most important resource". This is premised on the assumption that social and economic development would require empowerment of the people for active participation in the policy process.

It is, therefore, important to recognise the commitment to co-operative governance by the new political élite, but, as shown in the analysis that follows, this commitment has been derailed by the adoption of a neo-liberal economic policy, which by its very nature does not provide for consultative processes. At this juncture, it is important to take cognisance of the fact that a confluence of events conditioned the need for participatory and consultative decision-making in South Africa. The first related to internal conditions, that is, the need to overcome apartheid's legacy of secretive, technocratic and authoritarian modes of decision-making. The second was the need to re-integrate into the global economy after years of sanction-imposed isolation at a time of intensified globalisation of social and economic activities. As noted above, this process emphasises liberalisation, privatisation, flexible labour markets and co-operative governance, in order to achieve global competitiveness, sustained economic growth and equitable development. South Africa is part of a global phenomenon, although this is also reinforced by its own domestic imperatives. These conditions, according to some commentators on the South African transition, such as Houston *et al.* (1998), have given rise to a public-policy environment that promotes consultative and participatory decision-making. However, such a celebratory tone overlooks the challenges that have faced co-operative governance since 1994. This chapter is an attempt to explore the creative tensions between co-operative governance and economic reforms, which are at times contradictory and at others complementary and reinforcing in a divided and inegalitarian society like South Africa. The paradoxical relationship between liberal economic reforms and co-operative governance will be explored in detail below.

The establishment of a number of consultative forums, the most prominent being a statutory body, the National Economic and Labour Council (Nedlac), created by an Act of Parliament in 1994 to promote consultative decision-making, has marked the post-apartheid period. In order to explore the challenges that market economic reforms pose for co-operative governance, this chapter will focus on Nedlac's activities, and major policy decisions taken outside its ambit, as a glimpse of the functioning and vitality of participatory governance in South Africa.

This chapter attempts to present an overview of co-operative governance in post-apartheid South Africa. It reviews the debate on globalisation and co-operative governance, discusses the institutionalisation of co-operative governance, using Nedlac as the basis of such an analysis, and considers the effects of economic reforms on co-operative governance in the post-1994 period. Against this background, the chapter concludes by providing some suggestions on how co-operative governance can be consolidated in South Africa.

An overview of the globalisation and governance discourse

In an era of globalisation, scholars and development agencies alike are increasingly emphasising the importance of co-operative governance to democratisation and economic transformation. Globalisation here implies the intensification and integration of economic, socio-cultural and political relations and activities across regions and continents, with profound effects on governance. At the same time, the significance of co-operative governance, that is, the interlocking of the state and societal groups in a mix of public-private policy networks in the formulation and implementation of public policy, is also being trumpeted. Co-operative governance can take two forms: either that interest groups are directly represented in negotiating forums or that their interests are internalised within regulatory regimes that subject the activities of private agents to self-imposed discipline. This is what Evans (1995) calls synergy, involving both co-operation and competition among stakeholders in society in a positive-sum relationship. This implies the participation of citizens and interest groups in policy making and implementation with the aim of impacting on the quality of such policies.

As Dani Rodrik (cited in Prakash, 1999) has argued, co-operative governance gives voice to various actors, thereby enhancing the legitimacy of the system, which is key to economic growth. Collaborative relationships are also crucial in the provision of social insurance and other collective goods – human capital, education and health. In particular, it is argued that due to economic, political and cultural globalisation, the world is characterised by governmental and democratic deficits (that is, the state is less effective because power is shared by diverse forces and agencies at local, national, regional and global levels); and while nation-states are restricted to geographical borders, the processes they are supposed to govern, and the problems they are supposed to solve, have important global dimensions, trans-boundary in nature (Lubbers & Koorevaar, 1999; Held, 2000). The emerging issues that individual nation-states or the state cannot resolve alone include information and financial flows, HIV/Aids, environmental problems, global terrorism, the global criminal underworld, etc. – all of which require the co-ordination of activities across nations and continents. The democratic deficits manifest as the government reduces its social commitment to citizens and focuses more and more on facilitating the flow of global capital (Bakker, 1999).

In a multicentric/globalised world, governance, it is argued, involves complex interactions among governments and other state actors, sub-state actors, supranational organisations, non-government organisations, the private sector and interest groups of concerned citizens who operate across jurisdictional and national boundaries. Governance is conceived not in terms of hierarchical control, as was the case previously, but in terms of co-operative modes of interaction where the state and non-state actors participate in mixed public-private networks (Mayntz, 1998; Weiss, 1998). The United Nations Development Programme (UNDP) has succinctly summarised it thus:

> Governance is the exercise of political, economic and administrative authority in the management of a country's affairs at all levels. Governance comprises the complex mechanisms, processes and institutions through which citizens and groups articulate their interests, mediate their differences and exercise their legal rights and obligations. Good governance has many attributes. It is participatory, transparent and accountable. It is effective in making the best use of resources and is equitable. And it promotes the rule of law.

> Governance includes the state, but transcends it by taking in the private sector and civil society. All three are critical for sustaining human development. The state creates a conducive political and legal climate. The private sector generates jobs and income. And civil society facilitates political and social interaction – mobilizing groups to participate in economic, social and political activities. (UNDP, 1997)

The new governance system, while acknowledging the changing role of the state, stresses that government, civil society and markets all have important roles in public governance – achieving social good and minimising social ills. All these actors must adhere to basic norms of good governance: transparency, accountability and absence of corruption.

The UNDP definition tends to confine the role of the state to that of night-watchman, providing a conducive climate for private agents to function. However, it is argued here that governance does not imply the impotence or the end of the state, as asserted by scholars such as Ohmae (1990), but a reconfiguration of the state and its governance capacity (Sassen, 1995; Held, 2000). It is especially so as the state is a major agent of some of the transformations that are taking place in the global arena. In addition, the enforcement of most international laws and agreements is left with national legal systems. Therefore, the state is not a passive recipient or respondent but an active player in facilitating and shaping the processes of globalisation. Governmental and democratic deficits are being overcome through regional and international bodies and agreements, as well as by co-operative governance between the state, market agents and civil society bodies at the national and local levels.

The focus of this chapter is, however, at the national level – how states respond to globalisation to enhance governance capacities to meet their needs. As governments reduce their role due to the privatisation of previously public functions, civil society organisations have sprung up to fill the gap in the supply of basic services. Also, new global problems have engendered the revival of civil society organisations, including human rights organisations, environmental groups, the feminist movement and HIV/Aids advocacy groups. These groups have become important actors.

It is, therefore, argued that the emergence of new social actors and new problems calls for co-operative governance. The argument is that through intense linkages between the state and civil society (that is, co-operative governance), the state agencies are able to gather sufficient information and co-ordinate policy formulation and implementation and, by extension, enhance the robustness of the state apparatus. Co-operative governance thus provides a mechanism for feedback, information sharing and co-ordination between the government and civil society organisations. Where civil society participates in the agenda setting, and the formulation and implementation of policy to address the issues of social exclusion engendered by corporate globalisation, it enhances its belief that the policies will actually work in its favour. Another justification for co-operative governance is that it enhances openness and transparency in the formulation and implementation of socio-economic policy, as well as increases incentives for participation in public life and, consequently, lessens the distance between citizens, communities and the state. In turn, this has the potential to minimise the social exclusion and polarisation of societies.

Participatory processes, conceived this way, have profound developmental implications. As Manor (1998:127) puts it:

> They make it more likely that government agencies and institutions will become more responsive to the felt needs of grass-roots communities, and more capable of perceiving, understanding, and incorporating "local knowledge" about the management of resources and the conduct of society's business. They make it more likely that policy innovations will be realistic … and creative to ordinary people. They tend to increase the flow of information between state and society, in both directions. They enhance the chances that popular cynicism about any government initiative will be broken down or *minimized*. They make it likely that groups at the local level and *indeed at all levels* of society will develop a sense of ownership about development projects, so that such projects become more sustainable because such groups make efforts to sustain them. (emphasis added)

As an inclusive process, co-operative governance not only enhances associational activities but also gives greater legitimacy to democratic regimes, their policies and outcomes, which are products of inter-class accommodation, compromise and at times consensus, rather than those based on the exclusion of key sectors of society, be it business or civil society, which in turn fosters conflict among competing interest groups. Co-operative governance, therefore, has the potential to minimise conflicts in society. Furthermore, because co-operative governance is based on institutionalised (that is, structured and rules-based) relationships around specific policy areas, it enhances the capacity of the collective (organised interest groups), while imposing constraints on individuals in the design and implementation of public policy, and thus minimises corruption. This improves the chances of success of a transformative project. In this regard, co-operative governance is not an end in itself but a means to an end, enhancing social and economic development, and ultimately improving the standard of living of people.

Co-operative governance stands in contrast to the clientelistic and paternalistic relationships that characterised most postcolonial states in Africa. Clientelistic relations are based on the award of personal favours, and at times coercion, by the ruler – the patron – to the citizens, who are the clients. Scholars of African development have attributed the developmental failure of the continent to the lack of co-operative governance. As aptly argued by Bratton and Van de Walle (1997), citizens and their organisations were seldom consulted about public policies. At best, only societal interests with approved membership were consulted by the state. Citing Kashir, Bratton and Van de Walle conclude that post-colonial African states tried to circumscribe political participation by shrinking the public arena. In most of postcolonial Africa, the state-society relations can at best be described as paternalistic. Unlike in the Nordic countries, African business associations and trade unions, and indeed civil society, due in part to their repression, were relatively weak, fragmented and with limited resources to effectively engage the state. As a consequence, post-colonial African states demonstrated very little transformative capacity.

However, clientelistic politics is not the preserve only of African states or the developing world. It is also found in developed countries. Putnam's (1993) study of Italy is illustrative. His research findings show that in certain regions of Italy, "citizens are enmeshed in patron-client networks. They typically pass the chance to express an opinion on public issues, since for them the ballot is essentially a token exchange in an immediate, highly personalized relationship of dependency" (Putnam, 1993:96). This is in contrast to the developed regions of Italy whose politics he describes as programmatic. Programmatic politics is founded on collective deliberation on public issues and is characterised by dense networks of civic associations.

Co-operative governance is being cast in celebratory tones and is being touted as the only solution to the political and economic problems of developing countries, including South Africa. The title of Karl Wohlmuth's (1998) colloquium presentation *Good Governance and Economic Development: New Foundations for Growth in Africa* is suggestive of the positive light in which participatory decision-making is being presented. Its proponents, including international development agencies such as the UNDP and the World Bank,[2] have made a fetish of co-operative governance, which is seen as a means to overcome governmental deficits, reduce information gaps, build consensus around policy, lead to smoother implementation of state policies, and enhance the credibility and sustainability of programmes. Participation in decision-making, as well as in implementation, means that stakeholders can hold the government accountable for public policy and services. It is also conceived of not only as the most effective way to provide services to local communities, but also as the basis for global competitiveness. Developing countries are thus being urged to embrace co-operative governance in finding solutions to the challenges of national development. The purpose of this chapter is to interrogate the links between neo-liberal economic reforms and the participatory component of governance (that is, co-operative governance) that are being advocated by institutions such as the World Bank and by neo-liberal academics.

Thus far, the debate on globalisation and participatory governance has been projected in positive terms, and its contradictory dynamics have been overlooked. What are the tensions and contradictions of participatory governance in the context of globalisation? As scholars such as Paley (2001) note, participatory processes and structures have the potential to demobilise civil society and legitimatise the neo-liberal agenda. Civil society organisations that participate in agenda setting and implementation are more unlikely to protest against such policies. Quoting Veronica Schild, Paley argues that the real motive of the World Bank in promoting co-operative governance is to ensure political support by civil society organisations for neo-liberal economic reforms, which might be against the interests of their members. Stakeholders that participate in policy formulation and implementation are less likely to be critical of such policies, even when it is against the interests of their members. Co-operative governance also has the potential to refocus and derail the agenda of stakeholders, especially civil society organisations. As civil society leaders become increasingly preoccupied with policy forums and the implementation of policies, they are increasingly far removed from their members and, thereby, their accountability within civil society organisations is reduced. In this respect, civil society organisations are legitimising agents of neo-liberal socio-economic policies. And unwittingly, civil society organisations end up contributing to the contraction of the state and its shift from "securing the welfare of citizens to facilitating the flow of global capital" (Bakker, 1999:50). In the long term, this may contribute to the delegitimisation of the state in the eyes of the electorate.

Another point that is often overlooked by the proponents of co-operative governance is that it might give undue influence to powerful stakeholders, and could help to entrench inequalities in society, especially if those with access to the policy process are interest groups that represent the élites. In addition, its proponents inadequately address a range of technical challenges including co-ordination and capacity problems that arise. It may also undermine parliamentary autonomy. One variant of this argument is that participatory structures give stakeholders, who have not submitted themselves to the test of election, too much influence on government and this could undermine democracy (Friedman & Reitzes, 1996). From this perspective, democracy is better served through parliamentary and electoral reforms that make elected officials more accountable than participatory processes that involve organs of civil society. This position sees co-operative governance as usurping the decision-making powers of elected structures. This is a misreading, as parliament remains the final decision-making authority. Therefore, participatory and consultative processes and their relations to parliament should not been seen in a zero-sum game. Indeed, they could complement one another.

However, a fundamental concern in this chapter is the inherent conflict between neo-liberal economic reforms and co-operative governance. In a global world that privileges investors, what hope is there for participatory decision-making? The imperative to attract foreign investment, liberalise and deregulate national economies, so as to integrate into the global economy, is making states across the globe more responsive to the needs of the private sector and more likely to become guarantors of capital accumulation. This has been coupled with the privatisation of public goods. These developments, the privileging of investor interests and the state withdrawal from its role as provider of social insurance to its population, are likely to strain the relationship between the state and civil society organisations (CSOs), especially labour. On the other hand, the need for the government to reduce social exclusion by meeting its democratic commitments to the electorate through job creation and provision of social services, which require some form of state intervention, is likely to strain state-business relations with its adverse effects on participatory governance. These conflicting imperatives of globalisation are likely to hamper participatory processes and structures. Is co-operative governance able to deal with real political conflicts and its sources? This is a question that begs to be answered.

Structures and the role of Nedlac

It is pertinent to note that the origins of the institutionalisation of participatory and consultative decision-making in South Africa (including the establishment of Nedlac) lie in the trade union struggle, especially that of the major union federation, the Congress of South African Trade Unions (Cosatu) to prevent the apartheid regime in its dying days from unilaterally imposing social and economic policy. Two specific struggles are significant. The first struggle resulted in the restructuring of the National Manpower Commission (NMC), a body that was focused on labour-market issues, to include representation from the progressive trade unions. The second struggle led to the establishment of the National Economic Forum (NEF), a body established to give labour and business not only a voice but also formal representation in the formulation of macroeconomic policy. It is, therefore, important to note that the origin of consultative decision-making in the South African context was not about strengthening governance capacity but about reducing state capacity.

Nedlac[3] was launched in 1995 with the primary aim of building consensus between the state and its social partners on social and economic issues. The Nedlac Act of 1994 explicitly states that the council must:

- strive to promote the goals of economic growth, participation in economic decision-making and social equity;
- seek to reach consensus and conclude agreements pertaining to social and economic policy;
- consider all proposed labour legislation relating to labour markets before it is introduced in parliament;

- consider all significant changes to social and economic policy before they are implemented or introduced in parliament; and
- encourage and promote the formulation of co-ordinated policy on social and economic matters.

The council is made up of delegations from the government, organised business, organised labour and civic/community organisations. Thus, unlike corporatist arrangements in the Nordic countries, representation in Nedlac goes beyond the golden triangle of business, labour and the government to include representation from broader civil society, called the community constituency. It is also different from the corporatist institutions in the Nordic countries in that it addresses social issues that are not addressed by these institutions. Furthermore, the participatory nature of Nedlac is unlike the experience of East Asian developmental states, where state-society relations were limited to the inclusion of business in the policy process (to the exclusion of civil society organisations).

The government's representation in the council is drawn from the four core economic ministries, the Ministry of Finance (now called the National Treasury), the Department of Trade and Industry (DTI), the Department of Labour and the Department of Public Works. On occasion, other ministries participate in Nedlac activities. It is important to note that the council's highest decision-making structure, the Annual Summit, is presided over by the State President or the Deputy President, in compliance with the Act that established it. In the council, Business South Africa (BSA) and the National African Federation of Chambers of Commerce and Industry (Nafcoc) represent organised business. BSA represents the interests of predominantly White organisations such as the South African Foundation (SAF), the Afrikaner Handelsinstituut (AHI) and the South African Chamber of Business (Sacob). In turn, Nafcoc represents businesses, provincial and sectoral chambers, with predominately Black membership. The organisation of business associations along racial lines has rendered them ineffective in shaping social and economic policy through the platforms provided by Nedlac and other participatory decision-making processes and structures. This, however, is not to argue that business, especially the White business conglomerates and foreign capital, do not wield enormous influence on post-apartheid economic policy. Indeed, as will be argued, business has used the threat of capital flight to ensure that its interests predominate in the post-1994 period. For its part, organised labour is represented by the three trade union federations: Cosatu, the Federation of Unions of South Africa (Fedusa) and the National Council of Trade Unions (Nactu).[4]

The community constituency is made up of the South African Youth Council (SAYC), the Women's National Coalition (WNC), the South African National Civic Organisation (Sanco), Disabled People of South Africa (DPSA) and, most recently, the National Co-operative Association of South Africa (Ncasa).[5] The community constituency can be described as the junior partner in Nedlac, because it is not represented on all structures of the council.[6] However, Edigheji and Gostner (2000:86) aptly observe:

> Although the community participation is presently confined to certain structures and compared to the other social partners, it has "less social power" and has a much more narrow base, it is able to utilize its participation to promote and protect the interests of its constituencies. In the process, issues that would have been ignored if representation at NEDLAC were limited to the labour, business and government are brought to the fore of NEDLAC's programme. In addition, through participation in NEDLAC civil society organizations other than labour and business have their representatives nominated to statutory bodies that deal with industrial relations and minimum employment standards, and to governing councils of universities.

It is this dynamism of Nedlac, and the influence of the community constituency, that is not appreciated by scholars like Nattrass and Seekings (1998), who describe its representation as tokenistic. Indeed, participation in the Management Committee (Manco) and Executive Council (Exco) has enabled the community constituency to exert influence on the council's decisions.

The main structures of Nedlac are the Annual Summit, which is presided over by the State President or the Deputy President; the Exco made up of the four core economic ministers and their Director Generals, the Presidents and General Secretaries of the three union federations, eight senior representatives from organised business and two representatives from the community constituency; and the Manco comprising top government bureaucrats including Director Generals, the General Secretaries of the union federations, top businesspersons and two representatives of the community constituency. These structures are assisted by a small secretariat of about 14 staff members whose primary role is to facilitate consultative processes including co-ordination and research background for its work.

The council work is organised around four chambers, namely, the Monetary and Fiscal Policy Chamber, the Trade and Industry Chamber, the Labour Market Chamber and the Development Chamber. Against this background, some of the processes and policies negotiated in the council will now be discussed.

Labour-law reforms and affirmative-action policies

The history of the struggle against apartheid would be incomplete without an acknowledgement of the pivotal role played by the trade unions. Combining strike action, mass mobilisation and, later, strategic participation in policy making, the trade unions struggled for the improvement of working conditions and for a non-racial multiparty democracy. This earned them the label of "social-movement unionism" (Webster, 1988), challenging both employers and the state. Given its strategic role in the struggle against apartheid, Cosatu's alliance with the ANC, and the need to address inequalities and discriminatory labour laws, the democratic government tabled a range of labour-law reforms as part of its broader project of societal transformation. The emphasis was to move away from the adversarial labour-market relations and inequities of the apartheid period to a co-operative, consultative and equitable labour-market dispensation. The reform initiatives resulted in a number of progressive pieces of legislation that represent a major victory for workers and the trade unions. These include the Labour Relations Act (LRA) of 1995, the Basic Conditions of Employment Act (BCEA) of 1997, the Employment Equity Act (EEA) of 1998 and the Skills Development Act of 1998. This legislation was intended to fundamentally transform the labour market through democratising the workplace, promoting workers' rights to organise and bargain collectively, promoting equity and greater access for people from disadvantaged communities in the workplace, ensuring equitable representation in all occupational categories and levels in the workforce (affirmative action in employment), and promoting and protecting the right to strike and the right to freedom from victimisation.

Beginning with the Labour Relations Bill on 4 May 1995, these were the first pieces of legislation tabled by the government, through the Department of Labour, at Nedlac. Understandably, the council was preoccupied with these laws in its first few years of existence. Labour-law reforms have been one area where the trade unions have had an overbearing influence on policy making. This is partly because the Nedlac Act requires all major labour laws to be tabled in the council for negotiation and consensus seeking, before being tabled in parliament; as such, union input is a prerequisite. In addition, the trade union movement has very skilled negotiators on labour law issues. However, with the tabling of, and subsequent negotiations around, the labour-law reforms came the first serious test for the council, with major impact on co-operative governance in the democratic dispensation. The section that follows provides a brief summary of the consultative process at Nedlac, with the aim of capturing some of the dynamics and tensions thereof.

With respect to the LRA, the key demands of the trade unions were compulsory, centralised bargaining at the national level, the establishment of workplace forums that were union-based, the prohibition of lockouts, the banning of scab labour during strikes and lockouts, the allowance of solidarity strikes over individual dismissals, and increased severance packages – all of which were conceived of as an attempt to fundamentally transform the South African labour market. Business, on the other hand, took reactive positions to those of organised labour – opposing compulsory, centralised bargaining, supporting lockouts, the use of scab labour during strikes and the dismissing of workers on legal strikes, and arguing that employers should have the discretion to establish workplace forums or not. The White business strategy was an attempt to ensure that its interests predominated in the labour reforms and to cast the debate and negotiations in a way that was favourable to it; and if that failed, to block the labour-law reforms (through the consultative processes at Nedlac). By so doing, it aimed to undermine the developmental project of the new government and, thereby, maintain the status quo of racial discrimination and inequality in the world of work. Its opposition was firmly located within the neoclassical paradigm, that is, that the reform initiatives would lead to negative labour-market outcomes and inflexibility in the labour market, prompting low growth, low investment and impediments to job creation.

Given the doggedness of the business and labour constituencies, it was inevitable that a deadlock would ensue, forcing the latter to embark on mass protests and stay-aways to press for its demands, especially for centralised bargaining and the outlawing of scab labour. These protests, combined with behind-the-scenes ANC-led alliance meetings, resulted in compromises that led to the resumption of negotiations. After 149 hours of negotiations, spanning a period of ten weeks, the trade unions and business could not reach a compromise on some aspects, including the right to lockouts and solidarity strikes over unfair dismissals. Consequently, the Nedlac report to parliament noted the areas of agreement and disagreement.

Although the LRA finally passed by parliament did not meet all the unions' demands, it was a major victory for workers, and has been hailed by commentators as one of the most progressive labour laws in the world. For the first time in South African history, the LRA covers all workers, including public servants, farm workers and domestic workers, who were historically excluded from the ambit of earlier labour laws. Further, it protects workers' rights to solidarity strikes and entrenched centralised bargaining. The LRA also provides for the establishment of workplace forums aimed at promoting participatory decision-making at the enterprise level. The forums are also meant to ensure that employees' participation goes beyond union members at the enterprise level. They are effective mechanisms for joint consultation and decision-making between workers and employers. The significance of the LRA was not lost to Cosatu, which celebrated it thus:

> for us it represents a resounding victory for workers, a radical departure from the past ... a new dispensation for the management of industrial relations. It also demonstrated the determination of the ANC and its allies to lead a process of transformation of the workplace. Some of the last minute changes would not have been effected without the support of the ANC. (cited in Coleman *et al.*, 2000)

With respect to the BCEA, the trade union movement demanded a 40-hour week and 6-months paid maternity leave, and opposed downward variation of employment standards and the provision that an employee could work up to 12 hours a day without receiving overtime pay. These were the major sticking points in the negotiations, as business opposed these proposals. As a result of a deadlock in negotiations at Nedlac, especially over the demand for a 40-hour working week and 6-months maternity leave, Cosatu embarked on multiple strategies to further its demands. Through mass mobilisation, bilateral negotiations with the ANC and the direct briefing of ANC parliamentarians, it was able to achieve a breakthrough resulting in resumption of negotiations. Although the trade unions did not achieve all their demands, such as 6-months maternity leave (the Act provided for 4-months maternity leave), the BCEA, like the LRA, was pro-workers.

This reform process, which was a product of consultation, has produced mixed results. On the one hand, it has created a stable industrial-relations regime, as evidenced by the low levels of strikes and workdays lost; for example, workdays lost due to work stoppages and strike action fell from 3.9 million in 1994 to 0.5 million in 2000 (Andrew Levy and Associates, 2001). However, because the labour-law reforms did not privilege investors' interests, the business community – especially White business – has continued to oppose these laws and, consequently, has been reluctant to invest, as can be seen in the low level of fixed domestic capital formation, which declined by 6% between 1998 and 1999 alone (SARB, 2000). Holding the economy to ransom contingent upon liberalisation of the labour market is tantamount to an investment strike by the business sector.

While acknowledging that these are progressive labour laws, it is important to point out the contradictions and the possible effects on their mass base of leaders who are preoccupied with negotiations. The labour-law reforms brought to the fore the growing gap between the leadership and its base, both in form and aspirations, giving credence to those who are concerned about the demobilisation effects of corporatism, as leaders are drawn into élite, tripartite institutions, leaving behind their members. This was very evident during the LRA negotiations. Ordinary members, shop stewards and organisers accused the leadership of not providing proper briefings about the ongoing negotiations. It was, therefore, not surprising that, while union leaders regarded the LRA as a major victory for workers, shop stewards and organisers slammed it as a miserable compromise (see Von Holdt, 1995). The same situation also applied to the business constituency, as some of its members opposed the LRA and took their opposition to parliament. This raises an important question: When organisations are unable to carry their members along in negotiations, what is the source of their mandate during negotiations? At the heart of this is the issue of internal democracy, transparency and accountability to which these organisations laid many claims. As has been shown in the discourse on co-operative governance, its success is considerably dependent on the capacity of leaders to mobilise members around a common goal and to restrain members when necessary. However, if the link between leaders and members breaks down or is weak, it adversely affects the degree to which organised groups can impact on policy formulation and implementation. In addition, it leads to a situation where leaders enter into agreements that do not necessarily accord with the interests of their members.

The labour-law negotiations highlighted the divisions within the stakeholders, especially within organised business, and the differing agendas between White and Black business organisations, with major adverse implications for consultative decision-making. For example, given the division of organised business along racial lines, it makes it difficult for business to co-ordinate and speak with one voice on important policy and legislative issues within and outside Nedlac. Thus, while organised White business was vociferous in its opposition to the various proposed Acts, organised Black business was either conspicuous by its silence or supportive of major aspects of the policies. Likewise, White business has remained opposed to Black economic empowerment favoured by Black business groups. These different positions reflect the sharp division between big capital and small businesses represented by Nafcoc. Underscoring these different positions is the class and race nature of the South African political economy. Thus, the opposition of White business to these laws must be understood in the context of its need to preserve its class and racial interests. Its opposition to the labour laws has widened the gulf between White and Black business, on the one hand, and has created suspicion and mistrust between the government and White business, on the other. As one of South Africa's leading businesspersons and chair of Anglo American, Julian Ogilvey-Thompson (1998) noted, this raises questions about whether White business is "sufficiently committed to transformation". The famous two-nation speech of then Deputy President Thabo Mbeki to parliament in May 1998 illustrated this point. According to Mbeki (1998):

> In the majority of cases, the call for transformation of both public and private sector institutions and organizations, in particular to address the issue of racial representivity, has been resisted with great determination by *the white community especially white business*. Indeed, one of the issues of great agitation in our politics is the question of affirmative action. To ensure that it does not happen, some of what is said is that, black advancement equals a white brain drain and black management equals inefficiency, corruption and lowering of standards. (emphasis added)

However, the proposed merger between Black and White business associations, although riddled with crises so far, has the potential to strengthen the voice of business in its engagement with the other social partners in the country.

The labour-law reforms also brought to the surface questions about the efficacy of Nedlac as an institution for seeking consensus and reaching agreements between the major stakeholders. In particular, organised business claimed that "Nedlac is too labour biased"[7] to be an effective structure for consensus seeking and positive-sum agreements. As another business delegate to Nedlac put it, "the best deals for business are not being struck at Nedlac". Citing the example of the most recent labour law amendments, she noted that "the initial proposals by government were more business-friendly than what was finally agreed upon at Nedlac".[8] The government had tabled amendments to the labour laws to address what Minister of Labour Membathisi Mdladlana referred to as their "unintended consequences". This was a tacit acknowledgement that the labour laws had a negative impact on investment, hence the need for amendments that would be more business-friendly. However, these amendments represent a victory for workers, giving workers the right to strike over retrenchment and requiring employers to consider alternatives to job shedding. Organised business has received these amendments with reservations, fearing that they could deter investment.

The negotiations over the labour-law amendments were deadlocked at Nedlac. It took the intervention of the Millennium Labour Council (MLC) to break the deadlock, and it was only when agreements had been reached by business and labour at the MLC that the negotiations resumed at Nedlac. What this shows is that the non-formalised elements of co-operative governance are important to the success of the formalised consultative processes and structures, but that non-formalised processes are less effective in the absence of a formal process. The MLC is a bi-partite institution, launched in the second half of 2000 with twelve representatives each from business and labour. Business representation in the council is made up of captains of industry and representatives of organised business, Sacob, Nafcoc and Fabcos (Foundation of African Business and Consumer Services). The three union federations are formally represented in the MLC. The council seeks to find solutions to the problems of high unemployment, job losses, poverty and inequality in the country, as well as to develop a shared analysis of the crisis of the South African economy, with a view to finding common solutions (MLC, 2000). The MLC facilitates informal discussion between the parties, and agreements reached have to be formalised at Nedlac. Thus, it pledges to work collaboratively with Nedlac. In other words, an informal structure, the MLC, has been established to complement the work of a formal structure of consultative decision-making, Nedlac. It is a truism that because of the formalised nature of Nedlac, where delegations are under mandate and discussions are minuted and transcribed, negotiations drag on endlessly and delegates are unwilling to speak their minds even when they disagree with the mandated positions of their respective constituencies. The MLC is not faced with similar constraints and, because of its flexibility, agreements are likely to be reached speedily. This was the case in the negotiations on the amendments to the labour laws.

The trade unions were able to ensure that the amendments were favourable to their members, because they were represented by seasoned negotiators, unlike the captains of industry who participated at the MLC in their individual capacities, with no such negotiating experience, and who did not participate in Nedlac processes. At the MLC negotiations on the labour-law amendments, the labour delegation was able to outmanoeuvre the business delegates, and achieved agreements that were not favourable to the business community, according to a business delegate to Nedlac, Friedi Dowie.[9] Once such agreements were reached at the MLC, the business delegation to Nedlac was placed in a difficult position that it had to accept.

Business would have preferred the original government proposals and a non-consultative process, or bilateral negotiations with the government, to the inclusive processes at Nedlac, but this is not peculiar to organised business. As shown in the case of the negotiations on both the LRA and the BCEA, labour (especially Cosatu) also turned to bilateral negotiations with the ANC (which ultimately influenced the policy outcomes), when it was unable to achieve its goal through Nedlac. There are important lessons to be derived from this. The alliance between the ANC and Cosatu made the enactment of labour-friendly labour laws possible. By implication, to stem the negative effects of globalisation, an alliance between a progressive government, workers, domestic capitalists (who are threatened by corporate globalisation, and would like some form of protection) and the poor[10] is a necessary condition. Such an alliance, based on a common project, would strengthen the hand of the state in negotiating with capital. Of course, the business community would oppose such an alliance on the ground that it is counterproductive to co-operative governance. This argument resonates within South African business circles. Parsons' position is illustrative; according to him, Cosatu's alliance with the ANC is hampering co-operative governance, and casts a shadow over Nedlac.[11]

This raises an interesting point. By virtue of the fact that government, labour and community constituencies, as well as Nafcoc, are represented in the ANC-led alliance, it is clear that most of these initiatives would have been discussed in the alliance. By the time such issues were tabled at Nedlac, the negotiations degenerated into a confrontation between the ANC partners, on the one hand, and White business, on the other. The Nedlac labour-law process was a culmination of other bilateral processes between the government and social partners during the preparations of the Green Paper and the draft bills that preceded it.

Finally, the labour-law reforms brought the debate about the role of co-operative governance in policy formulation to the surface. Nedlac has been criticised on the basis that it usurps the powers and undermines the sovereignty of parliament and turns it into a rubber-stamp institution. The South African Institute of Race Relations has eloquently captured this point: "The current requirement that economic and labour legislation be referred to NEDLAC prior to its tabling in parliament is undemocratic. Law making is the province of the people's elected representatives in parliament" (Business Day, 4 September 1997).

What these critics failed to realise is that Nedlac played an important role in the policy process. It enabled the government to ensure stakeholders' buy-in and gave credibility to its programmes. The importance of Nedlac to the labour-law reforms cannot be overemphasised. In recognition of this, Parsons noted: "if we did not have Nedlac, we would have to invent it"; although he would prefer that Cosatu break its alliance with the ruling party. The central point here is that Nedlac has complemented parliament in the policy process. The problem, however, lies in the fact that Nedlac negotiates details of legislation and parliament is told that it cannot make any changes to agreements reached at the council. Such a situation allows conflict between parliament and Nedlac. The council would contribute more meaningfully to the policy process if it confined itself to negotiating and reaching agreements on the broad framework of policy reforms rather than preoccupying itself with the minute details of legislation. It should be recognised, nonetheless, that since the supremacy, autonomy and independence of parliament to enact laws for the country are constitutionally guaranteed, nothing in principle or by law prevents parliament from modifying, amending or rejecting draft legislation tabled through Nedlac or any other process. Rather, the difficulty arises politically, because of the dominance of the ANC-led alliance in the government, Nedlac and parliament. Interestingly, while this aspect appears to be a problem in the context of procedural democracy, it may be desirable from the point of view of the alliance attempting to define a hegemonic agenda and being able to execute it unequivocally.

Global economic integration: The social clause and the competition policy

Consultations at Nedlac are becoming a framework for South Africa in defining the nature of its engagement with the global political economy. One significant development in this regard has been the adoption of "the social clause" that commits the government to:

> propose to its partners in bilateral trade negotiations a side-letter to trade agreements, or a memorandum of understanding jointly committing the contracting parties to ratifying and observing the core ILO conventions, and to collaborate at the multilateral level to achieving same. (Nedlac, 1996)

This is an important agreement by the social partners, as it provides a basis for South Africa's engagement with the globalisation process. In particular, the country's engagement is to be conditioned by respect for human and workers' rights. This leads Adler and Webster (2000) to assert that Nedlac is the institutional basis for what they call "bargained liberalization". They argue that while bargained liberalisation involves accepting the need for economic liberalisation, it does, however, set the terms upon which liberalisation takes place and, at the same time, establishes new rules to regulate engagement with the global political economy. The council also provides national stakeholders with a voice in South Africa's engagement with the global order. Although a compromise, the social clause represents a victory for the trade unions. However, Nedlac negotiations have highlighted the inherent conflict in the need to provide suitable conditions for global competitiveness and to do so in a manner that protects the rights of workers, in particular, and human rights, in general.

The trade unions tabled a position on the social clause, predicated on its history and on the need for international solidarity and the mitigation of adverse social effects of globalisation. It aimed to use market access as an instrument to promote fair competition and fair labour standards. It proposed that the government include a social clause in all bilateral and multilateral trade agreements, including the South African Customs Union Agreement, which would bind the parties to accepting the right to form and belong to trade unions without victimisation, the right to bargain collectively (including the right to strike), freedom from child labour and freedom from discrimination on the basis of race and gender (Labour Caucus, 1995), in consonance with the broad human rights thrust of the South African Constitution.

The position tabled by business is a clear manifestation of the zeal to liberalise without regard to its social effects. It tried to do so through a combination of implicit threats and blackmail, in an attempt to place its interests at the centre stage of the economic reform process. Accordingly, business argued that insistence on social clauses in trade agreements would further isolate South Africa and that it could be perceived as an attempt to protect local industries, such as textiles and clothing, which are facing competition from global industry. Further, it was suggested that South Africa cannot impose its democratic values on other countries.[12] In its view, a social clause should only be pursued at the multilateral level through the World Trade Organisation (WTO). Its position on representation at the WTO also reflected the degree of its commitment to consultation and inclusive policy making. In contrast to the trade union movement, which advocated the reform of the WTO through representation of business and trade unions in its governing council, business opposed the extension of co-operative governance to the global level (Business Caucus, 1995). This illustrates the point that business prefers an undemocratic solution that will continue to marginalise most of the developing world and exacerbate global inequalities, as long as its interests remain dominant.

For its part, the government adopted a gradualist, cautionary and conservative approach to the social clause. Consequently, its initial response was to reject the incorporation of the social clause in trade agreements (Nedlac, 1995). It is surprising that a government led by the ANC, which called for economic sanctions against the apartheid regime, would propose an alternative social clause that delinked economic/trade issues from labour and human rights on the flimsy ground that such an approach might reinforce protectionism against developing countries. It argued further that: "In view of the political obstacles they posed, unilateral approaches based on simplistic invocations of moral judgments about the fairness or not of other countries' labour standards are best avoided" (Government Caucus, 1995). Instead, it proposed that South Africa ratify core ILO conventions, campaign for the promotion of labour standards at the global level, beginning in the Southern region, Africa and WTO level, rather than concentrate on putting social clauses in trade agreements. By so doing, the government jettisoned the moral principles on which the ANC struggle against apartheid was based in order to achieve global competitiveness. Such a disempowering conception of globalisation has reduced the degree to which South Africa can be a major force in changing the global governance and trading regime. Then Minister of Labour and current Reserve Bank Governor Tito Mboweni eloquently articulated this position when he asserted:

> No matter how we might detest them, they (international capital) are nevertheless so powerful that we have to accept them as constraints within which we have to operate, for we are in the global economy no matter what we think of ourselves in the moments of self congratulation and national pride. (cited in the *Sunday Tribune*, 14 July 1996)

Such defeatist and self-imposed constraints have limited the scope for South Africa to champion the transformation of multilateral institutions such as the WTO and to promote co-operative governance at the global level. However, the government seems to have moved from this defeatist position and has become a leading advocate of change, building international coalitions for the reform of the global trading system and multilateral institutions. South Africa's leading role in promoting the New Partnership for Africa's Development (Nepad), the formation of the African Union (AU), as well as its leading role in the most recent meetings of the WTO, are indications of the change in Pretoria. In spite of these changes, however, Pretoria has not abided by the content of the social clause in all its trade agreements.

Nonetheless, it is significant to note that Nedlac has provided an institutional framework for South Africa to engage the globalisation process, and has facilitated the co-ordination of inputs into the recent WTO negotiations. This has entailed the inclusion of business, trade union and civil society representatives as part of South African official delegations to meetings of multilateral organisations. As Edigheji and Gostner (2000:89,90) have observed:

> NEDLAC has also served as a national base for the formulation and articulation of South African positions in multilateral institutions. This has been most clearly evidenced in the engagement of the social partners in the ministerial meetings of the World Trade Organization (WTO). In both the Geneva and Seattle ministerial meetings of the WTO, representatives of business, trade unions and community were active participants of the SA government's delegation, enabling South Africa to speak with one voice in international fora and to strategically engage with global processes. In this context, social dialogue offers opportunities for developing countries like South Africa not only to respond to globalisation but also to shape its forms and outcomes.

By implication, through co-operative governance, countries can maximise their engagement with the globalisation process in a manner that could change undemocratic global governance and the exploitative trading system it has engendered. The focus on giving developing countries greater access to the developed economies is partly attributed to agitation by developing countries, among which South Africa has played a leading role since the late-1990s.

Competition policy is an area that confirms the bargaining liberalisation thesis. However, it brings to the fore the problems of co-operative governance, especially in a divided and inegalitarian society like South Africa. In the RDP, the ANC committed itself to promoting a policy that would create more competition and a dynamic business environment. The aim was to discourage pyramid schemes that lead to an over-concentration of economic power and the interlocking of directorships, as well as to abolish anti-competition practices such as market domination and abuse, and to prevent the exploitation of consumers. The draft policy tabled at Nedlac by the Department of Trade and Industry (DTI) was in accord with this goal. While it aimed to conform to global standards of promoting competitiveness and efficiency, it also was unique in striving to ensure access to people from disadvantaged communities, who had been precluded from an equal opportunity to participate in the economy (DTI, 1997).

The social partners were able to adopt a policy with such broad objectives, thus supporting the thesis that economic reform is possible through co-operation (Nedlac, 1998). However, it highlighted the tensions between neo-liberal economic reforms and co-operative governance, as disagreements soon emerged between the social partners. One area of disagreement was the proposal granting the Minister of Trade and Industry the power to review decisions on mergers on a number of grounds, namely, their effects on employment, industrial sector or region, Black economic empowerment and global competitiveness. Because the trade unions favour a strong developmental state, they supported this proposal, which was opposed by the business sector on the basis that granting such powers to the minister would impinge on the free operation of market forces and would "compromise good governance". Furthermore, business opposed the proposal entitling the competition tribunal to order divesture practice by dominant firms, which could not otherwise be corrected or which repeated previously prohibited conduct.

The subsequent Competition Act of 1998, although a compromise between the need to meet social goals and to effect market reforms, continued to be met with scepticism. The criticisms from both business and the trade union movement can be interpreted in the following ways. First, they are indicative of the different understanding of the role of the state in the era of globalisation. Second, they reflect the limitations of trying to meet social needs and to undertake market reforms through consultative processes in an inegalitarian society, where the nature of transformation remains contested. These criticisms have been succinctly summarised by Browne (2001:28):

> On the one hand, the business community continued to criticise the inclusion of social goals in the Act, the perceived underlying hostility towards conglomerates and cross-shareholding, ... the granting of discretionary powers over merger decisions to the Minister ... On the other hand, trade unions have argued that the Act "simply promotes competition for its own sake", and does not go far enough in associating it with clearly stated developmental goals; that in attempting primarily to prevent anti-competition conduct it does not explicitly introduce tools aimed at breaking up inherited patterns of concentration of ownership and control, that the scope of the ministerial review discretion should be widened to intermediate mergers, and that the powers of the Commission and related institutions be reinforced.

The business position is located within a perspective that views competition policy in "technical and apolitical terms", and interprets globalisation as requiring less government intervention in the economy in order to attract foreign investment. Creating a business-friendly environment should thus take primacy in any competition policy (Roberts, 2001). Accordingly, business opposed both any form of state intervention in the economy through the Competition Act and any deviation from their narrow interpretation of "global standards and norms". Consequently, business called for "independent competition institutions". These positions were backed by implicit threats that any deviation from "international best practice" would be met by an investment boycott. The unions, on the other hand, backed the proposal granting ministerial discretion on mergers. However, the business position prevailed. The ministerial review power over merger decisions was dropped, and replaced with the lesser right of the minister to make representations on public interest grounds; and, unlike in the apartheid period, an independent Competition Commission was established.

Consultative and inclusive decision-making, as in this case, has enabled business to exert influence limiting the state's ability to address the existing concentration and control of the corporate sector by White business, as well as to intervene in the economy in order to achieve its broad socio-economic goals. As Roberts (2001:23) has argued, "the resultant focus on a technocratic approach with independent institutions effectively limited the ability of the ANC government to use competition policy to address the entrenched positions of the dominant conglomerates and their behaviour". Furthermore, through their participation in the Nedlac processes, the trade unions legitimised a neo-liberal competition policy, and by so doing also de-legitimatised an interventionist state. In spite of their progressive rhetoric, once in the confines of negotiations, the trade unions had to be "reasonable and logical"; hence, they accepted a competition policy that fundamentally departed from their original position. Participation and agreements, therefore, carry the danger of demobilising civil society, and "limit the extent to which the working class can advance its own interests" (South African Communist Party, 2002b). Consultative processes can produce outcomes that compromise the trade unions, while reinforcing the values and interests of global financial institutions and international and local investors. Having been party to the agreement, the unions are now in a difficult position to mobilise their members against a competition policy that tends to reinforce the existing ownership patterns.

For its part, the ANC-led government, in spite of its continued advocacy of a developmental state, missed a unique opportunity to intervene in the economy by locating its competition policy within the market orthodoxy. Instead, through the competition policy, the state advanced the interests of the dominant White conglomerates. As shown in Table 3.1, the Johannesburg Securities Exchange (JSE) market capitalisation control of the top five groups has actually increased from 54.7% in 1998 (when the Act came into effect) to 61.4% in 2000. In the same period, the JSE market capitalisation of Black groups has decreased from 9.6% in 1998 to 5.6% in 2000. It can be concluded that the Act has not promoted Black economic empowerment, as was originally envisaged by the government.

The political economy of macroeconomic policy

By early 1996, pressure began to mount on the government to restructure the economy and to stabilise the falling rand. The pressure was so intense that the incumbent President, Nelson Mandela, had to go to hospital to get a certificate of a clean bill of health.[14] The pressure on the government also reflected the ideological division between the trade unions and the business sector, and the consequent contestation over the nature and vision of transformation. In early 1996, the South African Foundation, which represents 50 of the largest business groups, released its *Growth for All* economic framework. It

Table 3.1: Summary of JSE market capitalisation control, 1995–2000 (%)

	1995	1996	1997	1998	1999	2000
Group						
Anglo American Corp.	37.1	27.5	22.6	17.4	22.3	23.0
Sanlam	12.4	11.0	10.6	9.9	11.2	11.6
Rembrandt (Inc. Riche & G/Field)	11.2	10.2	11.4	8.8	10.7	10.8
Directors	11.4	10.0	10.6	16.2	13.0	10.9
Liberty Life/Standard Bank	7.3	11.1	11.9	9.5	4.9	5.2
Black groups13		6.3	9.3	9.6	4.7	5.6
Foreign	4.1	4.1	4.0	3.9	4.0	3.8
Institution/Unallocated	1.7	0.8	0.7	4.2	9.3	11.6
RMB/Norwich	1.0	1.7	1.8	4.8	3.6	2.9
Sasol	1.9	2.1	2.8	2.2	2.6	2.6
Investec/Fedsure	0.9	1.1	2.4	3.3	2.6	0.6
Naspers	0.3	0.4	0.5	1.2	0.8	1.3
Anglovaal	2.9	3.0	1.5			
Total	100	100	100	100	100	100.2
Top five groups control (excl. directors)	82.3	72.7	66.4	54.7	59.9	61.4

Source: McGregor's (2001)

contained neo-liberal economic prescriptions – a lean state, full-scale privatisation, flexible labour markets, deregulation and liberalisation. The trade unions responded with their own framework, Cosatu's *Social Equity and Job Creation*. Located within a neo-Keynesian framework, it called for labour-intensive growth, an active industrial policy, an interventionist state and social insurance, and stressed that privatisation be examined on case-by-case basis and that job creation should be accorded utmost priority.[15]

The ANC-led government had to respond to give policy direction and certainty to the markets; but in a manner reminiscent of Thabo Mbeki's announcement of the privatisation plans, Finance Minister Trevor Manuel, while unveiling the government's Growth, Employment and Redistribution (GEAR) policy, proclaimed its fundamentals to be "non-negotiable" (*Sunday Tribune*, 23 June 1996). This raised the hackles of organised labour, which had been briefed about the contents and objectives of the plan only shortly before Mr Manuel's announcement. As will be shown shortly, this supports the thesis that neo-liberal economic reforms and consultative and inclusive decision-making are incompatible.

GEAR represents a complete turn around in ANC economic policy: the RDP, neo-Keynesian in orientation and a product of extensive consultation with the trade unions and civic organisations, was replaced by GEAR, an orthodox neo-liberal macroeconomic policy. As one leading commentator notes:

> Overall GEAR's substantive abandonment of the RDP is indicative of the panic response to the recent exchange rate instability and a lame surrender to the policy dictates and the ideological pressures of the international financial institutions and domestic conglomerates. The proposed growth framework and policy scenarios are analytically flawed, empirically unsupportable, historically unsuitable for this country, and if implemented, will lead to disappointment and failures in achieving the RDP objectives of fundamentally transforming the inherited patterns of inequalities. (Adelzadeh, 1996:3)

The government circumvented the Nedlac processes in drafting the GEAR document. It was drafted in secrecy by a hurriedly constituted 17-member technical team. The team was made up of six academics, two officials of the World Bank, three officials of the Development Bank of Southern Africa, two officials of the South African Reserve Bank and four government officials, one each from the Ministries of Finance, Labour, Trade and Industry, and the Deputy President's office (Department of Finance, 1996). The proclamation of GEAR's fundamentals as being non-negotiable negated the basic principles of the RDP, the socio-economic programme under which the ANC came to power, which stressed the need for consultation between the government and civil society. It also raised questions about the government's commitment to participatory and consultative decision-making. As one business representative at Nedlac put it, "it is difficult for the government to say it is committed to participatory governance when its major policy is not discussed by stakeholders."[16] Indeed, GEAR marked a fundamental shift from *people-driven* to *technocratic-driven* processes, with the marginalisation of civil society organisations in the policy process and the predominance of the interests of market agents, both local and global, in policy objectives.

A question of critical importance is: Why did the government bypass Nedlac in the GEAR process, and in so doing undermine co-operative governance? To answer this question, there is a need to understand that the ideological battle within the ANC, and between the ANC-led alliance and the business sector, over the economic direction of the country was unresolved, in spite of the demise of apartheid and the consequent adoption of the RDP. Despite its public support by the alliance, the RDP did not garner the high degree of consensus it is claimed to have had. Indeed, some elements that were not fully supportive of it are currently staunch proponents of neo-liberal orthodoxy and the deification of market values. In the absence of another policy forum that brings all the major stakeholders together, Nedlac has become an ideological battleground for contesting the nature and direction of social and economic policy. Given such ideological division and the lack of a common vision of transformation, it would have been impossible to reach consensus around GEAR at the council. The overall business convenor in the council, Raymond Parsons (1999) points out that: "Nedlac has not yet been able to develop a shared economic vision. This has exacerbated underlying ideological divisions about economic policy and makes it very difficult to have an agreed growth and employment policy." There was, therefore, an implicit recognition by the government that, given the fundamental departure from the RDP in GEAR and the likely opposition it would have faced from labour at Nedlac, it was imperative not to go through a consultative and participatory process in the council. There was, indeed, recognition from all the stakeholders at Nedlac that there was no way that the government would have successfully secured a buy-in on GEAR from the trade unions. In the words of Parsons, "the government knew that Cosatu in particular would have killed GEAR at Nedlac."[17] Thus, as in many other countries, the government resorted to unilateralism to impose an unpopular macroeconomic policy. In this respect, South Africa's preference for a technocratic and secretive approach to making macroeconomic policy is part of the repertoire of structural adjustment programmes (SAPs) administered or influenced by the World Bank/IMF.[18]

As a "panic response", the government needed to urgently come up with a macroeconomic policy. It would have been impossible to reach a consensus on the policy at Nedlac, which has been criticised for being overly bureaucratic and for slowing down policy formulation. Without a doubt, this is a major weakness of the organisation, as decisions are delayed while the social partners try to reach workable compromises. In some instances, because of the fast pace at which issues arise and because negotiators work under broad mandates, the delegates have to revert to their principals before reaching decisions. All these instances cause major delays. Certainly, this is frustrating to a government that is confronted with major social and economic backlogs. Where consultative processes become obstructive to policy formulation and implementation, the government must move ahead with policy formulation and implementation itself (Parsons, 2002). The government is under a mandate to govern, argued DTI official Paul Jourdan.[19] The "government must govern thesis" sees in co-operative and consultative decision-making obstacles, nuances and impediments to market economic reforms. The primary shortcoming of the "government must govern thesis" is when it becomes an excuse not to take major decisions through consultative processes and to impose unpopular policies on the population, as in the case of GEAR, and by so doing to promote unilateralism, which amounts to bad governance. From the foregoing analysis, it is clear that neo-liberal economic reforms and consultative and inclusive decision-making are antithe-tical.

Further, the government clearly recognised that it was not obliged to go through a participatory process, as the Nedlac Act makes consultation mandatory only for social and labour policies. The "20%/80% principle" advanced by Parsons is important in understanding this point. This principle implies that only 20% of socio-economic policies are processed through Nedlac. 80% are products of technocratic decisions by the state, bilaterals between the state and business, state and civil society and state and labour, or other combinations at different consultative processes and structures. The important point, however, in the case of GEAR, is that the government acted unilaterally. Without attempting to explain away this action, the other social partners have also undertaken unilateral actions – work stoppages, strike actions and mass protest by the trade unions, investment strikes by business, and direct lobbying of parliamentarians and government by business, trade unions and civil society – in pursuit of their goals.

Whatever reasons are advanced, it is obvious from the way GEAR was formulated and announced that, in its attempts to reintegrate South Africa into the global economy, the government did not want interference from any quarter, not least the labour movement. If this is the case, the government's commitment to co-operative governance can be seriously questioned. It is also safe to assert that this poses a potential danger to consultative decision-making in South Africa, as it encourages the other social partners to resort to unilateralism with the potential to create a climate for social and economic instability.

Whether the government made the right decision to bypass the council on this important policy is debatable. On the one hand, in spite of the fact that GEAR was unilaterally adopted by the government, it has been embraced by business – it sent out the right signals to local and foreign investors. After all, business across the globe is notorious for its opposition to consultative processes. Given the business sector's history of unilateralism and repression *vis-à-vis* labour, South African business welcomed a unilateral approach to policy making, especially since it furthered its interests. On the other hand, the South African trade union movement has rejected GEAR.[20] The rift between the government and labour, especially Cosatu, around this policy continues to reverberate at the council. The Public Finance and Monetary Chamber of Nedlac, where the Department of Finance is the lead ministry, has been virtually paralysed as labour and department officials do not see eye-to-eye. Furthermore, the non-consultative process of GEAR has adversely affected the ANC-led alliance, becoming a subject of public acrimony between the ANC government and Cosatu. The ANC's position of non-negotiability has constituted a recipe for antagonism between the government and the unions. Nedlac has proven to be ill-suited to addressing the political fall-out, especially between Cosatu and the government; it has also not been able to bridge the ideological divide between the unions and business.

Neo-liberal economic reforms and co-operative governance are conflictual. Contrary to the assertion of most of the existing literature, such reforms (as the process leading to the adoption of GEAR has shown) undermine consultative processes and thereby threaten co-operative governance, as the government bypasses the consultative process in order to impose an unpopular policy on society.

Of fundamental importance was the fact that the ANC was unable to create a political coalition in support of GEAR, as it was not discussed within its own structures or with its alliance partners, Cosatu and the South African Communist Party (SACP). Had GEAR gone through a consultative process within the alliance, and then been taken to Nedlac (even if the contents remained the same), it would probably still not have received trade union and civil society endorsement (especially given Cosatu's ideological leaning), but the opposition would have been less vociferous and possibly more manageable. A recognition of this underlined Cosatu's call for an accord between it and the government to enable both parties to negotiate as a united front with business at Nedlac (Cosatu, 1996). Unfortunately, the state has not accepted this proposal, preferring instead to mediate between the interests of labour and capital. Some analysts have observed that the fact that both business and trade unions are not sufficiently strong or comprehensively organised accounts for the absence of a social accord (Nattrass & Seekings, 1998). However, it will be argued later that in the absence of a shared project by the ANC-led alliance, it is impossible for the government to reach an accord with the other social partners. As the history of the East Asian developmental states has shown, a social accord is possible only when the ruling élite articulates a project of national transformation and then mobilises societal actors around such a project (see Evans 1995; Weiss, 1998).

At this juncture, it is pertinent to note that neo-liberal economic reforms (in the form of GEAR) have reconfigured the alliances between the state and socio-economic actors. As evident from the discussion above, while the ANC draws its political support from workers and the poor, it is the business sector, initially suspicious of the democratic government (because of its original ideological orientation), which has embraced the government by supporting its macroeconomic policy. GEAR advances the interests of business. Thus, contrary to Baskin's (2000) assertion that the national liberation movement's agenda would determine the direction of the country, in reality business interests seem to be driving economic policy, and with this comes a reconfiguration of alliances. Moreover, the waning influence of civil society and the trade union movement is evident from this analysis. The expectation in the early 1990s that the trade unions would have considerable influence on the democratic government seems not to have been met, due in part to what the Deputy General Secretary of the SACP, Jeremy Cronin (2002), refers to as the marginalisation of the left within the ANC. Critical observers of South Africa's transition should not be surprised by these developments. They should recall Minister Trevor Manuel's earlier warning that "the trade unions would have limited ability to influence macroeconomic policies" in the new dispensation (cited in Desai & Habib, 1995). If Manuel's pronouncement is anything to go by, then we must reflect on the cautionary observation by Desai and Habib that Cosatu (and indeed the labour movement as a whole) could be reduced from a major player to a marginalised and bureaucratised onlooker in the process of public-policy making in the country.

In analysing this shift in policy orientation, it is important to understand the internal dynamics and contestation within the ANC and the alliance over policy making. To a large degree, the unity against apartheid was race-driven, and a section of the ANC has a long history of an anti-socialist, petty bourgeois orientation. In a recent address, President Thabo Mbeki reasserted the ANC's non-socialist orientation when he argued that "our movement, like all other national liberation movements throughout the world, is inherently and by definition, not a movement whose mission is to fight for the victory of socialism" (Mbeki, 2002). The year 1996 marked a monumental period in ANC history, as it represented a unique opportunity for the "national bourgeois" wing of the ANC not only to seize complete control of the macroeconomic policy-making process but also to entrench itself as the dominant force within the party.[21] An incisive account of how this shift occurred is provided by Marais (1998). As Gillian Hart (2002) has poignantly argued, the petty-bourgeois bloc "centered around Thabo Mbeki consistently invokes 'globalisation' to circumvent any questioning of neoliberal nostrums and policies, or their alignment to capital".

Closely linked to the above is a process of the "unravelling" of the liberation agenda; today, the ANC-led alliance and government have no coherent developmental framework. Before the introduction of GEAR, the alliance was united around the RDP, and even mobilised the whole nation around it. That unity and identification with a common vision have been unravelled. It is desirable, then, that the ANC mobilise its members and the alliance partners around a joint project of national transformation, and then consult and negotiate with business on such a project. Some members of the ANC share this position, and it is eloquently articulated by Langa Zita (2002), an ANC parliamentarian and a former member of the central committee of the SACP. According to him, the principal objective of the ANC should be to marshal its forces around a common project, which should form the basis of consultative processes with other social actors. In the same vein, the SACP (2002c:8) argues: "One of the critical challenges … is the need to unite the democratic forces through a common growth and development strategy and to face both global and domestic capital with a united voice and approach."

Regrettably, this has not been the case, partly because the national bourgeois wing of the ANC sees itself as more secure and powerful today than it was in 1994, and will press forward with its agenda. However, because much of South Africa is still strongly defined by racism – sometimes subliminal, sometimes overt – the ANC's identification with those for whom class oppression and marginalisation have a racial underpinning still projects it as a "revolutionary" force. Nevertheless, it is thoroughly bourgeois in its class orientation and character, and will increasingly brook less left-wing opposition. A social accord may be impossible; even if the government manages to enter into one with the major social partners, such an accord is unlikely to be successful without the ANC-led alliance first defining the transformation project and uniting and mobilising its supporters around it.

Consequently, two types of pact have emerged in the post-1994 period – an official political pact between the ANC and Cosatu, and an unofficial economic pact between the ANC government and business. These two types of alliance have made co-operative governance extremely difficult, as the two contending forces, business and labour, try to maximise their interests irrespective of the consequences for the national economy. As De Villiers and Anstey (2000) argue, participatory decision-making is successful only where there is an "abandonment of maximalist demands" by the social partners; but, in the absence of a shared project, maximalist demands from all the stakeholders have dominated the post-1994 period.

From the foregoing discussion, it can be argued that co-operative governance has little or no influence over economic policy, since a product of unilateralism has conditioned the macro environment. As a result, consultations and negotiations at Nedlac can only achieve limited results – to create pockets of efficiency, without being able to shape the broad framework of transformation (negotiations and agreements at Nedlac have to be within GEAR's parameters). It needs to be stressed that the victory won by the unions through decades of struggle to have a say in economic decisions is now being revised by a government (which union members voted into power) that is pursuing unilateral policies that privilege the interests of capital.

Privatisation, economic liberalisation and co-operative governance

The manner in which privatisation policy was formulated and subsequently announced has put considerable strain on co-operative governance in the post-1994 period. The government first signalled its intention to circumvent participatory decision-making processes in December 1995, when the incumbent Deputy President Thabo Mbeki announced government plans for the wholesale or partial privatisation of some parastatals, including South African Airways, Sun Air, Telkom (the telecommunications company) and Eskom (the fifth-largest electricity utility company in the world), without consulting with its ally, the major national trade union federation, Cosatu. The subsequent outcry and mass mobilisation (including a one-day strike) by the trade unions made the government enter into negotiations with Cosatu (*Sunday Times*, 28 January 1996). These negotiations resulted in the signing by the government and labour of the National Framework Agreement (NFA), which set the framework for the restructuring of public assets. The NFA implicitly requires that the restructuring of public enterprises be carried out only after due consultation with all stakeholders, particularly labour.

Significantly, the NFA is a product of bilateral negotiations between the state and the trade union movement, rather than of an inclusive process as represented by Nedlac. However, the implementation of this agreement has become the subject of a public spat between the unions and the government, with the former arguing that the latter has failed to abide by the contents of the agreement. As noted by the SACP (2002a:17):

> Although, in the NFA, we have a remarkably progressive national agreement on the kinds of processes required to ensure effective and strategic restructuring – in practice, the NFA is not working well. The NFA continues to be dysfunctional with labour dissatisfied with the lack of commitment shown to the NFA by managers of public enterprises in particular. Government seems unwilling in most cases to direct these managers and ensure that the NFA is adhered to.

The lack of a consultative process around such important policy measures has become the major source of tension between the ANC-aligned Cosatu and the ANC-led government, and "makes a mockery of consultative processes and consequently participatory democracy" (Cosatu, 2002). A former trade unionist and now ANC Secretary General, Kgalema Motlanthe, recently admitted this when he agreed that "restructuring was indeed the big problem and the major source of tension not only within the ANC-led alliance but between the government and the unions " (*Business Day*, 2 October 2001).

The government is under increasing pressure from business and the international investment community to privatise. Consequently, the ANC has shifted from its electoral mandate to "reverse privatisation programmes that are contrary to the public interest" (ANC, 1994:91). Instead, it is forcefully going ahead with the privatisation policy, without consulting with its alliance partners, the SACP and Cosatu. The government argues that privatisation is aimed at promoting Black economic empowerment (BEE), ensuring efficient and effective service delivery, promoting human-resource development, stimulating local and foreign investment, promoting private-public partnership, and raising funds in order to reduce the state debt and improve the country's credit rating (Ministry of Public Enterprises, 2000; National Treasury, 2001). This argument is hinged on neoclassical economic theories that conceive of markets as the most efficient allocator of resources, and that view privatisation as enabling the government to provide basic social and physical services to the poor.

While the Ministry of Public Enterprises' policy framework continues to stress the importance of a developmental state, a closer examination of the framework shows that there is greater reliance on market agents. Through this reliance, privatisation is leading to the hollowing out and disempowerment of the state in relation to the private sector. As aptly captured by Cosatu, privatisation "increases the voice of capital in social and economic policy. It takes assets out of the control of the democratic government and turns them over to private interests. It reduces the capacity of the state" (Cosatu, 2001). By the same token, BEE has become a euphemism for the creation of a Black bourgeoisie. In itself, there is nothing wrong in creating a Black business class. However, by outsourcing government services, rolling-back the state, employing cost-recovery social policy and commodifying basic services, privatisation as an instrument of BEE further disempowers the majority of the Black population and thereby widens social and economic inequalities among Blacks.

The South African trade union movement, although without a coherent policy on BEE, anticipated these adverse effects of privatisation. Cosatu, in particular, is vehement in its opposition to privatisation, and favours public-sector provision of public services and the decommodification of basic services. It argues that privatisation will lead to downsizing in the public sector (see Table 3.2) and will make basic services unaffordable to the poor majority. A point that is often overlooked by proponents of privatisation is that it makes the poor subsidise business and the rich. As illustrated by a report of Cosatu's research arm, the National Labour and Economic Development Institute (Naledi), the price of local telephone calls charged by Telkom is projected to increase by 35% while, at the same time, the costs of international calls have fallen by 40% in real terms. Thus, the poor subsidise business and the rich with respect to telephone rates.

The cost of electricity is estimated to increase by 50% after the partial privatisation of Eskom (Naledi, 2001). Partly due to arrears and the inability to pay – all linked to the question of affordability, as privatisation is premised on cost recovery – thousands of poor households have experienced electricity cut-offs. In early 2001, an estimated 20 000 poor households per month had their electricity disconnected (Fiil-Flynn, 2001), with major adverse effects on their living standards.

What is discernible from the foregoing is that privatisation has led to the maximisation of the interests of the privileged group, while placing the burden of economic reforms on workers, the poor and the marginalised. The South African democratic victory, a victory for the working class and the marginalised, is being revised through policies such as privatisation that advance the interest of capital. It must be acknowledged, however, that the government has made major strides in extending social and physical services to the poor, through the provision of telephone, water, electricity and housing services. Indeed, the new government has the enviable record of having constructed 1.1 million low-cost houses between April 1994 and January 2001 (Department of Housing, 2001). Still, the government's cost-recovery social policy and the commodification of basic services are undermining progress in the delivery of social services.

Significantly, privatisation is giving impetus to "globalisation from below", as the trade unions mobilise their members and forge alliances with a range of community organisations including churches, the South African Non-Governmental Coalition (Sangoco) and the South African National Civics Organisation (Sanco) in anti-privatisation campaigns in the form of mass protests, strike action and stay-aways (the most recent being a two-day stay-away in August 2001). This is already manifesting in conflictual relations between the trade unions and the state – due to economic reforms, this time the privatisation of public enterprises, conflict is replacing co-operation and consultative processes. Instead of trust and reciprocity, state-society relations are based on distrust and the consequent conflict between the state and societal actors. This can hardly be described as co-operative governance.

Table 3.2: Job losses in selected public enterprises and the public service

	1995	**2001**	**Number of job losses**[22]	**% decrease in employment**
Transnet	115 317	78 708	36 609	-32
Denel	11 243	6 363	4 880	-43
Telkom	58 793	46 000[23]	12 793	-22
Eskom	39 952	37 311[24]	2 641	-7
Public service	1 176 545[25]	1 042 392	134 153	-11
	1 401 850	1 210 774	191 076	-14

Source: Naledi (2001)

The process of privatisation seems irreversible, as the government is committed to it in spite of the trade unions' opposition. As with GEAR, the government has made it clear that it will brook no opposition in its drive for privatisation. This was succinctly expressed by then President Nelson Mandela when, in May 1996, he asserted that "privatisation is a fundamental policy of the ANC and would be implemented as a government policy" (*Financial Mail*, 19 January 1996). Like GEAR, privatisation has been presented to the alliance as a *fait accompli*. At best, and reflecting their waning influence, the unions have only managed to slow down the privatisation process.

The White business community has used the slow pace of the privatisation exercise to question the government's commitment to the process. In addition, it has been used to account for low domestic investment, which stood at 14.9% of GDP at the end of 2000 (South African Reserve Bank, 2001). This has important implications for economic growth and job creation, particular goals of GEAR. Its architects estimated a 6% GDP growth rate and the creation of 400 000 jobs. To achieve these targets, it was estimated that gross domestic investment as a percentage of GDP would have to increase to 26% annually by 2000. External factors, such as the global economic crisis in 1997 (dubbed the Asian financial crisis) and the global financial meltdown exacerbated by the events of 11 September 2001, are important factors to consider in explaining post-1994 economic performance. Account must also be taken of the fact that investment flows have increased between the triadic Europe, Asia and the US. The African continent as a whole has witnessed decreasing inflows of capital, a factor that those blaming the slow pace of privatisation in South Africa often overlook in their zeal to make the government a scapegoat. Critical analysts, even those who are opposed to the privatisation programme in principle, would welcome the caution with which the government has proceeded with the process, especially following September 11 and the consequent downward spiral of the global economy and technology stocks, in particular. Under such circumstances, it would have amounted to economic suicide to proceed, for example, with the early sale of Telkom, given that the government would have received lower prices for the shares.

The privatisation exercise has had other important implications for co-operative governance. One such outcome was that some entrepreneurs who acquired privatised enterprises were opposed to national labour legislation upholding workers' rights, and in some instances attempted to blackmail the government to set aside prevailing labour legislation. This situation has led to a continuation of conflictual relations between the state and civil society, thus undermining co-operative governance in the country. Commenting on the trend in southern Africa, Fashoyin (1998:9) observes that "the new employers ... are taking advantage of liberalization policies ... to introduce new employment conditions which are ... substandard and usually at variance with national legislation". In South Africa, which has the most progressive labour regime in the region, organised business and a host of individual businesspersons continue to oppose the current labour legislation (and to exert pressure for its amendment), citing it as one factor for the low investment and growth rates.

The government argues that economic liberalisation is a necessary condition for global economic competitiveness, the attraction of foreign direct investment and job creation.

Liberalisation has occasioned the decentralisation of political and economic power to several actors, which in part erodes the powers of the traditional social partners, government, business and labour. Partly because of the rapid decline in formal-sector employment, the individualisation of work, the growing informal sector and increased unemployment in South Africa (due in part to the privatisation programme), the traditional organisational base of the trade union movement is being eroded, and trade union membership represents a declining fraction of the labour force.[26] The membership of the three union federations that participate in Nedlac constitute only 35% of the formally employed, while business representation accounts for about 30% percent of the total number of active businesses in the country (CDE, 1999).[27] This situation is unlike classical corporatist arrangements, whereby both business and labour represent a higher proportion of their constituencies (encompassing societal interest groups). This makes it easier for governments in the Nordic countries, for example, to negotiate and forge agreements with trade unions and business associations, on the understanding that such agreements tend to reflect wider interests than is the case in South Africa. The community constituency, which should represent the non-formal sector, is the least representative and weakest constituency in Nedlac, reflecting the narrow base of all Nedlac stakeholders except for the government, which enjoyed greater than 60% support from the electorate in the 1999 general election.

Of concern, furthermore, is the inability of the trade unions to organise those in the informal sector, including the Self-Employed Workers Association (SEWA), led by a former trade unionist, Ms Pat Horn, and the large number of the unemployed. The same is true of the employers' associations, which have not shown any willingness to organise or bring into their fold those small entrepreneurs who are not affiliated. In addition, neither the trade unions nor business have been able to articulate the concerns of the poor and the unemployed unless such interests coincide with their own interests. Perhaps we should ask why the trade unions are not adequately representing the interests of the unemployed and the poor. Given the election of a democratic government with a developmentalist orientation, the union movement recognised at the beginning of the transition that it would be inappropriate for the movement to represent wider interests than those of its members. In other words, the movement made a strategic choice to focus on the interests of its members (see Friedman & Shaw, 2000); but by so doing, it has subjected itself to criticism for representing a narrow and privileged group. In the context of an approximate 35% unemployment rate, the employed are considered an élite group.

As part of the globalisation of economic activities, businesses in South Africa are becoming footloose as they delist from the JSE and relocate their head offices in Europe and North America, in what some have referred to as the "recolonisation" of South Africa (Carmody, 2001), whereby companies take decisions on their operations at their headquarters abroad with major effects on the national economy. In this regard, South Africa represents a significant departure from the European experience, where most companies were nationally based and tied their success to that of their national economies, and were therefore committed to co-operative governance. The emergence of transnational corporations (TNCs) in South Africa and the delisting of local companies have meant that these companies are less committed to co-operative governance, as they do not see their success as being connected to the national economy. In this context, as well as due to the fact that the unions are getting weaker, Nedlac is an inappropriate structure for co-operative governance, as it provides few incentives for business to take part in state co-ordinated consultative decision-making.

It is also pertinent to consider the capacity of the organised sector to represent and promote the interests of the poor and of marginalised groups such as women. Here we should look at the capacity of the National Women's Coalition (NWC), which claims to represent South African women in the structures of and agreements at Nedlac.

Lacking human and material resources and not being able to adjust to the imperatives of the democratic dispensation, the NWC has been incapable of effectively representing the interests of women in the council. Gershater's (2001) study captures the situation. It is observed that in its first few years of existence, the NWC made a significant contribution to democracy by increasing the number of women participating in the multiparty negotiations and by developing a women's charter, which influenced the interim constitution. Since 1994, however, although it has continued to claim to be the representative structure for women, the NWC no longer has the vibrancy of its early days, partly because it has lost its key leaders to government, has limited funding and lacks a strategic vision, and because there is an absence of consensus among women's groups.[28] Thus, questions have been raised as to the continued relevance of the NWC.

Closely linked to the above is the question of gender. An examination of Nedlac's main decision-making structures and agreements is revealing in this regard. For example, of the 31 delegates attending its Manco meetings in the 2000/2001 financial year, not one was a woman (Nedlac, 2001). This, in part, is a reflection of the male dominance of the internal structures of the various social partners. Allied to the low female participation rate is the marginalisation and non-mainstreaming of gender in the council's activities. An examination of major Nedlac agreements reveals that, apart from the labour laws, gender has not been an integral dimension of its activities. Most of the agreements are not disaggregated by gender so as to assess the implications for women and men. These factors explain the non-engendered nature of co-operative governance, in spite of the commitment of the ANC to non-sexism and the fact that South Africa has one of the highest representations of women in parliament and the cabinet in the world.[29]

The new dispensation of liberalisation has had adverse effects on trade unions and community organisations. As these civil society groups adjust to market imperatives, the question of individual maximisation has come to the fore. Trade unions and community groups have their human resource capability depleted as trade unionists and leading community activists move in droves into the public and private sectors, where they receive higher material rewards. Organs of civil society have been robbed of an experienced cadre of leaders and activists to engage in all the intricate and complex issues at Nedlac. Consequently, the labour and community constituencies have been unable to maximise their participation not only in the council but in other avenues of influence to the political economy of the country. As Alence (1999) demonstrates in his empirical work on policy making in the post-1994 period, the trade unions exert more influence on labour-market policies than on macroeconomic policy, where they have limited capacity and where technocratic policy making has prevailed.

This situation has led some analysts of the South African political economy to question the effectiveness of the participation of CSOs in public-policy processes. As Meer (1999) argues, participation in the policy process has rather had a demobilising and delegitimising effect on organs of civil society. This is because those that participate in the policy process have little time to consult with their constituencies on all issues, in spite of the fact that agreements reached at these negotiations are expected to be binding on the organisations. Of critical importance is that accountability and transparency, central elements of the strength of civil society organisations, are being undermined as a result. Again, on occasion, there is little co-ordination and reporting back by the delegations to the various Nedlac processes. However, it should be emphasised that civil society, through its participation and vigilance, has made the process of governance more transparent and elected officials more accountable, as well as ensured that the government has remained committed to the goals of development. Furthermore, as evident through the anti-privatisation protests by Cosatu, South Africa's civil society has not legitimatised neo-liberal economic policy and has not become a puppet of the government in spite of its alliance with the ruling party and its participation at Nedlac. Similarly, it can be argued that the trade unions' vociferous opposition to privatisation is partly due to the fact that they were not consulted and partly due to their principled and outright stand against privatisation as an economic policy (Cosatu, 2001).

Conclusion

The analysis in this chapter has highlighted some major challenges of globalisation on governance in South Africa, which could be generalisable. To begin with, while some academics and international development agencies stress that the need for economic reform requires consultative and inclusive decision-making, the actual practice of public policy leaves much to be desired. As the South African case has shown, there is a tendency by the government to unilaterally impose unpopular policies and, thereby, marginalise and exclude the other social partners from major policy concerns such as macroeconomic and privatisation policies. Globalisation thus breeds undemocratic practices, as the neo-liberal reforms associated with it are not conducive to consultative processes. These contradictory processes of neo-liberal economic reforms and consultative/participatory policy processes, which multilateral institutions are asking developing countries to embrace, have often been overlooked in the existing literature. However, such undemocratic practices by the state have led to an intensification of conflict – strikes and mass mobilisation by civil society and trade unions, on the one hand, and investment strikes by the business community, on the other. These actions pose potential threats to the socio-political stability that has been experienced since 1994, as well as to the economic growth and development prospects of South Africa.

The concern that then arises is that if social partners (in this case business, labour and broader civil society) are excluded from participating in and negotiating macroeconomic policies that define the broad environment for economic management, it is of little importance for them to participate in and be consulted on social policy and labour-market policy, which are conditioned by the macroeconomic environment. As the analysis above has shown, where such broad and defining policies are taken outside the ambit of consultative processes, gains achieved at the micro level, such as labour-market policy, are eroded through increased pressure to change such policies in the name of global standards.

The neo-liberal economic reforms have also diminished the capacity of the state to implement policies that would improve the living standards of its population, as we have seen in the case of privatisation. However, this is leading to the formation of alliances of trade unions, church groups, civics and non-governmental organisations in resistance to corporate globalisation, to reverse the race to the bottom. Globalisation from below could strengthen the hand of the state in implementing progressive economic policy; but the ANC government has not shown the political will to develop a common project of transformation with its alliance partners and civil society that could constitute the bedrock of such a progressive policy. Nonetheless, another trend is that participatory mechanisms have resulted in the legitimisation of neo-liberal economic policies, while at the same time delegimising the state in the eyes of the electorate (see the poll results discussed in Chapter 2), as witnessed in the formulation of the competition policy.

Co-operative governance has other mixed results. On the one hand, it provides stakeholders with a voice in national policies and a platform to set the conditions to engage with the global economy. On the other hand, consultative processes, if not properly managed, could undermine the internal democracy of societal actors like trade unions and business, as civil society's negotiators become preoccupied with the issues before them in forums and have no or little time to consult with their members. In this respect, they could enter into agreements that are in conflict with their members' interests. Striking a balance – engaging in negotiations and ensuring regular consultation with members to seek mandates – is therefore one of the major challenges confronting South Africa's stakeholders involved in consultative decision-making.

Another paradoxical feature of globalisation is that while it has lead to the enactment of public policies that promote and protect workers' rights, the economic reform process that furthers labour-market flexibility and privatisation has resulted in the retrenchment of workers and a consequent decline in union membership. Therefore, the economic reforms are eroding the organisational base of trade unions and their capacity to engage in consultative processes. In order to address these challenges, the union movement needs to broaden its representative base. Towards this end, it will have to include and organise the growing numbers of workers in the informal sector or in atypical forms of employment, in order to give them a voice to protect their interests and to shape the future developments of the country. This is in addition to the unions' already noted need to strengthen their alliances with other organisations of civil society.

The argument is not to deny the importance of co-operative governance to economic transformation, but rather to contend that for co-operative governance to be successful different sets of conditions are required. The ruling political alliance has to define its transformative project (as discussed by Mhone in Chapter 2) and, on the basis of such a project, negotiate with local and international capital. This should be the foundation for co-operative governance. Such a project must move away from neo-liberal orthodoxy, in order to secure the support of civil society organisations. All of this calls for "a different kind of politics"[30] – the state forging alliances with progressive civil society; business associations broadening their representational base by organising and bringing into their fold the large number of SMMEs; and trade unions establishing alliances with civics, NGOs and community organisations. Central to a different kind of politics is the need for self-empowerment by individuals, communities, localities and countries, so that citizens can claim their right to develop themselves and society, and by so doing "roll back the gods of the market" that have been so disempowering and exclusionary, and reverse the market's pervasive values of individualisation, commodification and monetisation of life. This is particularly pertinent in the new South Africa, in order to overcome the racial and gender inequalities and political exclusion bequeathed by apartheid. Therefore, rather than being treated as clients and consumers, South Africans must first and foremost be treated as citizens for whom politics should primarily be aimed at enhancing human welfare. This would see a shift from the politics of exclusion and élitism to the politics of active citizenship and popular participation.

Finally, social partners, particularly the trade union movement and civil society groups, have to pay greater attention to their lack of capacity; this shortcoming has hampered their effectiveness in engaging in consultative processes. These are the challenges that stakeholders must face head-on for co-operative governance to continue to be an important mechanism for socio-economic reform.

Endnotes

1   Thanks to Guy Mhone, Jonathon Moses and Jimi Adesina for their feedback on this chapter. However, I am solely responsible for any error in the chapter.

2   While the World Bank urges countries to embrace co-operative governance, on its part, it has continued to push policies (such as its Structural Adjustment Programmes) that are not formulated through participatory and transparent processes. Neither do such policies have any modicum of accountability.

3   Nedlac represents a merger of the NMC and the NEF.

4   It should be noted that these three union federations are divided along political lines. For example, Cosatu is aligned to the ANC while Nactu is aligned broadly to political parties of the black consciousness movement. There is a huge ideological gap between these two political camps. This ideological divide has been the major stumbling block to the unification of the federations, in spite of recognition by all that a united federation would be more desirable. Like business, this division among the union federations has also hampered their effectiveness. Thus, on occasion, it is not surprising to see the federations taking different positions rather than presenting a common front in negotiations with the other partners.

5   The National Rural Development Forum stopped participating in Nedlac activities about three years ago when it ceased to function as an organisation.

6   The community constituency is represented in the Management Committee and Executive Council and, except for the Development Chamber, participates on an ad hoc basis in the activities of other chambers on issues it considers relevant to its constituent organisations.

7   Author interview with Raymond Parsons, 13 February 2002.

8   Author interview with Friedi Dowie, 15 January 2002.

9   Ibid.

10 The representation of the poor in such an alliance would not be without its problems, given their lack of resources, not being organised and being dispersed. Their effective participation requires their being mobilised and organised into a broad-based coalition. This would enable them to share and utilise resources for common goals.

11 Author interview with Parsons, overall business convenor at Nedlac, 13 February 2002.

12 Ironically, it is the same business sector that advocates that the South African government should intervene in Zimbabwe in order to safeguard democracy.

13 These include all groups that have significant Black influence.

14 One reason advanced for the falling rand was that President Mandela was sick and it was feared that his death would have adverse effects on the economy. He went to hospital to quell the speculated attack on the rand.

15 The GEAR document has much more in common with the SA Foundation's prescriptions than those of Cosatu.

16 Author interview with Raymond Parsons, 13 February 2002.

17 Ibid.

18 The contention that GEAR is home-grown SAP is misleading. The World Bank and IMF impose their policies through various means including through seconding their personnel to work as members of teams that draft economic reform policies in African and other developing countries. Through such methods, they exert enormous influence, and indeed do impose SAPs on developing countries.

19 Author interview, 26 October 1999

20 The Community Constituency supported the unions' position, basically for two reasons. First, its position accorded with that of the unions. Second, they lacked the resources, both human and financial, to be able to develop their own extensive response to GEAR.

21 Thanks to Jimi Adesina for drawing my attention to this point.

22 This figure does not include local government and other parastatals.

23 Estimate.

24 Figure for 1998.

25 Figure for 1996.

26 This is not a one-way process, as some of the new civil society organisations collaborate with the trade unions to fight for a common cause. The alliance between Cosatu and the Treatment Action Campaign (TAC) over the provision of Nevirapine is one such example.

27 The organisations that make up the community constituency also represent a low proportion of civil society organisations in the country. It is also important to note that the peak civil-society organisation, Sangoco, is not represented in Nedlac.

28 The initial exclusion of women from the multiparty negotiations created an imperative for the establishment of the NWC – there was a consensus among women's groups to be part of the negotiations. After the 1994 election, the NWC has not been able to identify a common cause for women.

29 A third of parliamentarians are women.

30 Thanks to Harry Boyte with whom I have exchanged ideas on this concept. The exchanges have assisted me in developing my ideas on the subject. This concept will be further elaborated in future research.

References

Adelzadeh, A. (1996) "From the RDP to GEAR: The Gradual Embracing of Neo-liberalism in Economic Policy", NIEP Occasional Paper Series, No 3.

Adler, G. & Webster, E. (eds) (2000) *Trade Unions and Democratisation in South Africa, 1985–1997*. Johannesburg: Witwatersrand University Press.

Alence, R. (1999) "The Informational Politics of Democratic Consolidation: A Quantitative Analysis of Economic Policymaking in South Africa." Paper prepared for HSRC seminar on public policy analysis. 4 November. Pretoria

African National Congress (1994) *The Reconstruction and Development Programme*. Johannesburg: Umanyano Publications.

Andrew Levy & Associates (2001) *Annual Report*. Johannesburg.

Bakker, I. (1999) "Neoliberal Governance and the New Order." In *Working Papers in Local Governance and Democracy*. Istanbul: World Academy for Local Government and Democracy. 99/1.

Baskin, J. (2000) "Labour in South Africa's Transition to Democracy: Concertation in a Third World Setting." In Adler, G. & Webster, E. (eds) *Trade Unions and Democratisation in South Africa, 1985–1997*. Johannesburg: Witwatersrand University Press.

Browne, C. H. (2001) "Big Business and Wealth Creation of South Africa: Policy Issues in the Transition from Apartheid." Centre for International Politics, University of Pennsylvania. Working Paper Series #00—01.

Business Caucus (1995) "Business Position in Respect of the Social Clauses in International Trade Agreements as proposed by Labour." Business Submission to Nedlac, 5 July.

Business Day (2001) "ANC grapples with alliance tensions." Johannesburg, 2 October.

Carmody, P. (2001) "Between Globalisation and (Post) Apartheid: The Political Economy of Restructuring in South Africa." Unpublished paper. Department of Geography, University of Vermont.

Centre for Development and Enterprise (1999) "Policy-Making in a New Democracy: South Africa's Challenges for the 21st Century." Johannesburg, August.

Bakker, I. (1999) "Neoliberal Governance and the New Gender Order." Istanbul: World Academy for Local Government and Democracy. Working Paper No 1.

Bratton, M. & Van de Walle, N. (1997) *Democratic Experiments in Africa: Regime Transition in Comparative Perspective*. Cambridge: Cambridge University Press.

Coleman, N., Bodibe, O., Tregenna, F. & Creamer, K. (2000) *Accelerating Transformation: Cosatu's Engagement with Policy and Legislative Processes during South Africa's First Democratic Governance*. Cape Town: Cosatu Parliamentary Office.

Cosatu (1996a) *Social Equity and Job Creation: The key to a stable future*. Johannesburg.

Cosatu (1996b) "A draft programme for the Alliance presented to the Exco." Cosatu discussion paper, 22 November.

Cosatu (1997) "The Report of the September Commission on the Future of the Unions." Johannesburg, August.

Cosatu (2001) "Position Paper on Privatisation" tabled at Nedlac, 30 July. http://www.cosatu.org.za/docs/2001/privatpp.htm.

Cosatu (2002) *Cosatu Weekly*. 17 May 2002. http://www.cosatu.org.za/news/weekly/20020517.htm

Cronin, J. (2002) Interview with Helena Sheenan. http://www.comms.dcu.ie/sheenanh/za/cronin02.htm

Deegan, H. (1999) *South Africa Reborn: Building a New Democracy*. London: UCL Press Ltd.

Department of Finance (1996) *Growth, Employment and Redistribution: A Macro-Economic Strategy*. Pretoria.

Department of Trade and Industry (1997) *Proposed Guidelines for Competition Policy. A Framework for Competition, Competitiveness and Development*. Pretoria.

Department of Housing (2001) Database.

Desai, A. & Habib, A. (1995) "Cosatu and the Democratic Transition in South Africa: Drifting towards Corporatism", *South Asia Bulletin, Comparative Studies of South Asia, Africa and the Middle East*. Vol. XV, No.1.

De Villiers, D. & Anstey, M. (2000) "Trade Unions in Transitions to Democracy in South Africa, Spain and Brazil." In Adler, G. & Webster, E. (eds) *Trade Unions and Democratisation in South Africa, 1985–1997*. Johannesburg: Witwatersrand University Press.

Edigheji, O. & Gostner, K. (2000) "Social Dialogue: The South African Experience", *Labour Education*, Vol. 3, No. 120. International Labour Office, Geneva.

Evans, P. (1995) *Embedded Autonomy: States and Industrial Transformation*. Princeton, New Jersey: Princeton University Press.

Evans, P. (1997) (ed.) *State-Society Synergy: Government and Social Capital in Development*. California: University of California at Berkeley.

Fashoyin, T. (1998) "Industrial Relations in Southern Africa: The Challenge of Change", ILO/SAMAT Policy Paper, No. 5. Harare, Zimbabwe.

Fiil-Flynn, M. (2001) "The Electricity Crisis in Soweto", *Occasional Papers Series*, No. 4. Municipal Services Project. www.queensu.ca/msp.

Friedman, S. & Reitzes, M. (1996) "Democratisation or Bureaucratisation? Civil Society, the Public and the State in Post-Apartheid South Africa", *Transformation* (29).

Friedman, S. & Shaw, M. (2000) "Power and Partnership? Trade Unions, Forums and Transition." In Adler, G. & Webster, E. *Trade Unions and Democratisation in South Africa, 1985–1997*. Johannesburg: Witwatersrand University Press.

Gershater, D. (2001) *Sisterhood of a Sort: The Women's National Coalition and the Role of Gender Identity in South African Civil Society*. Research Report No. 82. Johannesburg: Centre for Policy Studies.

Government Caucus (1995) "Towards a Policy and Strategy for South Africa on Social Clauses (Labour Standards) in Trade Agreements." Government submission to Nedlac.

Hart, G. (2002) *Disabling Globalisation: Places of Power in Post-Apartheid South Africa*. Pietermaritzburg: University of Natal Press.

Held, D. (2000) "Regulating Globalisation? The Reinvention of Politics", *International Sociology*, Vol. 15, No. 2.

Hethy, L. (2000) "Hungary: Social Dialogue Within and Outside of the Framework of Tripartism", *Social Dialogue Papers ,4*. Geneva: ILO.

Houston, G., Mpanyane, J. & Liebenberg, I. (1998) "Policy-making in the new South Africa: A case study of the National Economic Development and Labour Council." Paper presented at the South African Sociological Association Congress, 30 June–3 July. Rand Afrikaans University, Johannesburg.

Labour Caucus (1995) "Labour Submission on the Social Clause to Nedlac", 8 June.

Lubbers, R. F. M. & Koorevaar, J. G. (1999) "Governance in an Era of Globalisation." Paper presented at the Club of Rome Annual Meeting. Vienna, 26–27 November.

Manor, J. (1998) "Democratisation and the Developmental State: The Search for Balance." In Robinson, M. & White, G. *The Democratic Developmental State: Politics and Institutional Design*. New York: Oxford University Press.

Marais, H. (1998) *South Africa: Limits to Change: The Political Economy of Transition*. London/Cape Town: Zed Books/University of Cape Town Press.

Mayntz, R. (1998) "New Challenges of Governance Theory." European University Institute; Jean Monnet Chair Paper RSC No. 98/50. http://www.iue.it/RSC/Mayntz.htm.

Mbeki, T. (1997) "Reconciliation and Nation Building." Statement at the opening of the debate in the National Assembly. Cape Town, 29 May.

Mbeki, T. (2002) Statement of the President at the ANC Policy Conference. Kempton Park, 27 September.

McGregor's. (2001) *Who Owns Whom in South Africa?* 21st edition. Grant Park, South Africa: Purdey Publishing.

Meer, S. (1999) "The Demobilisation of Civil Society: Struggling with New Questions", *Development Update*, Vol.3, No.1. Johannesburg: Interfund.

Millennium Labour Council (2000) *Millennium Agreement*. Johannesburg, 7 July.

Ministry of Public Enterprises (2000) *An Accelerated Agenda Towards the Restructuring of State Owned Enterprises: Policy Framework*. http://dpe.gov.za/docs/policyframework01.htm.

Ministry of Finance (1996) *Growth, Employment and Redistribution: A Macro-Economic Strategy*. Pretoria.

Naidoo, J. (1999) "Message from the Former Executive Director", *Nedlac Annual Report 1 April 1998 to 31 March 1999*. Auckland Park: Nedlac.

National Treasury (2001) *Budget Review.* Pretoria.

Nattrass, N. & Seekings, J. (1998) "Democratic Institutions and Development in Post-apartheid South Africa." In Robinson, M. & White, G. *The Democratic Developmental State: Politics and Institutional Design.* Oxford: Oxford University Press.

Nedlac. (1995) "The Government Rejects the Social Clause in Trade Agreements". Report from the Trade and Industry Chamber Labour Caucus, 9 October.

Nedlac. (1996) "Framework Agreement on Social Clause." Adopted 28 June 1996.

Nedlac. (1998) Report on Competition Policy. http://Nedlac.org.za/docs/agreements/competition_policy.html.

Nedlac. (2001) *Annual Report 1 April 2000 to 31 March 2001.* Auckland Park.

Ogilvey-Thompson, J. (1998) "Anglo American Corporate Chairman's Statement 1998." Johannesburg, 22 June.

Ohmae, K. (1995) *The End of the Nation State.* London: Harper Collins Publishers.

Paley, J. (2001) "The Paradox of Participation: Civil Society and Democracy in Chile." Working Paper #01–09e. The Centre for Migration and Development, Princeton University.

Parsons, R. (1999) "Message from the Overall Business Convenor", *Nedlac Annual Report 1 April 1998 to 31 March 1999.* Auckland Park: Nedlac.

Prakash, A. (1999) "Governance and Economic Globalisation: Continuities and Discontinuities." Paper presented to the United Nations General Assembly. New York, 30 September.

Putman, R. D. (1993) *Making Democracy Work: Civic Traditions in Modern Italy.* Princeton, New Jersey: Princeton University Press.

Republic of South Africa (1994) *National Economic Development and Labour Council Act,* No. 35.

Republic of South Africa (1995) *Labour Relations Act,* No. 66.

Republic of South Africa (1998) *Employment Equity Act,* No 55.

Republic of South Africa (1998) *Competition Act,* No. 89.

Republic of South Africa (1998) *Skills Development Act,* No. 97.

Roberts, S. (2001) "Competing Expectations and Contested Policy: The Political Economy of Competition Policy in South Africa." Unpublished paper. School of Economics and Business Sciences, University of the Witwatersrand.

Sassen, S. (1995) *Losing Control: Sovereignty in an Age of Globalisation.* New York: Columbia University Press.

South African Communist Party (2002a) "Growth, Development and Social Dialogue." SACP Discussion Note towards the Alliance Summit.

South African Communist Party (2002b) *Draft Political Programme of the SACP for Consideration by the 11th Congress.* Rustenburg, 24–28 July.

South African Communist Party (2002c) *Political Report to the 11th Congress of the SACP.* Rustenburg, 24–28 July.

South African Foundation (1996) *Growth for All.* Johannesburg.

South African Reserve Bank (2000) *Quarterly Bulletin.* December.

United Nations Development Agency (1997) *Governance for Sustainable Development.* http://magnet.undp.org/policy/summary/htm

Von Holdt, K. (1995) "The LRA Agreement: 'Workers Victory' or 'Miserable Compromise'?", *South African Labour Bulletin.* Vol. 19 No. 4.

Webster, E. (1988) "The Rise of Social-Movement Unionism: The Two Faces of the Black Trade Union Movement in South Africa." In Frankel, P. *et al.* (eds) *State, Resistance and Change in South Africa.* London: Croom Helm.

Weiss, L. (1998) *The Myth of the Powerless State: Governing the Economy in a Global Era.* Cambridge: Polity Press.

Wohlmuth, K. (1998) *Good Governance and Economic Development. New Foundations for Growth in Africa.* Berichte aus dem Weltwirtschaftlichen Colloguium. Der University Bremen, Nr. 59, December.

Zita, L. (2002) "Is South Africa the Weakest Link in the Imperialist Chain?", *The African Communist.* No 159. South African Community Party.

4 The Power Behind the Desk: Democracy, Collective Bargaining and the Public Service in South Africa

Ebrahim-Khalil Hassen

Introduction

Outsourcing, privatisation and rightsizing are issues that have seen the government and unions take divergent stances. Each has claimed that their policies are best for improving the effectiveness of the public service and meeting the developmental challenges that are faced by the democratic South Africa. The divergences are embedded in contrasting interpretations of transformation, democracy and service delivery. This contest for the direction of transforming the public service and, in particular, changing power balances tells a story of profound shifts in governance.

This chapter explores the relationship between the restructuring of the South African public service[1] and the modes of governance operative in South African society. The chapter begins by locating the public sector reform projects within international debates, and focuses on the relationship between governance and public service restructuring. Next, the collective bargaining experience in South Africa is assessed. This section sketches the key events, and attempts to explain the bargaining outcomes. Finally, the socio-economic impacts of restructuring are discussed, including the relative power of classes and interest groups in society.

Before entering this discussion, one feature of this chapter requires explanation. Bargaining arrangements by their very nature involve employers and employees. This excludes the rest of civil society. A discussion on governance, however, needs to account for the roles and expectations of parties outside the bargaining arena. The chapter thus consciously seeks to explore responses and implications for actors outside the formal bargaining arrangements.

Governance, restructuring and the developmental state

The terms "restructuring", "developmental state" and "governance" are all open to a variety of meanings, which in turn legitimise different political projects. This section develops a conceptual model contrasting "new managerialism" and "developmental restructuring". It begins with a discussion of these models, and proceeds by contextualising the rise of new managerialism in developing countries. Finally, governance as a relational concept is proposed as the means for analysing changes in the public service, and in evaluating the outcomes of collective bargaining.

New managerialism and developmental restructuring

Major shifts in the types of governance have occurred due to the restructuring of the public sector. Reconfigurations of citizenship, the distribution of resources and the relative influence of actors have occurred whenever the public sector has been restructured. Two major approaches to restructuring – each with many variants – have resulted in substantively different configurations of state-society interaction and the nature of democracy. These approaches have been called "new managerialism" and "developmental restructuring" respectively.

The developmental restructuring model seeks to reorientate public organisation towards its external mission and increase the voice of the citizenry. In practice, this has meant more team-based work, the devolution of frontline decisions to frontline workers, and increasing community participation. Multi-tasking of the workforce, the introduction of outcomes-based appraisal systems and greater interdepartmental co-operation are part of this system.

In the South African context, Cosatu (2000) has argued for developmental restructuring in the following terms:

> The developmental approach rejects the idea that only independent agencies – whether state owned or private – can deliver services efficiently. Rather, the public service must rely on a combination of strong administrative measures, appropriate decentralisation, and mobilisation of employees, and improved oversight and participation by the public and by major stakeholders.

The "Tilburg model" in the Netherlands has demonstrated that this kind of internal restructuring can lead to improvements in service delivery. In the Tilburg case, trade unions and the government agreed to a restructuring and decentralisation process. Rightsizing was achieved without retrenchments (Martin, 1996).

Porto Alerge in Brazil is one of the most effective examples of reorienting insulated bureaucracies. The local authority has created a budget council with representatives from the different wards in the community. The council receives a mandate from community meetings, and communities play a significant role in monitoring public works pro-grammes. The trade-offs of a limited budget are thus managed in a democratic manner. The impact on the bureaucracy has been profound, with increases in productivity, improving quality of government services and better-managed public institutions (Navarro, 1998).

The second approach to restructuring, new managerialism or the "contracting model", has appropriated progressive analyses of changing work organisation and has emphasised a "small and lean" state. This model favours outsourcing non-core services, corporatising bureaucratic work and isolating structures according to budgets, with the purpose of intro-ducing private finance, expertise and an entrepreneurial ethos into the bureaucracy.

Paul Hoggett (1996) argues that in Britain three fundamental but interlinked strategies of control have been implemented, specifically in universities. These strategies are:

- a pronounced shift towards the creation of operationally decentralised units with a simultaneous attempt to increase centralised control over strategy and policy;
- the employment of the principle of competition as the dominant method of co-ordi-nating activities of decentralised units; and
- the development of processes of performance management and monitoring.

Taken together, Hoggett concludes, these strategies do not describe a simple movement from a bureaucratic to post-bureaucratic form; rather, they combine strong elements of innovation with the reassertion of a number of fundamentally bureaucratic mechanisms. One of the features of the new managerial paradigm is a "one size fits all" solution. The processes described by Hoggett have occurred more widely in the public service, and in very different contexts.

This model has been applied in New Zealand, where reform initiatives sought to fragment the bureaucracy into smaller units, with a corporatised management structure. The restructured bureaucracies now "bid" to provide services. This has led to a decline in the state's capacity to respond to crises and to ensure equity in public spending (Schick, 1996).

The "exit idea" is associated with public choice theory. According to this school of thought, market forces are best suited to induce creative and continuous quality improvements. Clients can exit from a transactional relationship if they are dissatisfied. This analogy of the client has been applied to the public service. The main problem with the public service – or so the theory goes – is that the public is forced to receive services from one provider, the state. It argues that multiple providers would give the public more options. Market forces would ensure that the best service provider survives. Citizens could exit a particular service relationship at any time (Savas, 1987).

The idea of multiple providers is justified in the name of competition. International experience suggests, however, that this is a rare outcome. Competition usually means replacing a public monopoly with a single private sector operator. Various means of introducing private sector participation exist, ranging from long-term contracts (concessions) to private sector management (management contracts).

The rise of new managerialism

Many developing countries have gone the route of new managerialism. Several factors have influenced this major shift in the policy of public sector reform. Internal and external factors have shaped the shift, and this has resulted in changes as to how governance is conceptualised and practised.

At the core of these changes is a redefinition of the developmental state under the rubric of "good governance" since the early 1990s. Postcolonial states, particularly in Africa, adopted an assertive posture to achieve economic growth and development. The word "governance" is sometimes used to indicate a new mode of governing that is distinct from hierarchical control, tending towards a more co-operative mode where state and non-state actors participate in a mix of networks (World Bank, 1997). This sense of the word implies both an aspiration for what governance should mean, and a prescription for realising this aspiration. Utilising the word "governance" in this way not only conflates the ends and means of governance, but also ignores the fact that the term is used by a range of actors to legitimise different political or social projects.

This is aptly seen in the use of the term "good governance" by international financial institutions. Landel-Mills and Serageldin (1991:15), senior staffers of the World Bank in Africa, argue that good governance denotes "a minimum core of characteristics that are generally agreed upon". This minimum core is a liberal democracy with free markets. In turn, this means the establishment of property rights, separation of powers between judiciary, executive and legislature, and a formal multiparty democracy.

The lack of distinction between different regime types characterises much of the literature on governance. This is not surprising, as the term has been appropriated to endorse a specific political project, associated with the reduced role of the state, and a redefinition of the developmental state.

In response, critics of the international financial institutions have argued that governance is an ideological construct. Adrian Leftwich (1993:612) writes:

> The idea of democratic good governance is not simply the new technical answer to the difficult problems of development, although some of its proponents sometimes like to present it in that light. Democratic good governance is better understood as an intimate part of the

emerging politics of the New World Order. And clearly, the barely submerged structural model and ideals of politics, economics and society on which the contemporary notion of good governance rests is nothing less than that of Western liberal (or social) democracy – the focal concern and teleological terminus of much of modernisation theory.

The idea of good governance is thus seen as a reincarnation of previous failed polices in the developing world, notably structural adjustment programmes. The reincarnation of previous policy prescriptions is explained through the rise of neoclassical economics and the decline of the Soviet bloc. In such a setting, it is argued that the term "good governance" legitimises the continuation of a set of policies associated with neoclassical economics.

The failures of national development plans across most of Africa since liberation have played a major role, however, in the reconsideration of public service reform initiatives. Picard and Garrity (1997), for instance, see the establishment of over-centralised and under-implemented developmental states in Africa as a consequence of limited developmental management capacity and the absence of decentralisation programmes. The failure of both socialist and market models of development in Africa has created pessimism that the state cannot lead a long-term and sustainable developmental plan. In turn, the public service is today widely viewed as part of the problem, and not the solution.

However, the reform agenda has not been merely about internal weaknesses of implementation. The reform agenda in Africa has often been imposed by external forces such as international financial institutions, including the World Bank and the International Monetary Fund (IMF). Moharir (1997) indicates that there has been a move away from a narrow focus on macroeconomic stability towards sectoral reforms. Two areas in particular have been identified for reform initiatives, the public enterprise sector and the salaries of civil servants.

The establishment of "good governance" has been paralleled by profound changes in the international political economy. These changes have been loosely described as globalisation. The process of economic integration is a major aspect of South African society, and has been part of the developing world since colonial times. Indeed, it is sometimes suggested that the capital flows today are less than they were in previous periods. The process of globalisation, however, refers to the technological changes and the changes in production that characterise our society. As governments move towards market and formal sector based models, the need to attract foreign direct investment becomes all too pervasive, necessitating changes in tariff regimes, the opening of public and private markets to international competition and the shifting of policies to improve the countries' international competitiveness.

The impact has been direct, with the World Trade Organisation (WTO) explicitly creating markets for public services under the General Agreement on Trade and Services (GATS). The redefinition of public goods as "trading services" fundamentally changes the relationship between citizens and government into a transactional one. Moreover, this tilts the balance of power away from citizens, social movements and progressive government towards multinational corporations and international financial institutions.

At the same time, the need to extend services has become even more crucial. Many development indicators in Africa have regressed or remained stable, with only marginal improvements in some areas. The need to elevate the poor from poverty is a major impetus to reform public services. Unfortunately, this impetus is aligned with neoclassical economics, which seeks market solutions in conditions were the majority of people reside and work outside the formal economy.

The coalescing of internal weaknesses, globalisation and poverty, at a time when neoclassical economics remains dominant, has seen the rise of new managerialism in many developing countries, especially across the African continent. These policies have consisted of pay-decompression in the public service, in an attempt to create a highly skilled and smaller public service across the developing world. Bangura (1999) has indicated that such changes have often led to retrenchments in the public service, and have not necessarily improved service delivery.

Governance as an analytical concept

The rise of new managerialism in the developing and developed worlds is located within changes in the political economy. These changes reflect profound shifts in the power of different groups and in who drives different agendas. Analysing these changes in the South African context requires some clarity on what we mean by governance and, in particular, a relational notion of governance.

At the outset, this requires that one transcend the straightjacket of the "good governance" debate. This is because stepping outside this paradigm allows us to better understand the political project that underlies "good governance". The proponents and opponents of "good governance", however, share an unintended complicity, despite their many differences. The complicity is to prescribe a peculiar political meaning to the term "governance". This renders the term virtually useless in understanding society, as one is confined to assessing whether some preconceived idea of governance is being implemented and what its outcomes are. Many unanswered questions arise from adopting such an approach: Why are particular modes of governance operative? What changes in the social distribution mechanisms are envisaged? What are the impacts on the various societal actors?

Liberal democracy and market principles are a crude, but largely accurate, description of the political project that has grown internationally. Under the banner of "good governance", this project is attempting nothing less than a redefinition of the developmental state, as a mirror image of neoclassical economics and formal liberal democracy. There is a danger in creating a straw man of the "good governance" project, as advanced by the international financial institutions. After all, reviews of recent documents advance participation, a role for civil society and the importance of context in different countries (World Bank, 2000).

Ernesto Laclau and Chantal Mouffe (1985), however, warn that one of the basic strategies of the "New Right" is the appropriation of terms, and recasting them to meet a specific political project. It is advanced here that the term "good governance" appropriates the progressive meaning of a developmental state. This is done through the mechanisms of the state itself, and through incorporation of civil society into its programmes.

The term "governance" needs to transcend this narrow debate, and analytical methods that have comparative value and lend themselves to practical concerns must be adopted. There is a growing literature that attempts to develop schemas to assess different regime types. One approach is to assess the modes of governance operative in society. Jorgenson (1993) focuses on the value orientation, by which he means the "political aspects of public organisation". The basic question asked is: Who do the public organisations serve? Do they serve politicians, the general public, organised actors other than politicians or the primary users? Jorgenson defines four basic forms of state (the hierarchical state, autonomous state, negotiating state and responsive state). The importance of such a categorisation is that the concept of governance is placed within the wider political economy.

The work of Goran Hyden (1992) is instructive. Hyden develops an understanding of governance as a "relational concept". Practical judgement seems to be the basic message of Hyden's relational notion of governance. To this end, a complex analytical framework to understand governance is presented. This analytical framework consists of three major, and sequential, schemas. Hyden starts by identifying the basic concept of governance as consisting of an actor dimension, a structural dimension and the governance realm. Four properties are identified in the governance realm – authority, reciprocity, trust and accountability. Having crafted an understanding of what constitutes governance, Hyden then explains different regime types; communitarian, libertarian, corporatist and statist regimes are identified. Moreover, each of these regime types faces different types of crises, with none being necessarily superior to the other. Hyden then makes a case for the relationship between governance and development. Explicitly, he suggests that the empirical dimensions of governance (viz. citizen influence and oversight, responsive and responsible leadership, and social reciprocities) are the focus of analytical activity, supposedly because they would lead to good judgement within a certain context.

Another nascent strand in the literature is to define governance as a combination of state strategies directed towards the democratisation of social distribution (Albo *et al.*, 1993). Governance can then be understood as comprising institutional and political power to ensure the effective management of resources for development, and the means for legitimating allocation and distribution decisions. This strand of enquiry holds promise for critical social enquiry as it raises questions of redistribution and voice in society. In so doing, power relations between state and society and within the state are brought to the centre of analysis.

This chapter attempts to apply an approach to governance that has analytical value and lends itself to practical concerns. Consequently, the chapter builds on the writings of Jorgenson and Hyden, and advocates a relational understanding of governance. At the same time, the political project advanced under the rubric of "good governance" is utilised as one, albeit important, current in shaping governance in South Africa. The state strategy to democratise social distribution thus becomes important in assessing the winners and losers in restructuring processes. A double movement is proposed. First, governance as a concept must transcend the narrow debate on "good governance" if it is to blossom intellectually. The first aspect is thus one of appropriating the term. The second dimension concerns understanding governance as a relational concept that is open to shifts in power.

A typology for analysis

Achieving a system of analysis for the reform of the public service, and in particular focusing on collective bargaining, poses several challenges. Transcending the strictures of the "good governance" debate is only the first step in constructing a relational notion of governance. Key questions facing such an approach are: Is collective bargaining a form of popular participation? In whose interests does the public service act? What are the main features of change and development in society? Three major propositions will guide this analysis.

First, the public sector acts as an agent of change in society and reflects existing power structures in society. The public sector as a structure seeks to empower the marginalised through many of its statements and programmes; however, at the same time, public sector capacities are limited in terms of the societal balance of forces.

Second, restructuring both reflects and shapes governance modes. The restructuring process has winners and losers. The restructuring process thus seeks to establish a form of governance, but reactions to restructuring impact upon the modes of governance that develop. The point being stressed here is a more modest one – as systems of governance break down, the new systems both inherit from the old and build new forms of governance.

Third, the restructuring process is linked to assumptions on the nature and functions of the developmental state and specific political projects. In turn, these have differential impacts on society, democracy and service delivery.

The typology presented in Table 4.1, drawing on the discussion of new managerialism and developmental restructuring, provides a schema for the analysis of public sector reform in the democratic dispensation in South Africa.

Table 4.1: New managerialism and developmental restructuring – a comparison

	New managerialism	**Developmental restructuring**
Structure	Decentralised	Flatter structures
Management	Pay for performance Private sector techniques	Team-based structures Performance measured at institutional level
Method	Separate policy making from implementation	Strengthen delivery capacity of the state
Policy making	Market decision Managerial prerogative	Consultative Social accords with labour
Public interest	Low cost	Involvement Consultation
Size	Small Highly skilled	Linked to service delivery needs
Wages	High for managers Increase wage differentials	Provide living wages for all Establish career paths for public service
Collective bargaining	Decentralised bargaining	Centralised bargaining for common issues, together with bargaining at sectoral level.

The collective bargaining experience in South Africa

As a consequence of South Africa's transition to democracy, public service workers enjoy trade union and collective bargaining rights for the first time in the country's history. The engagements between unions and the government on the restructuring process for the public service can be conceptualised in four phases. Phase one was marked by the formation of a coalition by the government and the unions around issues of transformation. The second phase was characterised by a unilateral implementation of wages in 1999, and indicated increasing tensions between the government and unions. Phase three was characterised by a contradiction. On the one hand, social dialogue processes occurred. On the other hand, government laid the basis for the introduction of the new managerial paradigm. Phase four has been marked by an agreement on restructuring between the unions and the government that combines elements of developmentalism and new managerialism. It is still too early to ascertain the outcomes of this phase. However, before proceeding with an examination of these phases, it is important to discuss the apartheid inheritance, in order to set the context for the restructuring of the post-1994 period.

The apartheid inheritance

The new government inherited a public service based on apartheid racial structures, coupled with a rule-based and hierarchical work organisation (FitzGerald, 1995). The central characteristics of this system included:

- Fragmentation: The public service consisted of a plethora of institutions – provincial administrations, administrations in the self-governing territories and racially based administrative structures (McLennan, 1995; Patel, 2000). Different institutions had different pay systems.

- Pay determination: Salaries were set by a commission, without formal negotiations. Staff associations, especially the Public Service Association (PSA), which predominantly represented White workers in the public service, were consulted. Unions organising Black workers, however, were excluded.

- Discrimination: Salaries and benefits differed according to race and gender (DPSA, 1999).

- Career progression: Incentives and benefits were aimed at ensuring long tenure. Systems for career development were not established. Instead, public service workers received a mixture of benefits, merit awards and training that were not linked to increased responsibility or an improvement in their competencies.

The apartheid regime adopted an authoritarian governance system. Trade union rights, with the exception of certain White unions, were denied. It was only in the 1980s that public servants gained limited representational rights, but this was on a racially and occupationally divided basis. The government adopted a system of bounded consultation, which provided limited representational rights to staff associations, but marginalised trade unions organising Black workers.

In 1989 and 1990 a series of strikes were organised in the public service. Teachers, health workers, police and prison warders all engaged in strike activities, but these were confined to the homeland administrations. Over the next few years, the number of unions and unionised membership increased dramatically. Negotiations on a system of labour relations began after the strikes, and culminated in the Public Service Labour Relations Act of 1993 (PSLRA), which put in place a system of labour relations in line with that governing the private sector (Machun & Psoulis, 2000).

The new system of labour relations for the public service reflected the wider change in society: from apartheid to democracy. The establishment of trade union rights in the public service heralded a new era. Much optimism characterised this phase. In particular, the combination of a democratic state led by the ANC, and strong unions aligned to the Congress tradition, created the expectation of a "coalition for change" emerging in the public service.

Building a coalition for change

The period between 1994 and 1999 was characterised by the development of a coalition for change. The expectations of unions, utilising the wider political alliance to forge a progressive agenda of public service transformation, were heightened with the release of the *Reconstruction and Development Programme: A Policy Framework* (RDP) (African National Congress, 1994). The RDP argued for people-centred development, participatory democracy and an accountable developmental state.

However, there were ambiguities in the RDP document in relation to the public service. In particular, the clauses on rightsizing and privatisation were left open. The RDP argued that the democratic government would have to assess whether to increase or decrease the size of the public service. In a similar vein, it suggested that nationalisation or privatisation would be determined on a case-by-case basis.

In the period under consideration, the government and unions attempted to forge a common agenda that would take on board the needs of all parties. The government adopted strategies to improve the protection of workers and to introduce a reform programme for the public service. These first steps proved successful. The integration of different administrations proceeded relatively smoothly and ambitious poverty eradication programmes were initiated. On the labour front, the government and unions captured their understanding in the *White Paper on the Transformation of the Public Service*. The main agreements reached included increasing the minimum wage to R1 500 by 1997, reducing wage differentials, the development of career paths and improving the working conditions of women and people with disabilities.

These agreements were buttressed with the promulgation of the Labour Relations Act of 1995 (LRA). For the first time, a single law regulated labour relations in both the public and the private spheres. The LRA provided specific measures for the public service, including the establishment of the Public Service Co-ordinating Council (PSCBC). The PSCBC was established as the central negotiating body to replace different negotiating forums set up by different pieces of legislation.[2] The intention was to establish an industry-wide bargaining system for the public service.

However, the government was already experiencing the pressures of transforming the public service. For instance, the *White Paper on Transforming Public Service Delivery*, under the rubric of *Batho Pele*,[3] fundamentally redefined citizenship. Citizens were equated with customers. To treat citizens as customers according to the *Batho Pele* white paper implied:

- listening to their views and taking account of them in making decisions about what services should be provided;
- treating them with consideration and respect;
- making sure that the promised level and quality of service was always of the highest standard; and
- responding swiftly and sympathetically when standards of service fell below the promised standard.

The shift from citizen to customer reflected a shift from citizens who participate to customers who receive service. In South African parlance, this marked a shift from an active citizenry to a passive citizenry.

On other fronts, the government felt the pressures of a rising wage bill, wide disparities in personnel (e.g. teachers) between rural and urban areas and the need to improve efficiency to meet developmental goals. The major attempt to reach a compromise was through the signing of a multi-year agreement with the unions. The agreement, signed in 1996, and often referred to as the "three-year agreement", attempted to balance the need for worker security with that of transforming the public service. The agreement introduced a system of voluntary severance packages (VSPs) aimed at rightsizing the public service. Moreover, large wage increases for workers were provided for over a three-year period, to be funded in part from personnel leaving the service due to VSPs. This reflected a mode of governance that sought to find ways in which the government could work with the unions in realising developmental objectives.

In practice, the agreement did not last more than a year. In the second year, the state argued that the envisaged savings had not been achieved (Baskin, 2000). Unions did not resort to strike action but, instead, agreed to reduce the wages specified in the original agreement. Moreover, two months after the completion of negotiations on the agreement, government announced its macroeconomic strategy. The new strategy, christened *Growth, Employment and Redistribution: A Macroeconomic Strategy* (GEAR), adopted a tight fiscal stance. In terms of this strategy, public service delivery would need to be balanced with affordability and macroeconomic consistency. The situation reflected an inherent contradiction. On the one hand, unions and the government were attempting to create a coalition for change; on the other hand, the emergence of the macroeconomic model indicated that a wide divergence on economic policy and on governance was emerging between unions and the government.

Despite the contradictions between bargaining agreements and the needs of macroeconomic policy, the principles of the agreements remained in place. The three-year agreement ended in 1998. The new salary agreement of 1998/1999, however, reflected a deepening of the contradiction between macroeconomic stability and the public service transformation agenda. In this agreement, unions and the government agreed to reduce the employer contribution to the Government-Employee Pension Fund (GEPF), as a way to finance the wage increases. This was a measure introduced to meet the goal of the government to spend less on salaries, while meeting the demands of workers. The spirit of cooperation still continued, with agreement being reached on joint government-union processes in producing skills, service delivery and personnel audits. These audits would be the basis for determining human resource allocation in the provinces, and would inform strategies for restructuring.

Competing values and directions

A key feature of balancing the tensions between macroeconomic choices, the need to improve efficiency in the public service, and attempts to keep unions on board were the informal channels created through the alliance between unions in Cosatu and the ANC. While mechanisms were created to ameliorate tensions in the public service, a profound divergence on the development path in South Africa was playing itself out. The government contended that the GEAR strategy was necessary in the current context and would lead to sustained growth and development over the longer term. Cosatu responded by arguing that increased job losses and reduced social spending would see a weakening of the reconstruction and development agenda.

The second democratic elections in South Africa proved a turning-point. The new president, Thabo Mbeki, quickly moved to develop an agenda of accelerating transformation. This agenda included transforming the public service rapidly. The president appointed Geraldine Fraser-Moleketi as minister to lead this process.

Early into the second term of democratic government, unions went out on strike over wages for the 1999/2000 financial year. The first national strike in the public sector was undertaken and placed unions and the government at loggerheads. All 12 of the public service unions, which included traditionally White unions, sought to bring pressure to bear on the government. A largely successful two-day strike was held.

Layered over the traditional debate on the merits of increases, a profound political discussion ensued. Senior leaders in government questioned whether the trade union movement was acting in the wider societal interest. Minister Fraser-Moleketi (1999), for instance, argued:

> The amount the government pays its 1.1 million workers accounts for 51 percent of its budget, after meeting interest payments. If the wage bill continues to rise, we will put at risk even the meagre social services offered by the government. Very few South Africans will agree to cuts in the education budget – which will mean even greater difficulty in providing stationery and books – or the critical school building programme.

In reply, unions argued that they were indeed acting in the wider societal interest. The answer to this question, unions argued, must take account of a wider set of issues, including that:

- over 80% of public sector workers are employed directly as service providers (e.g. teachers, police persons, nurses, emergency service workers);
- most areas where the state directly provides services or seeks to extend services are labour intensive; and
- the cost of extending services has been rising, while the budget has been decreasing in real terms.

After the strike, the government argued that no settlement was possible with the unions, and chose to implement wages unilaterally. This action marked a pivotal moment in labour relations between the government and unions.

First, it indicated a shift from co-operative decision-making to the state asserting its authority and acting unilaterally. The primary reason for this change lay in the state's attempt to shift power balances in public service labour relations. Through demonstrating that it would act without the unions, it sought to transform the relationships that existed between the government and unions.

Second, the dispute reflected changes in the role of the state. The initial goals of the democratic state were the removal of discrimination carried over from the previous regime, the narrowing of wage gaps and the introduction of affirmative action. Today, the state's mandate is more complex. For instance, the state is increasingly arguing that the reduction of wage gaps must be balanced against the need to retain skilled staff. Furthermore, the state argues that the unions need to make choices between protecting employment and wage increases. The driving forces for this change are the straightjacket of fiscal discipline, and a commitment by the state to concentrate on "core functions".

Third, unilateral implementation indicated a value judgement on the role of the government. The message, however, was not one of the government governing, but rather that government had the legitimacy to act in the wider societal interest. The meaning of this approach for the forms of governance are profound, for it indicated that the government was prepared to make hard choices, even if it excluded the most organised sections of civil society. Moreover, these actions effectively sent a message that the rules of engagement had substantively changed; the co-operative arrangements that had characterised previous engagement processes ceased to exist.

The unilateral implementation reflected one component of a wider strategy for transforming the public service. A key aspect of this emerging strategy was the empowerment of managers at departmental level. The Public Finance Management Act (PFMA), for instance, empowered departmental managers to serve as accounting officers responsible for departmental outputs. The Department of Public Service and Administration (DPSA) also introduced the Senior Management Service (SMS), providing for a flexible pay structure and performance contracts for managers. These changes in financial management and salary structures indicated the rise of managers as the drivers of restructuring processes in the public service.

This ascendancy of managers was given even more credence as the government withdrew from the skills, services and personnel audits. The reason provided by the government for this was that a joint process between labour and the government effectively limited managerial autonomy in deciding on issues. Instead, the government established a process by which departments would formulate management plans, without necessarily involving the participation of either organised labour or the community. The major impact on labour was that, should this process be one of unfettered discretion for managers, unions would be fighting battles in a fragmentary manner, outside of the protection and strength that collective bargaining provides. The direction of the public service in South Africa, thus, increasingly conformed to the new managerial paradigm.

However, the unions attempted to reopen discussion on the reform agenda, and called for the Public Service Jobs Summit (PSJS). The PSJS was held in Pietersberg in January 2001. After a frantic negotiation process, the government and unions reached agreement on a number of issues. One of the major agreements reached was on the objectives of transforming the public service. This reiterated policy on extending services, the state playing a developmental role and the need to ensure equity in employment.

The agreement on objectives provided a framework for restructuring, and the restructuring components of the agreement called for further negotiations. Further, the agreement called on government and labour to reach agreement within the framework of the PSJS. Yet, the spirit of the agreement (as well as the substantive clauses) provided a platform for negotiations on restructuring in the public service. The agreement, for instance, provided for joint union-employer teams to receive and comment on strategic plans, and called for "constructive engagement" on these plans and the implementation thereof. Importantly, the plans of departments could be a negotiable matter (i.e. it was defined as an issue of mutual agreement). Further, the dispute mechanism agreed to emphasised a strong co-determination process in the public service. The unions interpreted this agreement as the reassertion of their influence over the restructuring agenda.

The wage negotiations following the PSJS indicated that unions might have been correct in this interpretation. In the 2001/2002 wage negotiations, the government agreed to create an additional 20 000 jobs. Moreover, the government and unions initiated processes towards drafting a final restructuring agreement.

After the PSJS, two significant agreements were entered into between unions and the government. The first was the signing of another multi-year wage agreement in 2001, which covered wage negotiations for the next three years. The defining feature of the agreement is that it links wages to the inflation rate. Consequently, wages would be set at inflation plus an agreed percentage that fluctuates between 0.5% and 1.5% for the period of the agreement. This has effectively meant that wages are being aligned to the macro-economic policy of the government.

Second, and even more profound, was the signing of a restructuring agreement on human resources. This agreement provides for ways to determine the organisational structure of the public service, and for procedures in the case of employees who are in excess of requirements. The agreement attempts to match personnel to the strategies of organisations. Simply stated, the agreement attempts to move personnel and determine posts needed to meet the mandate for accelerated delivery of services. The intention of the agreement, thus, should have the full support of all progressive organisations, as wide inequities exist between rural and urban areas, and between predominately Black and White areas, in terms of teachers, nurses and other personnel. Removing these inequities is a crucial step to building the capabilities of the poor. The process to be adopted is to first develop strategic plans for the different departments. These plans would identify the posts needed to effectively provide services and improve service delivery. The managements of different departments are responsible for developing these plans. Unions will be consulted on the plans. Once the human resource strategy is developed, a process of matching people to posts is initiated; those in excess of posts will then either be re-deployed in the public service, or will be offered an opportunity to be retrained. Once an employee is deemed to be in excess of the entire public service, either the employee can apply for a voluntary severance package (VSP) or the employer may initiate retrenchment proceedings.

The agreement sees a continuation of the trend towards empowering management and decentralising restructuring decisions. Moreover, it reflects a profound shift in power relations between unions and the government, as unions have accepted the main tenets of an approach that earlier they had opposed.

The causes and effects of this restructuring process are to be found in a combination of the macroeconomic context, delivery challenges facing government and state-society interactions. These factors have fundamentally reshaped the power relations between the state and unions, and consequently the governance paradigm in South Africa. However, resistance to this emerging governance paradigm will still arise.

Macroeconomic dimensions

The macroeconomic impact on public service wage negotiations is profound. Since the advent of GEAR, macroeconomic policy has sought as a main objective in public remuneration to reduce the share of recurrent expenditure and to increase the share of the budget allocated to capital expenditure.

Moreover, containing costs of personnel is a means to that end. The wage agreement that links wages to inflation essentially provides a means to contain wages. Using data from the 2001/2002 budget, Table 4.2 demonstrates the alignment of wages and inflation rate. These projections are being realised in practice today.

Table 4.2: Estimates for personnel expenditure, 2001–2004 (R millions)

	2000/2001	2001/2002	2002/2003	2003/2004
	92 376	98 905	104 170	109 302
% increase	–	7.1	5.3	4.9
Projected inflation (CPI)	–	5.6	4.8	4.5
Real increase	–	1.5	0.5	0.4
Average % increase over the Medium-Term Expenditure Framework (MTEF) period	5.8			
Average real increase over the MTEF period	0.8			

Source: Inflation estimates and wage projections drawn from Budget Review 2001/2002. Note: Inflation rates used are CPI.

The convergence of macroeconomic projections and bargaining outcomes has resulted in a wage containment strategy. Wage containment is not necessarily good for service delivery. Evidence seems to support the following arguments from trade unions. First, wage containment in Africa has usually been associated with a decrease in public service capability, a point that has been highlighted by a researcher at the IMF, Ian Lienert (1998). He observes that although cutting costs by squeezing real wages contributes to macroeconomic stability, beyond a certain point it becomes counterproductive. According to Lienert the "squeeze of real wages" results in demoralisation of the public service, absenteeism, moonlighting and increased corruption. The Ugandan experience, which has seen the practice of severe wage restraint in the public service, is illustrative: "The civil servant had to either survive by lowering his standards of ethics, performance and dutifulness or remain upright and perish. He chose to survive" (quoted in Mukherjee *et al.*, undated). Wage containment comes at a cost. If that cost is reduced effectiveness and probity in the public service, it is a cost that South Africa can ill-afford.

Second, a severe wage containment strategy will impact on attempts to improve service delivery. After all, wage containment places a limit on employment. However, increased employment is needed in selected areas (e.g. early childhood development, an integrated justice sector and professional skills in the health sector). The blunt objective of containing wages could detract from building up key areas to equalise services among race groups and to extend services to previously disadvantaged communities. Many in the government do not see this reality, and argue that "the government cannot be an employment agency". This is a convenient way to reduce a very important debate to the level of rhetoric. Sophisticated analyses of the public service, however, will reveal major areas of under-staffing, over-staffing and areas with gross inequities in the distribution of skills. Thus, the debate is not about the government's status as an "employment agency", but rather about the need to find ways to equalise and extend services. This will entail redeployment and retraining, but strategic increases in employment are unavoidable if services are to be improved in working-class areas.

Third, the personnel expenditure projections do not support the development of a motivated, disciplined, ethical and career-oriented public service. Folscher (1999) indicates that the current growth in the wage bill is insufficient to support improving capacities in the public service. Funds for career and skills development are key areas that are likely to be compromised under the current budget projections.

Delivery challenges facing the government

The trend towards empowerment of managers and decentralisation of restructuring reflects a strategy to cope with the delivery challenges facing the government. Since 1994 the government has adopted a series of ambitious poverty eradication programmes. These programmes have seen a significant increase in outputs. However, the outcomes of developmental programmes have resulted largely in negative externalities. Disconnection from the water supply and downward raiding (where individuals who benefited from the housing subsidy sell their newly acquired houses to individuals or companies at a discount) in the low-income housing sector are some examples of the negative externalities, points highlighted in the chapters by Edigheji, and Habib and Kotzé in this book.

Rural communities still suffer from staff shortages in key social programmes. Figure 4.1 shows the unequal distribution of nurses, educators and other public service workers across provinces. The graph indicates the acute shortages of staff – when compared to population – in rural provinces. Thus while the Eastern Cape has a large number of educators, staff shortages still exist in key areas (e.g. maths and science). Moreover, the numbers of nurses in the rural provinces are wholly inadequate to deal with the health needs, particularly as government moves towards primary healthcare systems. The need to equalise services across the country is a central problematic to meeting delivery challenges. Shifting personnel to areas of need is, thus, a crucial driver of the restructuring agenda in the public service.

At the same time, there has been a push to reduce the public service on the basis that it is bloated and overstaffed. The underlying feature of this argument is the need to reduce personnel costs to meet the macroeconomic targets suggested. This is an approach that

Figure 4.1: Distribution of public servants

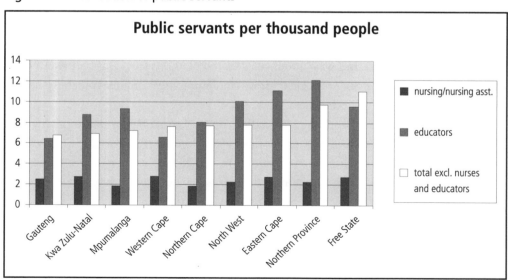

Source: Department of Public Service and Administration, Persal database, 2001

seeks to reduce the public service on grounds of economic efficiency rather than a wider developmental perspective.

Yet, the overall size of the public sector decreased by 11.4% between 1996 and 2001 (Hassen, 2001). Specifically, losses have occurred in lower skilled jobs, which are the target of retrenchment pressures. The underlying rationale is to move to a smaller and highly skilled public service, which is in line with the managerial paradigm.

There are two schools of thought on rightsizing the public service. One school attempts to match skills and needs, while the other sees it as a cost-cutting exercise. Nonetheless, government policy seems to be moving towards a wider developmental agenda, with unions and the government agreeing to create 20 000 jobs in the public service, but the emergence of a narrow cost-cutting agenda cannot be underestimated.

Black economic empowerment

A key driver of the reform agenda is Black economic empowerment. Powerful actors in government and business see the reform process as being central to opening opportunities and markets to Black economic empowerment. In its wider sense, the term refers to the upliftment of Black people, particularly the poor, and encouraging their participation in the mainstream economy. Restructuring the public service to provide and extend services to the poor, and the reform of social security are examples of realising this wider vision of empowerment.

In the narrow sense, it refers to the emergence of a "patriotic bourgeoisie" (i.e. a capitalist class that acts in the wider societal interest). The major form of empowerment has been through introducing affirmative action principles into government procurement policies, such as the 10-point plan by the Department of Public Works. The department is aiming to create an enabling environment for small and emerging businesses (especially those run by Black people) to participate in government procurement programmes.

The other form of empowerment is through creating markets in the public sector. In the public enterprises and local government, several lucrative privatisation contracts have been awarded to Black empowerment consortiums. While this trend is not yet observable in the public service itself on major restructuring deals, the wider political phenomenon does impact on restructuring in the public service. At issue is not simply the privatisation agenda, but rather whether the restructuring process serves the interests of a particular class. Through making the public service operate on business lines, fragmenting the public service and introducing public-private partnerships, the restructuring agenda is meant primarily to serve the interests of emerging Black capital.

Globalisation

The process of globalisation has had a profound impact on restructuring in South Africa. The ability of nurses and other skilled personnel to move to other countries is one example of this change. Furthermore, the need to reduce spending on personnel to meet the requirements of credit rating agencies and international financial institutions has been palpable in government's adherence to fiscal discipline. Another example of influence is large donor support for restructuring initiatives.

Thus, the process of globalisation has directly impacted upon the public service. A main feature of globalisation is the adoption of models from the developed world. Differences in context obviously render such direct importation of models inappropriate. The South African government has made some changes to the models, but the values of the models have remained intact. This has seen the imprint of public choice theory on the restructuring initiatives. In a sense, the restructuring process aligns itself to the changes and underlying values that have guided restructuring elsewhere.

Impacts and implications

This experience indicates several implications and impacts for governance. The major trend towards empowerment of management and decentralisation of decision-making will have fundamental consequences for democracy, service delivery and civil society. These are discussed in turn. However, major changes in public policy have occurred under the guidance and initiative of civil society.

Democracy

The rise of the manager as a champion of restructuring is now a feature of the South African restructuring agenda, with profound implications for democratic governance. Bardouille (2000:92) argues that encouraging entrepreneurial risk taking and democratic stewardship are irreconcilable:

> Consider the ramifications of a public entrepreneur who thinks they own the policy process or a particular programme. As a result he/she risks becoming a power-wielding tyrant. The manager is then no longer a servant of the people, as probity, truthfulness, equity and fairness become significantly undermined in the pursuit of the bottom line.

The process being described here is the shift of power away from elected leadership and communities to public service managers. However, some see public entrepreneurship as creating more effective government, or assume that warnings about the rise of the manager are alarmist and misplaced. Yet, the very real increase in the power of bureaucrats must be a warning for democratic and participatory governance.

The South African case has indicated different views and strategies. On the one hand, macroeconomic policy choices have been insulated and left to a largely bureaucratic process. On the other hand, civil society organisations have managed to impact on key policy choices in government. The increases in the child support grant and the provision of anti-retrovirals to pregnant women are cases in point. Moreover, the general thrust of extending services is supported by most of the population, although the type of service delivery is contested.

The question raised by the restructuring experience is whether citizens will be able to influence and guide bureaucratic decisions. The strength of civil society, or what Putnam (1992) calls social capital, will be a crucial counterbalance to rising managerialism.

However, the objection from a democratic standpoint is more fundamental. Managerialism transforms citizens in demobilising ways. The shift from citizen to client, where the state interacts with clients, is the most observable and immediate. What, however, happens to clients, mostly from the Black community, without money? Managerialism, furthermore, transforms a collective (citizens) into a singular entity (client). In so doing, the ability of communities to intervene on specific issues is made more difficult, for their treatment by the public service is not as a collective but as individual clients.

From the foregoing analysis, it can be concluded that managerialism has profoundly adverse effects on the deepening of democratic governance and the promotion of development. The supporters of managerialism would contest these ideas. The foundation for managerialism, they argue, is a democratic mandate to deliver; as such, the most important value is one of outputs, as opposed to outcomes of public policy (Paine, 1999). As noted above, the most fundamental problem with managerialism is its impact on democracy. The model transforms citizens into clients. The interaction between the government and its clients is largely seen as transactional. A wider conceptualisation of citizens as active participants in delivery is absent.

Contractors usually view elected officials, as opposed to service users, as their primary clients. Officials are, after all, the ones who could stop a contract. Good and well-meaning elected officials do exist. They try to ensure that contractors deliver according to specification. However, less honest officials, who are open to corruption, also exist. In either case, the supposed benefits of a market arrangement are not achieved. Several studies of American cities point to the informal agreements reached between élites in government and élites in contracting organisations, which have severely negative effects on the poor and marginalised (Squires, 1989; Leitner & Garner, 1993).

Service delivery

This section attempts to assess the likely impacts on service, starting with the matching of human resources to services. Next, the likely behaviour of public service managers is assessed, with particular reference to budgeting choices. Finally, an assessment of the impact of the labour relations environment is provided.

Managerialism values management's perspective as the only rational and legitimate one. The perspectives of users and workers are often ignored. Systems and techniques are seen as ends in themselves. Business plans, vision statements and zero-based budgeting are par for the course. Ends are defined, but managers having the discretion to decide on the means.

The central weakness of this model in South Africa relates to context. Managerialist approaches have mainly been applied in the developed countries. In those countries, the challenges are about improving existing services. In South Africa, where the primary goal is the extension of services, managerialist perspectives could lead to distorted results. Experiences in housing policy are a case in point. The delivery of 800 000 housing opportunities is a significant achievement. However, it is widely acknowledged that delivery has failed to integrate cities or stimulate economic recovery. In the managerialist paradigm, the figures would be all important. Wider social impacts are ignored.

The new restructuring framework will have significant consequences for extending services to the poor. Increasing private participation in public services is a likely outcome of the push to managerialism. A central weakness here is that contracting blunts the state's role in the pricing of services. In rural areas, 80% of income is derived from public expenditure and this generates limited disposable income. This is not conducive to private profit. Through contracting arrangements, the state inevitably loses some of its capacity to establish redistribution mechanisms.

Economists who support contracting suggest that service costs will be reduced due to the superior techniques used by private sector agents. These efficiency improvements, it is argued, will lead to surpluses that could be used to cross-subsidise poorer areas. This means lower profits for private operators, but also that access becomes increasingly contingent on the profit motive. These contingencies relate to the capacity of public managers to negotiate and enforce contracts.

The management of contracts requires skilled regulators, adequate legal frameworks and effective monitoring systems. Current capacity in all these areas is extremely limited. Examples can again be found in housing delivery, where large numbers of the houses being built are substandard. Unscrupulous builders are, however, only part of the problem. The public institution charged with upholding standards is equally at fault. Consequently, a great deal hinges on the behaviour of managers.

The service delivery implications of the restructuring agreement are more difficult to assess, as the agreement still awaits implementation. Ostensibly, the rationale for this agreement, is that a better match between organisational strategy and service delivery, on the one hand, and human resources, on the other hand, is achieved. The goal is a laudable one, as many areas of the public service require substantive restructuring. The prevailing orthodoxy in the public service, however, is based on the practice of new managerialism. Examples of this approach can already be seen in some government departments. The majority of plans are thus likely to reflect this approach to restructuring, and are likely to include public-private partnerships.

Consider the following scenario. Department X decides that it is more cost-effective to provide cleaning and security services through a management contract. Consequently, its new organisational structure does not create positions for cleaning and security. Unions protest against the management contract, but the plan goes ahead, as this is not necessarily a matter for dispute under the new restructuring agreement, which has been codified in the Public Service regulations. The plan is implemented, and workers are placed on the list of excess staff. Moreover, Department X still lacks contract compliance capacity. Under this scenario, service delivery is unlikely to improve. A more positive scenario could see the same proposal being mooted, but with Department X building in contract compliance capacities, so that services might improve, although the costs of providing the services are likely to be high, and may result in negative externalities.[4] The central point is that there is nothing in the agreement that a priori supports improved service delivery. It is the implementation of the agreement that will (hopefully) improve service delivery.

Moreover, many proposals for increased private participation in public services are unlikely to be realised. This poses challenges to the unions' anti-privatisation stance. In other words, a question may be raised as to whether the pending agreement will strengthen the unions' hand in arguing for more inclusive public sector alternatives to improve service delivery. This is not a simple question, as the negotiation process is overlaid and informed by a contest between developmental restructuring and new managerialism. The pending agreement will probably mark the continued ascendancy of new managerialism, as it is the preferred model of many in government, and space for unions to contest departmental plans is extremely limited.

Crucial to realising improved service delivery through the agreement will be the behaviour of public service managers. Two major responses are likely to characterise this terrain. First, public service managers will attempt to move with speed. In most cases, the groundwork for restructuring has already been laid, as departments have developed plans. This movement to restructure must be encouraged by progressive trade unions, and unions can be certain that political pressure to support restructuring will occur. Leaving aside the question of private participation in service delivery, progressive unions will need to support a transformative agenda.

Second, budget constraints and budget restructuring will play a huge role, some of it positive. Some questions in this regard are:

- The mantra of "doing more with less" pervades much of the public service restructuring; however, will a situation arise where posts are reduced simply to bring expenditure in line with declining budgets?

- If capital expenditure is prioritised over personnel spending, will this result in a smaller, more highly skilled public service? Differently stated, will lower-ranked workers be explicitly excluded in a future restructuring arrangement?

- Will the costs of restructuring (i.e. social plans, relocation costs) undercut an emerging expansionary stance in government?

The informal rules of budgeting at a departmental level are likely to be substantively changed. Whether these new informal rules will impact positively on service delivery to the poor is an open question.

Given managerial behaviour and the wider context of restructuring, will sound labour relations emerge? The question is value-laden, as it assumes that sound labour relations are necessary for speedy implementation of the agreement. However, this is a value not necessarily shared, as labour is often seen in government circles as an obstacle to change. Labour cannot negotiate plans, and the plans are not a matter of mutual interest, thus it seems likely that disputes about the plan will not necessarily bear on the employee-employer relationship. However, the implementation process may be conflict-ridden.

Government managers will argue that the agreement provides them with a set of tools to better manage resources. Moreover, they will argue that the agreement decentralises restructuring to the departmental level, and thus removes red tape in the restructuring process. One sincerely hopes that this will be the outcome of this agreement, and not a simple strategy of further containing costs.

A point that needs to be stressed is that restructuring at a departmental level is a logical choice for transforming services. This is due to the public service being a large entity, needing large-scale restructuring to improve its efficiency and to improve equity in society. Restructuring at the level of departments (i.e. not at institutions like hospitals or schools) provides a basis for deliberate and sustainable reforms. This, however, poses challenges to the capacity and organisation of unions to participate at this level. There are, after all, over 200 departments in South Africa. More and better management at institutional level is indeed a requirement for improved service delivery, but the process of new managerialism aims to strengthen head-office managers, at the expense of district and institutional level managers.

Women

One of the significant features of the restructuring experience has been women's involvement in the restructuring process both within and outside the bargaining arena. Inside the bargaining arena, women constitute the largest number of employees in lower grades and key professional occupations (e.g. nursing and teaching), and senior management is becoming increasingly representative. Some gains have been made for women (e.g. maternity leave), but female workers in lower grades still remain the most vulnerable of all workers, as they are employed in "non-core" activities such as cleaning. These female workers are likely to be the first causalities of restructuring processes due to the current restructuring agreement. This reflects a curious picture, with unions attempting to engender bargaining arrangements, but not providing sufficient protection to women.

Outside the bargaining arena, several important interventions have occurred. The Women's Health Project, which works on health issues from a gender perspective, has made vital interventions in the restructuring of healthcare. Similar initiatives focussing on women's issues and the reform of the public service have been undertaken. One of the significant projects has been on assessing public expenditure in South Africa through the Women's Budget Initiative (Budlender, 1996).

Trade unions

Global changes coupled with the democratic transition in South Africa have provided significant challenges to the trade union movement. The public service unions have attempted to develop new strategies to meet these challenges.

Adding complexity to this picture are the very distinct traditions of White unions and Black unions. Staff associations, which are predominately White, have been criticised for not advancing a transformative agenda (Grawitsky, 2002). These unions come from a tradition outside the liberation movement, and generally have sought not to engage in the wider restructuring agenda. Insularity from social movements and concern with bread-and-butter issues have remained their main focus. This reluctance of the predominately White unions to engage in wider societal issues can be explained by the traditions that the unions come from, as well as the fact that their membership are largely skilled and are potential winners in the restructuring process.

In contrast, the Black unions, mostly affiliated to Cosatu, have attempted to engage in wider societal transformation issues. Moreover, there has been an attempt to utilise bargaining to advance a progressive developmental agenda. Social unionism[5] has emerged as the professed orientation of Cosatu. The term "social unionism" has been outlined by the September Commission (Cosatu, 1997) as follows:

> Social unionism is social in the sense that it is concerned with broad social and political issues, as well as the immediate concerns of its members. It aims to be a social force for transformation. Its goal is democracy and socialism. Its influence on society is based on its organised power, its capacity to mobilise, its socio-economic programme and policies and its participation in political and social alliances.

Social unionism thus implies at least that progressive trade unions:

- redefine their constituencies to include the broader working class;
- attempt to strengthen the interconnectedness between worker struggles and societal transformation;
- seek to use a mixture of negotiation, mass action and policy intervention to advance the cause of the working class; and
- have a social project, which seeks to destroy racial, class, gender and other forms of discrimination.

The Cosatu affiliates have attempted to entrench this wider agenda in bargaining. Yet, at the same time, the wider societal interest has been redefined and recast in the image of the government. A long process of political engagement has seen the government accuse unions of acting in a selfish interest, and not allowing it to govern. The argument is that the government represents a wider interest, and this has been used in legitimising the restructuring programme. Thus, unions entered into the agreement through a coalescing of the common need of the government and unions to transform services.

Moreover, the utilisation of strikes and other methods of mass mobilisation has been blunted, due to the ever-present and growing threat of retrenchments in the public service. Unions have calculated that such retrenchments are inevitable and that it is better to manage retrenchments than oppose them. An open question is whether this tactical consideration will lead to the public service unions no longer focusing on wider societal issues, and retreating to ameliorate the consequences of restructuring.

The shift to departmental-level bargaining will test the limited capacities of unions to engage with the technical detail of restructuring proposals. A major consequence for unions is that capacity at the shop floor (i.e. within departments and institutions) will need to be strengthened if labour is to exercise its limited role in a strategic manner.

Conclusion

The period 1994 to 1999 was characterised by an attempt to meet the goals of improved efficiency in the public service, improved working conditions and the development aims of a nascent democratic state. This process saw the emergence of strategies that sought to meet multiple goals. Since 1999 there has been an ascendancy of efficiency as the main criteria for restructuring. This, in turn, has led to the eminent possibility of retrenchments in the public service, as well as the declining influence of elected politicians and citizens over the restructuring process. Moreover, building management capacity at the coalface will be marginalised as centralising tendencies in the bureaucracy are reinforced. The litmus test for the programme of restructuring is improvements in and the extension of services to the poor. The evidence suggests that the interaction between centralisation and standard restructuring models across sectors will kill innovation and hamper attempts to deliver services more effectively, efficiently and efficaciously. The trend emerging is the consolidation of power over the nature and content of reform behind the desks of head-office managers. This trend is likely to reduce the degree to which unions will influence the restructuring of the public service.

Endnotes

1 The scope of the chapter is on the public service (i.e. national and provincial government). The term "public sector" includes the public service, local government, state-owned enterprises and other institutions of state, and is used in this sense.
2 Prior to the LRA, teachers, police and the general public service negotiated in different councils, under different pieces of legislation. See Adair & Albertyn (1999).
3 *Batho Pele* is a Sotho term meaning "People First".
4 Evidence suggests that costs of services to the poor increase once the private sector is brought into the delivery of public services. This is discussed in the report from the Naledi conference on Alternatives to Privatisation.
5 The term "social unionism" is contested within the ranks of Cosatu. More recent documents of Cosatu have spoken about transformative unionism, implying that unions must fight for a wider change in society, and attempt to locate the concept within a socialist, as opposed to social democratic, framework.

References

Adair, B. & Albertyn, S. (2000) "Restructuring Management in the Public Service: Implications of New Legislation." In Adler, G. (ed) *Public Service Labour Relations in a Democratic South Africa*. Johannesburg: Witwatersrand University Press.

Albo, G., Langille, D. & Panitch, L. (1993) *A Different Kind of State: Popular Power and Democratic Administration*. Canada: Oxford University Press.

African National Congress (1994) *The Reconstruction and Development Programme: A Policy Framework*. Johannesburg: Umanyano Media.

Bangura, Y. (2000) *Public Sector Restructuring: The Institutional and Social Effects of Fiscal, Managerial and Capacity-Building Reforms*. Occasional Paper 3, United Nations Research Institute for Social Development, Geneva.

Bardouille, N. C. (2000) "The Transformation of Governance Paradigms and Modalities: Insights Into the Marketization of the Public Service in Response to Globalization", *The Round Table*, Vol. 353, January.

Baskin J. (2000) "Public Service Wage Bargaining: An Assessment of the Three-Year Agreement." In Adler, G. (ed.) *Public Service Labour Relations in a Democratic South Africa*. Johannesburg: University of Witwatersrand Press.

Budlender, D. (ed.) (1999) *The Forth Women's Budget*. Cape Town: Institute for Democracy in South Africa.

Cosatu (1997) *Report of the September Commission*. Johannesburg.

Cosatu (2000) *Labour Position on the Restructuring of Public Services*. Input to the Public Services Jobs Summit.

Department of Finance (1996) *Growth, Employment and Redistribution: A Macroeconomic Strategy*. Pretoria: Department of Finance.

Department of Public Service and Administration (1997) *White Paper on Transformation of the Public Service*. Pretoria.

Department of Public Service and Administration (1999) *Annual Report*. Pretoria.

FitzGerald, P., McLennan, A. & Munslow, B. (1995) *Managing Sustainable Development in South Africa*. Second edition. Cape Town: Oxford University Press.

Folscher, A. (2001) *Time to Rehabilitate Personnel Expenditure*. Budget Brief No. 63. Cape Town: Idasa.

Fraser-Moleketi, G. (1999) "Social Services at Risk if We Let Public Servants' Wages Run Riot", *Sunday Times*, 15 August.

Grawitzky, R. (2002) "Is it Crunch Time for the Public Service?", *Labour Bulletin 26*, 3, pp. 38–40.

Hassen, E. K. (2001) "A Dwindling Pie? Implications of the 2001/2002 Budget for Public Service Bargaining." National Labour and Economic Development Institute: Johannesburg.

Hoggett, P. (1996) "New Modes of Control in the Public Service", *Public Administration* 94, pp. 9–32.

Hyden, G. (1992) "Governance and the Study of Politics." In Hyden, G. & Bratton, M. (eds) *Governance and Politics in Africa*. Colarado and London: Lynne Reinner Publishers.

Jorgenson, T. B. (1993) "Modes of Governance and Administrative Change." In Kooiman, J. (ed.) *Modern Governance: New Government-Society Interactions*. London: Sage.

Laclau, E. & Mouffe, C. (1985) *Hegemony and Socialist Strategy*. London: Verso.

Landel-Mills, P. & Serageldin, I. (1991) "Governance and the Development Process", *Finance and Development*, September.

Leftwich, A. (1993) Governance, Democracy and Development in the Third World", *Third World Quarterly,* 24, 3, pp. 605–624.

Leitner, H. & Garner, M. (1993) "The Limits of Local Initiatives: A Reassessment of Urban Entrepreneuralism", *Urban Geography*, Vol. 14.

Lienert, I. (1998) "Civil Service Reform in Africa: Mixed Results After 10 Years", *Finance and Development*, Vol. 35, No. 2.

Macun, I. & Psoulis, C. (2000) "Unions Inside the State: The Development of Unionism in the South African Public Service." In Adler, G. (ed.) *Public Service Labour Relations in a Democratic South Africa*. Johannesburg: University of Witwatersrand Press.

Martin, B. (1996) *European Integration and Modernisation of Local Public Services Trade Union Responses and Initiatives*. A report for the European Federation of Public Service Unions.

McLenan, A. (1995) "Into the Future: Restructuring of the Public Service." In Fitzgerald, P., McLenan, A. & Munslow, B. (eds) *Managing Sustainable Development in South Africa*. Second edition. Cape Town: Oxford University Press.

Moharir, V. (1995) "Civil Service Reform in Africa: Problems and Prospects." In Fitzgerald, P., McLenan, A. & Munslow, B. (eds) *Managing Sustainable Development in South Africa*. Second edition. Cape Town: Oxford University Press.

Mukherjee, A., de Tommaso, G. & Schiavo-Campo, S. (Undated) *Government Employment and Pay in Global Perspective: A Selective Synthesis of International Facts, Policies and Experiences*. Public Sector Management and Information Technology Team, The World Bank.

National Treasury (2001) *Budget Review*. Pretoria: National Treasury.

Navarro, Z. (1998). *"Affirmative Democracy" and Redistributive Development: The Case of "Participatory Budgeting" in Porto Alegre, Brazil [1989-1997]*. Cartagena: Programas Sociales, Pobreza y Participatión Ciudadana.

Patel, I. (2000) "Growing Pains: Collective Bargaining in the Public Service." In Adler, G. (ed) *Public Service Labour Relations in a Democratic South Africa*. Johannesburg: University of Witwatersrand Press.

Piccard, L. A. & Garrity, M. (1995) "Development Management in Africa: Issues for South Africa." In Fitzgerald P., McLenan, A. & Munslow, B. (eds) *Managing Sustainable Development in South Africa*. Cape Town: Oxford University Press.

Paine, G. (1999) "Dark Side of a Hot Idea", *Siyaya*, Issue 6.

Putnam, R. D. (1992) "Democracy, Development and the Civic Community: Evidence from the Italian Experiment", *World Bank Conference on Culture and Development*, Washington D.C., 2–3 April.

Savas, E. S. (1987) *Privatisation: The Key to Better Government*. New Jersey: Chatham House Publishers.

Schick, A. (1996) *The Spirit of Reform: Managing the New Zealand State Sector in a Time of Change*. Wellington: State Services Commission/Treasury.

Squires, G. (1989) *Unequal Partnerships: The Political Economy of Urban Redevelopment in Postwar America*. New Brunswick: Rutgers University Press.

World Bank (1997) *World Development Report 1997: The State in a Changing World*. Washington D.C: Oxford University Press.

World Bank (2000). *World Development Report 2000: Poverty Eradication*. Washington D.C: Oxford University Press.

Part Two

Decentralisation and Development

5 Housing Provision through Co-operative Government in Post-apartheid South Africa

Kirsty McLean

Introduction

This chapter examines housing delivery in the context of co-operative government.[1] In particular, it will look at how the practice of co-operative government in the housing sector differs from the legislative and the constitutional model of co-operative government. This chapter will also explore whether these differences, if any, are in any way attributable to an ill-conceived constitutional model premised on co-operation rather than on inherent conflict. Chapter 2 of the 1996 Constitution[2] lays down the overarching principles of co-operative government, yet the precise detail of how this co-operation is to work is left to future legislation and policy documents.[3] There is still much uncertainty about the roles of the different spheres of government, particularly in the light of the restructuring of local government and in the Thabo Mbeki government's emphasis on trying to devolve service delivery down to this level.

Housing is a concurrent competence of national and provincial government,[4] yet local government has emerged as one of the major developers of housing. This demonstrates a shift from the developer-driven policy of the National Housing Forum (1993–1994), the "Botshabelo Agreement" of the National Housing Summit on 27 October 1994 and the White Paper on Housing (1994), towards greater state involvement in initiating and developing housing programmes. This shift is clearly demonstrated in the 1997 Housing Act.[5] Another clear trend within housing delivery is the principle of subsidiarity – that the lowest sphere of government capable of undertaking housing delivery must do so. These two developments (of private to public, and of provincial to local) have resulted in increased emphasis on the role of local government in housing delivery, and a corresponding need to clarify the residual role of the provincial government where local government has become more active in housing delivery. It should be noted that this chapter focuses on the "vertical" intergovernmental relations between national, provincial and local government, rather than on the "horizontal" relations between different provincial governments and different local governments. This is because, at present, there appears to be little in the way of horizontal co-operation in the housing sector. In the future, however, horizontal co-operation will hopefully become a greater feature of intergovernmental relations in the development of more efficient and better quality methods of housing delivery.

The methodology used in this chapter was, first, to examine the two notions of the right to housing and the principle of co-operative government at an ideal or normative level, through legislation, policy documents and case law. The second aspect of the study was to gather more qualitative data on the functions and role of the various spheres of government, as well as on problems experienced in housing delivery, through a series of interviews with academics, government officials and other participants in the industry, such as consultants and members of non-governmental organisations (NGOs). In this way it was hoped that problems in the relationships between the various spheres of government would be revealed, facilitating an evaluation of the practical functioning of co-operative government within the area of housing delivery.

In the course of this research, 23 interviews were conducted. These included a broad range of interviews in both the public and the private sectors, and across all three spheres of government. This facilitated a balanced and comprehensive view of the opinions and perceptions of policy makers and those involved in the field. The interview process, however, was both frustrating and enlightening. Amongst government officials, there is widespread confusion about the role of the various spheres of government, in particular that of local government. While some point to the Constitution and the fact that housing is a concurrent national and provincial competence, many local government officials are actively engaged in developing housing policy, despite the absence of a clear constitutional or legislative mandate. A further complication is introduced where a significant proportion of housing development is privately initiated and undertaken, where private developers identify a potential scheme and beneficiaries, and apply to provincial government for funding, with local government approval.

Ultimately it appears that the problems encountered within housing delivery are less a function of co-operative government (although there certainly are problems in this area), than a result of lack of managerial experience, finance and capacity. These weaknesses are to be found across all spheres of government, but are particularly prevalent at local government level. Many developers and building contractors have also experienced problems of this nature, which have led to time delays and poor quality building work.

Many normative issues surrounding the constitutional right to housing and housing delivery through co-operative government have been clarified in the watershed Constitutional Court case of *Grootboom*,[6] and this chapter will start in by examining the court's analysis of these two issues, beginning with a brief discussion on socio-economic rights, in order to contextualise the right to housing and the debates around judicial enforcement of socio-economic rights. The idea of co-operative government will be discussed in detail in the second part of the chapter; the third part deals with the constitutional and legislative vision for housing provision through co-operative government; and the fourth part discusses the accreditation process for local government, and the implications this may have for the existing model of co-operative government. Finally, the chapter concludes with some reflections on the present functioning of co-operative government in housing delivery.

It has become increasingly clear throughout the research undertaken for this paper that it is extremely difficult, perhaps even impossible, to lay down a rigid template for the practice of co-operative government. The various provinces and municipalities have had vastly different roles and experiences in housing delivery, all of which are provided for in the Housing Act. This should not be seen solely as a flaw of the Housing Act. Rather, it is this fluidity within the principles of co-operative government laid down in the Act that will allow the different spheres of government to develop their own best practices over time. Until this happens, however, there will continue to be confusion over the roles and duties of the various spheres of government. Furthermore, allowing different departments to develop their own systems will lead to diverging practices, which may result in conflict in future. Co-operative government in South Africa is still in its infancy, and the remarks and conclusions drawn at the end of the chapter will therefore necessarily be tentative observations on this dynamic network of relationships.

Grootboom and the right to housing

International and constitutional law distinguish between civil and political rights (so-called "first generation rights") and socio-economic rights ("second generation rights").[7] These are also referred to as "negative" and "positive" rights respectively, since the former are said to place restrictions on the use of power by government, while the latter place positive obligations on the state. Yet this distinction can be criticised as highly artificial, since "all human rights impose a combination of negative and positive duties on states" (Liebenberg, 1999:41-25) and the enforcement of "negative obligations" frequently requires states to undertake positive obligations.[8]

The question of whether the new South African Constitution should include socio-economic rights gave rise to much debate during its writing.[9] It is the "positive" nature of socio-economic rights that makes them controversial, particularly when it comes to the proper enforcement of these rights by courts. Opponents of socio-economic rights argue that it is undemocratic for unelected judges to be able to direct how the state is able to allocate resources, and that this involves a violation of the "separation of powers" doctrine. This counter-majoritarian argument was rejected in principle by the Constitutional Court in the first *Certification Judgment*, in which the court held that "it cannot be said that by including socio-economic rights within a bill of rights, a task is conferred upon the Courts so different from that ordinarily conferred upon them by a bill of rights that it results in a breach of the separation of powers".[10] This means that socio-economic rights are justiciable in principle and, at the very least, courts can protect the negative invasion of a right, that is, courts can stop the state from introducing what have been called "deliberately retrogressive measures", measures that impact directly on the right and involve a denial or restriction of an existing right.[11] More controversial is the enforcement of the positive aspect of the obligation, and the separation of powers doctrine again becomes relevant to the issue of appropriate orders of courts. This is discussed more fully below.

The South African Constitution entrenches both civil and political and socio-economic rights, and the interconnectedness of these two sets of rights has been recognised by the Constitutional Court.[12] The two most important socio-economic rights in the Constitution are s 26 and s 27 – the housing and health care rights respectively. Other socio-economic rights include s 25(5), which deals with land redistribution; s 28, which provides for various children's rights; s 29, which provides a right to education; and s 35, which provides various rights to arrested and detained persons (see De Waal, *et al.*, 2000:433).

To date, there have been three significant socio-economic rights cases. The first was *Soobramoney v Minister of Health, KwaZulu-Natal*,[13] in which Mr Soobramoney applied to the High Court for an order directing a state hospital to provide him with an expensive dialysis treatment. His claim was based in part on s 27(3), which provides that "[n]o one may be refused emergency medical treatment". In rejecting his appeal to the Constitutional Court, the court held that the right did not extend to providing treatment for an ongoing, chronic condition, and that the state's policy to limit the availability of dialysis treatment to specific patients was reasonable in the circumstances.

The second and most recent case is that of *Minister of Health v TAC*,[14] again dealing with the right to healthcare. In this case, the Court held that a government policy concerning the prevention of mother-to-child transmission of HIV/Aids that provides for the distribution of anti-retroviral drugs only to selected state hospitals around the country is unreasonable and infringes the right to healthcare of HIV-positive women and their babies born in the public health sector, outside of these pilot sites. Limiting the programme for the prevention of mother-to-child transmission of HIV to pilot sites for a research period before deciding whether to expand the programme nationally was also found to be, in the circumstances of the epidemic in South Africa, unreasonable and in breach of this right.

The third socio-economic rights judgment is that of *Grootboom*. This decision of the South African Constitutional Court represents the first attempt by a court to provide judicial protection for a socio-economic right in a politically sustainable way by not violating the separation of powers doctrine. Cass R. Sunstein (2002) explains this as follows: "for the first time in the history of the world, a constitutional court has initiated a process that might well succeed in the endeavour of ensuring that protection [of socio-economic rights] without placing courts in an unacceptable managerial role". The court achieved this through what Sunstein describes as an "administrative law model of socio-economic rights", involving a form of judicial review of government action.

Grootboom involved a community who had invaded private land that they named "New Rust", after leaving the deplorable conditions of their previous settlement. The owner of the land sought and obtained an eviction order under the Prevention of Illegal Eviction From and Unlawful Occupation of Land Act 19 of 1998, and the community then sought shelter on a municipal sports field. After requesting assistance from the relevant local government authority to no avail, the community then sued the municipality in the Cape High Court for an order granting temporary shelter, relying on s 26(1) and (2), and on s 28(1)(c), of the Constitution. Davis J granted an order in terms of s 28(1)(c), which instructed the present appellants to provide shelter for the children in the community and their parents. The state then appealed against this order to the Constitutional Court and, after the intervention of an *amicus curiae*, the claim based on s 26(1) and (2) was also reargued.

The court (at paras 94, 95) held that the right in s 26, and in s 28, did not entitle "the respondents to claim shelter or housing immediately upon demand", yet emphasised that socio-economic rights are nevertheless justiciable "rights", which can be enforced by courts in certain circumstances. Rather than directly regulating the way in which the government fulfils it duty to provide housing, the court handed down a declaratory order to the effect that the state must have in place a reasonable plan to realise the right to housing over time and within its budgetary constraints, and that this programme must include relief for those in desperate need.

In examining the right to housing, this chapter will focus on s 26(1) and (2), and will not consider the relationship between this right and the protection granted against arbitrary eviction in s 26(3), the right of the child to shelter in s 28(1)(c), or the right of detained persons to adequate accommodation in s 35(2)(e). Section 26(1) and (2) provides as follows:

(1) Everyone has the right to have access to adequate housing.

(2) The state must take reasonable legislative and other measures, within its available resources, to achieve the progressive realisation of this right.

Section 26(1) and (2) should be seen as constituting one distinct right, rather than the two subsections creating separate rights. This interpretation is based on the text itself, where s 26(2) speaks of "this right" in a clear reference to s 26(1). Furthermore, the Constitutional Court has expressly stated that that the two subsections "are related and must be read together" (para 34), and analyses s 26(1) and (2) as a single right. The court went on (at paras 34–46) to interpret s 26(1) as outlining the scope of the right, and implying a negative obligation on the state not to interfere with the right to housing, and s 26(2) as delineating the state's duty with regard to housing provision.[15]

Section 26(1) does not provide a right to housing itself, but only a right to have *access* to adequate housing. Clearly the wording of this provision was intended to limit the state's obligation to provide housing (see Liebenberg, 1999:41-26), but the exact scope of the right and the extent of the state's duty is unclear. Gina Bekker (2000:122) explains what this right means as follows:

Section 26 is formulated in such a manner that a right of "access to" adequate housing is provided for rather than a right to housing. The obligation placed on the state is therefore to create an enabling environment in which individuals are able to realise the right for themselves. The state has to ensure for example that people are protected against forced evictions and that there are housing subsidies available. However, this does not mean that the state is absolved from all responsibility of actually providing housing. In instances where due to floods or other natural disasters or other situations in which people find themselves in a position where they do not have a roof over their head, the state is required to step in and provide them with housing.

This quote is typical of pre-*Grootboom* analysis (see also Liebenberg, 1997:345–349) and reveals a forced separation of s 26(1) and (2). While this interpretation is consistent with the structure of the right in the constitutional text, it has led to confusion, demonstrated in the quote above, where commentators have tried to make sense of the distinction between s 26(1) and (2). This resulted in a more conservative reading of the state's obligation than the one given by the court.

The wording of the duty in s 26(2) indicates that the right is more extensive than the duty merely to provide "an enabling environment for the individual to realize the right on his/her own accord" as Karrisha Pillay (2000:2) has interpreted it. Rather, s 26(2) points to a duty on the state to provide housing itself, albeit progressively and within its financial constraints. As s 26(2) identifies the right as being the same in s 26(1), perhaps a wider reading of "access" is necessary. Indeed, the word "access" appears to be redundant, since the housing right is already qualified by s 26(2), and it is thus unnecessary to try to qualify it further by the word "access" in s 26(1).

The above quote also demonstrates the difficulty of trying to read s 26(1), (2) and (3) together. While protection against arbitrary eviction is clearly a "housing right", thus appearing at first glance to fit neatly within s 26, it is suggested that it would have been preferable to have had the s 26(3) right within s 25, before s 25(5), the parallel provision to s 26(2), providing for access to land. This is justified given the very close connection between land and housing, particularly in rural areas. In the context of eviction, whether one locates the right as a right to housing or as a right to land seems moot. Sections 26(3) and 25(5) would then bear a similar relationship to that between s 26(1) and (2). This interpretation, however, has not been borne out by the Constitutional Court, which (at para 34) interpreted s 26(3) as an extension of the "negative right" in s 26(1).

In *Grootboom*, Yacoob J defines the right to "access to adequate housing" in s 26(1) by contrasting it with the right to "adequate housing" found in the International Covenant on Economic, Social and Cultural Rights (ICESCR). His definition, however, initially begins by describing the content of the right as opposed to its scope, that is, it describes what constitutes *adequate* housing rather than what *access* to adequate housing means. It is only at the end of the paragraph that Yacoob J deals with the limitation the word *access* places on the scope of the right.

The right delineated in s 26(1) is a right of "access to adequate housing" as distinct from the right to adequate housing encapsulated in the Covenant. This difference is significant. It recognises that housing entails more than bricks and mortar. It requires available land, appropriate services such as the provision of water and the removal of sewage and the financing of all of these, including the building of the house itself. For a person to have access to adequate housing, all of these conditions need to be met: there must be land, there must be services, there must be a dwelling. Access to land for the purpose of housing is therefore included in the right of access to adequate housing in s 26. A right of access to adequate housing also suggests that it is not only the state that is responsible for the provision of houses, but that other agents within our society, including individuals themselves, must be enabled by legislative and other measures to provide housing. The state must create the conditions for access to adequate housing for people at all economic levels of our society. State policy dealing with housing must therefore take account of different economic levels in our society (*Grootboom*, para 35).

The court thus recognised that the state's obligation must be context-sensitive: its policy must cater both for those who can afford to pay for adequate housing themselves, and for those who require state assistance. Consideration must also be given to whether the person requiring assistance lives in a rural or an urban area, and there may be differences across provinces and cities. The court's interpretation, however, in dismissing the interpretation of the ICESCR, contradicts the national government's policy laid down in the Housing Code, which expressly accepts the interpretation given by the ICESCR. In explaining what the word "adequate" means in s 26(1), the Code states that:

> [t]he wording of the housing right provision corresponds with the International Covenant on Economic, Social and Cultural Rights (1966). In that context, "adequate housing" is measured by certain core factors: legal security of tenure; the availability of services; materials, facilities and infrastructure; affordability; habitability; accessibility; location and cultural adequacy. South Africa's housing policy concurs with this concept of housing. (National Housing Code, 2000:7)

Thus, Yacoob J's interpretation of what constitutes adequate housing is more conservative than the interpretation given by the National Department itself. This means that there is now a level of normative confusion, since the interpretation given by the Constitutional Court is different to the one set out in national legislation and policy documents.

Section 26(2) places a duty on the state to take "reasonable legislative and other measures" towards the realisation of the right in s 26(1). This obligation is qualified in two main ways: it must be within the state's "available resources" and it must be progressively realised. In interpreting "reasonable measures", the Committee on Economic, Social and Cultural Rights (General Comment 2, 1990:para 2, cited in *Grootboom*) has held that this means that the state must show that it has taken steps which are "deliberate, concrete and targeted as clearly as possible" towards fulfilling that right. The primary means through which the state has sought to meet this obligation is through legislation, such as the National Housing Act read with the Housing Code, as well as through national subsidies.

In discussing what constitutes "reasonable legislative and other measures", the court held (at paras 39,40) that this must be determined within the context of co-operative government:

> What constitutes reasonable legislative and other measures must be determined in the light of the fact that the Constitution creates different spheres of government: national government, provincial government and local government ... The Constitution allocates powers and functions amongst these different spheres emphasising their obligation to co-operate with one another in carrying out their constitutional tasks. In the case of housing, it is a function shared by both national and provincial government. Local governments have an important obligation to ensure

that services are provided in a sustainable manner to the communities they govern. A reasonable program therefore must clearly allocate responsibilities and tasks to the different spheres of government and ensure that the appropriate financial and human resources are available.

Thus, a co-ordinated State housing programme must be a comprehensive one determined by all three spheres of government in consultation with each other as contemplated by chapter 3 of the Constitution. It may also require framework legislation at national level ... Each sphere of government must accept responsibility for the implementation of particular parts of the program but the national sphere of government must assume responsibility for ensuring that laws, policies, programs and strategies are adequate to meet the State's s 26 obligations. In particular, the national framework, if there is one, must be designed so that these obligations can be met. It should be emphasised that national government bears an important responsibility in relation to the allocation of national revenue to the provinces and local government on an equitable basis. Furthermore, national and provincial government must ensure that executive obligations imposed by the housing legislation are met.

Co-operative government is dealt with in detail in the following section, yet it is worth making a couple of remarks at this stage: in the first paragraph above, Yacoob J states that housing is a concurrent national and provincial competence, and that local government has a role to play in service provision. It is unclear whether he means that local governments have a role to play in the provision of houses or in the provision of services associated with housing such as those laid down in Part B of Schedules 4 and 5. The latter would accord more with the constitutional competencies laid down in Schedules 4 and 5, and this interpretation is reinforced by the last sentence in the second paragraph, where Yacoob J highlights the role of the executive in national and provincial government. Yacoob J, therefore, appears to emphasise the role of national and provincial government, an interpretation closest to the constitutional model of co-operative government.

Yacoob J then remarks that all spheres of government must consult with one another in the development of a housing delivery plan, "as contemplated by chap 3 of the Constitution". The Constitution does not actually require that there be consultation in the development of programmes, only that the various spheres of government must consult "on matters of common interest" (s 41(1)(h)(iii)).[16] In fact, there was initially little, if any, consultation between national and local government regarding housing provision.

In further interpreting what constitutes "reasonable measures", Yacoob J emphasises that the programme itself must not only be reasonable, but must also be "reasonably implemented" (para 42), and this must in turn be considered in its "social, economic and historical context" (para 43). The programme should address the short-, medium- and long-term housing needs of the community, and must cover all sectors of the community: "[a] program that excludes a significant segment of society cannot be said to be reasonable" (para 43). Lastly, the idea of reasonableness must be assessed with reference to the Bill of Rights.[17]

The duty on the state to take reasonable legislative and other measures is qualified in two ways: the right needs only to be progressively realised, and the state needs only to act within its available resources.[18] In interpreting the term "progressive realisation", the court referred to General Comment 3 of the ICESCR Committee, finding that the phrase in our Constitution has the same meaning as that in the covenant. The court noted that this provision did not mean the state could simply take as long as it liked in realising the right, and that it must "move as expeditiously and effectively as possible towards that goal".[19]

The qualification that the state needs only to fulfil its duty within "available resources" is notably different to the wording of Article 2(1) of the ICESCR, which provides that a state must take steps "to the maximum of its available resources".[20] In a discussion on the nature of State Parties' obligations under Article 2(1), the Committee argued for a "minimum core obligation" in order to meet the "minimum essential levels of each of the rights" in the ICESCR. This means that in order to meet its obligation, a State Party "must demonstrate that every effort has been made to use all resources that are at its disposition in an effort to satisfy, as a matter of priority, those minimum obligations".[21] This idea was rejected by the Constitutional Court in *Grootboom* (at para 32) because of the significant differences in the wording of the two provisions and because there was not sufficient information before the court. While it is recognised that there is a significant difference in the wording of the two provisions, the court should have taken into consideration the fact that national housing policy has already shown a willingness to conform to the norms laid down by the ICESCR, demonstrated above in the discussion of the interpretation of the term "adequate housing". The court's justification is also questionable, as the court, in accepting an international norm, would not need to reassess the content of a minimum core obligation in the context of South Africa, as the Committee of the ICESCR has laid down a minimum standard to be applied irrespective of local conditions (General Comment 3, 1990:para 10). The minimum core obligation is not meant to be a flexible standard, but to "describe the minimum expected of a State in order to comply with its obligation under the Covenant" (*Grootboom*, para 31).

To conclude: the court's analysis of s 26(1) and (2) is a fairly restrictive reading of the right, often ignoring a more practical and progressive understanding of the state's duty laid down in national legislation and policy documents. Similarly, the Constitutional Court's analysis of co-operative government, on the whole, concurs with the constitutional vision of concurrent national and provincial competencies, rather than with the more flexible legislative model laid down in the Housing Act and the Housing Code. This has exacerbated the normative conflict in the interpretation of s 26 and the understanding of co-operative government. In the following section, the differences between the constitutional and legislative models for co-operative government in housing delivery will be explored in greater detail.

Principles of co-operative government

Chapter 3 of the Constitution sets out the principles of co-operative government. The positioning of this chapter within the Constitution, before chapters on individual branches and spheres of government, indicates that the drafters of the text considered it to provide an overarching concept, or context, within which later chapters must be understood.[22] Chapter 3 provides as follows:

40. (1) In the Republic, government is constituted as national, provincial and local spheres of government, which are distinctive, interdependent and interrelated.

    (2) All spheres of government must observe and adhere to the principles in this Chapter and must conduct their activities within the parameters that the Chapter provides.

41. (1) All spheres of government and all organs of state within each sphere must –

    (a) preserve the peace, the national unity and the indivisibility of the Republic;

    (b) secure the well-being of the people of the Republic;

    (c) provide effective, transparent, accountable and coherent government for the Republic as a whole;

    (d) be loyal to the Constitution, the Republic and its people;

    (e) respect the constitutional status, institutions, powers and functions of government in other spheres;

    (f) not assume any power or function except those conferred on them in terms of the Constitution;

    (g) exercise their powers and perform their functions in a manner that does not encroach on the geographical, functional or institutional integrity of government in another sphere; and

    (h) co-operate with one another in mutual trust and good faith by –

        (i) fostering friendly relations;

        (ii) assisting and supporting one another;

        (iii) informing one another of, and consulting one another on, matters of common interest;

        (iv) co-ordinating their actions and legislation with one another;

(v) adhering to agreed procedures; and

(vi) avoiding legal proceedings against one another.

(2) An Act of Parliament must –

(a) establish or provide for structures and institutions to promote and facilitate intergovernmental relations; and

(b) provide for appropriate mechanisms and procedures to facilitate settlement of intergovernmental disputes.

(3) An organ of state involved in an intergovernmental dispute must make every reasonable effort to settle the dispute by means of mechanisms and procedures provided for that purpose, and must exhaust all other remedies before it approaches a court to resolve the dispute.

(4) If a court is not satisfied that the requirements of subsection (3) have been met, it may refer a dispute back to the organs of state involved.

Section 40(1) of the Constitution provides that "in the Republic, government is constituted as national, provincial and local spheres of government which are distinctive, interdependent and interrelated". This represents a radical shift from the centralised governmental structure of the apartheid era, where relations between the different tiers (now spheres) of government were redefined. Local and provincial governments are now independent spheres of government. Their powers and status are dependent on the Constitution itself.

South Africa's commitment to decentralisation, however, was not always a given. During the multiparty negotiations between 1992 and 1994, the ANC was initially opposed to a "federal" model of government, believing "that only a centralized, unitary state could have the strength and resources to engage in the massive process of social and economic transformation that lay ahead. Fragmenting and dispersing authority would make decision-making more difficult and undermine the capacity to achieve reconstruction and development" (Murray & Simeon, 2000:5). Federalism, associated with the bantustans of apartheid, and championed by secessionist parties, was seen as undermining the goal of a majoritarian democracy (Haysom, 2001:44). Yet over time, the parties opposed to a federalist model began to see the advantages of decentralisation for effective and accountable government.

In part, the ANC had to accept a multilevel system as part of the bargain, but some ANC leaders came to see advantages in effective regional governments both for the delivery of services and for the empowerment of citizens. Their exposure to foreign models of federalism, especially in Germany, convinced them that regional governments could be combined with strong leadership from the centre (Murray & Simeon, 2000:note 56 at 6).

Due to the controversy surrounding the word "federalism", parties to the negotiations decided to move away from a debate focussed solely on whether or not federalism was appropriate, and instead decided to "embark on an inquiry into an appropriate system of constitutional government whose objective would be to promote nothing other than good and effective government" (Haysom, 2001:note 57 at 45). One of the defining characteristics of this process was the creation of a form of regionalism with concurrent powers, along with a set of "override" powers should this be necessary in the national interest. This approach differs markedly from the traditional federal model in which there is a clear division of roles (Haysom, 2001:47).

Under the final Constitution, this concept of concurrent powers was developed with the addition of the notion of co-operative government. In so doing, the Constitutional Assembly followed the lead of the German model of federalism, as opposed to the "competitive federalism" of countries such as Canada (Haysom, 2001:52). Thus, the nature of the relationship between national and provincial governments in South Africa, which was created out of the negotiation process, is neither truly federalist nor unitary, and has been described as "decentralised or regional with strong central control" in nature (Murray, 2001:note 3 at 68).

The constitutional conception of co-operative government is premised on the independence of the various spheres of government, while recognising that the government, in order to function effectively, needs to function as a coherent whole. This emphasis on co-operation represents a significant departure from the practice of most modern states, where intergovernmental relations are characterised by conflict (Levy & Tapscott, 2001:1). The South African model for intergovernmental relations has been described as a *political approach towards managing tensions in government*" (Levy & Tapscott, 2001:11), yet the very creation of independent spheres of government has given rise to a series of new tensions as a result of competition for political credibility and acknowledgement. This is exacerbated by the fact that the different spheres are not truly equal, as the Constitution provides for extensive override provisions, and overseeing roles, particularly in the sphere of local government. These override provisions have the effect of allowing the national sphere to dominate (Gutto, 1998:para 8).

Despite the careful and detailed analysis of intergovernmental relations in the certification process,[23] there has been surprisingly little decided case law in this area. This is due in some part to the constitutional mandate in s 41(1)(h) to the different spheres to avoid litigation, to the dominance of the ANC at both national and provincial level, as well as to the political nature of many of the disputes themselves.[24] Nevertheless, there have been some significant cases brought before the Constitutional Court, demonstrating the willingness of provinces to litigate if necessary to uphold their legislative independence.

These cases will be discussed in chronological order.

In the *NEP Bill*[25] case, the Constitutional Court had to decide whether a bill that allowed a national minister to implement policy infringed provincial legislative competence. Chaskalson P, in finding (at para 33) that the bill was not unconstitutional, allowed national government considerable leeway in enforcing co-operation, to the extent of withholding financial incentives: "[i]t cannot therefore be said to be contrary to the Constitution for Parliament to enact legislation that is premised on the assumption that the necessary co-operation will be offered". This case demonstrates the court's emphasis on co-operation, rather than on competition or conflict.

In *Premier, Western Cape v President of the Republic of South Africa*,[26] the Western Cape Provincial Government challenged certain amendments to the Public Service Act for encroaching on provincial executive competence. While the case was ultimately decided on the issue of competence, the Western Cape had also argued that the amendments were a violation of co-operative government. At paras 89–94, Chaskalson P examined the Public Service Act in this regard, again indicating the court's willingness to find Chapter 3 justiciable.[27] Similarly, in *Executive Council of the Western Cape*[28] the Western Cape and KwaZulu-Natal provincial governments challenged national legislation[29] that attempted to regulate the establishment of municipalities as a violation of their and municipal constitutional competencies.

In the *Liquor Bill* case,[30] the Western Cape argued that the proposed Liquor Bill was unconstitutional as it encroached upon the exclusive legislative competence of the Western Cape. The court, per Cameron AJ, held that while provinces did have some exclusive competencies, this was subject to a national government override, where the requirements of s 44 of the Constitution have been met. And in *DVB Behuising*,[31] the court, per Ngcobo J, partly overturned an order of the court *a quo*, which found a provincial proclamation declaring unconstitutional racist land laws to be *ultra vires*.

Finally, in *National Gambling Board*,[32] the court (at para 33) emphasised the obligations which s 41(1)(h)(vi) places on organs of state to avoid litigation: "[t]he obligation to settle disputes is an important aspect of cooperative government which lies at the heart of Chapter 3 of the Constitution. If this Court is not satisfied that the obligation has been duly performed, it will rarely grant direct access to organs of state involved in litigation with one another."

These cases have dealt almost exclusively with disputes concerning provincial legislative competence between national and provincial governments, and demonstrate the Constitutional Court's sensitivity to the principles and values of co-operative government set out in the Constitution. As Murray and Simeon (2000:note 56 at16) point out, it is critical that future decisions flesh out the tests to be used to decide disputes concerning concurrent executive competence. The decisions also point to the fact that rather than prescribing a rigid model for co-operative government and the different competencies of the provincial and national governments, the constitutional model, as interpreted by the court, is enabling, preferring to prescribe policies and goals (Levy & Tapscott, 2001:note 63 at 2).

The discussion above has focussed on the constitutional model for co-operative government, as interpreted by the Constitutional Court. The next section will examine the legislative model, which differs from the constitutional model primarily through its emphasis on local government and on the principle of subsidiarity.

The White Paper on Local Government (1998) is arguably the foremost policy document on co-operative government, and provides the following list of what co-operative government involves:

- collectively harnessing all public resources behind common goals and within a framework of mutual support;

- developing a cohesive, multi-sectoral perspective on the interests of the country as a whole, and respecting the discipline of national goals, policies and operating principles;
- co-ordinating activities to avoid wasteful competition and costly duplication;
- utilising human resources effectively;
- settling disputes constructively without resorting to costly and time-consuming litigation; and
- rationally and clearly dividing the roles and responsibilities of government, so as to minimise confusion and maximise effectiveness.

It also deals extensively with co-operative government and service provision. In this context, national government is to provide a "strategic role", and is:

> responsible for setting the overall strategic framework for the economic and social development of the nation, and for all spheres of government. It should ensure that local government operates within an *enabling framework*[23] and is structured and capacitated in a way that best enables it to promote the development of citizens, local communities and the nation. (White Paper on Local Government, 1998:39)

This directive is based on s 154(1) of the Constitution which states that "[t]he national government and provincial governments, by legislative and other measures, must support and strengthen the capacity of municipalities to manage their own affairs, to exercise their powers and to perform their functions". National government is also to "[e]nsure that provincial legislation with respect to local government is formulated within a national legislative framework" (White Paper on Local Government, 1998:39). Lastly, the White Paper states that national government must monitor and oversee the functions of provincial and local government. Thus, national government's role in service delivery is to introduce national legislation, formulate policy and monitor provincial and local government to ensure that they function within national government policy.

Provincial government's role is similar with respect to local government and includes developing an integrated framework for economic, social and community development within the province, and ensuring that municipal policy frameworks are co-ordinated across the province and are in line with provincial policy.

The White Paper also states that provincial government should include local government in decision-making, thereby enhancing co-operation between provincial and local governments. Provincial government should also encourage co-operation between municipalities. As is the case for national government, provincial government has an important monitoring role in local government service delivery.

In terms of the constitutional model for co-operative government, s 139 of the Constitution provides for provincial executive interference in a municipality where a municipality is unable or unwilling to fulfil an executive obligation. Thus, while the Constitution embraces a "federalist" notion of co-operative government, the roles allocated to each sphere of government are far from clear and immutable. With regard to local government in particular, the national and provincial override provisions are extensive.

The White Paper's vision for municipalities is that they are required to "work with provincial and national government in their respective areas of jurisdiction, and enhance the effectiveness of national and provincial programmes" (White Paper on Local Government, 1998:46). The detail of local government's role is not spelt out any further than this broad principle to co-operate with provincial and national government in their developmental policies. The White Paper envisages vertically integrated departments in which all spheres co-operate to realise nationally established goals. It sees local government as critical for effective service delivery, a partner with national and provincial government. The exact relationship between the spheres, particularly between provincial and local government, is left to the different spheres to work out for themselves. This allows for a flexible model in which the different provinces can work out their relationships with the various municipalities, depending on the circumstances of each sphere. Lastly, the White Paper emphasises devolving service delivery down to local government level, if this would lead to it being more effectively implemented.

The constitutional model for co-operative government, on the other hand, tends to emphasise to a greater degree the independence of the three spheres of government and mechanisms for conflict resolution, particularly in the area of concurrent national and provincial legislative competence. Nevertheless, the Constitution still places a strong emphasis on co-operation, and provides broad principles of co-operative government to support this.

Thus, the constitutional and legislative models for co-operative government are substantially the same, both placing emphasis on the need for the different spheres to co-operate in order to achieve effective service delivery. There is, however, one important difference: the legislative model, as set out in the White Paper on Local Government, emphasises the role of local government and the need to devolve functions down to this level far more than does the Constitution. This principle of subsidiarity emerges even more strongly in the context of housing delivery discussed in the following section.

Co-operative government in housing provision

Having considered the principles of co-operative government in service delivery in the previous section, this section will examine South Africa's housing policy more specifically. Essentially, the legislation and policy documents on housing delivery follow the legislative model of national government providing the broad framework and policy, provincial government overseeing planning and facilitating development, and local government being involved in development itself, where its capacity enables this.

Discussions around South Africa's new housing policy began prior to the democratic elections with the establishment of the National Housing Forum. The findings of this "multi-party non-governmental negotiating body" (National Housing Code, 2000:3UF) were used by the Government of National Unity in formulating South Africa's National Housing Policy. In October 1994, a National Housing Accord (known as the "Botshabelo Agreement") was signed by "a range of stakeholders representing the homeless, government, communities and civil society, the financial sector, emerging contractors, the established construction industry, building material suppliers, employers, developers and the international community" (National Housing Code, 2000:4UF), and in December 1994, the White Paper on Housing was promulgated, establishing the basic housing policy for post-apartheid South Africa. The White Paper represented the first time that South Africa would have a universal housing strategy applicable to the entire country.[34]

The current policy documents central to housing are the Constitution, the Housing Act and the Housing White Paper. Other influential documents are the Reconstruction and Development Programme, the Growth, Employment and Redistribution Strategy, the Urban and Rural Development Frameworks, and various other white papers on local government and the public service (National Housing Code, 2000:5UF).

The preamble to the White Paper on Housing (1994:para 1 at 4) claims to approach housing, not by setting up a list of rules, but through "the search for the creation of an enabling environment". This approach seeks to "contribute to the certainty required by the market, as well as give the Provincial and Local Governments their capacity to fulfil their Constitutional obligations". A co-operative "partnership" between the various spheres of government and between government and private investment is seen as essential for delivery of houses, and effective housing delivery is posited as "one of the cornerstones of rebuilding our social structures and regenerating the economy".

In a consideration of the roles of the various spheres of government, the White Paper on Housing, discussing Schedule 6 of the Interim Constitution, argues that while national and provincial governments are given concurrent legislative capacity, "[t]he intent, however, is clearly that appropriate housing functions and powers should be devolved to the maximum possible extent, to the provincial level".[35] (A detailed summary of the various roles of government set out in the White Paper is listed in the Appendix below.)

By the time the Housing Act 107 of 1997 was enacted, however, there was a shift to including local government in housing delivery to a far greater degree, and to devolving power down to local government. In so doing, it was following the new paradigm laid down in the White Paper on Local Government (1998) and the Development Facilitation Act 67 of 1995 in establishing "development principles" to be followed by all spheres of government. This new position is set out in the National Housing Code (2000:Part 1 at 8) as follows:

> A critical policy challenge for the governance of housing is to facilitate the maximum devolution of functions and powers to provincial and local government spheres, while at the same time, ensuring that national processes and policies essential to a sustainable national housing development process are in place. The Housing Act, No. 107 of 1997, determines roles in respect of such devolution, and defines key national and provincial responsibilities with respect to empowerment at the provincial and local spheres of government.

This "shift in policy" also appeared to be legitimating an already existing situation. Local governments, such as the Greater Johannesburg Metropolitan Council (GJMC) and Durban Metropolitan Area (DMA) had already recognised the socio-political imperative to build low-cost housing, and had taken the initiative to undertake development. Politically, housing was seen as a substantial service and important to develop political credibility in the new political era.

Speaking of the draft Housing Bill in May 1997, the Minister of Housing, Ms S. D. Mthembi-Mahanyele, laid down the department's vision for the role of local government in housing delivery:

> Municipalities have a major role to play in planning, budgeting, managing, administering and maintaining services once capital investment has taken place, but we cannot expect municipalities to have a hands-on approach to housing delivery if they are not in control of the factors which have an impact upon it.
>
> The draft Housing Bill ... empowers provincial and local government to administer national housing programmes for the first time. It makes sense to devolve to local government those housing matters, which could most effectively be administered locally.

Housing is about fulfilling a basic human need, the availability of land, the affordability of basic services, economic growth, social development and the environment. The draft Housing Bill proposes that municipalities be obliged to deal with each of these issues, while giving priority attention to the basic needs of the communities.

Therefore, I wish to announce that I, together with the MECs, have approved guidelines for the accreditation of municipalities. These guidelines take effect immediately. Municipalities will now be able to offer new homeowners the best value for money by introducing more competition. (Hansard 6 May 1997, 7 1997 col. 2169 at 2170,1)

In this speech, the minister announced that she seeks to "devolve" power to local government through the accreditation process, provided for in s 10 of the Act. In the Housing Code (2000:Part 2 at 110), it is argued that this devolution is constitutionally mandated:

It is the constitutional responsibility of both national and provincial government to assign to a municipality the administration of matters such as housing if that matter would be more effectively administered at a local level, and if the municipality has the capacity to administer it. In this regard, and in keeping with the spirit of devolution, the Housing Act provides for the accreditation of municipalities to administer national housing programmes.

The principle of subsidiarity, however, is not one that is clearly constitutionally mandated. Section 156(4) of the Constitution, the section that allows for the assignment of various functions to municipalities, reads as follows:

The national government and provincial governments must assign to a municipality, by agreement and subject to any conditions, the administration of a matter listed in Part A of Schedule 4 or Part A of Schedule 5 which necessarily relates to local government, if –

(a) that matter would most effectively be administered locally; and

(b) the municipality has the capacity to administer it.

The wording of s 156(4) thus allows for the devolution of specific national and provincial competencies where this is agreed upon, and does not amount to a general principle of subsidiarity. The devolution of power through the accreditation process and its meaning for co-operative government is discussed in further detail below.

The Housing Act is the central piece of national legislation regulating housing policy. At the heart of the Act is the aim to "provide for the facilitation of a sustainable housing development process". "Housing development" is defined in s 1 as:

the establishment and maintenance of habitable, stable and sustainable public and private residential environments to ensure viable households and communities in areas allowing convenient access to economic opportunities, and to health, educational and social amenities in which all citizens and permanent residents of the Republic will, on a progressive basis, have access to –

(a) permanent residential structures with secure tenure, ensuring internal and external privacy and providing adequate protection against the elements; and

(b) potable water, adequate sanitary facilities and domestic energy supply.

The Housing Act lays down "general principles" for housing development. These include prioritising the needs of the poor (s 2(1)(a)), consulting with affected parties (s 2(1)(b)), and regulating affordable and sustainable housing development (s 2(1)(c)) through the principles of co-operative government set out in s 41 of the Constitution. This Act describes in detail the powers and duties of the various spheres of government, and the ways in which they should interact and co-operate in order to give effect to s 26.

The Housing Act sets out the role for national government. This is similar to that provided for in the White Paper on Local Government and the general constitutional vision for national government's role in service delivery. In order to "establish and facilitate a sustainable national housing development process" (s 3(1)), the Minister, after consulting with Members of the Executive Council (MECs) and Organised Local Government (OLG), must *inter alia* "determine national policy" (s 3(2)(a)), set national goals and facilitate provincial and local government goals (s 3(2)(b)), monitor the performance of national, provincial and local governments against these goals (s 3(2)(c)), and assist provinces and local government to fulfil their duties under the Act (s 3(2)(d) and (e)). Section 3(4) allows the Minister to regulate funding among the various spheres of government to these ends.

Section 4 of the Act prescribes that the Minister must publish a National Housing Code containing the national housing policy and guidelines regarding the implementation of this policy. Section 5 establishes the South African Housing Development Board to "advise the Minister" (s 5(2)(a)) and "monitor the implementation of national housing policy" (s 5(2)(b)). The Director-General of Housing, in accordance with s 6, must also establish a national housing data bank and a national housing information system.

Section 7(1) provides that provincial government, after consulting with OLG, must "do everything in its power to promote and facilitate the provision of adequate housing in its province within the framework of national housing policy". In order to achieve this, all provincial governments must develop a provincial housing policy (s 7(2)(a)), draft legislation to "ensure effective housing delivery" (s 7(2)(b)), and "co-ordinate housing development in the province" (s 7(2)(d)). Provinces must also draft "multi-year plans" regarding national and provincial housing schemes within the province (s 7(2)(g)).

With regard to a province's relationship with local government, s 7(2)(c) mandates provincial government to "take all reasonable and necessary steps to support and strengthen the capacity of municipalities to effectively exercise their powers and perform their duties in respect of housing development". There is also a duty to support municipalities directly in this regard (s 7(2)(e)). When municipalities fail to perform duties under the Housing Act, provincial government must "intervene by taking any appropriate steps in accordance with s 139 of the Constitution, to ensure the performance of such duty" (s 7(2)(f)). Section 139 of the Constitution is a general clause allowing provinces to "issue directives" or to "assume responsibility" themselves when "a municipality cannot or does not fulfil an executive obligation". Note that s 139 of the Constitution is permissive: provinces have discretion to intervene, while s 7(2) of the Housing Act mandates intervention.

Thus, the Housing Act is fairly flexible in allowing for different configurations in the relationship between the different spheres, particularly with regard to local government's involvement in housing delivery. This framework is closest to the legislative model for co-operative government.

The accreditation process: Shifting competencies

This section will discuss the accreditation process and the implications this would have for the constitutional model of co-operative government. Section 10 of the Housing Act sets out the "accreditation" process for municipalities in order to administer a national housing project. Section 10(1) of the Housing Act entitles a municipality to apply to the MEC to be accredited to administer a national housing programme, subject to directions of the MEC (s 10(3)(a)). In order to do this, the municipality "may exercise such powers and must perform such duties of the relevant provincial housing development board as are necessary for the administration of such national housing programme" (s 10(3)(b)).[36] In essence then, it appears as if, once accredited, a municipality may effectively take the place of the provincial government within the municipality's jurisdiction.

There are two levels of accreditation. The first is that local government can apply to control the administration of non-credit linked individual subsidies; the second is far more substantial, involving the administration of a broad range of projects, including non-credit linked subsidies, project linked subsidies, project linked consolidation subsidies, institutional subsidies, residual amounts of non-credit linked subsidies, and individual consolidation subsidies (Strategic Housing Framework for the Durban Metropolitan Area, 1999:43). At present, no municipalities have been accredited, and there is still much confusion over how the process is to be administered. It appears as if the different provinces are administering the process separately.

According to a local government official, once accredited, local government would then deal directly with national government, by-passing provincial government completely.[37] Until such time as the GJMC, for example, is accredited, the Gauteng provincial government controls the purse strings to housing development. Currently, the Gauteng provincial government has invited local governments within the province to detail a housing scheme and to apply to it for funding. (This does not preclude the province from initiating a scheme if it chooses to.) A selection committee set up by the provincial government then assesses the scheme and decides whether to approve it or not and, if approved, enters into a contract with the local government authority, which then runs the project. The provincial government monitors the funding by controlling how payment is made at various stages of the development. In Gauteng, therefore, it is seen as preferable for local government to administer schemes as, according to a provincial government official, the provincial government does not have the capacity to do so itself.[38]

This statement is interesting in the light of the existing constitutional override provisions, which allow a higher sphere of government to override a lower one, when that government sphere is unable to fulfil its functions. In this case, the provincial government is arguing that since it does not have capacity, the administration of housing projects should be devolved downwards. This would appear to invert the constitutional model of co-operative government.

The minister for housing establishes the criteria for accreditation in consultation with the MEC, and provided that the MEC is satisfied that these criteria are fulfilled, the MEC must accredit the relevant municipality. The GJMC has not yet been accredited, and was aiming to have achieved this within 18 months of the coming into operation of the Housing Strategy at the end of 2001.[39] Yet, by June 2003, the GJMC had still not received these criteria, despite requests to that effect. (In June 2001 the author was informed by a provincial government official that the provincial department was still developing a framework for deciding on the accreditation criteria, and that there was no deadline as to when this had to be completed.) One of the reasons hinted at for delays in the accreditation of the GJMC, is that once the Gauteng MEC approved accreditation of the GJMC, provincial government would no longer have a role to play in the housing delivery programme within the jurisdiction of the GJMC. "By being accredited the GJMC will be able to carry out the function of the Provincial Housing Development Board within its area of jurisdiction. The GJMC will in effect become the Provincial Housing Development Board in the Greater Johannesburg Metropolitan area."[40] The Gauteng housing department's main recent policy document, the Strategic Plan 2002–2005, interestingly also seeks to place greater emphasis on Gauteng's role in housing delivery, placing province at the centre of the delivery process, trying to ensure that it will not become marginalised in the future, once the GJMC is accredited.

The delay in the provision of criteria is perhaps the clearest example that has emerged in the course of the research done for this chapter of non-co-operation and political tension. The Strategic Plan has even been described by a local government official as the province's response to the GJMC's application for accreditation, and as a potential obstacle in the future accreditation process.

This seeming reluctance of the Gauteng provincial government to relinquish power over housing is interesting in the light of debate over the role of provinces in South Africa and a questioning of whether provinces are at all necessary. With the consolidation of municipal power and the increased capacity of local government to provide services, these questions will certainly become more prominent in political debate, as they were in the drafting negotiations for the 1993 and 1996 constitutions. Murray and Simeon reiterate this ongoing debate over the status of provinces:

> Indeed, it [that is, the question of whether South African was to be a federalist country] became one of the central issues in the final certification process before the Constitutional Court. And it remains contested, as provinces and local spheres of government struggle to establish and consolidate entirely new political institutions and processes. While multilevel government is embedded in the constitutional design, it has yet to become fully internalised as a basic fact of government in the eyes of leaders and citizens. Some South African voices call for the abolition of the provinces, and President Mbeki has signalled that significant changes in the federalist regime may be necessary. (Murray & Simeon, 2000:note 56 at 1)

> For some, especially in the ANC, these developments [in local government] foreshadow an "hour-glass" system in which the national and local spheres become the dynamic elements, and the role of provincial governments is reduced, if not eliminated. The argument is that three spheres of government is one too many, and that most of the political and policy benefits of multilevel government could be achieved by a strong local sector working closely with the national government, by-passing the provinces. Such developments are attractive to the governing party because they seem to address national frustration over provincial capacities and its longstanding hostility to federalism. On the other hand, this view may be wishful thinking, as local government is presently in disarray, under-resourced and itself enormously lacking in capacity. The hourglass model therefore remains a dream rather than a reality. (Murray & Simeon, 2000:23)[41]

Thus, the debate over federalism still simmers, and will continue to surface as local governments become better organised and emerge as a force to be contended with by provincial governments. Another argument for re-evaluating the way in which provincial and local governments relate is the artificiality of dividing related competencies between these two spheres.[42]

Housing is viewed as one of the major "services" within provincial competence,[43] unlike other more traditional areas such as water, electricity and gas, which are clearly understood and classified as local government matters. Yet this hierarchy of competence is misleading: local government, apparently frustrated at the lack of effective service delivery, has initiated many of its own housing projects, often funded out of its municipal budget.[44] Furthermore, the GJMC has established its own policy of housing delivery, going so far as to propose its own subsidy mechanism in addition to that of the national government, with different criteria attached. While there is some recognition by the GJMC that there is no real legislative basis for local government housing initiatives, the council nevertheless passes its own resolutions and acts in accordance with these resolutions.

The implications of devolution of power through the accreditation process on the competencies laid out in Schedules 4 and 5 of the Constitution are unclear. The accreditation process would appear to place the accredited municipality in the position of the province. Whether this would then confer the same legislative capacity on local government that the province would have had remains to be seen. Clearly, should litigation arise involving an accredited municipality's housing policy, one of the most important issues will be whether that municipality in fact has the capacity to enact such a policy.

The fact that the GJMC has found it necessary to initiate and fund its own housing projects, despite having no clear legislative basis upon which to do so, also calls into question the wisdom of dividing service delivery between provincial and local competence. Clearly, national departments are desirable and necessary to formulate national policy, set standards, establish budgets, goals and so on, but the practice of housing delivery and the interaction between the Gauteng government and the GJMC indicates that provincial government may not only be unnecessary, but obstructive. The GJMC is seen as being more powerful than the Gauteng provincial government, and better resourced in terms of skills and finances.[45] According to a former housing developer/manager, the White Paper on Local Government sets out an integrated vision of co-operative government, but delivery is hampered by confusion over powers and functions of the various spheres of government. Since the objectives are not clearly spelt out, co-operative government often results in a power struggle. He is particularly critical of provincial government, arguing that while provinces are supposed to be co-ordinating planning, they are not doing this adequately. There is no shared vision or strong leadership coming from the provincial government.[46] He is also critical of the national government for not having a broader planning vision for housing in the country.

Finally, this section will end by examining some of the financial mechanisms for housing delivery, as well as the implications of the accreditation process on the control of money between the different spheres. National housing policy has focussed on the granting of a once-off capital subsidy in terms of the National Housing Subsidy Scheme to qualifying beneficiaries. Originally the subsidy of R15 000, later increased to R16 000, was intended for the building of the house itself. This was done by the national government making funds available to provincial authorities for allocation. A practice developed, however, where more and more of the subsidy was used to finance infrastructure and services. For this reason, the national government then capped the amount to be used on services at R7 500, with the remainder to be spent on the top structure.[47] It should be noted that this subsidy is presently insufficient and other finances are needed. This has led many local governments to contribute to the subsidy out of their own budgets, rather than compromise on the quality of the top structure or services.

The Housing Act is unclear on the financial responsibilities of local government. Many local governments feel that they have been left with the bulk of the work, and argue that requiring local government to participate in housing development amounts to an unfunded mandate.[48] In a discussion of these responsibilities, the Strategic Housing Framework for the Durban Metropolitan Area argues that there are two ways in which this can be interpreted: first, local government can be seen to be responsible only for financing its "planning and facilitation" role; alternatively, since the Act gives all spheres of government "joint responsibility for housing", local government's role includes "the expectation of financial contribution".[49] The DMA Strategic Housing Framework then argues that the latter interpretation is preferable, given the fact that national government is limiting the amount in the subsidy to be spent on services, as well as the perception that "national government is frustrated by the fact that housing delivery appears to be entirely central government subsidy-driven with very limited gearing, and are looking to local authorities and to individuals to make top-up contributions".[50] Clearly, requiring local governments to allocate funding to housing schemes can lead to an inequitable situation as a result of the vastly different financial capabilities of the different municipalities.

Accreditation will also impose an additional financial burden on local governments where they have to take financial risks in acting as a developer, as well as bearing the administrative costs of organising housing development. The Act, however, does make provision for accredited municipalities to be given an agency fee for administering such housing programmes.

The Housing Act empowers local authorities to establish separate business entities to manage housing development, in order to alleviate some of the financial and administrative burden. For example, the GJMC has established the Johannesburg Development Agency (JDA), a s 21 company created out of the recognition that the GJMC lacked the skills and capacity to take on large-scale development. The JDA enables the GJMC to fulfil its mandate at arms' length, outside of local government politics and the strictures of the tender environment.

The financial, political and legal implications of the accreditation process are far from clear. There is the potential for significant change in the relationship between provincial government and an accredited municipality, which may go as far as placing the local government in the position of provincial government, assuming the powers and functions that the provincial government would have had. The ramifications of this process on the legislative competence of local government and the application of conflict resolution mechanisms are issues that will have to be addressed by provincial authorities in defining the powers to be devolved through accreditation.

Conclusion

This chapter concludes by making some observations on three broad areas, namely, the present state of co-operative government, the development of housing policy, and the division of various constitutional competencies. First, the model for co-operative government laid down in the Constitution and in various pieces of legislation is far from rigid. Co-operative government is still crystallising into various patterns, which will emerge in the future. While this "fluidity" has led to some confusion over the various roles, powers and functions of the different spheres of government, it is submitted that it is nevertheless preferable to a prescriptive or rigid model. This is because the thorough-going shift brought about by the Constitution in intergovernmental relations requires time to consolidate and for "best-practices" to emerge. An attempt to force a prefabricated matrix on the various government departments would lack the subtlety and flexibility necessary to cater for the different needs and capacities of the various spheres of government. Of course, in the interim, this fluid model creates the potential for the various departments to develop diverging policies that may lead to political and legal conflict in the future.

Second, the research undertaken through the interview process shows that housing policy itself is developing in all three spheres of government as departments learn from their previous mistakes and political imperatives shift. This is aptly demonstrated in the Gauteng Housing Department's Strategic Plan (2001:15), which outlines the province's new housing policy, through a criticism of previous policy:

> The [previous housing] strategy was driven by an approach of chasing numbers, a mass housing approach. However, in order to deliver at scale, developmental criteria were disregarded. Houses were built everywhere where land could be acquired cheaply. Through this approach, urban sprawl was perpetuated, and quality was compromised. With a view to obtaining cheap land, avoiding local political opposition and escaping costly delays arising from legal action against proposed developments, most new housing developments were located further away from job opportunities, schools, medical services and shops than had been the case under

apartheid. In the course of maximising the output (a million houses), the desired outcome of
a better life for all, and a decent house for all, was not realised.

The state's housing policy to date has been far from perfect. There have been significant
problems in proper planning, in the quality of the building work, and in the rate at which
housing projects are completed. There have also been a number of project-specific problems due to political rivalry, defaulting building contractors, and so on. Despite this, the
national housing department has achieved its target of a million houses within the first five
years and is more or less satisfied with the continued rate of housing delivery.

One aspect of the housing policy sector is important to note for the purposes of this
chapter: to date, there has been hardly any large-scale planning on a national or provincial basis. Local governments have been required to put together an Integrated
Development Programme (IDP), but there has been no similar provision at provincial
level. In 2002, provinces were required to present their strategic plans for housing, and
national government has stated that it wants to consolidate all these municipal plans to
create a nation-wide housing strategy.[51] This process is interesting, as it will effectively
invert the existing top-down decision-making process. It will also enable national government to have access to much more information from local governments before co-
ordinating the national strategy, which is expected to culminate in a second housing
white paper (Strategic Housing Framework for the Durban Metropolitan Area, 1999:63).

Thus, the state is taking steps to identify and remedy the problems experienced by the
various housing departments. Yet it should be noted that none of the specific problems
identified in housing delivery relate directly to problems in co-operative government.
This is not to say that there are not strained intergovernmental relationships, but rather,
that these cannot be identified specifically, and can only be spoken of in general terms, as
no consistent problems (other than the lack of inter-provincial planning and co-ordination) have emerged in the course of the research undertaken for this chapter.

In addition to intergovernmental relations between the various provincial housing
departments, there is also a need for greater co-operation between the different
departments. While interdepartmental co-ordination between departments such as
housing, education and health does occur on an informal level, there is no clear legislative framework in which this can be facilitated. This would perhaps be best organised
at provincial level to ensure adequate planning across departments and municipal
jurisdictions.

The third observation relates to the competencies outlined in Schedules 4 and 5 of the
Constitution. The fact that housing is a concurrent competence of national and provincial government means that provinces are empowered to enact their own housing policy,

which may differ substantially from national policy, provided national government cannot demonstrate that it is in the national interest for housing to be centrally regulated.[52] At present, provincial housing policy has replicated national policy to a large degree, so there has not been significant conflict, particularly in provinces controlled by the majority party. In Gauteng, for example, the Gauteng Housing Act 6 of 1998 is substantially the same as the national Housing Act. Indeed, one of the objectives listed by the Gauteng Housing Department's Strategic Plan (2001:61) is to enact "Provincial Housing Legislation that is in line with National Legislation". Nevertheless, there remains the potential for provinces to enact substantially different housing legislation, and national policy should be wary of simply assuming this will never be done.

Furthermore, specifying housing as a national and provincial competence does not provide sufficient clarity in the event of conflicting municipal policy. It is not unrealistic to suggest that a local government authority that has been accredited would create its own, conflicting housing policy. The GJMC, for example, has already suggested a different subsidy mechanism, where the GJMC will grant a top-up subsidy of R4 000 in addition to the national subsidy if beneficiaries have made a contribution themselves (GJMC Housing Strategy, 2000:19, 31). Should a different policy result in conflict, the question would obviously arise whether local government is indeed empowered to make such a decision in the first place and, if so, what the procedure is for determining which policy or legislation trumps the other.

In conclusion, while the research undertaken has not revealed glaring conflicts and problems in intergovernmental relations in the context of housing delivery, it has nevertheless revealed that there are some tensions and confusion over the roles of the . various spheres of government. Co-operative government can best be described as rather haphazard and, in some cases, competitive. The responsibility undertaken by the various municipalities depends largely on their capacity and willingness to undertake housing development. Many municipalities are unwilling to take on housing delivery as a responsibility for fear of being saddled with an unfunded mandate. The bigger metropolitan centres, on the other hand, have eagerly taken on housing as a core function, viewing it as politically crucial in the power struggle with provinces and for political credibility. The model of co-operative government provided for in the Housing Act allows for all of these possibilities, laying down principles rather than prescriptive frameworks. While this system provides the necessary flexibility, it also potentially allows certain spheres of government to abdicate responsibility. Once again, it needs to be emphasised that co-operative government is still in its formative stages, and as the specific roles and duties of the different spheres become clearer, more concrete tensions may emerge.

Appendix

The White Paper on Housing (1994:para 5.2.1) sets out functions for the national department of housing as follows:

- Setting broad national housing delivery goals and negotiate provincial delivery goals in support thereof;

- determining broad national housing policy, in consultation with relevant other national departments and provincial governments where relevant, in so far as it relates to:

  - Land development and use (especially in respect of State land holdings),

  - land title and registration systems,

  - minimum national norms and standards,

  - national subsidy programmes,

  - fund allocation to provinces,

  - fund allocation to national facilitative programmes,

  - mobilisation of funds for land acquisition, infrastructural development, housing provision and end user finance,

  - guidelines for the spatial restructuring of cities and towns and rural settlement patterns;

- adopting or promoting legislation to give effect to national housing policies;

- establish a national institutional and funding framework for housing;

- monitoring national and, in liaison with provincial governments, provincial performance against housing delivery and budgetary goals and accounting to the national parliament in this regard;

- overseeing and directing the activities of national statutory advisory and facilitative institutions and accounting to national parliament in this regard;

- negotiate for the systematic increasing of the national apportionment of State budget to housing; and

- account to national parliament for the performance of the sector against set targets and efficiency/effectiveness parameters.

The following role is envisaged for provincial government (at para 5.2.2):

- Setting of provincial housing delivery goals and performance parameters within the context and in support of national delivery goals;

- determining provincial housing policy (within broad national guidelines), so far as it relates to:

  - Minimum housing norms and standards in the province,

  - development priorities and programmes,

- urban and rural development,
- land identification and planning within the province, including performance criteria,
- urban spatial restructuring,
- rural settlement restructuring;
- monitoring provincial housing delivery and accounting to the provincial legislature in this regard;
- overseeing and directing the housing activities of provincial statutory advisory and executive bodies, local authorities as well as the activities of provincial facilitative institutions, and accounting to the provincial legislature in this regard;
- liaising and negotiating with the National Ministry and Department as well as national statutory and facilitative bodies in respect of:
  - Fiscal transfers for housing to the province,
  - provincial priority status in respect of national facilitative programmes for housing, and
  - national housing policy and programmes.

It is recognised that provincial governments are accountable to the people who have democratically elected them in the provinces, for the delivery of housing. A leading role for these governments in enabling sustained delivery of housing in the provinces, within broad national housing policy guidelines, is envisaged. At the same time, it has to be recognised that the Minister of Housing is accountable to Parliament for overall sectoral performance. A balance between the functions and powers at national and provincial level to reflect these accountabilities, will be vital to success.

Finally, the White Paper (para 5.2.3) has the following to say on the role of local government:

The physical processes of planning and housing is very much a local community matter. The role of metropolitan and especially local government in enabling, promoting and facilitating the provision of housing to all segments of the population in areas under their jurisdiction, can therefore not be over emphasised. The absence of legitimate, functional and viable local authority structures will jeopardize both the pace and quality of implementation of housing programmes.

The following housing functions are envisaged to be performed at metropolitan and/or local level:

- Setting metropolitan / local housing delivery goals;
- identification and designation of land for housing purposes;
- the regulation of safety and health standards in housing provision;
- the creation and maintenance of a public environment conducive to viable development and healthy communities;

- the mediation of conflict in the development process;

- the initiation, planning coordination, promotion and enablement of appropriate housing development;

- facilitative support to housing delivery agencies;

- planning, funding and provision of bulk engineering services;

- provision and maintenance of revenue generating services (if not provided by specialised utilities / suppliers);

- provision of community and recreational facilities in residential areas;

- welfare housing;

- land planning in areas under their jurisdiction (in terms of laid down performance criteria, possibly at provincial and even national level); and

- regulation of land use and development.

Endnotes

1 The term "co-operative government" is used in a narrow, technical sense in this paper, and refers to the model of government laid down in Chapter 3 of the South African Constitution. Exactly what is meant by this idea is discussed in greater detail below. Furthermore, the word "government" is used throughout in preference to the word "governance", in order to conform to the terminology used in the Constitution itself.

2 The Constitution of the Republic of South Africa, Act 108 of 1996.

3 Section 41(2) of the Constitution makes provision for Parliament to enact legislation to regulate "structures and institutions to promote and facilitate intergovernmental relations". There has, as yet, been no specific legislation in this area, yet many related pieces of legislation have been passed, such as the Housing Act 107 of 1997, which deals with co-operative government in the area of housing. The White Paper on Local Government (1998) is also a good example of a policy document that aims to flesh out the State's policy on co-operative government. Christina Murray (2001:76) points out that the "Budget Council and the Committee of Education Ministers are the only major intergovernmental relations institutions established by statute" and that there is no legislation dealing specifically with this area.

4 "Housing" is listed in Part A of Schedule 4 to the Constitution, which lists areas of concurrent competence of national and provincial government. This means that both national and provincial governments are competent to enact legislation to regulate housing.

5 Act 107 of 1997. The Housing Act was assented to on the 27 November 1997 and came into force on 1 April 1998.

6 *Government of the RSA and Others v Grootboom and Others* 2001 (1) SA 46 (CC); 2000 (11) BCLR 1169 (CC), hereafter referred to as *Grootboom*.

7 The Bill of Rights also protects collective "third-generation rights". This includes the collective right to environmental protection in s 24(b) of the Constitution, and certain rights to self-determination and protection of minorities in s 30 and s 31 of the Constitution.

8 See, for example, *August and Another v Electoral Commission and Others* 1999 (3) SA 1 (CC); 1999 (4) BCLR 363 (CC) at para 16, where Sachs J held that "[t]he right to vote by its very nature imposes positive obligations

upon the legislature and the executive. A date for elections has to be promulgated, the secrecy of the ballot box secured and the machinery established for managing the process." Furthermore, s 7(2) of the Constitution places an obligation on the state to "respect, protect, promote and fulfil the rights in the Bill of Rights", further indicating both the positive and negative implications of all rights.

9   See, for example, Basson, D. (1989); Dlamini, C. R. M. (1990); Sachs, A. (1990); Haysom, N. (1992); Mureinik, E. (1992); Davis, D. (1992); Corder, H. *et al.* (1992); SA Law Commission (1994:180–199); and De Villiers, B. (1994:599).

10   *Ex Parte Chairperson of the Constitutional Assembly: In re Certification of the Constitution of the Republic of South Africa, 1996* 1996 (4) SA 744 (CC); 1996 (10) BCLR 1253 (CC) at para 77.

11   In the *Maastricht Guidelines on Violations of Economic, Social and Cultural Rights* (1997) at para 14, a number of examples of negative violations are provided:

" (a)   The formal removal or suspension of legislation necessary for the continued enjoyment of an economic, social and cultural right that is currently enjoyed;

(b)   The active denial of such rights to particular individuals or groups, whether through legislated or enforced discrimination;

(c)   The active support for measures adopted by third parties which are inconsistent with economic, social and cultural rights;

(d)   The adoption of legislation or policies which are manifestly incompatible with pre-existing legal obligations relating to these rights, unless it is done with the purpose and effect of increasing equality and improving the realization of economic, social and cultural rights for the most vulnerable groups;

(e)   The calculated obstruction of, or halt to, the progressive realization of a right protected by the Covenant, unless the State is acting within a limitation permitted by the Covenant or it does so due to a lack of available resources or force majeure;

(f)   The reduction or diversion of specific public expenditure, when such reduction or diversion results in the non-enjoyment of such rights and is not accompanied by adequate measure to ensure minimum rights for everyone."

12   *Grootboom* at para 23: "[a]ll the rights in our Bill of Rights are inter-related and mutually supporting. There can be no doubt that human dignity, freedom and equality, the foundation values of our society, are denied those who have no food, clothing or shelter. Affording socio-economic rights to all people therefore enables them to enjoy the other rights enshrined in Chapter 2."

13   1998 (1) SA 765 (CC); 1997 (12) BCLR 1696 (CC).

14   *Minister of Health and Others v Treatment Action Campaign and Others*, a decision of the Constitutional Court handed down on 5 July 2002, CCT 08/02, as yet unreported.

15   It may perhaps have been preferable for the Constitutional Assembly not to have separated s 26(1) and (2), but to have drafted them as one right. This would also have helped to prevent confusion on the relation between s 26(2) and (3), in *Betta Eiendomme (Pty) Ltd v Ekple-Epoh* 2000 (4) SA 468 (W) at para 7.3, for example.

16   Section 41(1)(h)(iii) provides that the different spheres of government must co-operate by *inter alia* "informing one another of, and consulting one another on, matters of common interest".

17   In this judgment, the court was at pains to emphasise the inter-relatedness of the rights in the Bill of Rights.

18   This analysis of the state's obligation as a duty to take reasonable measures with two qualifiers is slightly different to the Constitutional Court's analysis of the structure of s 26(2), which sees s 26(2) as consisting of three elements: "[t]he extent of the State's obligation is defined by three key elements that are considered

separately: (a) the obligation to 'take reasonable legislative and other measures'; (b) 'to achieve the progressive realisation' of the right; and (c) 'within available resources'." Little turns on this distinction.

19 General Comment 3, 1990:para 9, cited in *Grootboom* at para 45.

20 Article 2(1) of the ICESCR states that '[e]ach State Party to the present Covenant undertakes to take steps, individually and through international assistance and co-operation, especially economic and technical, to the maximum of its available resources, with a view to achieving progressively the full realization of the rights recognized in the present Covenant by all appropriate means, including particularly the adoption of legislative measures.'

21 General Comment 3, 1990:para 10. The importance of the minimum core obligation to the Covenant is demonstrated in the following extract: "[i]f the Covenant were to be read in such a way as not to establish such a minimum core obligation, it would be largely deprived of its *raison d'être*".

22 Chapter 4 of the Constitution deals with Parliament; Chapter 5, The President and the National Executive; Chapter 6, Provincial Government; and Chapter 7, Local Government.

23 See *Ex Parte Chairperson of the Constitutional Assembly: In re Certification of the Constitution of the Republic of South Africa, 1996* 1996 (4) SA 744 (CC); 1996 (10) BCLR 1253 (CC) and *Ex Parte Chairperson of the National Assembly: In re Certification of the Amended Text of the Constitution of the Republic of South Africa, 1996* 1997 (2) SA 97 (CC); 1997 (1) BCLR 1 (CC).

24 Murray (2001:note 3 at 76). Murray also points out that this tendency is well illustrated by the Liquor Bill case (*Ex Parte the President of the Republic of South Africa In re: Constitutionality of the Liquor Bill* 2001 (1) SA 732 (CC); 2000 (1) BCLR 1 (CC)), "the most important case concerning the division of powers between the national and provincial governments", where the matter was not referred to the Constitutional Court by a sphere of government, but by the President who was concerned about the bill's potential unconstitutionality.

25 *Ex Parte Speaker of the National Assembly: In Re Dispute Concerning the Constitutionality of Certain Provisions of the National Education Policy Bill 83 of 1995* 1996 (3) SA 289 (CC); 1996 (4) BCLR 518 (CC). Note that this case was heard under the Interim Constitution.

26 1999 (3) SA 657 (CC); 1999 (4) BCLR 382 (CC).

27 Obeng Mireku (1999:565–568), in a comment on this case, criticised the court for defining co-operative government hierarchically, and for undermining the many forms of horizontal arrangements of government power. With respect, it is submitted that this criticism is not justified from a reading of the case.

28 *Executive Council of the Western Cape v Minister of Provincial Affairs and Constitutional Development of the Republic of South Africa; Executive Council of KwaZulu-Natal v President of the Republic of South Africa* 2000 (1) SA 661 (CC); 1999 (12) BCLR 1360 (CC).

29 The Local Government: Municipal Structures Act 117 of 1998.

30 *Ex Parte the President of the Republic of South Africa In re: Constitutionality of the Liquor Bill* 2001 (1) SA 732 (CC); 2000 (1) BCLR 1 (CC).

31 *DVB Behuising v North West Provincial Government and Another* 2001 (1) SA 500 (CC); 2000 (4) BCLR 374 (CC).

32 *National Gambling Board v Premier of KwaZulu-Natal and Others* 2002 (2) SA 715 (CC); 2002 (2) SA BCLR 156 (CC).

33 These words are italicised in the original text to indicate that there is a definition provided in the glossary at the end of the White Paper, and not in order to emphasise them. The definition provided is as follows: "An enabling framework is a legal, regulatory or institutional framework which makes certain activities possible through removing obstacles to initiating those activities, or providing support for those activities. An enabling

framework does not oblige anyone to perform specific actions or prescribe the details of how activities must be performed. Rather, an enabling framework creates a supportive space in which activities can be initiated."

34 See Gutto (1998:para11, note 65). The Development Facilitation Act 67 of 1995 was also pivotal in bringing about the new approach to housing development. The Act aimed to "facilitate and speed up the implementation of reconstruction and development programmes and projects in relation to land" (Preamble to the Development Facilitation Act).

35 White Paper on Housing (1994:para 5.2.1.1 at 35). No reasoning is provided for this assertion in the document itself. See *DVB Behuising* (para 17, note 76) where the Constitutional Court held that there is no presumption in favour of national or provincial competencies.

36 These powers and duties are subject to various accounting regulations in s 10(4).

37 This interpretation is different to that given by Doreen Atkinson "Local Government in Intergovernmental Relations: Towards Co-operative Governance?" in Atkinson & Reitzes (eds) (1998:27). Atkinson argues that even after accreditation no decision-making powers will be allocated to local government: "What this means, in practice, is that accredited local authorities would have the power to deal with all the paperwork surrounding applications for subsidies – without the actual power to allocate those subsidies. This power would remain with the Provincial Housing Boards, who will continue to follow strict Departmental regulations. The main purpose of this arrangement is to bring the paperwork closer to the beneficiaries." With respect, it is submitted that this interpretation is incorrect.

38 This view was contradicted by another Gauteng provincial housing official, who claimed that Gauteng presently has greater capacity to be involved in housing delivery, but it is preferable that this be done at local government level.

39 Previously, in an interview with another official from the GJMC Department of Housing, at the beginning of 2001, this date was set at three years within the coming into operation of the Housing Strategy (2000), which was not yet in force at that date.

40 GJMC Housing Strategy (2000:50). When questioned on this issue, one local government official said that "[a]ccreditation may be a threat to some Provincial officers hence the investigation by a firm of auditors, which has been commissioned by the National Government". Unfortunately, it was not possible to follow up this cryptic remark.

41 See also Haysom (2001:note 57 at 57,58) for a similar observation.

42 For provincial government to develop a housing scheme, for example, the land must be correctly zoned and municipal co-operation is required for water, electricity and sewage provision, and so on. Urban planning also requires that schools, hospitals and business districts be accounted for.

43 Other areas of national and provincial competence, such as health and transport, appear to be similarly "staked out" as provincial matters.

44 According to the figures published in the "Budget Guide for Residents: 2000/01", R199 957 000 is allocated to "housing", out of a total operating budget of R7 293 433 000.

45 For example, the budgets of the GJMC (Johannesburg) and DMA (Durban) exceed those of their respective provinces (Murray, 2001:note 3 at 75).

46 This weakness is recognised by the Gauteng Department of Housing in an evaluation of its strengths and weaknesses. As one of the "threats" to housing delivery, it states that "[t]here is no coordinated approach at provincial level to ensure that integrated development is achieved" (Strategic Plan 2002-2005: Gauteng Co-Investment Partnership for Housing, 2001:26).

47 National Department of Housing Norms and Standards. The Norms and Standards further provide that a minimum of 30 square metre top structure must be built.

48 See also Strategic Housing Framework for the Durban Metropolitan Area (1999:42): "[t]he issue of whether or not the [Housing] Act implies an unfunded mandate to local authorities is a question which has engendered much recent debate."

49 Strategic Housing Framework for the Durban Metropolitan Area (1999:42).

50 Ibid.

51 The Gauteng Strategic Housing Framework, which has already been referred to above, is an example of a document outlining the provincial housing strategy.

52 Case law has demonstrated that it is relatively easy for national government to meet the requirements set out in s 146 of the Constitution for national legislation to prevail over provincial legislation. The cases discussed above dealing with disputes in areas of concurrent national and provincial competence illustrate this point well.

References

Atkinson, D. & Reitzes, M. (eds) (1998) *From a Tier to a Sphere: Local Government in the New South African Constitutional Order.* Johannesburg: Heinemann.

Basson, D. (1989) "Economic Rights: A Focal Point in the Debate on Human Rights and Labour Relations in South Africa", 4 *South African Public Law* 120.

Bekker, G. (nd) "The Right of Access to Adequate Housing and Children's Right to Basic Shelter." In *Report on the Realisation of Socio-Economic Rights – 2000.*

Bremner, L. (2000) "Post-Apartheid Urban Geography: A Case Study of Greater Johannesburg's Rapid Land Development Programme", 17 *Development Southern Africa* 87.

Budget Guide for Residents 2000/01 for Greater Johannesburg.

Chaskalson, M., Spitz, D., Woolman, S., Kentridge, J., Klaaren, J. & Marcus, G. (eds) (1999) *Constitutional Law of South Africa.* Kenwyn: Juta.

Community Agency for Social Enquiry (CASE) (nd) "Intergovernmental Relations and Provincial Government", report available at http://www.case.org.za/htm/intgov3.htm.

Corder, H., Kahanovitz, S., Murphy, J., Murray, C., O'Regan, K., Sarkin, J., Smith, H. & Steytler, N. (1992) *A Charter for Social Justice: A Contribution to the South African Bill of Rights Debate.* Unpublished.

Davis, D. (1992) "The Case Against Inclusion of Socio-economic Rights in a Bill of Rights Except as Directive Principles", 8 *South African Journal on Human Rights* 475.

Davis, D., Cheadle, H. & Haysom, N. (eds) (1997) *Fundamental Rights in the Constitution: Commentary and Cases.* Kenwyn: Juta.

De Villiers, B. (1994) "Social and Economic Rights." In Van Wyk, D., Dugard, J., De Villiers, B. & Davis, D. (eds) *Rights and Constitutionalism: The New South African Legal Order.* Kenwyn: Juta.

De Villiers, B. (ed.) (1994) *Birth of a Constitution.* Kenwyn: Juta.

De Villiers, B. (1997) "Intergovernmental Relations in South Africa", 12 *South African Public Law* 197.

De Waal, J., Currie, I. & Erasmus, G. (2000) *Bill of Rights Handbook.* Kenwyn: Juta.

Dlamini, C. R. M. (1990) "The South African Law Commission's Working Paper on Group and Human Rights: Towards a Bill of Rights for South Africa", 5 *South African Public Law* 91.

Friedman, S. & Humphries, R. (eds) (1993) *Federalism and Its Foes.* Johannesburg: Westro.

Gauteng Department of Housing's housing policy and projects. See http://www.housing.gpg.gov.za/

Gutto, S. (1998) "Housing." In *The Law of South Africa* 11 (First Reissue) 1. Durban: Butterworths,

Haysom, N. (1992) "Constitutionalism, Majoritarian Democracy and Socio-Economic Rights", 8 *South African Journal on Human Rights* 451.

Haysom, N. (2001) "The Origins of Co-operative Governance: The 'Federal' Debates in the Constitution Making Process." In Levy, N. & Tapscott, C. (eds) *Intergovernmental Relations in South Africa: The Challenges of Co-operative Government.* Cape Town: Idasa.

Housing Strategy of the Greater Johannesburg Metropolitan Council (2000).

Levy, N. & Tapscott, C. (2001) "Intergovernmental Relations in South Africa: The Challenges of Co-operative Government." In Levy, N. & Tapscott, C. (eds) *Intergovernmental Relations in South Africa: The Challenges of Co-operative Government.* Cape Town: Idasa.

Liebenberg, S. (1997) "Housing." In Davis, D., Cheadle, H. & Haysom, N. (eds) *Fundamental Rights in the Constitution: Commentary and Cases.*

Liebenberg, S. (1999) "Socio-Economic Rights." In Chaskalson, M. *et al. Constitutional Law of South Africa.* Kenwyn: Juta.

Meyer, J. (1998) *Local Government Law.* Johannesburg: Butterworths.

Mireku, O. (1999) "No Victor, No Vanquished? A Comment on *Premier, Western Cape v President of the Republic of South Africa",* 15 *South African Journal on Human Rights* 563.

Mureinik, E. (1992) "Beyond a Charter of Luxuries: Economic Rights in the Constitution", 8 *South African Journal on Human Rights* 464.

Murray, C. (2001) "The Constitutional Context of Intergovernmental Relations in South Africa." In Levy, N. & Tapscott, C. (eds) *Intergovernmental Relations in South Africa: The Challenges of Co-operative Government.* Cape Town: Idasa.

Murray, C. & Simeon, R. (2000) "Multilevel Governance in South Africa: An Interim Report." Unpublished Paper.

National Department of Housing's housing policy and projects. See http:www.housing.gov.za/

National Department of Housing (1997) "Living Cities: Urban Development Framework."

National Housing Code (2000) National Department of Housing.

Pillay, K. (2000) "The Rights to Accomodation, Housing and Shelter in the South African Constitution." In Bekker, G. (ed.) *A Compilation of Essential Documents on the Rights to Accommodation, Housing and Shelter, Economic and Social Rights Series,* Volume 5. Centre for Human Rights, University of Pretoria.

Pimstone, G. (1998) "The Constitutional Basis of Local Government in South Africa." Occasional Papers, Konrad-Adenauer Stiftung.

Sachs, A. (1990) "Towards a Bill of Rights in a Democratic South Africa", 6 *South African Journal on Human Rights* 1.

SA Law Commission (1994) *Final Report on Group and Human Rights* (Project 58).

Sealey, S. (ed.) (2000) *HRC Quarterly Review: Local Government The First Five Years.* Johannesburg: Human Rights Committee.

Sparks, A. (1994) *Tomorrow Is Another Country: The Inside Story of South Africa's Negotiated Revolution.* Johannesburg: Struik.

Strategic Housing Framework for the Durban Metropolitan Area (1999)

Strategic Plan 2002–2005: Gauteng Co-Investment Partnership for Housing (final draft 21 November 2001).

Sunstein, C. (2002) "Social and Economic Rights? Lessons from South Africa." In Chicago John M. Olin *Law and Economics* (2nd series) 12 Constitutional Forum 2.

Van Wyk, D., Dugard, J., De Villiers, B. & Davis, D. (eds) (1994) *Rights and Constitutionalism: The New South African Legal Order.* Kenwyn: Juta.

6

Decentralisation and its Impact on Service Delivery in Education in Post-apartheid South Africa

Anne Mc Lennan

Introduction

In 1994, just prior to the election of an African National Congress (ANC)-led Government of National Unity (GNU) in South Africa, the ANC articulated the following vision for the governance of the future education and training system:

> Governance at all levels of the integrated national system of education and training will max-imise democratic participation of stakeholders, including the broader community, and will be oriented towards equity, effectiveness, efficiency, accountability, and the sharing of responsi-bility. (ANC, 1994a:22)

Over the next few years, this vision of governance became the focal point of a set of policies to transform an education system characterised by inequalities in resource allocation according to race, class and geographical area. This particular view of governance as democratic participation reflected a fundamental concern to enhance the legitimacy and quality of an increasingly decentralised education system.

The governance approach adopted incorporated several key assumptions that reflected global understandings about education change, as well the unique context and history of South African education. The first assumption was that education enhances and sustains national development. Education was seen as central to the process of "nation building" and the economic, social and political development of the country, because it empowered people "to participate effectively in all processes of democratic society, economic activity, cultural expression and community life" (Department of Education, 1995:5). A second assumption, linked to this focus, was that improved, efficient and decentralised management would ensure delivery at all levels in the education system. The apartheid education system had been managed neither effectively, in the sense of ensuring delivery of services, nor efficiently, in the sense of saving and utilising limited resources. A third assumption was that democratic participation was key to education change and delivery. The apartheid governing structure had been characterised by a non-participative, hierarchical and secretive ethos that was neither accountable nor democratic. The many stakeholders (parents, learners, educators and local communities) making up the education system had had limited voice in decisions that affected their development. In addition, the various delivery systems lacked political, financial and management accountability as a result of an over-centralisation of control and the limited legitimacy of the political authorities. The emphasis on participation was motivated by the crisis of legitimacy and accountability that confronted education. However, it was also aimed at endorsing the democratic principles that had formed the basis of the struggle against apartheid education (ANC, 1995). Finally, it was assumed that democratic governance would ensure equity and redress. Equity concerns were directed at quantitative issues such as the redistribution of resources, universal access and improved provision and facilities, often (but not always) at the expense of considering the social relations of power and domination that comprised education.

These principles – education for development, effective and efficient management, democratic accountability, shared (democratic) responsibility and equity – which underpinned the approach to education governance and transformation in South Africa, incorporated a linear conception of development, dependent on the responsible and legitimate action of education stakeholders in government and communities. The policy adopted, in particular the South Africa Schools Act 84 of 1996, reflected a worldwide trend to transfer powers to local levels on the assumption that it provided greater opportunities for the regulation, and technical and financial support of development. In the South African context, it was assumed that education stakeholders would fill the gap created by the reduced role of the state as provider of education. This approach reflected an attempt to move away from a hierarchical system of organisation to one that enabled and supported local school development. Schools had greater responsibility in the new education system, but education departments continued to have a major task in assisting and supporting schools to create the conditions for effective teaching and learning.

This approach reflected the more fundamental changes that took place after April 1994 when the democratic elections heralded the development of new governance systems, which represented the negotiated compromises of the political settlement. In the first few years of democratic government, a new semi-federal state system emerged from the fragmented apartheid systems of the past, which had included race-determined parliaments, departments and territories. In the first five years of democracy, the national Department of Education (DoE) developed a comprehensive framework for the governance and delivery of education in South Africa. Policy focused on building a national (high quality and equal) education system whilst simultaneously decentralising decision-making to the lowest possible level in the system.

This chapter explores the relationships between globalisation, development and democratic governance in the South African education sector by tracking the process and implications of decentralisation. It is argued that a combination of globalisation and the particular history and context of education development seems to limit policy choices and operational boundaries for the state in education delivery. In particular, the adoption of the form or mantle of globalisation, without engaging the content or context of education change in South Africa, seems to result in limited capacity at all levels in the system to achieve redistribution or democratisation. This raises the question of whether it is possible to achieve effective service delivery (for development) in impoverished contexts through decentralisation and minimal state intervention.

The chapter briefly reviews some of the key theories and assumptions that underpin understandings about globalisation and governance. This is followed by a description of the forms and structures of the South African education system at the end of apartheid and under the democratic dispensation. Finally, the chapter explores in some depth two key assumptions about the impacts of decentralisation, specifically, its likely effects on development and democratisation. In particular, these final sections explore the tensions and contradictions that emerge from the influence of globalisation on governance practices in South Africa. It is argued that the emphasis on equity, decentralisation of authority, self-managing schools, professionalism, outcomes-based learning and quality assurance, evident in the approach to education governance, was a consequence of the particular history of education development in South Africa, as well as the tendency to utilise global knowledge and understandings.

Decentralisation and globalisation

Many developing countries have focused on education as a primary tool for national development. This fits a popular conception of the modernisation process as involving the development of an educated middle class, through (usually Western-style) education expansion, to sustain economic growth and social transformation (Saqeb, 1985; Stadler, 1987). Education growth and delivery expanded dramatically between 1950 and 1970, but declined in the 1980s due to economic crises in the developing world (Graham-Brown, 1991). Despite a growing sense of disillusion with the ability of education systems to enhance and sustain development, many aid agencies and nation-states continued to view education as a panacea for underdevelopment and poverty. This is evident, for example, in the World Bank and United Nations Educational, Scientific and Cultural Organisation (UNESCO) policy of "education for all". In addition, many marginalised groups still see education as a means to escape the limitations of poverty and exclusion. South Africa, emerging from a history of racial oppression is no different from other newly independent states in decades past, in asserting the promise of "education for all" as a commitment to future development and a means of improving the legitimacy of the new government. However, given the global context, the expanded delivery of education must take place within a context of economic crisis, increasing polarisation between different racial, ethnic and religious groups and a reduction in the purpose of education to the production of human capital to feed economic growth (Graham-Brown, 1991).

The governing structures of emerging national education systems, traditionally, are centralised and hierarchical. Popkewitz (1996) suggests that the construction of the modern Swedish welfare state brought a collection of education actors, providers and institutions under the professional and administrative machinery of the state. He argues that this type of governing, which reserves responsibility for planning and evaluation for the central state ministry and it bureaucracies, embodies certain ideals of social engineering through the application of a universal traditional knowledge and neutral professional expertise to regulate educational affairs. Lauglo and McLean (1985) argue similarly that a degree of centralised control of educational processes seems necessary for modernisation and nation building. Certainly, many developing countries, in an attempt to expand access and encourage social and economic development have placed a strong emphasis on central planning and hierarchical forms of control in education and other social service systems (Mutahaba *et al.*, 1993; Graham-Brown 1991). Centralised control does seem to have the benefit of standardisation of curricula, examinations and qualifications, equity of provision and efficiency. Lyons (1985:87) also suggests that centralisation builds national unity and creates management efficiencies. However, centralised governing systems were criticised for being unable to deal with school level problems resulting in a large degree of inertia and stasis in education provision (Popkewitz, 1996). In addition, it is suggested that such systems tend to reduce teachers to the level of skilled operatives in a bureaucratic system, required to follow rules and regulations, which stifles innovation and creativity.

Given these perceived limitations of centralised and hierarchical governing structures, there has been a tendency, in line with the opening up of the concept of governance more broadly, to shift authority and responsibility both down and out of the education system. Lauglo (1996:40) suggests that this process is motivated by three values – notably "a politically-legitimate dispersal of authority, efficiency in using available resources, and improvement in the quality of service provided". The first is achieved through a process, which is directed towards democratising educational decision-making through the estab-lishment of school governing councils with parent and community participation (Fullan, 1997; Schaeffer, 1996 and 1997). This worldwide phenomenon is motivated in part by a political rationale to improve democratic participation in education provision. However, it is also linked to a managerialist trend to make education services more responsive and accountable to the communities they serve. Most governing councils at the school level assume a liberal democratic notion of representation of stakeholders and are assumed to contribute to the quality of education delivery at the school level. Decentralisation can bring about a closer relationship between education and development and improve the quality of schooling by making it more relevant to local needs (Shaeffer, 1997). Rondinelli (1989) argues that central governments are primarily concerned with macroeconomic issues and maintaining their power base, and only secondarily concerned with the provi-sion of services such as education. Central government ministries see themselves as direct-ly accountable to their bureaucratic superiors and are less responsive to the needs and demands of the people being provided with the service. Creating a sense of community ownership of schooling would make local communities more willing to take on the costs of education delivery and planning (Shaeffer, 1996).

The decentralisation of the control of education is related to a particular country's political and ideological commitment to democratisation and extending participation in decision-making about educational processes (Lauglo & McLean, 1985; Shaeffer, 1997). In support of the decentralisation of authority down the education system, the sharing of responsibility with other actors and the provision of greater management autonomy to the school, Shaeffer (1997:225) suggests that the decentralisation of control improves the quality of education and its relevance to local conditions and needs. He asserts that bring-ing decision-making about education closer to the level where the decisions will make real differences will encourage local innovation, increase local accountability with regard to the provision and quality of education and stimulate community participation and own-ership of education. These purposes are evident in, for example, the local management of schools initiative in Britain and in the shift to school councils in Canada, Russia and many other countries worldwide (Fullan, 1997). Lauglo and McLean (1985:1) suggest that these developments indicate "some loss of faith in the value, validity and monopoly of state education systems and a willingness to broaden or change the distribution of edu-cational power". Many of these decentralisation initiatives are mooted as a means to ensure a wider representation of legitimate interests in education, but also as an attempt to share the growing costs of education provision (Graham-Brown, 1991). There is a gen-eral acceptance that education stakeholders have the right to participate in decisions that affect their education services. However, the extent of decentralisation of control over issues such as the provision of education, school organisation, curriculum content and process, teacher management and resourcing is contested.

There is no direct evidence to support the assumption that the decentralisation of power and authority improves democratic interaction or development at the school level. In many cases, it seems to exacerbate interest group conflict, especially in a context of diminishing resources for education investment. Some argue that the shift in the locus of control of education forms part of an attempt to diffuse responsibility for intractable education problems. Structural adjustment, with its emphasis on cost recovery and efficiency, resulted in reduced spending on public services, price increases and continued economic stagnation in many developing countries. A consequence of this process, for many newly independent countries with recently won victories in the universal provision of basic education, was reduced spending on education. The hardest hit were impoverished rural communities who lacked the basic resources to fill in the.gaps created by reduced public expenditure and provision (Graham-Brown, 1991).

Shifting responsibility to local schools and school communities for the financing and support of education, in a context of scarce resources, can therefore be seen as an attempt to "privatise" education provision and the conflicts that may arise. Often, traditional arguments for decentralisation, as involving a redistribution of power, greater efficiency and sensitivity to local communities, disguise a more basic rationale of legitimisation (Lauglo & McLean, 1985). A consequence of this marketisation of education services, especially in developing countries, is the increasing impoverishment and marginalisation of poor communities. In fact, Graham-Brown (1991) argues that it has shifted emphasis away from the broader issues of education development, particularly the concern to promote equity and social well-being, by being narrowly focused on economic growth. In this context, then, the decentralisation of education is seen less as an attempt to improve responsiveness and democracy, and more as a strategy to abrogate financial and political responsibility for education provision.

Finance and resourcing, in particular, raise issues with regard to the equality of education provision. In societies with discrepancies in socio-economic status, local responsibility for education usually means that poor communities continue to have less access to education, as they are unable to take on the burden of financing education provision. Furthermore, poor communities tend to lack access, resources, information or organisational skills to appropriately influence decisions about education or other social services (Barberton et al., 1998). Decentralisation in countries with large socio-economic differences has often been described as attempts to pass on the growing costs of education to local communities. These are disguised as attempts to improve management efficiency and democratic participation by extending responsibility and accountability (ownership) to local communities. However, most often these strategies exacerbate a range of inequalities in and between communities, as impoverished communities worldwide tend to lack the social and economic resources required to support participative development processes (Barberton *et al.*, 1998).

For those countries with a strong ideological and political commitment to local autonomy and decision-making, a compromise is reached by enabling local school communities to control the use of educational resources provided by central or provincial authorities. Mostly, however, this enables higher levels of government to maintain a fairly strong level of control over educational allocation. This tension, implanted in decentralisation initiatives, is embedded in the approach to education governance in South Africa. On the one hand, equity objectives assume the need for a strong central government role in redressing past imbalances, while, on the other hand, a commitment to democratisation assumes autonomous local control over education.

Current writing on the impact of globalisation on education reflects similar considerations. A number of scholars have suggested that there are two related but distinct processes that drive globalisation (Astiz *et al.*, 2002; Davies & Guppy, 1997). Economic globalisation involves the intensification of international economic competition across national boundaries. This has the effect within states of structuring social and economic policy to meet the requirements of global competition. Institutional globalisation or global rationalisation is characterised by convergence toward a uniform model of polity and rationalisation. This process also impacts on the state by framing possible policy and service delivery strategies. The current dominance of new public management or managerialism in the structuring of public services internationally is an example of this.

Benjamin Levin (1997), for example, argues that the most common rationale for recent large-scale education reform in the developed world has been the need to maintain and improve economic welfare in order to compete in a global market. While equity and individual social mobility are also cited goals, the economic emphasis has been given greater importance. This has been accompanied by a declining faith in the ability of national education systems to address social problems, a distrust in the ability of public institutions to reform themselves and an unwillingness to spend more on education (Levin, 1997:255; Smith, 1997). Given this global shift to market oriented provision, reforms have stressed a greater curricular focus on workplace knowledge and skills, decentralised or local management of schools (to reduce the power of officials) and an increasing emphasis on market choice, user fees and efficiency. Decentralisation has therefore been accompanied by a greater emphasis on testing through national examinations, public regulation and accountability (Levin, 1997; Popkewitz, 1996; Brown, 1996).

The impact of institutional globalisation is evident in the organisational forms and management strategies adopted by states to govern the distribution and delivery of education. Despite the tendency of educational systems to follow patterns determined by their structural reality, there has been a general shift from hierarchical forms of organisation in education governance and management to market or exchange-based systems, at national and institutional levels (Mc Lennan, 2000). This is indicated in a general tendency, at national level, to decentralise authority to local, district or school level. It has been accompanied by an emphasis on community participation and more democratic forms of organisation at the school level. In management terms, there has been a shift away from mechanistic forms of organisation and control to more managerialist solutions indicated in a growing emphasis on effectiveness and efficiency at the school level. School quality, performance and value for money are growing considerations in the literature and practice of education.

Popkewitz (1996) suggests that this reflects part of a shift in global governing technologies used to manage education. It is evident, for example, in a shift from the regulatory certainty of a defining hierarchical authority to the professional certainty of a problem-solving educator élite. The discourses of standards and professionalism operate in lieu of the state as a monitoring and steering system for education provision. This assumes, of course, that the expertise exists for managing more fluid and less bureaucratically centralised administration of schools. His primary point, however, is that educational governance does not simply operate in the realm of the state and the state administrative system. Instead, it comprises the broad set of relationships, institutions and practices, which construct modes of behaviour and practice that are considered normal. These are supported by knowledge systems and understandings, such as whole school development, site-based management or democratic participation, which co-ordinate various sets of actors in the education sector. In other words, the concept of school improvement is made possible by assumptions about teachers who are able to design curricula, work collaboratively with local communities and assess performance. This, in turn, is made possible by a set of institutions and relationships that reward professional initiative, school competition and certain types of school performance.

Most education systems are a mix of centralised and decentralised governance and management systems and relations. Margaret Archer (1984) suggests that educational interaction in centralised systems is patterned in ways dissimilar from that in decentralised systems, and that the basic structural tendency of an education system is resilient. Once established, structures tend to remain because of the interests vested in their maintenance. While clearly it is essential to understand the education system in its broad political and socio-economic context, there is no simple correspondence between the political and economic systems in a country and the particular form of education governance. In his study of education control in Eastern Europe, Tomiak (1985) argues that even the existence of a common ideological commitment (such as Marxism) can produce radically different education models such as the democratic centralism of the former Russia and the "self-management" of former Yugoslavia.

Education service delivery in South Africa

Two processes seem to define education service delivery in the new South Africa. Firstly, economic and institutional globalisation have partially delineated the policies and strategies selected to drive education delivery. Secondly, the context and content of governance and delivery have structured relationships historically in ways that pattern distribution. This approach assumes that governance comprises the formal allocation of social services through the legitimate structures and practices of public institutions and public policy, as well as the social power relationships that pattern interactions and distribution between social groups (Mc Lennan, 2000). While public policy may aim, for example, to distribute resources more equitably, existing unequal patterns of distribution, embedded in the socio-economic structure and institutional context, may be reinforced. This notion of institutional context as constitutive of the relationships, which define authority and voice in public contexts, is similar to recent understandings of the function of discourse as playing a role in the normalisation of behaviour in institutions (Foucault, 1988; Young, 1990).

Discourse (briefly) refers to the systems of meanings, practices and processes that frame agency. This is not to suggest that the users of discourse simply submit to its meanings, but that commitment to a particular understanding of the world results in a lived reality, which to some extent limits the actions and behaviour of social actors (Bertelsen, 1998). Dominant discourses, or preferred meanings, tend to be taken as given and seen as truths. It is through these discursive lenses that individuals or groups accept forms of domination as "the way things are". These relationships create subjects whose conscious behaviour corresponds to established social norms. The agency of a group or individual is therefore defined but not necessarily limited by discursive practices and strategies of normalisation. Governance partly involves the use of methods that encourage consent for particular ways of understanding social distribution, which coincides with dominant interests (Mc Lennan, 2000). However, since the meaning of dominant discourses is fluid and adaptable to particular needs and interests, social actors mobilise around particular understandings and rearticulate these to different discourses. This enables social groups to fix the terms of the debate. In this sense, discourses have material and social consequences and become institutionalised. The contestation of meaning often results in a series of contradictions or paradoxes in the practice of service delivery that are difficult to resolve.

Given this approach, education delivery in South Africa is partly defined by a set of discourses that pattern post-apartheid distribution and the allocation of resources (Mc Lennan, 2000). The first discourse, "Separate Development and Scientific Administration", broadly represents the interests of the apartheid state in establishing a racially separate development and distribution process and the use of pseudo-scientific, administrative language to supervise unequal delivery. It corresponds, in form, to global discourses of scientific administration and expanded state control over distribution. The second, "Reform and Managerialism", represents the language used to justify the "reform" of the apartheid state to accommodate Coloureds and Indians (and exclude Africans), and the managerialist governing technologies used to justify limited public decision-making and authoritarian control. This discourse corresponds to global discourses related to the rise of neo-liberalism and limited state intervention. It assumes that only the "free" market can achieve efficient service delivery. The third discourse, "Resistance and Democratic Participation", is evident in the language and strategies of the struggle against apartheid and the subsequent emphasis on people's participation in the processes of service delivery and distribution. It draws largely on social democratic discourse, with an emphasis on civil society participation in public decision-making, and alternative forms of economic development. Many of the discourses contain contradictory elements, or discourses within discourses. They are also interrelated, as they were developed in reaction to or parallel to each other and are rooted in historically contained economic and political processes. Despite these limitations, they do provide a useful framework for analysing the limits of service delivery in local contexts.

The apartheid education system

Decentralisation as a process is not a new phenomenon in the South African education system. It has existed in various forms of racial or regional de-concentration and devolution with limited local involvement since the unification of South Africa in 1910 (Buckland & Hofmeyr, 1993). While the White education system had existed for some time, education systems for the African, Coloured and Indian groups were introduced by the National Party after 1948. The system as a whole was a curious mix of centralised and decentralised practices. There was some devolution of power to provincial departments in the White system and to regional centres in the Black Department of Education and Training (DET). As Figure 6.1 illustrates, there was no one department that exerted authority over the whole system.

These separate systems were linked through the overarching ideology of apartheid, based on White supremacy, and have been described as a "system of systems" (Buckland

Figure 6.1: The South African education system prior to 1994

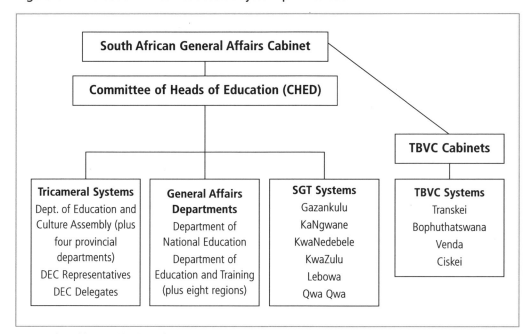

Source: Adapted from Buckland & Hofmeyr (1993)

& Hofmeyr, 1993), which remained in place despite being rejected by a wide range of community, especially the Black community, political and business organisations. Within these systems, the management culture in departments was hierarchical and authoritarian. The accountability of the different departments was constrained by problems of over-centralisation of control and the limited legitimacy of the political authorities. The result of this was that policy was formulated and implemented by the administrators within the system, with little public access to the process.

Although the education system appeared to be decentralised, the autonomy of the different departments was limited by a process of allocating funds, which was determined by the Cabinet of the National Party (NP) government. Key decisions taken in the Cabinet determined the expenditure on education for the country. The Cabinet also indirectly determined the amount of the grants for TBVC education departments, which were channelled through the Department of Foreign Affairs. The policy powerhouse of the bureaucracy was the Committee of Heads of Education (CHED), which advised the respective ministers on budget allocations. CHED comprised six members of whom four were White. The capacity of the self-governing territories (SGTs) to influence this bureaucratic process was limited, although attempts were made in the early 1990s to boost their status by providing more direct access to the Department of National Education (DNE).

Schooling systems were structured in a racial hierarchy of unequal provision, with White schools as key beneficiaries and Black schools as most disadvantaged. This is evident in the comparative statistics provided in Table 6.1. School leaving examination results indicated the generally poor quality of Black education with a 40% pass rate for Black candidates and over an 85% pass rate for White candidates in 1989 (Unterhalter, 1991:47). In Black schools, the inadequate supply, low qualifications and poor morale of teachers took their toll, creating despondency and apathy in many school communities. Many of these schools were "no-go areas" characterised by school boycotts, strong opposition and high rates of absenteeism (Hartshorne, 1990; Christie, 1998). A combination of poor physical and social facilities, organisational problems and damaged school/community relationships resulted in an impoverished teaching and learning culture in most Black schools. Education delivery in general was characterised by high repetition and dropout rates, particularly for Coloured and Black pupils (Hofmeyr & Mc Lennan, 1992). Education service delivery under a racially and ethnically fragmented and (centralised) decentralised apartheid governing system was grossly unequal and designed to exclude and separate parents from children, teachers from principals, and schools from state and community. The effects of this process on local school relationships continue to shape service delivery in the democratic dispensation (Mc Lennan, 2000).

A (new) decentralised delivery system in the post-apartheid period

While a decentralised education system was not new to South Africa, the form it took following the April 1994 elections was. The notion of (centralised) participatory democracy had been the mobilising glue behind calls to legitimise education governance. This was to remain a key concern of the new Ministry of Education, especially since the ANC's "Policy Framework for Education and Training" (1994a) assumed a strong national direction for education. However, the Interim Constitution, which reflected the compromises of the political negotiation process, placed structural constraints on the extent to which centralised participatory democracy could be achieved.

Both the Interim Constitution and the 1996 Constitution listed education as a concurrent power of both national and provincial departments. The nine provinces had power over all aspects of education with the exception of higher education. If national and provincial law were consistent, then both would apply. However, if they were inconsistent, provincial law would prevail except where minimum or uniform norms and

Table 6.1: Comparative education statistics, 1989

	White	Indian	Coloured	African
Student-teacher ratios	17:1	20:1	23:1	38:1
Under-qualified teachers (less than 12 years of schooling plus a 3-year teacher's certificate)	0%	2%	45%	52%
Matric pass rate	96%	93.6%	72.7%	40.7%
Per capita expenditure (rands)	3 082	2 227	1360	765

Source: Hofmeyr & Mc Lennan (1992:176)

standards were required to render an effective service or it materially prejudiced national interests and economic growth (Interim Constitution, 1993, Schedule 6; Constitution, 1996, Schedule 4).

This lack of clarity with regard to policy development and decision-making in the education arena left space for conflict over the responsibility for education provision. The constitutional model adopted for South Africa was neither centralised nor entirely federalised, which has been discussed in greater detail in Chapter 5 of this book. It was based on the principle of co-operative governance under which each sphere (not level) of government (national, provincial and local) retained its own unique character but could not function independently of the other spheres (Smith & Foster, 2000). In fact, the Constitution advocates that legislative conflicts between spheres should be resolved collaboratively. Formally, there is no hierarchy of government levels, because each sphere is required to co-operate with the other.

This tension in the structural arrangements that define education governance as neither entirely the responsibility of national nor of provincial government remains an enduring characteristic of intergovernmental relations in the education sector. Despite a commitment to "spheres" of government and co-operation, the relationship between the national department and the provincial departments is perceived in hierarchical terms (Mc Lennan, 2000). There is a continuous push and pull between these spheres as each attempts to establish authority over the distribution and allocation of resources. The constitutional arrangement is unusual but not surprising, given the compromises made in the political negotiations preceding 1994. The ANC favoured a strong centralised governing system, while the NP preferred a federalised system, which would have been more likely to protect White interests (Thompson, 1995). The increasing emphasis on decentralised systems reflects global rationality despite the fact that most newly "liberated" education systems are centralised to ensure equity and development.

A combination of historical compromise and global rationality has created a tension between a tendency to centralise authority and control (for development purposes) and an inclination to decentralise responsibility (for management purposes). White Paper One (DoE, 1995), developed soon after the democratic elections, reflected the compromises of the recently negotiated settlement. It articulated the range of discourses that had characterised the struggle for legitimate governance in the education arena. However, it lacked clarity about functions, authority and lines of accountability within and between systems of governance. It suggested that the new system of education would "be one single national system which is largely organised and managed on the basis of nine provincial sub-systems" (DoE, 1995:47). In this respect, it mooted a more centralised system of governance than was to emerge over the following few years.

A realisation that effective delivery required clarity about relationships of accountability and responsibility between the national and provincial education departments, as well as between the key stakeholders in the education and training process, resulted in the promulgation of the National Education Policy Act 27 of 1996. The National Party, Democratic Party and Inkatha Freedom Party challenged the constitutionality of the Education Policy Bill on the grounds that it impinged on the legislative competence and jurisdiction of provincial governments by giving unlimited authority to the Minister of Education. The Constitutional Court rejected the argument that the Bill gave the national minister unconstitutional powers. The court's findings did not endorse the dominance of the national department, and suggested instead that the Act gave the provinces the opportunity to address issues where they felt that the standard of national provision did not comply with the Constitution.

By late 1996, there were ten different operating education departments implementing their own regulations in terms of one national education act (DoE, 1996c) and several provincial acts. Only the provincial departments employed teachers and operated schools. Departments were still structured on gender and racial lines although the representation of Blacks in senior management levels had changed. Management systems had not changed as dramatically as implied by the new policy frameworks. While the formal structures were in place, that is, a national department, collaborative governing committees – Council of Education Ministers (CEM) and Heads of Education Departments (Hedcom) – integrated provincial departments and schools governing bodies, former institutionalised systems of delivery were relatively intact. Education departments were required to provide quality and compulsory education up to grade nine, within extremely deprived, uneven and racially unequal school and provincial contexts.

This was evident in both the Provincial Review Report (DPSA, 1997) and the Presidential Review Commission (1998), which assessed service delivery in the nine provinces of

South Africa. The 1997 review found that the centralisation of functions in provinces, particularly financial and personnel management, had a negative effect on the ability of departments to deliver services (DPSA, 1997). This, it was argued, resulted from a lack of a client-service approach by the central provincial departments (which still saw themselves in the main as controlling, not enabling, line departments), as well as a deficit of skills. Provinces were restricted by a lack of flexibility to respond effectively to local conditions. They were also hampered by an inability to restructure their departments around the needs of service delivery and the constraints placed upon them by budget formats.

Provincial education departments had different numbers of schools to manage under different geographical and socio-economic conditions (HSRC, 1997). The Northern Cape, for example, had only 531 schools, but these were located across an enormous geographical area. Eastern Cape, Northern Province and KwaZulu-Natal had the highest number of schools and school enrolments, and were also the most rural and economically disadvantaged provinces. The highest enrolments were in KwaZulu-Natal (2 690 950), followed by the Eastern Cape (2 231 865) and the Northern Province (1 934 101). Nationally, the majority of schools (62%) had enrolments less than or equal to 500, 30% of schools fell within the enrolment category of 501–1000, and 8% of schools had enrolments higher than 1000. In many cases, the new governing system (national and provincial legislatures) had simply been overlaid on existing racial and socio-economic patterns of distribution.

The School Register of Needs (SRN), completed by the Human Sciences Research Council (1997), showed that a small proportion of (formerly White) schools were well-resourced, while the vast majority of (mainly Black) children continued to be educated in impoverished and unequal conditions. Most schools lacked basic services. At 24% of schools in the country, there was no water available within walking distance from the schools. Less than half the schools (43%) in the country had electricity. In KwaZulu-Natal, North West and Mpumalanga less than 50% of the schools had telephones. 3.7% of schools had no student worktops and chairs, and 38% of schools were inadequately supplied. Three provinces where classroom shortages were extremely high were the Eastern Cape (15 538), KwaZulu-Natal (14 534) and the Northern Province (13 670).

The inability to fundamentally shift patterns of unequal service delivery was acknowledged by the new Minister of Education Kader Asmal, when he called the education community to action in response to a national emergency characterised by rampant inequality, low teacher morale, failures of governance and management and a poor quality of learning:

> The public believes that we have a crisis on our hands. Our people have rights to education that the state is not upholding. They have put their confidence in the democratic process, and returned their government with an overwhelming mandate. After five years of democratic reconstruction and development, the people are entitled to a better education service and they must have it. (Asmal, 1999)

His call to action, Tirisano (work together), utilised the language of resistance and democratic participation to mobilise actors to rebuild schools and make education work in the name of development and democracy. However, research indicated that the government failed to significantly improve education delivery between 1994 and 1999 despite a sustained focus on changing governing and managing structures and education practices (Taylor & Vinjevold, 1999; Chisholm & Peterson, 1999; Vally, 1999).

There were some improvements in the infrastructure of provision reported in the 2000 SRN. There was less overcrowding in institutions overall, with a decline in the average number of learners to a classroom from 43 (in 1996) to 35 (in 2000). Except for Mpumalanga, learner classroom ratios had decreased. Classroom shortages decreased from 49% (1996) to 40% (2000). In 1996, 40% of all schools had no access to water, and in 2000 this was reduced to 34%. There was a 68% improvement in the provision of sanitation, although 16% of learners continue to be without toilet facilities. However, the 2000 SRN also indicated that investment in physical infrastructure had not been sustained. The number of buildings in good condition declined from 9 000 to 4 000, with at least 12 000 buildings in need of repair.

Despite gains made towards improved equity and democratic practice in the 1989 to 2001 period, as shown in Table 6.2, education service delivery continues to be characterised by inequality and underdevelopment. Within provinces, privileged schools and school communities (especially the White community) are able to provide, in most cases, better quality education than under-resourced township schools (Black schools). A similar pattern operates at the national level. Better resourced departments such as Gauteng and Western Cape are able to provide better quality education than those like the Eastern Cape, KwaZulu-Natal and Northern Province departments, which began with huge deficits in basic resources and provision. This tendency for education delivery to remain

Table 6.2: Education statistics, 1989 (DET) and 2001 (National)

	1989	**2001**	**Variation**
Student-teacher ratios	38:1	35:1	25 to 40
Under-qualified teachers (less than 12 years of schooling plus a 3-year teacher's certificate)	45%	24%	10% to 34%
Matric pass rate	40%	60%	40% to 80%
Per capita expenditure	R765	R2 370	R1 947 to R3 740

Source: DoE (2002)

static has been perceived as a consequence of the challenges of globalisation, poor implementation and deep-rooted inequality. While these do affect the process of provision,
institutionalised social relationships and distribution patterns are a key and unacknowledged determinant of poor service delivery in South Africa. This will be explored in more
detail in the next sections.

Education for Development

Education development policy in the initial period following the democratic elections was
strongly rooted in the growth through redistribution approach of the Reconstruction and
Development Programme (RDP). However, over years that followed, this policy shifted
increasingly towards a marketised model of education development, with a growing
emphasis on decentralisation, user fees, choice and efficiency, and a decreasing emphasis
on redress and redistribution. Over time, the initial emphasis on education as a tool for
social and democratic development was superseded by a much stronger focus on education for economic development. While Minister Asmal has attempted in the post-1999
period to reintroduce stronger social development objectives through a focus on values in
education (DoE, 2001), the discourse of education delivery continues to be dominated by
an emphasis on building human capital to enhance South Africa's competitiveness in
global markets (Mc Lennan, 2000). In addition, the impact of economic globalisation is
evident in the effects of fiscal constraint on the scope of state services. There is an increasing tendency for the state to reduce its investment in education, while simultaneously
shifting the educational output to the skill requirements of globalisation.

The shift from state-led redistribution to a market-led approach was evident in broader
state development policy. The RDP was intended as an integrated socio-economic framework for the restructuring of government and its objectives. Its key purpose was to address
the inequalities caused by apartheid and it was premised on six basic principles (discussed
by Guy Mhone in Chapter 2 of this book). The RDP process was replaced in 1996 with a
more conventional development strategy known as the Growth, Employment and
Redistribution Policy (GEAR), which combined a series of strategies aimed at building the
economy rapidly, improving productivity, creating jobs, redistributing income and opportunities, providing social services and securing working and living environments. The
"growth first, redistribute later" strategy left unsolved the issue of how economic benefits
would trickle down to the majority of Black people who had been excluded by apartheid.
In both the RDP and GEAR, education, as a developer and a provider of skilled human
resources, was perceived as being at the heart of the development process. While the RDP
focused on the development of human resources for nation building and citizenship,

GEAR was more concerned with fiscal saving, human capital and efficient delivery. The RDP was rooted in the discourses of resistance and democratic participation, while GEAR arguably tended towards the reform and managerialism discourse.

In South African education policy, these discourses vied for dominance. While the former was necessary to secure legitimisation through redistribution, the latter was effective in dealing with fiscal constraint and global economic austerity. The complex overlapping of discourses resulted in a tendency to see education for development as necessary to build social capital and democratic consensus, as well as to produce human capital to fuel economic growth. The resistance discourse, in particular, was founded on an understanding of socialist community development ("people's" education) focused on redistribution and redress. This was implicit in the RDP, which notes that the three key features of apartheid education and training were racial and ethnic fragmentation, lack of access and exclusion of key stakeholders from decision-making (ANC, 1994:58). The writers suggested that the:

> fragmented, unequal and undemocratic nature of the education and training system has profound effects on the development of the economy and society. It results in the destruction, distortion and neglect of the human potential of our country, with devastating consequences for social and economic development. (ANC, 1994:58)

The ANC recognised early that redistribution would be a challenge given local economic conditions. Despite a commitment from the government to shift state expenditure towards social services, the Department of Education was required to expand and improve services within tight fiscal constraints. An ANC Education Finance Task Team had acknowledged the need to charge user fees in order to meet the shortfall required for education redistribution. It was felt that the total education budget of R24 billion was already high and that there was a need to reprioritise within existing limits (Chisholm, 1994). Funding for upgrading Black education and addressing backlogs in provision would have to be limited to what was affordable within existing budget allocations and what could be generated from redistribution (from the White education system) and other sources such as the RDP fund and international donors. Finally, a major limitation in achieving development was the high percentage allocation of education expenditure to personnel costs – up to 90% in some cases (DoE, 1996d).

Within these constraints, budget reform initiatives began to focus on options for achieving equity within existing fiscal limits by redefining teacher-pupil ratios, pooling resources, modifying teacher pay scales, improving unit costs and productivity, user charges and seeking new funding partnerships (Greenstein & Mobagoane, 1994). However, despite a total education budget allocation of R32.2 billion, of which 85% went to provinces for school and college education, the 1995 enrolment increase of 3.5% meant that the amount available for each child in the system declined in the 1995/6 fiscal year. In addition, an attempt to redistribute funding allocations between provinces and a shift in per capita expenditure from White to Black children meant that some provinces were faced with cutbacks in new teaching posts and the scrapping of building projects and minor repairs (Chisholm, 1995). Furthermore, many of the provincial departments over-spent on their budget allocation by millions (Govender *et al.*, 1995).

All redistribution had to occur within budget limits through efficiency savings. The Report of the Medium Term Expenditure Framework (MTEF) Sectoral Team identified four sources of inefficiency in the education system – the flow-through of learners, levels of productivity among educators, provincial spending choices and institutionalised inequalities (DoE, 1997). The report indicated that learners stay in school too long in relation to their education attainments. The document suggested further that educators earned more than the average taxpayer. Their conclusion was that educator costs were high relative to the total education budget, taxpayers' incomes and work effort. In addition, spending in education was determined by tradition rather than by informed choices about what would improve learning. This was evident where the North West Province had unusually high matriculation pass rates, 20% higher than expectations based on per learner expenditure, yet the lowest educator qualifications profile. The Northern Province (Limpopo), on the other hand, had a slightly higher educator qualifi-cations profile but a pass rate 15% lower than expectations based on per learner expendi-ture.

In the 1995 to 1997 period, the Minister of Education had responsibility for provincial budgetary allocations and claims to have reduced inter-provincial inequity by almost 60% during this period (DoE, 2001). In 1997/8, provincial governments were allocated an "equitable share" of national revenue as a block grant and, for the first time, were respon-sible for dividing their own budgets among their line function departments. The minis-ter, therefore, had no control over the national redistribution process. This had implica-tions for achieving national equity in the education system, as better-resourced provinces, regardless of the redistribution formula, were able to do more with their resource base than poorer provinces.

Serious inequality in funding between provinces continued. Both Mpumalanga and KwaZulu-Natal, two of the poorer and previously under-funded provinces, reflected a fall in actual funding in the 1997/98 period. Real expenditure was usually higher than the budget allocation, which resulted in strenuous efforts by the national and provincial treas-uries to require the education departments to restrict budget projections in order not to overspend. This exercise resulted in demands for the retrenchment of large numbers of educators and extreme pressure on non-salary expenditure. As it stood, departments lacked the powers and the tools to prioritise expenditure, especially in the absence of a personnel retrenchment tool.

The MTEF was introduced in 1997 to ensure an equitable and planned distribution of expenditure. Specific constraints in the 1996 to 1998 period included an increase in the budget deficit (from 3.2% of GDP in 1980 to 5.5% in 1996), moderate economic growth in the context of global and local economic slowdown and the extensive devolution of executive authority to provinces for decision-making on expenditure. The MTEF was an attempt to get provincial education departments to prioritise their needs in a context of literally shrinking human and financial resources. It was assumed that provincial responsibility for the allocation of education resources would improve service delivery.

An inherent tension between the requirements of global competition and the needs of local communities and action groups was established. On the one hand, education was seen as a key driver of economic recovery; on the other hand, departments were crippled by contradictory relationships, which affected the prioritisation process. Unions, for example, had an unequal power in their ability to resist initiatives that reduced the personnel bill. While provinces were able to reflect positive changes in their 1999/2000 budgets, the budgets of the poorest provinces, usually with the largest enrolments, continued to be dominated by personnel expenditure leaving little over for developmental initiatives. Despite an improvement in inter-provincial inequity from 34% in 1995 to 14% in 2001 (DoE, 2001), poorer provinces with bigger and less predictable enrolment rates were unable to shift service delivery towards redistribution. This led to an increasing shift of education costs from the state to local communities.

The move towards a semi-privatised system of education delivery was evident in shifts in education policy over the 1996 to 1999 period. White Paper Two (DoE, 1996a) opted for a more decentralised system than that suggested by the Hunter Commission, established to assess school organisation in South Africa. White Paper Two also suggested that the implementation of a redress formula for schools based on need would lead to a decline in funding for privileged schools, which would "propel middle-class parents out of the public school sector and into the independent sector" (DoE, 1996a:Section 5.2). Acting on the advice of international consultants, the government argued that the exodus would be prevented by allowing governing bodies to set fees. It was suggested that a national income threshold be established, below which parents would be exempt from paying.

Following a round of negotiations and consultations, White Paper Two was reconstituted as the South African Schools Bill. The implications of the policy were that privileged communities (White and Black middle class), by means of the user-fee principle, would be able to exercise greater choice in the education of their children, through the use of their economic muscle. In developmental terms, the South African Schools Act 84 of 1996, enacted on 15 November 1996, had gone the route of semi-privatised delivery in the name of redress.

A key tension in the attempt to achieve equity was between the need for uniformity and the need to deal with redistribution. The South African Schools Act attempted to do both. On the one hand, schools were assumed to have the same form, structure and context for the purposes of eliminating differences and fragmentation. On the other hand, it was suggested that savings generated by limiting funding to privileged public schools would be redistributed to needy Black schools. In reality, developmental programmes were limited largely to those funded by the RDP budget or donors. Furthermore, quite a lot of the RDP funding was unspent, as many provincial education departments were unable to utilise the funding in the allocated time period.

It was only in October 1998 with the passing of the National Norms and Standards for School Funding (No. 19347 of 1998) that the education department took a definitive step in the direction of redistribution and redress. In fact, the document explicitly acknowledged that the user-fee policy had advantaged middle-class learners in already well-resourced schools. In terms of the new national norms, provinces would be required to set up five school quintiles from poorest to least poor. The poorest 40% of schools would then receive 60% of the provincial school budget allocation and the least poor 20% would receive only 5% of the resources. This latter group would be required to fund additional schooling resources through user fees. Regulations with regard to equitable criteria and procedures for the exemption of parents unable to pay fees were outlined.

The growing marketisation of education, resulting from a tendency to pass costs to local communities, led to a class- and race-differentiated schooling system where the children of those who could afford it (mostly Whites, given the historical and continuing concentration of income and wealth within this group, and the new Black élite) received good quality education. Provinces struggling to reduce high personnel costs tended to trade off priorities by enabling well-resourced communities to supplement the gap between basic provision and quality provision. This was usually facilitated through inaction rather than direct intervention (Vally, 1998). However, the implication of this strategy was that poorer communities (mainly Black) that desperately required quality education (in order to develop their human resources) would only be able to afford rudimentary provision. The Poverty and Inequality Hearings demonstrated that impoverished communities could not afford fees of less than R100 per year and this did not include other expenses such as uniforms, transport, food and excursions (Vally, 1998).

It is still too early to assess the impact of the School Funding Norms; however, it is likely that socio-economic conditions in local communities will continue to determine the quality of educational outcomes and the prospects of development in impoverished areas. Poor educational outcomes are not simply a consequence of inappropriate financing, but of deeply embedded and disrupted teaching processes that undermine appropriate learning. South Africa has very high repetition rates and poor levels of performance in national examinations. On average over the past few years, less than 50% of those taking final examinations have passed. Teaching and learning tends to be characterised by teacher-centeredness, learner passivity and rote learning (Taylor & Vinjevold, 1999).

The trade-off implicit in redistribution within a semi-privatised approach is that the most disadvantaged schools and learners are unlikely to benefit. This is because the market continues to be structured by race and class, which together underpin a high level of poverty. Even the redistributive formula implicit in the Norms and Standards for School Funding is unlikely to shift the legacy of unequal distribution, as the starting-points for the various schools are wide apart. Well-resourced public schools benefit not only from communities that can pay fees, but also from stable school-community relationships, which uphold a liberal conception of education as a foundation for individual social and economic development. Even with extra resources generated by the new funding system, for many schools the backlogs and deficits in terms of school relationships would be too large to redress over time.

Research into school governance indicates that high levels of commitment from the local school and parent community sustain decentralised governance relationships (Mc Lennan, 2000). This ensures that high levels of social and financial investment in the school are maintained. This is consistent with initiatives in developed countries and with theories about social capital (Putnam, 1992). A combination of socio-economic privilege and high levels of education have ensured the continuing success of privileged, and in most cases formerly White, suburban schools. The dynamics shift as the school communities become more diverse or poorer. In these schools, lack of trust, poverty, racial conflict or an embedded culture of resistance have diminished social capital. This has been evident in the struggles over scarce resources, which have occurred in under-resourced schools and communities. Governing bodies became sites of struggle for resources such as decision-making power, authority and entitlements. Often, parents in poor communities did not have the voice, authority or capacity to challenge the established interests of educators, learners or principals in schools (Mc Lennan, 2000).

The implications of this approach to governance are that privileged schools will continue to benefit from their better-resourced school communities, while poor schools will become increasingly disadvantaged. Given that Black schools are in the majority, this will not address the need of a globally competitive economy for a highly skilled workforce, nor the need to ensure political stability in a fledgling democracy. It would seem then that the commitment to economic growth through market liberalisation, implicit in the managerialist discourse, has worked its way into education policy through the structural limitations of economic concerns and the ability of minority interest groups to lobby the state system. However, as eloquently demonstrated by Bond and Guliwe in Chapter 10 of this book, despite a demobilisation of the mass democratic forces after the elections, civil society groups are remobilising to apply pressure on the government in the direction of redress.

Democratic governance in the education sector

The influence of global rationalisation is evident in the way service delivery systems and processes in education are being governed. Many of the strategies adopted in South Africa, like elsewhere, reflect a growing dominance of managerialism in the structuring of governing relationships and the emphasis on decentralisation and performance. However, in many cases, these discourses are superimposed on quite rigid hierarchical processes and serve to disguise the inherently undemocratic decision-making process. The move towards managerialism has led to a shift in policy away from the centralised and collaborative decision-making of the 1994 to 1996 period to more fragmented and decentralised processes.

A key aspect of decentralisation in South Africa and internationally is the need to disperse authority and voice among key stakeholders. The underlying assumption of this approach is that democratic governing structures at lower levels in the system enable those closest to the point of delivery to make decisions about education provision. It is also assumed that inclusion will result in improved education delivery and accountability. This notion of parental and community participation in South Africa incorporated the rallying call of "people's education for people's power", which mobilised the education resistance movement in the 1980s. However, despite an articulated commitment to participatory democracy, policy development and governance are premised on the principles of representation and consultation, rather than popular participation.

Even the collaborative structures established in terms of the National Policy Act (DoE, 1996b) were premised on the notion of representation. These included the Council of Education Ministers (CEM), a Heads of Education Departments Committee (Hedcom), stakeholder forums such as the South African Council of Educators (SACE), the National Education and Training Forum (NETF) and school level governing bodies (DoE, 1996b; 1996c). However, this consultation process tended to extend only to organised and mandated groups within the education arena with sufficient voice to "represent" specific interests. Even where popular consultation was institutionalised, in requests for submissions on white papers, public hearings or commissions, only policy-literate, well-organised groups such as trade unions, teachers' associations, education policy units, political parties or privileged parent associations were able access the formal pathways of policy consultation and negotiation.

The national department was responsible for setting norms and standards, the development of national policy and higher education. Provincial departments were responsible for delivery. This reflected a division of responsibilities implicit in both the scientific administration and managerialist discourses. However, whereas in these approaches the divide between politics and administration was one between ministries and departments, in the education system the divide was between national and provincial levels of government. This established a structural limitation in the governance of education delivery, which would potentially lead to conflict between the levels of government. The national department tended to abstract the complexity of educational problems in order to standardise educational delivery, while provinces were required to adapt these uniform norms to a diversity of contexts and social conflicts to ensure delivery.

Provinces were able to develop province-specific education policy but only within national guidelines. The gap between policy development and policy implementation continued to widen over the years. National policies became increasingly sophisticated and abstracted from on-the-ground realities, as international consultants and trends influenced policy development processes. Provinces became less willing to implement policy for which they had inadequate funding and little capacity. Furthermore, the large amount of policy developed in a range of areas such as teacher management, school restructuring and curriculum change gave provinces a sense of overload with inadequate guidance about how to prioritise implementation. They were all struggling to restructure and integrate racially fragmented departments and maintain basic levels of service provision, whilst attempting to undertake an ambitious transformation programme initiated by the national department.

The emphasis on consultation and collaboration enabled privileged stakeholders to re-articulate the discourse of democratic participation to further group interests and channel scarce resources. As a consequence, consultative relationships were characterised by high levels of distrust within the state, between provinces and within civil society. Finally, civil society was unevenly organised, and privileged interest groups were able to dominate the voices of the excluded. In these contexts, participatory processes tended to favour those groups within the state most able to manipulate the system to achieve their interests. Formal consultative and participative processes based on representation did not guarantee that all interests were considered. The less vocal and empowered provinces (and usually the poorest and least resourced) continued to be on the receiving end of a policy development process that favoured the national department and articulate provincial departments. As a consequence, the policy developed tended to favour the privileged middle class, and millions of poor rural children were excluded from the processes of education transformation (Tikly, 1997).

This was particularly evident at the school level. The South African Schools Act provided for the establishment of School Governing Bodies (SGBs), which would be responsible for school development through the provision of quality education. SGBs would comprise of parents, educators, non-educators and learners in secondary schools. The principal of a school would be an ex-officio member and community members could be co-opted onto governing bodies but could not vote (DoE, 1996c). While the intention of legislating SGBs was to enhance democratic participation at the school level, their composition and design was to ensure representivity. The South African Democratic Teachers Union (SADTU), in particular, expressed concern that parents were the majority group on SGBs and called for an equal representation for parents, teachers and students. This set the stage for the representation of interests, rather than collaborative decision-making, at school level.

The Schools Act set up a broad range of responsibilities, from the development of school policy to fund-raising and the maintenance of school infrastructure. Many of these responsibilities were beyond the capacity of under-resourced school communities. Most schools in South Africa had had very limited self-management or governance experience and tended to respond reactively to instructions from above. Many district or circuit level offices, which would have to provide much needed support, were still in the process of being established and staffed and also lacked experience and capacity. Local level educational offices had traditionally served as post boxes for passing on information, or as inspectorates. In addition, governing bodies could be allocated additional functions if they had the capacity to carry them out. These functions included maintaining and improving school property, buildings and grounds, deciding on extramural curriculum and subject choices, purchasing textbooks and educational resources and paying for services to the school.

Research on school governance in Gauteng indicated that there was a large degree of confusion about who was responsible for what (Mc Lennan, 2000). Schools with broken windows, toilets and facilities expected the department to fix them. However, district budgets for repairs were limited and districts assumed that schools would pay for minor repairs from school fees. This did occur in schools where governing bodies charged comparatively high fees and did extensive fund-raising. By virtue of the parent body being mostly of middle-class income and background, many SGBs had a wide range of skills and services to draw on. Parents with maintenance companies often completed the work required at cost. While the SGBs of disadvantaged schools were willing to assist by planting gardens or cleaning grounds, they often lacked the financial resources or skills for basic repair work. In some of the rural schools, parents were mostly farm workers and were unable to pay even R10 a year in school fees. They also lacked the time to work at the schools. Most worked from sunrise to sunset, six days a week, and liked to go to church or relax on Sundays. There was, therefore, a concern that decentralising functions such as maintenance would further disadvantage poor and under-resourced schools.

Many teachers and schools, still rooted in a culture of resistance, simply refused districts access. One reason for denying access was because the district failed to follow the due process for school visits, which involved notification and agreed dates. If a district official arrived unannounced, the school assumed that he or she was checking up on them and reacted defensively. In one case in Gauteng, staff and students stoned district officials.

> The district visited us when we were unprepared and produced a very negative report. We felt bad because we had accepted these people when we were not prepared and then they did a demolition job. When they visited again we decided not to let them in. They were stoned by the pupils. We had a bosberaad and since then things have improved. But their agenda was a witch-hunt, not support. (Mc Lennan, 2000:307)

There was no general acceptance of the right of the district not only to support schools, but also to monitor delivery. Another reason for refusing access was because the school was aware that high levels of staff and student absenteeism and substance abuse were affecting its work and wanted to hide the non-performance from the district. In many cases, district officials had to spend many hours courting stakeholders and the school before they were able to adequately provide services. A district official describing her work with one school said:

> The district realised that the defiance was so ingrained that change within this institution would not come from within. It was a difficult road to travel. I was not able to break the barrier in the sessions I spent with them. As DEC of the school, it was inevitable that I, as the department's representative, would be implicated as part of the process. When the investigation was announced intimidation began. I was not prepared for the severity of the intimidation. (Mc Lennan, 2000:307)

This statement highlights the tension in the decentralisation process. The Schools Act was consistent with major education policy shifts internationally, which had also moved increasingly to local school management. In England and Wales, for example, responsibility for school management and governance was devolved from local government, in the form of local education authorities (LEAs), to schools in the late 1980s. The role of LEAs became one of resource planning, monitoring performance and support. Schools were responsible for the development of three-year plans and budgets to ensure their sustainability (Arthur & Welton, 1997). In some LEAs, schools underwent a phased process of implementation, which involved increasing parent support, managing paper budgets and supporting school planning. Many of these schools began to make planning choices that affected education quality rather than school maintenance only ten years into the process (Hopkins, 1999).

While the framework for school management and governance in South Africa was not significantly different from those in developed countries, the institutional context was. South Africa had neither the capacity and support of local level education authorities nor the stable professional relations that existed in these countries. The framework was, therefore, a curious blend of international education management and governance trends and specific South African needs. The latter was evident in the accommodation of students in governance at school level given the large contribution they made in the struggle against apartheid education.

In many cases, it would seem that contrary to expectations, instead of improving democratisation, interest group conflict was exacerbated, especially in contexts of limited resources. This was evident in the formerly White ex-Model C schools, where the non-racial priorities of the education department clashed with the guaranteed right to autogenous education. The principle of non-racialism was a key aspect of the resistance discourse and was enshrined in the Freedom Charter as a commitment to a united but diverse South Africa with a single national identity. Much of the restructuring of the education system had been premised on an attempt to reduce the racial fragmentation and inequalities of the apartheid system through the development of a national system of education provision. However, Clause 32 (c) of the Interim Constitution also guaranteed the right to establish "where practicable" educational institutions based on a common culture, language or religion. Many Afrikaner nationalists re-articulated the racial discourse implicit to separate development by affirming their "cultural" identities and their right as parents to guarantee their children's heritage through education (Tikly, 1997).

The weight given to parental representation on SGBs exacerbated the potential for racial conflict at schools, as parent majorities utilised the powers given to SGBs to maintain their group identities. Conservative White parents of children at Potgietersrus Primary School, for example, attempted to bar Black children on the grounds of cultural incompatibility. When this was ruled illegal, they attempted to use language as an exclusionary mechanism (Mokgalane & Vally, 1996). Despite an official emphasis on non-racialism and co-operation, the decentralised and representative structure of education governance was better suited to reinforcing the principle of autogenous education, because it reinforced the principle of self-managing and self-sustaining community schools implicit to education policy. Entrenching and sustaining non-racialism required a more centralised and controlled commitment to redress historical legacies of inequality.

Decentralisation did not, however, simply exacerbate the potential for racial conflict at the school level. The devolution of responsibility for distributing scarce resources created a space not only for the inclusion of but also for competition between representative groups (parents, teachers, students and managers) with fixed identities and severed relationships. Furthermore, the devolution was not complete. Governing bodies were accountable for supplementing scarce resources and for quality improvement, while the state retained the right to decide about the development and distribution of teachers, resources and learners. In other words, while responsibility and accountability were decentralised, autonomy and control were not. Schools were expected to own the problems but not necessarily the solutions. The motivation to diffuse responsibility for intractable education problems was implicit in the Schools Act, as it made a governing body responsible for taking "all reasonable measures within its means to supplement the resources supplied by the State in order to improve the quality of education provided by the school to all learners at the school" (DoE, 1996c: Section 36).

This conception of democratic participation, as comprising partnership and the sharing of responsibility, reinforced the tendency to privatise the costs of education delivery. The definition of school level governance and the distribution of voice and authority implied inclusion not only in decision-making but also in bearing the costs and responsibilities that accompanied education provision. Partnerships between school stakeholders were seen as enhancing the quality of education by passing on some of the responsibility to parents and other groups. However, in contexts with large discrepancies in socio-economic status, local responsibility often meant that poor communities continued to have less access to education, as they were unable to take on the burden of financing quality provision. Furthermore, poor communities tended to lack the access, resources, information or organisational skills to appropriately influence decisions about education (Barberton *et al.*, 1998).

This tendency to pass on responsibility to local communities was disguised as an attempt to improve management efficiency and democratic participation by extending responsibility and accountability (ownership) to local communities. The assumption was that the responsibility for restoring the culture of teaching and learning did not lie with the government alone, but also with school communities. The government was required to provide the framework and resources, and SGBs were responsible for the rest. This level of decentralisation, in vastly unequal contexts, meant that government departments were able to pass the buck. In line with the depoliticising logic of managerialism, government was accountable for facilitating delivery, while school communities were accountable for actually achieving delivery.

Conclusion

This chapter argues that the effects of globalisation and the results of decentralisation are mixed. There is evidence that economic globalisation and global rationalisation, through their influence on the discourses used to define education change in South Africa, did have some influence on the content and process of education change. However, it is also evident that local historical and socio-economic conditions patterned policy and distribution in particular and unique ways. The South African education system has always been decentralised according to a racial logic derived from apartheid, and to some extent this structure has been perpetuated in a different form. The results of this intersection of global conditions and local contexts are contradictory, particularly with regard to adopting a policy of decentralisation in contexts of extreme inequality and poverty.

In order to explore the challenges of decentralised service delivery, the chapter examines the meaning and promise of democratic governance in the South African context. It is noted that the new policy adopted combined both global trends and local concerns, in an attempt to meet the demands for equitable education delivery in a competitive global economic order. It is suggested that this global-local blend is reflected in the structure and form of the new delivery system. In this regard, two key themes are explored in some depth – the notion of education for development and democratic governance.

Under the mantle of the influence of global capitalism, it is suggested that the South African state shifted its emphasis from a more holistic approach of social and economic development to a narrower focus on economic growth. In line with this shift, the extent of state intervention was reduced as it was assumed that school communities had the social, if not the financial capital, to take on the challenges of education delivery. However, a shift towards marketisation as part of a strategy to contain education costs tends to undermine both aspects of development. Often impoverished and fragmented school communities are increasingly required to take on the costs of development without sufficient support or institutional capacity.

Furthermore, under the influence of global rationalisation, two contradictory processes are in operation in education governance policy. On the one hand, there are decentralised decision-making structures in place, which assume that existing management processes and relationships are able to support and implement collective decision-making. On the other hand, many relationships are either rule-driven or shattered, and often undermine attempts to achieve greater accountability and democracy. These contradictory processes are evident in the legislated split between decision-making and management at all levels of the system and in the tendency to focus on structure rather than process, and representation rather than collaboration.

The attempt to institutionalise democratic governance in the South African education system has thus resulted in centralising and decentralising tendencies, which undermine the ability of the new education departments to implement policy. It also reinforces a dichotomy between politics and administration in broad decision-making processes and between levels of government. Politics is seen to operate in the consultative structures established at all levels, which are separated from day-to-day practices of management. This widens the gap between purpose and delivery. While the governing structure represents all the stakeholder groups, it is premised on a set of institutionalised relationships, which disrupt formal processes in the attempt to access scarce resources. These, combined with the unequal socio-economic circumstances of provinces, districts and schools, undermine attempts to achieve equality, quality and development in education.

The reason for this limitation on service delivery is neither only the effects of globalisation, which limit the choices of the state, nor simply a consequence of bad (as opposed to good) implementation, which can be remedied through re-engineering. Poor delivery is also a consequence of the nature of the social relationships and institutional contexts in the education arena, which pattern the distribution of authority and voice. There has been a failure to acknowledge and recognise both the limits and potential of these relationships as forces for change. This has resulted in the development of policy that cannot be effectively implemented because of a lack of institutional capacity at all levels. In the absence of this capacity, there is a distortion in service delivery as existing, locally defined and represented institutional interests define who gets what.

References

African National Congress (1992) *Ready to Govern. Policy Guidelines for a Democratic South Africa.* Johannesburg: ANC.

African National Congress (1994a) *A Policy Framework for Education and Training.* Johannesburg: ANC Education Department.

African National Congress (1994b) *Reconstruction and Development Programme.* Johannesburg: Umanyano Publications.

African National Congress (1994c) *Implementation Plan for Education and Training.* Johannesburg: ANC Education Department.

African National Congress (1995) *Freedom Charter.* Johannesburg: ANC.

Archer, M. S. (1984) *Social Origins of Educational Systems.* London: Sage.

Arthur, L. & Welton, J. (1997) "Education Management Development in England and Wales." In Foster, W. F., Smith, W. J. & Thurlow, M. (eds) *Supporting Education Management in South Africa: International Perspectives.* Volume 2. Montreal: CSAEMP.

Asmal, K. (1999) "Call to Action: Mobilising Citizens to Build a South African Education and Training System for the 21st Century", Press Statement.

Astiz, M. F., Wiseman, A. W. & Baker, D. P. (2002) "Slouching Towards Decentralization: Consequences of Globalisation for Curricular Control in National Education Systems", *Comparative Education Review* 46, 1.

Barberton, C., Blake, M. & Kotze, H. (1998) *Creating Action Space: The Challenge of Poverty and Democracy in South Africa*. Cape Town: Idasa and David Philip.

Bertelson, E. (1998) "The Real Transformation: The Marketisation of Higher Education", *Social Dynamics* 24, 2.

Brown, P. (1996) "Education, Globalisation and Economic Development", *Journal of Education Policy* 11, 1.

Buckland, P. & Hofmeyr, J. (1993) "Education Governance – Who Decides?", *People Dynamics*, March.

De Clercq, F. (1997) "Policy Intervention and Power Shifts: An Evaluation of South Africa's Education Restructuring Policies", *Journal of Education Policy* 12, 3.

Chisholm, L. (1994) "The Foundation of Reconstruction and Development of Education and Training", *EPU Quarterly Review* 1, 4.

Chisholm, L. & Peterson, T. (1999) "Education Policy and Practice on the Eve of the '99 Election", *EPU Quarterly Review* 6, 1

Christie, P. (1998) "Schools as (Dis)Organisations: The 'Breakdown of the Culture of Learning and Teaching' in South African Schools", *Cambridge Journal of Education* 28, 3.

Davies, S. & Guppy, N. (1997) "Globalisation and Educational Reforms in Anglo-American Democracies", *Comparative Review* 41, 4.

Department of Education (1994) *Draft White Paper on Education and Training*. Notice 1030 of 1993, Government Gazette.

Department of Education (1995) *White Paper on Education and Training in a Democratic South Africa*. No. 196, Government Gazette.

Department of Education (1996a) *White Paper on the Organisation, Governance and Funding of Schools*. No. 130, Government Gazette.

Department of Education (1996b) *National Education Policy Act*. No.27. Pretoria: Government Printers.

Department of Education (1996c) *South African Schools Act*. No. 84. Pretoria: Government Printers.

Department of Education (1996d) *Department of Education Annual Report June 1994 – December 1995*. Pretoria: Department of Education.

Department of Education (1997) *Medium-term Expenditure Framework: Report of the Education Sectoral Team*. Pretoria: Department of Education.

Department of Education (1998) *National Norms and Standards for School Funding*. Pretoria: Department of Education.

Department of Education (2001) *Values in Education*. Pretoria: Department of Education.

Department of Public Service and Administration (1997) *Provincial Review Report*. Pretoria: Department of Public Service and Administration.

Foucault, M. (1988) "The Ethic of Care for the Self as a Practice of Freedom." An Interview translated by J. D. Gauthier in Bernauer, J. & Rasmussen, D. (eds) *The Final Foucault*. Cambridge, Mass. and London: MIT Press.

Fullan, M. (1991) *The New Meaning of Educational Change*. London: Cassell.

Fullan, M. (1993) *Change Forces: Probing the Depths of Educational Reform*. London: Falmer Press.

Fullan, M. (1997) "Leadership and the Moral Mission of Schools in South Africa." In Smith, W. J., Thurlow, M. & Foster, W. F. *Supporting Education Management in South Africa: International Perspectives*. Montreal: CSAEMP.

Fullan, M. (1999) *Change Forces: The Sequel*. London: Falmer Press.

Govender, V., Greenstein, R. & Kgobe, P. (1995) "Policy Formulation and Practical Implementation", *EPU Quarterly Review* 3, 2.

Graham-Brown, S. (1991) *Education in the Developing World: Conflict and Crisis.* New York: Longman.

Greenstein, R. & Mabogoane, T. (1994) "The Challenges of Transformation: Policy and Conflict in South African Education and Training", *EPU Quarterly Review* 2, 2.

Hartshorne, K. (1990) "Post-Apartheid Education: A Concept in Process." In Schrire, R. (ed.) *Wealth or Poverty? Critical Choices for South Africa.* Cape Town: Oxford University Press.

Hofmeyr, J. & Mc Lennan, A. (1992) "The Challenge of Equalising Education." In Schrire, R. (ed.) *Wealth or Poverty? Critical Choices for South Africa.* Cape Town: Oxford University Press.

Hopkins, D. (1999) "School Improvement for Student Achievement." Workshop on Whole School Development, Graduate School of Public and Development Management, University of the Witwatersrand, 5–6 July.

Human Sciences Research Council, Education Foundation and Research Institute for Education Planning (1997) *School Register of Needs Survey.* Pretoria: Government Printers.

Jansen, J. (1995) "Effective Schools?", *Comparative Education* 31, 2.

Lauglo, J. (1996) "Forms of Decentralisation and their Implications." In Coombe, C. & Godden, J. *Local/District Governance in Education Lessons for South Africa.* Braamfontein: Centre for Education Policy Development.

Lauglo, J. & McLean, M. (eds) (1985) *The Control of Education.* London: Heinemann.

Lyons, R. (1985) "Decentralised Education Planning: Is it a Contradiction?" In Lauglo, J. & McLean, M. *The Control of Education.* London: Heinemann.

Levin, B. (1997) "The lessons of International Education Reform", *Journal of Education Policy* 12, 4.

Mc Lennan, A. (2000) "Education Governance and Management in South Africa." PhD thesis, University of Liverpool.

Mokgalane, E. & Vally, S. (1996) "Between Vision and Practice: Policy Processes and Implementation", *EPU Quarterly Review* 3, 3.

Munslow, B. & FitzGerald, P. (1995) "The Reconstruction and Development Programme." In FitzGerald, P., Mc Lennan, A. & Munslow, B. *Managing Sustainable Development in South Africa.* Cape Town: Oxford University Press.

Muthahaba, G., Baguma, R. & Halfani, M. (1993) *Vitalising African Public Administration for Recovery and Development.* Connecticut: Kumarian Press.

Popkewitz, T. S. (1996) "Rethinking Decentralisation and State/Civil Society Distinctions: The State as a Problematic of Governing", *Journal of Education Policy* 11, 1.

Presidential Review Commission (1998) *Developing a Culture of Good Governance.* Report of the Presidential Review Commission on the Reform and Transformation of the Public Service in South Africa. Pretoria: Office of the President.

Putnam, R. D. (1992) "Democracy, Development and the Civic Community: Evidence from an Italian Experiment." World Bank Conference on Culture and Development, Washington, D.C. 2–3 April.

Putnam, R. D. (1993) *Making Democracy Work.* Princeton, New Jersey: Princeton University Press.

Rondinelli, D. (1989) "Decentralising Public Services in Developing Countries: Issues and Opportunities", *Journal of Social, Political and Economic Studies* 14, 1.

Saqeb, G. N. (1985) "The Effects of Tensions Between Nationalism and Provincialism on Education Administration in Pakistan." In Lauglo, J. & McLean, M. *The Control of Education.* London: Heinemann.

Shaeffer, S. (1996) "Partnerships in Basic Education: The Facilitation of Teacher and Community Participation in School Improvement." In Coombe, C. & Godden, J. *Local/District Governance in Education Lessons for South Africa.* Braamfontein: Centre for Education Policy Development.

Shaeffer, S. (1997) "Supporting Local School Management: The Key to Successful Reform." In Smith, W. J., Thurlow, M. & Foster, W. F. *Supporting Education Management in South Africa: International Perspectives.* Volume 1. Montreal: CSAEMP.

Smith, W. J. (1997) "School Performance, Change and EMD." In Smith, W. J., Thurlow, M. & Foster, W. F. *Supporting Education Management in South Africa: International Perspectives.* Volume 1. Montreal: CSAEMP.

Smith, W. J. & Foster, W. F. (2000) *The Governance of Education in South Africa: An Analysis of the Legislative Framework.* Montreal: CSAEMP.

Stadler, A. (1987) *The Political Economy of South Africa.* London: Croom Helm.

Taylor, N. & Vinjevold, P. (eds) (1999) *Getting Learning Right.* Johannesburg: Joint Education Trust.

Thompson, L. (1995) *A History of South Africa* (Revised edition). New Haven and London: Yale University Press.

Tikly, L. (1997) "Changing South African Schools?: An Analysis and Critique of Post-Election Government Policy", *Journal of Education Policy* 12, 3.

Tomiak, J. (1985) "The Control of Education: Contrasting Interpretations of Marxism." In Lauglo, J. & McLean, M. *The Control of Education.* London: Heinemann.

Unterhalter, E. (1991) "Changing Aspects of Reformism in Bantu Education, 1953–89." In Unterhalter, E., Wolpe, H., Botha, T., Badat, S., Dlamini, T. & Khotseng, B. *Apartheid Education and Popular Struggles.* Johannesburg: Ravan Press.

Vally, S. (1998) "Education Policy and Implementation Developments, February to May 1999", *EPU Quarterly Review* 5, 4.

Vally, S. (1999) "Teachers in South Africa: Between Fiscal Authority and 'Getting Learning Right'", *EPU Quarterly Review* 6, 2.

Young, I. M. (1990) *Justice and the Politics of Difference.* Princeton, New Jersey: Princeton University Press.

7

Developmental Local Government and Decentralised Service Delivery in the Democratic South Africa

Thomas M. Mogale

Introduction

The closing decades of the twentieth century witnessed the disintegration of many one-party rule governments and the emergence of parliamentary democracies in most African countries. In southern Africa, Zambia and Malawi emerged from decades-long one-party rule under Kaunda and Banda respectively, and apartheid rule came to an end in South Africa. In West Africa, Nigeria and Ghana wrestled away from years of corrupt and abusive military rule and established democratically elected governments. However, the cases of almost problem-free African democratisation cited above beg for special attention and serious inquiry, particularly as it relates to answering questions not only of the fragility of the embryonic democracies and the difficulties they had to endure in the transition and consolidation phases, but also of the extent to which they have coped with development deficits while delivering tangible benefits to local communities.

Democratising African countries have to reckon with several difficulties that have continued to besiege their embryonic political models. These range from crushing economic pressures, increasing population growth rates, the Aids pandemic, exacerbated by accelerating globalisation forces, to a political culture borne out from authoritarian colonial experience and equally long post-independence one-party rule and military dictatorship. In this regard, Heller (2001:131) warns that "[i]n the developing world however, uneven capitalist development, resilient social cleavages and various forms of bureaucratic authoritarianism have blunted lower class collective action". Considering the newness and the weakness of the institutions of governance prevalent in these democratising societies, it is patently obvious that the gulf between theory and practice remains wide and needs to be bridged, while emerging democratic institutions must be strengthened.

Transition to democracy is a long and sensitive process involving preparing the legal and structural frameworks, setting up the requisite governance ethos for the functioning of all spheres of government, and consolidating the gains. Unfortunately, except for a few cases, no new democratising government can anticipate, nor be fully prepared to deal with, the teething challenges attendant upon the democratising process and the internalisation of a whole range of tasks and responsibilities associated with parliamentary democracy after years of authoritarian rule.

The present post-apartheid democratically elected government in South Africa inherited a bewildering hotchpotch of administrative, financial, economic and political structures emanating from the legacy of decades of apartheid rule. For example, the legal and administrative structures inherited were not intended to serve the broad population of the country but rather small divided ethnic or racial categories. The apartheid system was not known for upholding participatory norms of decision-making and, as a result, different sets of local government administrative structures for different racial groupings were imposed to operationalise discriminatory policies, rather than to deliver basic services to all.

"Apartheid policies have fundamentally distorted and damaged the spatial, social and economic environments in which people lived, worked, raised families, and sought to fulfil their aspirations" (White Paper on Local Government, 1998). Given this context and in the light of the urgent need to reduce historical socio-economic backlogs through acceleration of service delivery to local communities, it has become vital that a strong, synergetic partnership between central and local governments, civil society organisations and private and donor communities be galvanised to rectify associated inefficiencies.

Implicit in the above, is that local government in South Africa has undergone a process of transformation from apartheid's highly unequal, racially classified local administrative apparatus to a potentially integrated, developmental, equitable and sustainable form of government. This transformative process involved three phases of transition: the pre-interim phase, the interim phase and the final stage. In this context, and due to the country's recent legislative history, it is apparent that local governments are pivotal to reshaping and strengthening local communities and intensifying service delivery, especially to the poor and, thereby, deepening the foundation for democratic, integrated, prosperous and truly non-racial local communities. Hence, substantial assistance should be diverted toward provincial and local government capacity building and the institutionalisation of service delivery instruments within the jurisdiction of local governments.

This chapter explores the relevance of the notion of local governance in relation to addressing the challenges of poverty alleviation in the South African context through careful targeting of services to the weak and marginalised sectors of society. Specifically, it focuses on the efficacy of newly established local government structures and modes of governance in South Africa as the vital locus around which the challenge of poverty alleviation can be tackled. This form of decentralisation is designed to facilitate and open up the gradual process of enhancing opportunities for citizen participation, by placing more power and resources at a closer, more familiar, and more easily influenced level of government. Implicit in the chapter is an argument that posits that in environments with rich traditions of citizen participation such as South Africa, local governance heralds an important reinforcement of regular, predictable opportunities for citizen-state interaction and, hence, for addressing concerns close to the hearts of the local poor.

Despite its praiseworthy virtues, the theory and practice of participative local governance in most of the developing world suggest that it has not been unproblematic. In sub-Saharan Africa, its application has been limited, and the success recorded in terms of poverty reduction has been rather patchy. Available anecdotal evidence in South Africa would suggest that the same pattern is emerging. In this regard, the chapter attempts to draw and reflect on such experiences. It draws parallels with and explains peculiar South African challenges experienced thus far. In particular, the chapter will examine the general interface between different spheres of government and the resulting operational dynamics that either enhance or stifle local government capacity to fulfil the poverty reduction mandate. For instance, what is the central government authorities' attitude to granting popular voice by surrendering power, authority, and resources to local-level structures? What is the local government authorities' view on strengthening local-level institutions in integrated development planning, particularly institutions that enhance the democratic tradition at the grassroots level? Do government authority structures sufficiently extend to civil society/grassroots institutions that are the real agents of local governance?

In this respect, the chapter suggests that the main challenge for developmental local government in South Africa will be to ensure that existing decentralisation moves hand in hand with deliberate efforts to mobilise and strengthen civil society structures, processes and institutions at lower levels in a manner that would allow their relationship with central and sub-national governments to be more interactive and mutually reinforcing. That way, it is contended, the challenge of poverty reduction and extension of service delivery will not be reduced to government or individual responsibility but will be a joint responsibility addressed through partnership. In other words, poverty reduction requires recognition that a flourishing, strong civil society is an important prerequisite for any meaningful, vibrant, democratic, and decentralised governance system to address poverty. But for this to work, it is argued that the political environment ought to be perceived to be supportive of people's welfare through, for example, a demonstrably transparent, accountable and fair system of sharing resources and opportunities amongst the citizens to avoid the poorer members of civil society being more preoccupied with basic economic survival issues.

The chapter further argues that well-functioning local governments that have a holistic, integrated planning format as the mainspring of activities are best placed to make significant inroads in poverty reduction. Further, it concludes by highlighting the fact that poverty reduction is a realistic proposition where people for whom pro-poor interventions are targeted are allowed, through empowerment, to effectively participate in these interventions.

Theorising local governance and poverty reduction

Traditional conceptions of government and governance carried with them a duality which connoted meaning that characterised them as both synonymous and yet distinct. A textbook definition of government refers to formal institutions of the state with overall national responsibilities and which enjoy a monopolistic exercise of power. It further links them to formal institutions and processes operating at national level to maintain order, and often co-ordinating and facilitating national collective action. Viewed against that backdrop, government has the latitude to make wide-ranging decisions whilst enjoying legitimate means, including coercive power to enforce them towards the achievement of specific outcomes.

In recent years, a large amount of work has gone into distinguishing the concepts of government and governance, leading to a redirection of their use and import (Rosenau & Czempiel, 1992:3). Some scholars generally conclude that the term governance is open to a variety of uses and evokes several meanings (Stoker, 2002; Rhodes, 1996). Rhodes (1996:19) indicates that governance denotes "a change in the meaning of government, referring to a new process of governing; or a changed condition of ordered rule; or the new method by which society is governed". Ultimately, governance may lead to the setting up of conditions required for some form of ordered rule and collective action. In a similar vein, Stoker (1996:2) further argues that "the outputs of governance are not different to those of government. It is rather a matter of difference in processes". There is, however, a unanimous view that suggests that governance is about the development of a governing mode, which "blurs" the boundaries between and within public and private sectors. Hence, the essence of governance is about focus on governing mechanisms, which do not rest on recourse to government authority and sanctions. "The governance concept points to the creation of a structure or an order which cannot be externally imposed but is the result of the interaction of a multiplicity of governing actors and each influencing the other" (Kooiman & Van Vliet, 1993:64).

As implied above, however, this does not suggest that most of South African local government structures have reached a functioning, planning and understanding fit to be characterised in good governance terms. Nor should it be assumed that there is greater familiarity with concepts of governance for those White sections of the population accustomed to previous local government structures that served more as administrative units of the central apartheid state. Notions of a participative, accountable and developmental local government, whose prime responsibilities include resource mobilisation with redistributive mandates, are all too unfamiliar and poorly understood by most local actors. Under the present conditions, thus, for most local government actors, a major hindrance is the all-consuming preoccupation with what Friedman and Chipkin (2001) characterise as the politics of "identity coalition" even at the local level. Accordingly, in the new democracy, political loyalties and hence participation options for ordinary citizen groups in governance are not shaped by material interests but rather are conditioned by common identities even where this is unrepresentative of local groups. When this happens, Friedman and Chipkin argue, the links between various interest group formations or community organisations and local government representatives are likely to fall into disuse with dire consequences for the quality of governance.

Professed claims by political parties or organisations (largely made up of activists whose links to the grassroots are no more than that they came from similar backgrounds) of being inclusive of community organisations in local government business are increasingly beginning to sound highly questionable in the quest for good governance for most municipalities. Local communities are understood to be an amorphous and undifferentiated whole, devoid of distinct interests, values or political affiliation. The upshot is what Friedman and Chipkin (2001:27) refer to as a "substitute for public opinion, a set of politically well-connected organisations whose difference with the governing elite often consisted of the fact that the former formally held office while the latter did not". Inevitably, such structures have the practical effect of excluding the poor, women and other marginalised groups within governance frameworks. Further, and as a consequence of the above, the incentives for grassroots organisations to access representative organisations to which they could appeal or demand representation have been removed. Empirical evidence and interview informants during the integrated development plan (IDP) processes in Limpopo municipalities confirm the emergence of these patterns and the fact that representative institutions are no longer eager to consult, mobilise or coexist with grassroots organisations.

Local governance and citizen participation

The present developmental local government model is premised on recognition of the primacy of linkages between development, service delivery and local citizen participation, defined as the organised effort to increase control over resources and regulative institutions by groups and movements, especially of those excluded from such control (Stiefel & Wolfe, 1994). The White Paper on Local Government urges: "building local democracy is a central role of local government, and municipalities should develop strategies and mechanisms (including, but not limited to, participative planning) to continuously engage with citizens, business and community groups" (Republic of South Africa, 1998:33). Participation is mandated in four major senses: as voters to ensure democratic accountability, as citizens who through a variety of stakeholder organisations can contribute to policy processes, as consumers and end users who can expect "value for money" and affordable services, and as organised partners engaged in resource mobilisation for developmental objectives.

The theoretical foundation of notions of participatory development planning is premised upon and informed by the influential writings of development planning theorists such as Mumford (1968), Faludi (1986) and Habermas (1996) who underscored the primacy of such precepts as diversity, collaboration, communication and integration. Thus, the current practice locally, nationally and internationally in development planning has over the past century been in transition, moving away from old-fashioned and technocratic blueprint models to more integrated and comprehensive ones fostering inclusion and integration while welcoming diversity. In a real sense, therefore, the recent development planning experience in South Africa through local development objectives (LDOs) and latterly IDPs is a manifestation of this trend.

Central to this trend has been the need for integrated development planning based on the idea that development planning should be holistic and eschew the isolated and segregated models advocated by Mumford and Geddes in the early twentieth century. Integrated development planning in the new South Africa is to ensure integration and the undoing of divisions bequeathed by the apartheid state. Development planning under apartheid was about creating "separateness of races" both geographically and socially and the upholding of these divisions by force if necessary. The IDP framework, as part of the democratic reform, aims to bring people together in terms of space, economic and socially, especially at the local level.

Contemporaneously with this trend and much in evidence within the IDP model has been the gradual theoretical ascendancy of systems thinking and procedural rationalism, which characterises development planning more as an interconnected organic system of processes rather than merely as isolated and disjointed outcomes. What this suggests is that development planning is presently viewed as complex and messy, and confronting a complex whole of interconnected parts made up by people and societies interacting from diverse backgrounds that must be assessed holistically to achieve desired objectives. Indeed, this can hardly be overemphasised in contemporary South Africa, where challenges of diversity and management thereof are severe; the need to explore avenues and creative ways of moving forward as a unified entity is real and immediate.

Yet, for this to be achieved, there is a need to understand existing differences in backgrounds, be they religious, socio-economic, ethnic, race, political or any other; and this is best achieved through communication or what Healey (1995:237) describes as "communicative rationality". Accordingly, communicative rationality suggests that quite apart from scientific and formulaic approaches to achieving and reaching the truth, alternative ways can and should be found to uncover new "knowledges", which are socially and diversity sensitive. She warns against the complacency that comes with uncritically accepting scientific knowledge as necessarily superior truth, as this may represent an incomplete and partial worldview. There is merit in sharing knowledge based on a variety of backgrounds and accumulated through diverse methodologies. Ostensibly, this is brought about in an environment that creates space for the wilful sharing of knowledge, mediated by good communication and the ability of individuals and groups to come together and communicate about various issues and find solutions to problems.

However, inclusive communication and participation will not achieve much if it displays a poor grasp of the machinations of power relations among participants in the decision-making process. It is worth remembering that when communication and collaboration are conceived of as cornerstones of inclusive and participatory local government, issues of power relations among local actors should be brought to the forefront. Power in whatever form within the local development planning rhetoric is crucially important as it has the ability to define and manipulate the development agenda, and construct and create planning realities of the political élites that have scant bearing on the development challenges faced by the poor and marginalised groups.

The idea of communication, collaboration, debate and argument and, thus, integrated development planning is taken further here to include citizen participation in the resolution of societal problems. In theory, the notion of citizen participation presupposes the involvement of various groupings within society, including those Sandercock (2000) describes as "voices from the Borderlands", in local decision-making processes. This compels local government actors to be inclusive of all voices from the community; they should be sought, given cognisance of and included in the general rhetoric of planning, for to do so allows local government actors to learn from experiences that are generally unheard and unacknowledged.

A gendered perspective on integrated development planning

The idea of participatory development planning assumes a qualitatively broader meaning and significance when taken further to include gendered perspectives on local communities, particularly impoverished urban and rural women, and warrants investigation of its integration or lack thereof. Already, a considerable amount of work has gone into highlighting the saliency of gender inequalities in society (Sandercock & Forsyth, 1992). While studies have been undertaken to explore ways and means to open up and facilitate inclusion and integration of women's perspectives, opinions and theories on general development planning discourse and practice remain divided. If it is accepted that development planning has moved away from a segmented and disjointed mode of organising society to one that is comprehensive and integrated, it stands to reason that it can benefit from inclusion of diverse gender perspectives. There is then a compelling case to acknowledge and include knowledge(s), lessons and experiences drawn from women's lives, habits, preferences, lifestyles and ways of thinking, which can do much to enrich local development planning practice and hence society as a whole.

Diverse gendered perspectives, particularly those on poor women and issues that affect them, need to be seen, heard, recognised and most of all understood for ease of mainstreaming in local development plans. The increasing number of working women and female-headed households implies that more than ever before, women's integration as taxpayers and contributors to local economic development will have to be taken into consideration in development planning. In this regard, feminist theory of planning has much to offer in terms of how to think of spatial, economic and social relationships, language communication and methodology. Consideration of feminist spatial theories brings along diverse perspectives on economic and social relationships. The imperative of providing child care facilities close to places of work and their proximity to transport routes, and the need to schedule staff meetings during lunch as opposed to late afternoon when women collect children from aftercare, for instance, could be lost where planning institutions do not include and integrate women's concerns.

Increasingly, and as a result of general reflections and acceptance of gender perspectives (albeit mostly at rhetorical level) within theories of spatial, economic and social relationships, it is easier today for women's issues to be understood and included in development planning.

Because development planning has shifted to and centred around science and procedure, reason and subjectivity, feminist thinking has assumed an added significance around methodology. Sandercock and Forsyth (1992) assert that the insertion of feminist thinking has opened up notions of connected knowing, by which is meant the linking of rationality and scientific methodology. Accordingly, women are viewed more as emotional, sensitive and personal beings and as generally endowed with the ability to link and connect their worlds of work and research with their personal lives. The upshot is that women's insights lead to the expansion of the planning process, which enriches the planning perspectives beyond scientific and technical knowledge to other ways, means and avenues of knowing, learning and gaining experience. Feminist thinkers of this stripe assert that the discourse is enriched by inclusion of knowledge obtained from sources other than so-called scientific thought and research, and whose sources may include talking, gossip, expression of personal feelings and "petty" conversation, most of which are considered untrustworthy and trivial sources in the male dominated planning arena.

What the feminist discourse highlights is that there are many ways of knowing and obtaining or reaching the truth or a desired end, and this has to be included in local development planning. Not all ways of knowing, putatively considered valid and trustworthy, offered by male perspectives can lead to desired results; hence, female integration into development planning and implementation is crucially important not only for women but for society as a whole.

Participation politics and the rise of managerialism

The concept of the active citizen is not a recent invention nor one that can be applied naively even where the most favourable democratic conditions have been established. In his exploration of the complexities of grassroots participation within three transforming and democratic contexts, Heller (2001:133) suggests that "a favourable political alignment be maintained but that a delicate and workable balance between the requirements of institution building and grassroots participation be struck". For decades, development theorists and practitioners have underscored the centrality of decentralisation and participation of ordinary people in their own development as an article of faith. In much of local development experience, however, the conception of citizen participation has remained at a rather fuzzy and ideological level. Its conception and operationalisation have not been matched by practical analytical methods and sound theoretical underpinnings. Invariably, participation has degenerated into a kind of feel-good slogan coined to convince local audiences that local government has recognised the necessity of involving people in development activities. Our conception of participation is meant to denote a "fundamentally transforming exercise of state power" leading to an increase in the scope and depth of subordinate group participation, leading to authoritative and sustainable resource allocation (Heller, 2001:133).

To govern is by definition to exercise power, and even with institutionalised, formal and consolidated democratic practices such as those found in South Africa, no a priori reasons exist to suggest that grassroots demands for participation in localised government will always be met with sympathetic responses. Paradoxical though this may sound, recent history of much of sub-Saharan Africa is marked by decentralisation experiments orchestrated by centralised democratic states with strong commandist impulses. Despite a transformed constitutional environment and governance practice, inherited bureaucratic institutions may still harbour an authoritarian mindset and hence may be contrary to creating participation space for subordinate groups, especially those displaying an autonomous bent.

To understand the reality of participation in those contexts, it is crucial to ascertain the extent to which inherited bureaucratic institutions have changed modes of governance, their previous and preferred social partners and how developmental goals are prioritised. Without such in-depth review of transformation measures, local governments risk remaining distant from rather than being closer to the people, while initial reforms aimed at increasing the scope and depth of local participation may be superseded by unaccountable technocratic and managerial authority. Against this backdrop, Edmunds and Wollenberg (2001:232) warn:

> many approaches to multi-stakeholder negotiations mask abuses of power and more structural, enduring inequity. In doing so, they are prone to exaggerate the level of consensus reached through negotiations and expose disadvantaged groups to greater manipulation and control by more powerful stakeholders.

For some stakeholder groupings in contemporary South Africa, this is a reality. According to some accounts gleaned from interviews, by readily submitting to globalisation pressures and a neo-liberal strategy of economic management, with an attendant managerial outlook of local governance, South Africa has already succumbed to these tendencies. Friedman and Chipkin (2001:26) draw a similar conclusion from recent research, pointing to the relative weakness of representative democracy and the manifest inaccessibility of democratic institutions to grassroots parties and organisations. They furthermore cite the existence of a "deep gulf between policy preoccupation of the elite, … and the grassroots" and the fact that there already is a widespread perception amongst grassroots actors that their elected representatives and institutions are remote and unresponsive.

Such research observations simply confirm what has been a noticeable pattern in recent South African political economy, as the government has shifted from a preoccupation with the quality of democracy to the managerial competencies of managers and policy implementers. The transition has been described in such stark characterisation as "the era of policy making is over, what is now required is to deliver". Partly as a result of this, there has been a perceptible decline in the enthusiasm for political participation and a heightened degree of political cynicism among grassroots organisations, at a time when the role of managers and policy implementers has commensurably increased. Ironically, South Africa's embrace of the neo-liberal strategy of economic management is unlike that adopted by most of the developing world, in that it is not under intense pressure to liberalise and hence has much leeway to free up space for grassroots participation and to lessen local governance managerialism.

Further, local government participation has to be demonstrated to be all-inclusive, ensuring the incorporation of particular categories of people with a history of suffering marginalisation – women, the poor and minority groups. Equally important is the acknowledgement that participation often has to be asserted and not demonstrated. This can be achieved by creating space and allowing marginalised groups and the poor to examine participation indicators and what effects these have on them and wider development.

Whatever critics may say, the notion of participation has widespread common sense appeal and impact. In the South African local government context, citizen participation carries with it system-transformation expectations, in the sense of being closely tied up with equity and empowerment ideals. Rahman (1990:45–49) identifies several dimensions of empowerment that provide a good starting-point for understanding what participation can do for the poor and marginalised in asserting their position in local government decision-making. Firstly, participation encourages marginalised groups to be organised in structures under their control. Secondly, such organised structures bring with them knowledge of their social environment and process to the local government agenda in a way that no other structure can. Thirdly, participation will generally foster self-reliance – an attitudinal quality likely to engender solidarity, caring and the sharing of a collective identity. Fourthly, participation strengthens women's position, providing for articulation of their points of view and, thereby, spearheading progress in gender relations towards equality as assessed by women themselves. Overall, empowerment brought about by such participation would imply that there are "changes going on in the wider society as a result of grassroots changes: the development of human dignity, popular democracy, and cultural diversity" (Shepherd, 1998:180).

Nowhere are the virtues of citizen participation espoused above better understood than in South Africa, with a recent history of community organisation and mobilisation. Following the collapse of apartheid in South Africa, however, the once powerful civic movements and leaderships have either been incorporated or marginalised by the government, leading to the atrophy of organisational participation. Community organisations, labour movements and credit unions suffered capacity setbacks in the early post-apartheid years, as top and middle management cadres left in droves to join the new government. Those who remained found themselves severely incapacitated, pitted against drawn-out transitional local governance arrangements and under-resourced as donor money was diverted to assisting the fledgling government. Reflecting on the above, Cashdan (in Parnell *et al.*, 2002:170) remarks: "Demobilisation and confusion in community organisation, the inheritance of municipal staff, structures and ordinances from the previous regime, and recent emphasis on individual cost recovery, has given rise to a local state system which often has an uneasy relationship with poor communities".

Nonetheless, these organisations have by and large not only survived, they are proving to be major assets in the democratisation process by making inputs into government legislation and policy, including local government development plans. Increasingly, great strides are being made by local government officials and councillors to incorporate and empower organisations, and to engage them in pro-poor planning, restructuring and service delivery. Examples of such gestures include the provision of premises, finance and information, as well as training in participatory planning, budgetary processes and conflict resolution in support of marginalised people.

If the virtues of participation in a decentralising state occupy the centrepiece of the modernising-democratic discourse, the task of making the state responsive can be even trickier unless underpinned by a set of favourable conditions. For South Africa, a liberal foundational constitution and the strong political will of those in power in moving the locus of authority from central to other spheres of government proved pivotal. In this regard, the transitional phases and the will to bring about far-reaching institutional transformation measures laid the foundation for overcoming institutional inertia. Partly as a consequence of constitutional imperatives and government commitment, the Herculean task of passing new legislation, structural transformation and deployment of personnel has been completed, and resources, albeit woefully insufficient, have been channelled to relevant local administrative units. Capacity, however, remains the Achilles' heel of these processes.

Yet, South Africa is still fundamentally constructing a developmental state, and it is conceivable that political, skill, fiscal and organisational imperatives may force a re-examination of decentralisation, especially at local level. Quite apart from the fact that centralised top-down governance has largely fallen into disfavour worldwide, the realisation of severe capacity and fiscal deficits in most local governments in South Africa carries the temptation for a strong organisational bias, as evidenced by several guidelines on fiscal and performance management systems emanating from central government recently.

The challenge for the current local governance dispensation, thus, is to deepen and strengthen local democratic culture, including instances where this may lead to local divisions. This will enhance accountability and ensure that pro-poor developmental outcomes become a reality. When this happens, participation becomes synonymous with development and creeping cynicism about the concept will increasingly dissipate.

Legal and constitutional frameworks for local government

The local government elections of 5 December 2000 marked the culmination of the establishment of a democratic local government dispensation, which had been preceded by interim and transitional arrangements. In very important ways, the different phases marked important milestones in the gradual extension and translation of participative democratic ideals to local communities. Underpinning these efforts is a perspective that holds that the building of local governance is critical to energising local communities to participate in activities that may lead to individual and community development. Good local governance, characterised by transparency, accountability and participatory decision-making, is presumed to provide enabling conditions for poverty reduction measures. Available evidence in recent decades suggests that while economic growth is critical to local development and poverty reduction, it is insufficient unless buttressed by a constitutional and legislative scaffolding that provides material and philosophical support. In the South African context, the following legal and constitutional frameworks have emerged.

The Constitution

The signing of the new Constitution in 1996 heralded the adoption of local government as the epicentre of the government delivery system and at the heart of poverty eradication initiatives. The constitution further signified the adoption of the relatively new and innovative concept of "spheres" as opposed to "tiers" of government, manifesting itself through political and administrative systems and structures. This marked the establishment of new relations between public institutions, government structures and civil society. Specifically, s 40(1) of the Constitution stipulates: "In the Republic, government is constituted as national, provincial and local spheres of government which are distinctive, interdependent and interrelated". Chapter 3 of the Constitution deals with the notion of co-operative governance, by which is meant that all spheres of government must "exercise their powers and perform their functions in a manner that does not encroach on the geographical, functional or institutional integrity of government in another sphere" and "co-operate with one another in mutual trust and good faith" (s 41(1(g)).

Section 151(1) provides that "the local sphere of government consists of municipalities, which must be established for the whole of the territory of the Republic". While the notion of "sphere of government" is an innovative concept for South African local government, and harbours features of distinctiveness and independence, it is important to recognise that it does not connote autonomy for local government from both provincial and national spheres. Section 151(4) of the Constitution provides for a system of inter-governmental relations in which the rights of municipalities are protected and "the national or a provincial government may not compromise or impede municipality's ability or right to exercise its powers or perform its function". National government remains responsible for setting the broad policy frameworks, and monitors local government activities through provincial governments. Within this framework of checks and balances, and bearing in mind that never before in South African local government history has so much power been devolved, municipalities have been configured to discharge their duties and to be accorded recognition as a distinctive sphere rather than as local administrative arms of the national government.

Constitutional innovations introduced by these principles in the South African system oblige all spheres of government to help authorities in other spheres to build their legislative and executive capacities, including the capacity to empower civil society and to secure the well-being of citizens. In the case of municipalities, this approach is illustrated by s 154(1) of the Constitution: "the national government and provincial governments, by legislative and other measures, must support and strengthen the capacity of municipalities to manage their own affairs, to exercise their power and to perform their functions". The role of provincial government in this respect is an evolving one, originally from intervening in or supporting vulnerable municipalities (through financial transfers and secondment of staff) to monitoring and capacity building. With newly established municipalities based on arguably sound demarcation principles of viability, it should no longer be necessary (at least in theory) for provincial governments to perform municipal functions.

Most importantly, the Constitution regulates the transformation of the local government system, while providing it with a pivotal and distinctive role in underpinning and promoting social development and democracy at the local level. For instance, Chapter 7 of the Constitution explains the role of municipalities in the developmental local government process. Concomitant with the thinking above, for local government to fulfil the expectations of the people in respect of grassroots development, significant resources in material and human capital would need to be set aside for investment. With local government's constitutional frameworks in mind, it is appropriate to conceptually examine its nature and role assumptions associated with it, to better appreciate the complex and enormous underdevelopment burden to be addressed. It is to this that our discussion now turns.

The White Paper on Local Government

What does developmental local government mean in contexts of high socio-economic inequality and unrelenting poverty, and in the era of global spread of capitalism? The actual meaning of developmental local government is elusive, extremely imprecise, passing for manifold phenomena, and underpinned by vague theory. Against this backdrop, Bagchi (2000:398) defines developmental local government as one "that puts economic development as the top priority and is able to design effective instruments to promote such an objective". The instruments identified include, *inter alia*, forging new formal institutions, the weaving of formal and informal networks of collaboration between citizens and officials, and the utilisation of new opportunities for trade and profitable production. Developmental local government is not constrained by ideology, but is rather able to switch gears effortlessly from market- to government-directed growth, or vice versa depending on the contingent circumstances. Often, it combines both market and state direction in a synergistic manner when opportunity beckons. Bagchi's characterisation of developmental local government is best captured by sentiments contained in the White Paper on Local Government.

The basis for developmental local government in South Africa is founded on provisions set out in the White Paper on Local Government, published in March 1998. Taking its cue from the Constitutional provisions cited above and experiences of pre-interim and interim transitional local government phases, the White Paper asserts that local government should be developmental, in the sense not only of promoting growth and development, but also in a manner that maintains and sustains the process. This places local government at the centre of driving an ambitious developmental vision and programme designed to address developmental backlogs, the eradication of poverty, the promotion of sustainable development and the provision of safe and secure environments. Similarly, the instruments for pursuing these goals reflect the challenge of "seeking partnerships with all role players that contribute to the development of an area", thereby enabling municipalities to fulfil their "core responsibilities in a way that has a lasting and profoundly positive impact on the quality of life of the people they serve" (Coetzee, 2001). Specifically, it is a partnership logic that interlocks local government, civil society and the private sector.

The White Paper (RSA, 1998:33) recognises the local government sphere as primarily developmental in the sense of being "committed to working with citizens and groups within the community to find sustainable ways to meet their social, economic and material needs, and improve the quality of their lives". To this end, several approaches and trends have started to emerge over the post-apartheid years, setting the tone for local governments as sites for development and poverty reduction measures. Mostly, these approaches have manifested themselves in integrated development planning, urban renewal strategy, extension and improvement of service delivery, especially to the poor, and the adoption of local economic development measures.

In order to assist local governments to meet developmental requirements and speed up service delivery to the poor, extensive resource acquisition in terms of funding, human resources, appropriate institutions and, most importantly, the adoption of key and enabling legislative measures became essential, notably in the Municipal Demarcation Act, the Municipal Structures Act and the Municipal Systems Act. These legislative measures have become indispensable to operationalising the concept of developmental local government.

The Municipal Structures Act

The Municipal Structures Act provides for the determination of types of municipality. For instance, Category A municipalities are metropolitan areas with exclusive legislative and executive authority within their areas of jurisdiction, and Category B municipalities operate within the administrative boundaries of districts.

The Act provides for the establishment of two-tier local government outside the metropolitan areas, to facilitate the flexible exchange of powers and functions between the local and district municipalities. Where local municipalities have sufficient administrative and financial capacity, as is the case in localities with a history of municipality, they will execute all their powers and perform their functions. This is in sharp contrast to municipalities in relatively poor or rural areas, with a dearth of capacity and limited prospects of sustainability. Partly as a result of these deficiencies and weak institutions, such municipalities have generally been granted a reduced range of powers and functions. Where this has happened, district municipalities, with the acquiescence of local actors and the imperative to co-ordinate and streamline development initiatives, have assumed additional powers and functions on their behalf. This flexible approach is intended to capture the advantages of local representation with economies of scale in service delivery. A distinct potential shortcoming of this operational flexibility is the potential for undermining the legitimacy of local government structures. Another disadvantage is associated with costs, in the sense of poorer communities being unable to afford to support two-tier local government.

The Municipal Systems Act

The Municipal Systems Act provides for municipal operations and introduces management systems intended to strengthen municipalities. It further addresses financial and human resource management issues, and governs integrated development planning, municipal service partnerships and performance management in a holistic manner. In terms of this act, municipalities are obliged to produce integrated development plans (IDPs,) which set out their strategic plans in consultation with local communities. The municipal performance management system is intended to determine levels of service municipalities can render, based on their budgets. In terms of a municipal equitable share formula, the national minister can determine appropriate service levels.

Theoretically, municipalities are obligated to provide basic services to communities. They have the latitude, though, to provide a range of service levels to communities based on their IDP estimates and performance management systems. The value of IDPs is that they provide information regarding municipal strategic objectives to other spheres of government in regard to capacity, and they identify possible areas of supportive intervention to comply with minimum standards. Performance management, on the other hand, allows citizens to compare standards, levels and costs of services they receive in relation to neighbouring municipalities. Thus, under-performing municipalities will be under severe pressure to provide services cost-effectively.

The demarcation process has created fundamental building blocks for sustainable and viable municipalities. The Municipal Structures Act differentiates between several types of municipality to allow for different local conditions and political preferences. The Municipal Systems Act seeks to ensure that all South Africans have access to minimum standards of municipal services, but provides considerable leeway to municipalities to exceed those service standards through innovative service delivery, effective cost recovery and appropriate local taxation. The sum total effect of these sets of legislative measures is intended to build a framework by which local government will become truly developmental.

Service delivery within an integrated development planning context

With the demise of the apartheid system and its concomitant replacement by a democratic form of local government, the challenge for the newly established structures and elected councillors is to transform deep-rooted socio-political aspirations, particularly those of the poor and marginalised, into tangible, material improvements in living and working conditions. For these social groups, the struggle to dislodge the apartheid system and its practices and the promise of a "better life for all" could sound hollow were it not to be followed by the elimination of physical and economic discrimination, the creation of opportunities and consequent poverty eradication. This realisation has prompted the call for intergovernmental and departmental planning measures and schemes aimed at poverty reduction. Mostly, initiatives and endeavours to this end are focused on municipal planning approaches, job creation through local economic development funding, developing human capital, fostering community economic development through public works programmes, promoting small, micro and medium enterprises (SMMEs) and developing municipal capacity to retain and attract investment and market localities.

Integrated development planning is the overarching fulcrum around which local government developmental and regulatory responsibilities revolve, and has proven to be a vital tool in ensuring the integration of legitimate physical and economic needs of local communities with broad municipal goals. Briefly put, where properly designed and implemented, integrated development planning can be both integrative and distributive, a municipal planning tool aimed at integrating rich and poor neighbourhoods while distributing goods and services. Spatial plans would be mindful of connecting and binding existing towns with neighbouring townships and rural villages in a much more concrete way, by means of new housing, transportation and commercial development in intermediate buffer areas.

However, design and implementation of integrated development is not unproblematic. Given the entrenched apartheid legacy of unemployment, simultaneous transitional constraints, inherited expanses of underserved townships and rural areas, and housing backlogs, newly demarcated municipalities face the unparalleled challenge of large-scale underdevelopment and poverty way out of all proportion to the means at their disposal. Many local governments carry chronic budgetary deficits while experiencing unsustainable payments arrears, declining capital spending, increasing water and electricity consumption levels and spiralling housing backlogs. In some areas, observers have noted old-style apartheid taking on a new manifestation of "economic segregation". In those cases, any efforts by municipalities to integrate rich and poor neighbourhoods have been "met with incomprehension or opposition by property owners and developers" under the pretext that such integration brings with it the lowering of property values (Cashdan, in Parnell *et al.*, 2002:163). To newly incorporated communities, the benefits of integrated development planning are still marginal, as is accessibility to some of the local amenities, despite a purported right to them.

Across the country, great strides have been made in changing perceptions that a new municipal dispensation perpetuates a "business as usual" approach to municipal functioning. As a result of the strategic nature of integrated development planning processes, budgets are restructured, as is the desegregation of municipal spatial, institutional, administrative and development plans. Prosecution of integrated development plans is underway, as is the insistence that the process be founded on democratic governance, including the participation of local poor communities in needs assessments, prioritisation processes, implementation programmes and monitoring systems (SALGA, 2001:9). Underpinning this position is a rationale that is suggestive of the fact that such an inclusive municipal planning approach guarantees the generation of a holistic development strategy, by definition pro-poor and likely to mobilise the requisite sustainable political support.

Integrated development planning coincides with sustainable development principles, in the sense of being concerned about the need to harmonise local government economic growth and poverty eradication imperatives with safeguarding environmental integrity. Key to this commitment is ensuring that development "meets the needs of the present without compromising the ability of future generations to meet their own needs" (WCED, 1987:8). This means that, in contrast to apartheid township and village planning, attention is now paid to refuse and waste management, the creation of open and green public spaces, the greening of residential spaces, and the promotion of an affordable and environmentally efficient public transport system.

This chapter argues that integrated development planning has the potential to realign spatial, budgetary, institutional, administrative and development patterns into developmental and pro-poor instruments. The challenge, however, is that local municipalities are newly established and, with few exceptions, have severe capacity deficits. Newly elected councillors and appointed officials with responsibility to drive transformation processes, while politically committed, are very quickly swamped by complex technical, legal and institutional constraints and by an uncompromising bureaucratic mindset. To navigate around these challenges, they are forced to resort to the use of external service providers such as consultants whose advice may perpetuate old development patterns that hamper redistribution and integration goals. The result may be a betrayal of the aspirations of poor communities, women and other marginalised groups.

Municipal service delivery in an unequal society

Service delivery represents another avenue for municipal action in obtaining redress for previously excluded local communities and hence to address poverty reduction in South Africa. The White Paper on Local Government asserts that "[b]asic services enhance the quality of life of citizens, and increase their social and economic opportunities by promoting health and safety, facilitating access to work, to education, to recreation and stimulating new productive activities" (RSA, 1998:92). Providing services to newly incorporated communities is hard at the best of times, it is doubly hard where large sections of these communities are afflicted by high levels of unemployment and poverty, historical backlogs in infrastructure and services, and the uneven spread of economic resources.

Under these circumstances, notions of a constitutionally guaranteed "right to services" linked to full cost recovery become highly problematic, especially where service subsidies for the vulnerable are unavailable. The principle of cost recovery in municipal service provision is well-established, ostensibly to eliminate an entitlement mindset and to force service consumers to use only what they can afford to pay for. While subsidies to cushion the plight of the indigent are promised, the reality is that municipal policies and criteria take time to develop and implement and, consequently, few deserving cases have felt the benefits of this. In contrast, rich neighbourhoods and large-scale consumers continue their profligate consumption patterns not dissimilar to those enjoyed under the apartheid dispensation. The result is that tariffs and rates levied remain high and unaffordable for the poor, leading to growing alienation occasioned by the destruction of public facilities and what is euphemistically termed a "culture of service non-payment".

Different schools of thought have emerged and vigorous debates have taken place around the efficacy of pricing municipal services according to commercial criteria, and the effect this has on health, welfare, educational gains and social stability, especially for the poor. Pricing municipal services this way, it is asserted, renders socio-economic benefits beyond the reach of the vulnerable poor. In this vein, Cashdan (2002:165) argues:

> The private-goods approach also reduces citizens to individual consumers with income streams and preferences. Yet apartheid operated against whole communities and resistance was a collective effort. … Emphasis on 'economic pricing' and local competitiveness limits the potential for redistribution between communities, and within sectors such as water and electricity.

In contrast to the above, the sceptics advocate the primacy of market incentives and discipline, that is a minimum of non-economic distortion if respect for financial sustainability in service provision by municipalities is to be upheld (Friedman 1963, Hayek, 1990). In practice, this means municipalities should be able to recover the cost of service provision from consumers by insisting that all residents pay the full cost of services and, where possible, profits be generated for future capital spending. Where subsidies need to be obtained, they argue, central government should be the source without placing an undue burden on wealthier sections of the population.

For South African municipalities, the adoption of a hard-line attitude to cost recovery through the setting of rates and service charges has contributed to increasing social exclusion of the poor, while denying them essential services such as electricity and water. Cross-subsidisation of the poor by rich neighbourhoods has been attempted, although it has been met with alarm and resistance; Sandton ratepayers challenging a Johannesburg metro decision to increase rates in the area is a case in point.

In the face of resistance to cross-subsidisation and limited prospects of additional revenue streams for municipalities to support increasing and competing service requirements, local authorities are hard-pressed to promote redress and reduce poverty. Coupled with this is the lack of human capacity to generate and manage revenues. The perennial capacity constraints facing municipalities to accurately measure service consumption, and incorrect billing, have undermined communities' confidence in the ability of local municipalities to meet their service needs.

However, there are strong economic imperatives for the hard-line cost recovery attitude adopted by municipalities. The notion that competitiveness of localities, in terms of retaining and attracting industrial investment, is best enhanced by pursuing minimal distributive policies that do not upset current expenditure and other resource allocation patterns is all the more commonplace in the local economic development strategies of many municipalities today. This logic suggests that in order to enhance locational competitiveness *vis-à-vis* other localities, conditions for rich neighbourhoods have to be maintained, as this will lead to greater investment, which will bring about increasing job creation for the poor. Thereby, the conditions of the poor will be improved. There is, however, no assurance that rich local citizens will invest locally in proportion to municipal sacrifices made; this may just be a case of the poor subsidising the rich.

To the extent that burgeoning and competing service delivery needs have been unfolding in the past few years alongside a poor prognosis for additional revenue streams and human resource capacity, local authorities are presently challenged to quickly devise mechanisms, including fast-tracking capacity building of their personnel, to ensure that available resources are optimally utilised.

Reducing economic vulnerability through local economic development

The White Paper on Local Government argued for a local government role in boosting employment and improving local conditions for investment attraction. It further posited that local government is "responsible for promoting the social and economic development of communities. This provides municipalities with a mandate to provide special economic services, or to assist other agencies with the provision of such services, where appropriate" (RSA, 1998:25–26). The rationale for this and much of the local government literature underscores the connection between increased investment and job creation, expansion of the tax base, and ultimately significant inroads into poverty reduction.

Confounded by unexpected financial and human resource constraints and massive difficulties in attempting mere service delivery, many smaller local authorities are unable to embark on local economic development. Furthermore, national and provincial government departments have churned out policies, white papers and legislation, which need to be complied with. Understandably, some municipalities assume the "ostrich approach" (by burying their heads in the sand) to the external environment by merely continuing their previous roles and functions, whilst others aggressively grasp the "shot-gun" approach (of "shooting everything that flies"), hoping for something to fall down. The problem with both of these approaches is that neither will adequately lead to the "developmental" outcomes expected of local government. If the success of municipalities is to be measured in terms of their developmental outcomes, then local authorities should actively develop integrated development plans explicitly designed to factor in the poverty concerns necessary to effectively undertake their developmental mandate.

Awareness of the uneven impact of globalisation on localities and sectors in South Africa, and the threat of deepening divisions between the so-called "core" and "periphery", skilled and unskilled, and advantaged and disadvantaged, challenges municipalities to promote and facilitate local economic development. Unless municipalities seriously address questions of poverty, job creation and competitiveness in their localities, and unless they strengthen their strategies through networks and linkages, the existing unequal socio-economic landscape may be reinforced rather than altered. Local economic development will contribute to creating opportunities for regeneration and economic participation.

While boosting local conditions for investment retention and recruitment is neither cheap nor guaranteed of achieving desired outcomes, available literature is replete with examples of ambitious and over-optimistic local economic development strategies, reliant on the consumption of scarce and valuable resources, that have not generated a satisfactory quantity of jobs. A study of the local economic development process in Stutterheim, Eastern Cape, has indicated that despite inclusive, participative and entrepreneurial programmes, the development strategies have failed to arrest escalating poverty levels. Equally important to note is that, while municipalities have an understanding of local economic development, few have a conscious mindset that generates "structured and monitored" strategies to "ensure a systematic reduction in incidence of poverty and vulnerability" (DCD, undated:1).

Gender mainstreaming

We have already alluded to feminist thinking, which advocates the altering of perceptions and practices that have characterised development planning in the previous century. Although development planning in South African municipalities is still male-dominated, there is an increasing realisation that an increase in female inputs into the planning process will benefit society as whole. The ruling party, the ANC, has called for greater participation of women in the planning process in order to undo the legacy of apartheid.

Currently, local municipalities exhibit inadequate representation of women in leadership positions. "Although women constitute more than 50% of the population, only 20% of municipal councillors are women" (RSA, 1998:88). This issue is being addressed through training programmes targeted at councillors, relevant local government officials and community leaders. Officials, especially those involved with IDPs, have been invited to participate in these programmes, some of which were specific training programmes to empower women councillors on issues that are essential to their effective participation in local government affairs. The challenge is now to involve members of civil society in these issues.

Municipal service partnerships

The White Paper on Municipal Service Partnerships, released by the government in 2001, defines a municipal service partnership (MSP) as a "contractual arrangement with another body or organization for the delivery or performance of any municipal services" (http://www.dplg.gove.za). Given that some local municipalities are still weak in capacity and yet obliged to ensure sustainable delivery of services, councils are forced to consider the MSP option for meeting the particular municipal service needs of their communities.

This involves assessing the advantages and disadvantages of entering into a partnership with the private sector or other interested organisations, such as NGOs, community-based organisations (CBOs) and other municipalities, to provide the required municipal services for the community. There are various co-operative options that have been explored by providing information, piloting demonstrations, training local government staff and other stakeholders such as representatives of business, labour and communities. To further increase understanding about local government service partnerships, presentations have been organised by experts to share experiences from successful South African and international projects. Also, experiences of other government departments have been examined.

Provision of infrastructure services

Through the Municipal Infrastructure Investment Programme (MIIP), Extension of Municipal Services Programme (EMIP) and Consolidated Municipal Infrastructure Programme (CMIP), many projects have been completed that have extended sewerage and water to a number of areas, especially to disadvantaged communities. Cost recovery, however, is still a problem.

The CMIP grants include a portion to be used for capacity building. Whereas, this was previously allocated on a project-by-project basis, a province may now allocate a lump sum from the global allocation for capacity building generally (DPLG, 2000:1). In this way, provincial and local authorities, instead of it being restricted to a particular project, can now provide broader capacity building around infrastructure delivery, project management and so forth.

Globalisation and its implications for service delivery

Given the scope and dynamism of socio-economic and political transformation processes in South Africa over the past decade, it has become necessary to understand how these were impacted on and shaped by globalisation forces beyond the borders and control of the country. Key to this understanding are two contending world views of globalisation, namely hyperglobalist and sceptic (Held *et al.*, 1999; Gray, 1999). The hyperglobalists argue that the entire world has become global in the sense of being on the verge of becoming a single free market, untrammelled by any interference from previously sovereign states. For the hyperglobalists, nation-states have lost the power to control capital flows in and out of the national territories over which they exercise constitutional sovereignty. By contrast, the sceptics argue that the actual extent of globalisation has fallen short of the hyperglobalists' claims of the erosion of national sovereignty. They contend that the nation-state has never enjoyed complete sovereignty and has always confronted constraints imposed by both external conditions and internal opposition.

Therefore, globalisation has an important bearing on local government transformation, especially the extension of integrated service delivery to the poor in South Africa as in other parts of the globe. While the hyperglobalists view the world as an open economy, and nation-states as powerless and inactive spectators to the demise of their authority, the sceptical call for state intervention in the economy to produce distributive outcomes and thus mitigate negative impacts unleashed by globalising forces. According to the sceptics, the economy is still sufficiently closed to allow the nation-state a considerable margin of autonomy, and the talk of globalisation and its imperatives is nothing more than a disguise used by neo-liberal proponents to justify their policies. The nation-state still has the power to leverage resources via taxation and to embark on distributive measures whilst simultaneously pursuing sustainable growth policy. The fact that there is a global tendency to move away from the social market towards the free market signals the success of the ideological struggle waged by capital under the guise of globalisation, which, for the sceptics, can be reversed by the state.

Whatever the substantive differences are between the arguments raised above, there is no denying the fact that "contemporary processes of globalisation are historically unprecedented" and governments and societies at all levels are forced to adjust "to a world in which there is no longer a clear distinction between international and domestic, external and internal" (Held, *et al.*, 1999:7). A pattern of deep transformation in the contemporary processes of globalisation, which is neither singular nor linear but rather an essentially contingent historical process, is much in evidence. In this regard, predictive claims about the future trajectory of globalisation and its impact on sovereign nation-states are impossible, given that these are significantly shaped by hypothetical factors.

Further, advances in science and technology, especially in the fields of information and telecommunications, have promoted integration in a way that potentially can assist national and provincial spheres of government to facilitate effective decentralisation, while increasing the capacity of municipalities to better fulfil their functions efficiently and expeditiously. These advances link the centre to previously unreachable localities. In so doing, there are countless possibilities brought about by globalisation to integrate development plans vertically across spheres of government and horizontally within spheres and sectors of government.

The corollary of the view raised above, then, is that a nation-state like South Africa and various spheres of government still have significant authority to intervene against perverse consequences of globalisation and in favour of distributive actions and the promotion of local economic development initiatives to improve the lives of the poor and marginalised. What this suggests is that, far from emptying the state of all political relevance, as hyperglobalists suggest, globalisation has endowed struggles to influence state, indeed local government, policy with new and added significance, albeit in an environment marked by a pattern of deep transformation and significantly shaped by conjectural factors. By the same token, just as in the nineteenth and twentieth centuries the state had to adapt to the advent of the railroad, in the contemporary period the nation-state has to adapt to the arrival and influences of globalisation brought about by information technology (Graham & Marvin, 1996:61).

As has been highlighted, the advent of globalisation has crucial implications for the macroeconomic policy options for developing countries such as South Africa. The post-apartheid state has had its foundation and options pulled from underneath it, given that capital is now more mobile and South African companies are relocating their headquarters to international metropolitan centres. As a result, capital has found new ways to avoid contributing to the redistribution project being promoted by the post-apartheid state. Viewed against this backdrop, a process of role-reversal has ensued, in which globalisation enables capital to set the limits of feasible national macroeconomic policy.

Conclusion

One of the emerging observations in this chapter is that most of the writing and documentation on developmental local government does not make explicit connections nor interrogate the relationship between structural transformation, good governance, integrated planning and poverty reduction. The relationship appears axiomatic. There seems to be an underlying and unquestioned assumption that a focus on participative, integrated development planning, cost-effective infrastructural and partnership arrangements and local economic development strategies necessarily leads to beneficial "trickle down" effects on communities, especially the marginalised and poor. Yet, it is arguable whether municipalities have prioritised or developed a clearer conceptualisation of structural linkages that infuse poverty reduction concerns with economic growth promotion. Even more problematic is the fact that despite putative claims of political equality in the post-apartheid dispensation, one cannot naively assume that the poor and marginalised groups such as women and the disabled have as many opportunities for local participation as the educated, socio-economically well off and the urbanised. Empirical evidence drawn out from integrated development planning processes and assessment suggests that, apart from the periodic act of voting, the poor and marginalised, especially in rural provinces, not only suffer from a low level of political efficacy but genuinely lack the material resources and technical skills to organise effectively for collective action. Mindful of vastly varied levels of socio-economic development and inherent political inequalities between local government officials, councillors and marginalised groups, an urgent imperative is that disadvantaged groups and supporters be strategically engaged to achieve equitable and mutually beneficial outcomes.

Evidence from interviews conducted by the author further suggests that civil society and broadly marginalised groups and poor women, in particular, may not have a full awareness of the broad spectrum of anti-poverty reduction policy frameworks, instruments and opportunities. In extreme cases, this may also include some key municipality officials or councillors themselves. This is, however, hardly surprising, given the recent nature of the anti-poverty trends in policy work in South Africa. For instance, the first national anti-poverty document, the Poverty and Inequality Report, was only released in 1998. In addition, the poverty hearings initiated by the South African Non-Governmental Coalition partnership with the Gender Commission and Human Rights Commission helped to raise awareness about poverty.

The impact of globalisation on contemporary development planning in South Africa is that it has reduced the scope for the state to take independent action. The relationships that currently characterise capital, government and local communities' interaction reflect the effects of globalisation. Highly mobile domestic and international capital, as well as multilateral institutions have exercised significant leverage over the South African state, leading to the adoption of the Growth Employment and Redistribution strategy. Thus, while globalisation has generated unprecedented pressure on the South African state, in the process constraining its sphere of authority and limiting available options to deliver services to the poor, there is scope for the state to develop new ways of mitigating the negative effects of globalisation, including the promotion of local economic development strategies through municipalities.

While there is widespread awareness of local economic development and its potential to help stimulate economic development, the understanding of it, however, is varied and usually lacking in poverty focus. It is open to differing interpretations depending on political or ideological motives. Business sector actors, for instance, read into local economic development a justification for their opposition to the principle of cross-subsidisation of low-income communities under the pretext that such cross-subsidisation undermines local competitiveness. By the same token, community groups use it to exclude external competition in the local market by insisting that local businesses be given preferential treatment even where their efficiency and capabilities do not approximate those of external rivals. As a result of these competing interests, developing a coherent local economic plan becomes problematic, let alone attempting to give such a plan a poverty reduction focus.

Hence, the challenge of poverty reduction for local government is going to require genuinely vigorous partnerships between various stakeholders, local as well as national, governmental, private sector and civil society. These partnerships may assume different forms, formalised or loosely structured, and be of different duration. The key is that such partnerships be built on democratic principles, genuinely participative and transparent.

Development planning literature and documentation gleaned in this study frequently made references to the goal of poverty reduction at local level without establishing indicators. Briefly stated, "anti-poverty initiatives are as good as the evaluated outcomes of the development" (RSA, 2001:7). As local government is the sphere closest to people concerned with poverty reduction, the imperative of building their capacity to set indicators for the measuring, monitoring and evaluation of anti-poverty programme outcomes cannot be underestimated. Current training efforts for municipalities on performance management and measurement should go a long way to building capacities of anti-poverty target setting. Given vast variations among municipalities in terms of economic base, capacity, access to information and inter-group co-operation, it seems appropriate to suggest that provincial and national government assist in providing support and guidance.

References

Bagchi, A. K. (2000) "The Past and the Future of the Developmental State", *Journal of World System Research*, 6, 2, Summer/Fall.

Coetzee, M. J. (2001) "Developmental Local Government and Integrated Development Planning", D*emocratic Local Government; A Guide for Councillors*. Case Studies on LED and Poverty. Pretoria: Department of Constitutional Development.

Department of Constitutional Development (Undated) "Case Studies on LED and Poverty." Pretoria.

Department of Provincial and Local Government (2000) "LED Programme", Local Economic Development Manual Series 2/5. Pretoria.

Department of Provincial and Local Government (2002) "Vhembe District Municipality IDP Assessment Report Interviews" (Conducted by the author).

Edmunds, D. & Wollenberg, E. (2001) "A Strategic Approach to Multistakeholder Negotiations", *Development Change*, Vol. 1, No. 32.

Faludi, A. (1986) *Critical Rationalism and Planning Methodology*. London: Pion.

Friedman, M. (1963) *Capitalism and Freedom*. Chicago: Chicago University Press.

Friedman, S. & Chipkin, I. (2001) "A Poor Voice?: The Politics of Inequality in South Africa." Research Report No. 87. Johannesburg: Centre for Policy Studies.

Graham, S. & Marvin, S. (1996) *Telecommunication and the City*. London: Routledge Publishers.

Gray, J. (1999) *False Dawn – The Delusions of Capitalism*. London: Granta.

Habermas, J. (1996) *The Inclusion of the Other; Studies in Political Theory*. Frankfurt am Main: Suhrkamp.

Hayek, F. A. (1990) *Economic Freedom*. Cambridge, MA: Basil Blackwell.

Healey, P. "Discourse Integration." In Healey, P. et al. (eds) (1995) *Managing Cities, The New Urban Context*. Chichester: John Wiley and Sons.

Held, D., McGrew, A. G., Goldblatt, D. & Perreton, J. (1999) *Global Transformations: Politics, Economics and Culture*. London: Polity Press.

Heller, P. (2001) "Moving the State; The Politics of Democratic Decentralisation in Kerala, South Africa, and Porto Alegre", *Development Change*, Vol. 1, No. 32.

Hayek, F. A. (1990) *Economic Freedom*. Cambridge, MA: Basil Blackwell.

Kooiman, J. & Van Vliet, M. (1993), "Governance and Public Management." In Eliassen, K. & Kooiman, J. (eds) *Managing Public Organisations*. Second edition. London: Sage Publishers.

Mumford, L. (1968) *The City in History: Its Origins, Its Transformations and, Its Prospects*. New York: Harvest Books.

Parnell, S., Pieterse, E., Swilling, M. & Wooldrige, D. (2002) *Democratising Local Government. The South African Experiment*. Cape Town: University of Cape Town Press.

Rahman, M. A. (1990) "Qualitative Dimensions of Social Developmnent Evaulation. Thematic Paper on Evulating Social Development Project." In Marsden, D. & Oakley, P. (eds) *Development Guidelines* No 5. United Kingdom: Oxfam.

Rhodes, R. (1996) *Governing Without Government; Order and Change in British Politics*. Newcastle: Department of Politics, University of New Castle Upon Tyne.

Republic of South Africa (1998) "The White Paper on Local Government."

Republic of South Africa (2001) *Local Economic Development, LED Financing*. National Department of Provincial and Local Government.

Rosenau, J. N. & Czempiel, E. O. (1992) *Governance Without Government: Order and Change in World Politics*. Cambridge: Cambridge University Press.

Sandercock, L. (2000) "Negotiating Fear and Desire: The Future of Planning in Multicultural Societies", *Urban Forum*, Vol. 11.

Sandercock, L. & Forsyth, A. (1992) "A Gender Agenda, New Directions for Planning Theory", *American Planning Association Journal*.

Shepherd, A. (1998) *Sustainable Rural Development*. London: Macmillan Press Ltd.

South African Local Government Association (2001) *Integrated Development Planning: A Practical Guide to Munipalities*. (Supplementary to the IDP Guide Pack of the Department of Provincial and Local Government) Pretoria.

Steifel, M. & Wolfe, M. (1994) *A Voice for the Excluded: Popular Participation in Development; Utopia or Necessity*. London: ZED Books.

Stoker, G. (2002) "Governance as Theory: Five Propositions." Enjeux des debates sur La Gouvernance, Universite de Lausanne, 29–30 November, 1–8.

World Commission on Environment and Development (1987) *Our Common Future*. Oxford: Oxford University Press.

Part Three
Civil Society in the
Democratic Dispensation

Civil Society, Governance and Development in an Era of Globalisation: The South African Case

Adam Habib and Hermien Kotzé

Introduction

In recent years, there has been a growing academic and intellectual interest in South African civil society. Part of the reason for this is the perceived success of South Africa's democratic transition and the role of civil society organs therein. Part of it has to do with the fact that South Africa is a very useful laboratory for the investigation and understanding of social phenomena because of its changing nature, which ensures a hybrid character where the old and new coexist. Part of it has to do with the more universal interest in civil society or the so-called Third Sector, prompted by demoralisation with the state and the market. And part of it has to do with the fact that civil society has become the hope for all across the ideological spectrum. For those on the right, it is a support and service-delivery mechanism, while for those on the left, it is an agency to usher in a new social order.

This new interest in South African civil society is reflected in the conclusion of two multi-million rand research projects on the size and shape, and impact of the sector. The first (Swilling & Russell, 2002), part of the Johns Hopkins multi-country comparative project, and undertaken by the School of Public and Development Management at the University of the Witwatersrand, is the most comprehensive assessment of the size and shape of civil society in South Africa. It is a study that has some serious flaws, the least of which is that its theoretical and empirical sections are entirely divorced from each other. This is largely the result of a methodological flaw in the design of the project. But both sections of the final report make interesting observations and are thus useful in their own right. Moreover, despite the small sample size, the study does provide the most serious attempt to estimate the size and shape of civil society in South Africa.

The second study (Idasa/Core, 2001), undertaken by the Institute for Democracy in South Africa (Idasa) and the Co-operative for Research and Education (Core), is part of the Civicus multinational comparative research project on impact. Again, there is a serious flaw in the design of the project. The study investigates impact on the basis of question-naires, workshops and in-depth interviews with NGO[1] practitioners. It is useful for getting a general, impressionistic picture of the sector. But it is problematic from an analytical viewpoint, since the findings are based on NGOs' own perceptions of their roles, rela-tionships, performance and impact. There is thus no independent attempt within the methodology to verify NGO practitioners' assumptions about themselves.

In any case, the research reports of both projects identify a series of issues, which require further in-depth investigation. This includes impact assessment studies. The principal les-son, however, that needs to be learnt from both projects is the necessity of good research design and methodology, for without this, scholars and practitioners are simply in no position to make generalisations about the sector. This chapter does not do this; although grounded in empirical information, informed largely by the "Johns Hopkins" and "Civicus" studies, it is essentially a broad, reflective (some may even say impressionistic) analysis of the emergence and evolution of civil society in post-apartheid South Africa. It explores how globalisation and the transition to democracy influenced and shaped civil society and its relations with the state.

One of the major problems with studies of civil society is that their authors have a direct stake in advancing the case for, or presenting a positive image of, the sector. This may account, in part, for the popularity of organisational and institutional methodologies, which focus inward and tend to be descriptive and provide greatly exaggerated assess-ments of the sector and its impact.[2] Some recent studies, however, have corrected this and undertaken a more systemic analysis of civil society, its emergence and evolution. One example of this is Lester Salamon and Helmut Anheier's (1998) "Social Origins of Civil Society", which explains the Third Sector as a product of regime types, which are a result of the configuration of social forces within society.[3] Similarly, Terje Tvedt's (1998) *Angels of Mercy or Development Diplomats* focuses on the international aid system and investigates how it conditions the evolution of NGOs, their behaviour and operations.

This study follows in the footsteps of these pioneering works by explaining civil socie-ty from a systemic perspective. It investigates structural variables like the socio-economic environment, the political system and the prevailing flow of resources to explain the evo-lution of civil society in South Africa. The chapter is structured in five parts. Part two focuses on definitional issues, describing the international context and how it informs the evolution of civil society across the globe. Part three focuses on the export of neo-liberal-ism to South Africa and the evolution of the post-apartheid political economy. Part four reflects on how the post-apartheid socio-economic and political environment informs the evolution of civil society and impacts on its diverse components. Finally, part five, which serves as the conclusion, effectively tries to summarise the argument and to learn the political lessons thereof.

Definition and international background

For more than a decade, the notion of civil society has held central sway in official, academic and popular discourses about development, democracy and governance in the world. The last quarter of the twentieth century witnessed the democratisation of several authoritarian regimes, most notably in Africa, Asia, Eastern Europe and Latin America. In almost all of these instances, a wide array of non-state actors played an important role in the democratisation experiments. Analysts thus revived the concept of "civil society"[4] to explain these developments and the term moved rapidly from academic discourse to widespread popular use across the entire ideological spectrum. The power and importance of civil society was lauded by everybody from the World Bank to small, radical grassroots groupings and movements in the South.

This "rhetorical consensus" (Pearce, 2000:32) led to an oversimplification of the concept, which manifested itself in definitions that reduced civil society to an amorphous and homogeneous entity, generally assumed to be broadly progressive in nature and often almost exclusively associated with NGOs and CBOs. The oversimplification and depoliticisation of the concept facilitated what Jenny Pearce (2000:18) refers to as the "collective collusion in the myth that a consensus on development exists, or even that some clear conclusions have been reached about how to deal with global poverty". Increasingly, however, it is being recognised that there is a need to deconstruct this myth and to locate development discourse and practice in the complex reality of conflicting interests and opposing agendas.

Nowhere is this more necessary than in South Africa. The role of associational groups in bringing an end to apartheid has promoted an overly romanticised view of the sector among both scholars and activists. Almost all definitions of civil society in South Africa are afflicted with this malady and treat the sector as a homogenous entity ascribed with a progressive political agenda.[5] This, however, is clearly not academically or politically sustainable. Ideological and political heterogeneity must be a defining element of the concept of civil society. In addition, civil society must be conceptualised as distinct from both the market and state. Of course, traditional Hegelian definitions of civil society include the market. Jean Cohen and Andrew Arato's (1992) comprehensive and defining work on the subject, however, makes a coherent case for why the market should be excluded from definitions of civil society. In line with their recommendation, then, this study takes as its working definition of civil society the organised expression of various interests and values operating in the triangular space between the family, state and the market.

Of course, the configuration and evolution of this civic space is determined by the political socio-economic milieu within which it is located. And, this milieu is primarily defined by the Third Wave[6] of democratisation that so dramatically culminated in the collapse of the Berlin Wall in 1989. Although it is clearly impossible to construct a precise chronology of developments in the aftermath of the complex confluence of historical events that had propelled the Third Wave of democracies, the net effect of these was the coupling of democracy with neo-liberal economic prescriptions. This vision was advanced not only by Western powers and international financial institutions, but also by the mainstream academy in both the developed and developing world. It was implemented through the standard mechanism of conditional "governance" packages that Western governments, the International Monetary Fund (IMF) and the World Bank attached to foreign aid and loan programmes in the newly democratising societies. Thus, in a few short years, countries across the developing world were characterised by a shrinking state, a deregulated labour market, the lowering of trade and financial barriers, the streamlining of social expenditure and, above all, the establishment of an environment where the supremacy of the market went unquestioned.

In line with this vision, "civil society"[7] in developing countries was allocated the task of promoting democracy and engaging with the shrinking state. This was partly unavoidable, since civil society had been significantly legitimised as a result of the strong influence of people's power in the third wave of democracy. But it was also encouraged because CSO involvement implied "a diffusion of power both in state institutions and between the state and non-state actors" (Shubane, 1999:10) that fitted in neatly with neo-liberal thinking on the role and power of nation-states.

One significant element of civil society's new responsibilities was stepping into the social services delivery domain, partially vacated by the state in terms of the standard neo-liberal budgetary and fiscal directives. Basically, the official neo-liberal logic started with the "efficiency" argument that NGOs, unhindered by large bureaucracies and having closer links with beneficiary communities, would deliver a better, more efficient and cost-effective service than government departments. In order to do this, they were either contracted by government departments or funded directly by foreign donors to implement certain programmes on the state's behalf. The question that immediately arose was to whom these NGOs were accountable. The answer, generally, is that they became directly accountable to their donors and the government that had contracted them, thus becoming mere implementing agencies for the agendas and policies of other institutional actors.

Apart from the cost-cutting concerns though, there was also a strong element of social containment implicit in this project. It is well-recognised, even by the architects and technocrats of this economic order, that the prescribed cuts in governments' social expenditure and the job losses resulting from privatisation and the removal of trade barriers had a high social and human cost. If this cost rose too high, it would have led to political instability, which would have derailed the neo-liberal project. To avoid this consequence, and to help take the edge off increased poverty, inequality, unemployment and worsening basic living conditions, NGOs were expected to pick up the social costs of neo-liberal programmes.

The appeal was made in more technical and persuasive terms, of course; otherwise, not even the most deluded NGO would have taken on this impossible task. Clearly, not all the NGOs in the world, even if there were thousands more, could possibly address the underlying causes of global poverty and inequality. Their involvement, then, could at best be of a palliative nature, providing a social band-aid to the victims of the very system employing their services. Rather like doctors in a war hospital. Or to use the more graphic description of Stephen Commins (in Pearce, 2000:20), NGOs' role in the present order can only but be seen as "useful fig leaves to cover government inaction or indifference to human suffering".

Thus, NGOs took on a task, each in their own way and context, which simply could not be achieved. In doing so, they took risks and made compromises that are already starting to turn against them, not only in increasing cynicism from community constituencies and more radical grassroots groupings, but also in growing scepticism from official donors. Pearce (2000:20) states that:

> Perhaps what has encouraged the beginnings of an anti-NGO shift is that, unsurprisingly, NGOs were unable to offer the solution to the social cost of economic restructuring. Criticisms of NGOs have focused on their technical deficiency, their lack of accountability, and their excessively politicised and critical character. This "failure" has undermined their credibility among the technocrats within donor institutions, who demanded rapid and measurable outputs from investments in the NGO sector. And it weakened the influence of the pro-NGO social development advocates within those institutions.

In any case, if the bigger, more formalised NGOs, became mere implementers of donor and government development agendas, who was then responsible for generating the alternative development agenda? This responsibility appears to increasingly fall on the smaller, more radical grassroots organisations and movements, whose members and supporters experience the negative effects of neo-liberalism first-hand.

These moral dilemmas and choices, largely emanating from neo-liberal technocrats' desire to contain the state and transfer its responsibilities to non-state actors, have caused fragmentation and tension in the civil society sector. Civil society, of course, has never exactly been a model of harmony and homogeneity and neither is it expected to be thus. The new plans and funding preferences of technocrats, however, have led to more finger pointing and fiercer competition between NGOs, and have opened up a growing divide between the formal structures and their smaller grassroots-based counterparts.

This divide appeared quite early on in Latin America, where harsh distinctions were drawn between what were termed "neo-liberal" and "progressive" NGOs (see Kotzé, 1998 and 1999). Increasingly, this divide, which incidentally often seems to reflect the wider inequalities and divisions in societies, has manifested itself across the developing world. In recent years, there has been a tendency in developing countries for the smaller CBOs, which are truly closer to ordinary people's lives, to start organising around the human fall-out of neo-liberal programmes. They tend to organise around quite specific issues and identities, broadly related to issues of economic and social exclusion and exploitation. Social observers and analysts are always speculating about the significance of these developments and whether they have the potential to be harnessed into broader-based social movements with real potential to challenge the status quo.

The position of churches and trade unions on the effects of neo-liberalism and globalisation obviously varies between countries, but in most cases is also located among ordinary people. They have generally tended to be critical of the status quo. In South Africa, for example, the churches have in recent years become more vocal in campaigns to cancel international debt, and have publicly urged the government to address the growing poverty and inequality in the country. Cosatu, the biggest trade union federation, has also been extremely vocal in its anti-neo-liberal sentiments, but remains in an uneasy alliance with the ruling party.

It is unfair to apportion blame to this or that section of civil society. The issues and dilemmas raised here are complex and multi-layered and often not even clear in the minds of the individuals and organisations confronting the choices imposed upon them by the "new world order". Although many NGOs presumably became service delivery agents by choice, the majority probably ended up in that role either through considerations of survival or because of the lack of a proper grasp of the neo-liberal discourse and its practical implications.

Civil society is neither a homogeneous nor a static entity, so hopefully the growing international challenge to the neo-liberal paradigm will lead to radical self-analysis and a new commitment to pursue fairer alternatives in local and world development. An early positive indication is the fact that the World Bank is irritated not only with the technical deficiencies of CSOs, but also with what is perceived to be their excessively politicised and critical character. It is just possible that, in spite of all the forced conformism, something about the essential nature of CSOs has remained intact, and can form the basis for the rethinking that is urgently required. What is necessary now is peer pressure on CSOs to disentangle themselves from the "thought vacuum" they have tended to inhabit these last years and to move forward with more critical clarity and a new purpose.

Reflection and repositioning, however, is not only required on the side of civil society. Increasingly, the notion and practices of neo-liberalism and globalisation are being fundamentally challenged across the world. No longer is there only a confused retreat in the face of the "no alternative" mantra. Instead, there is a well co-ordinated and increasingly vocal and visible insistence on an alternative. Ironically, a large part of the growing success of the anti-globalisation movement is attributable to extensive use of new forms of electronic communication (the Internet and cell phone technology) that paradoxically contributed to enlarging corporate power in the first place (see Byers, 2000).

In any case, the core of this new social movement is constituted by a variety of diverse organisations, located across the developed and developing world, which question the ideological parameters of the existing world order. This has prompted a chorus of voices in international officialdom, which is now making consistent demands for more and better regulation of the world economy (see, for instance, Stiglitz, 1998). But it is also important for those CSOs critical of the world order to make a concerted effort at improving analysis and strategy, as well as developing real alternatives to the present economic orthodoxy.

South Africa: The end of exceptionalism?

The question then is: Are the same processes at play in South Africa? Are we bound to follow the same route and face the same dilemmas and choices or can we persist with our long-held delusion of being different? Do we even have a solid grasp of the dilemmas and choices confronting us? These are some of the questions and issues that will be addressed in this section.

South Africans have always had a tendency to see themselves and their country as different, exceptional even. The origins of this acute sense of exceptionalism, usually expressed as a blend of pride and defensiveness, can probably, at least partially, be found in the country's colonial history and distant geographical location at the southern-most part of the African continent, far from Europe and North-America but also strangely out of touch with what is generally referred to as "the rest of Africa". For a very long time, thus, there was South Africa, then the rest of Africa and, finally, the rest of the world.[8]

This mentality became nearly pathological during the isolation of the apartheid years, particularly in the case of many White South Africans, who responded to all challenges and criticism of the system with the lament that other people simply did not understand. Africans[9] were not entirely exempt from the exceptionalism tendency either, in that for many decades they had to face and fight apartheid daily, which in itself required a degree of single-mindedness. South Africans thus, each in their own way and for different reasons, became a dangerously inward-looking nation. We believe that what happened here had no parallel in the rest of the world (which is true in some respects) and that we were all different from everybody else.

The tendency peaked, in a more positive way, in the immediate aftermath of the successful and relatively peaceful general election in 1994. Millions of South Africans, including many who previously opposed majority rule, basked in the glory of the political miracle and the general sense of being at the centre of the world's attention. "Madiba magic", the short-reigning notion of the rainbow nation, major international sport achievements and the general opening up of South Africa to the world and vice versa, were just some of the many factors that contributed to a new sense of being special.

The developmental phase

On the political front, there was also euphoria enough, at least temporarily, to sustain the belief that we could and would do "our own thing", and on a grand scale, regardless of prevailing trends in the rest of the world. After 46 years of apartheid, the majority of South Africans were left poor, inadequately educated, badly housed, living far from their places of employment or job opportunities, and with little or no access to basic services like electricity, clean piped water and accessible health facilities. Any government serious about socio-economic justice and the consolidation of democracy needed a comprehensive development programme to address this multitude of needs and restore dignity and decency to the lives of the millions of ordinary South Africans who were the victims of apartheid. This was even more true for the ANC government, which came to power on a broad base of popular support that embodied the hopes and expectations for a better life of millions of people.

In response, the ANC and its allies developed the Reconstruction and Development Programme (RDP), which served as their electoral manifesto. The programme was premised on state-led development, informed by neo-Keynesian assumptions and policy prescriptions, which had lost favour in the World Bank and IMF. For a while, we were going to be different: we had a large and legitimate task to address the ills and backlogs of the past and had clearly earned the moral right to do it in our way.

The ruling party had strong social-democratic underpinnings, which at that time had already begun eroding, in the face of subtle pressures and persuasion from local and international business. Thus, whilst the RDP was on everybody's lips, popular expectations sky-high and government officials struggling to gear up for massive delivery, the balance of power turned out decidedly against such a programme. It should not be surprising to note that, already in December 1993, the ANC gave support to a small IMF Compensatory Financing Facility, to which the standard, neo-liberal, draft Letter of Intent was accepted by the ANC without any changes, and quite contrary to the advice of their own economic advisors at the time (Habib & Padayachee, 2000:10).

Nonetheless, and maybe indicative of the compromises, concessions and contradictions of the time, the RDP was adopted and, for some time, had the full support of politicians, ordinary South Africans and even some business people. Although there were subtle signs, even in the RDP document, of economic moderation (Habib & Padayachee, 2000:11), the programme was, and is still, better known for its more popular social-democratic vision. For the two years that the RDP was official policy, the government completely seized the "development initiative" that, under apartheid, had been the virtually exclusive preserve of development CSOs. In practice, the CSOs were almost completely crowded out of even the policy-making circles that they had participated in since the early nineties.[10] Moreover, many of the development projects, initiated over many years, experienced serious problems, as a result of confusion over direction, issues of scale of projects and problems over funding (Kotzé, 1998:176). The state claimed total control over the development agenda, a task it was often woefully unprepared for, but would not share with anyone, even old allies and erstwhile colleagues in CSOs.[11]

Despite all the centralised activity (endless workshops, strategic planning, hiring of consultants, meetings and business plans), it was clear quite early on that there were serious problems of capacity in state institutions. In retrospect, it was almost impossible to implement a programme of that magnitude from scratch and in such a short space of time, particularly given the massive restructuring and reorientation of the public service that had to take place. Government officials, particularly those attached to RDP units across the country, quite contrary to the public commitment to inclusiveness, turned inward (and to private consultants) to figure out ways of mastering the mammoth task. In the process, they generally became totally inaccessible to the very people they were supposed to help.[12]

The government's public commitment to "people-centred" development and to working closely with CSOs (see ANC, 1994) generally turned out to have been largely rhetorical. Early on, with all the people-centred rhetoric still officially around, there was already a discernible shift in the development discourse towards a more technical interpretation of development, commonly referred to as the "bricks and mortar approach". The more complex and circumspect human and social processes, generally associated with development projects in the "NGO world" worldwide, started falling by the wayside. When questioned about this, senior government officials often responded with irritation, stating that they need not consult with people about their needs, since they already knew their needs.[13]

Moreover, instead of drawing on the experience and expertise of thousands of CSOs and actively involving them in policy-making and, where appropriate, implementation of projects, the government tried to handle it on their own or assisted by consultants.[14] Ironically, given its generally anti-capitalist policies in the past, the new ANC government preferred a working relationship with the private rather than the third sector. In 1996 Thabo Mbeki, then Deputy President of South Africa, expressed this in his "The State and Social Transformation" document, where he argued for "a dialectical relationship with private capital as a social partner for development and social progress" (in Habib & Padayachee, 2000:17). In retrospect, however, it is clear that the growing courtship between big business and the government had begun much earlier, probably even prior to the formal onset of constitutional negotiations in the 1990s.

In any case, whether the tendency to exclude other development players was caused by sheer panic at the enormity of the task or by the inherent centralist tendencies of the ruling party (see, for example, Shubane, 1999:6–14) or even the early dabbling with the "efficiency discourse" (or a complex combination of these and other factors), the net effect was a major alienation between some CSOs and the state. In other cases, most notably in rural areas, development NGOs were left to play a kind of intermediary role between the government and communities, namely assisting in the preparation of business plans and other technical requirements imposed by the RDP Office and/or undertaking service delivery through sub-contracting arrangements with the state agencies. The result was a growing schism within civil society on precisely how to relate to the government and its developmental agenda.

The official arrival of neo-liberalism

In the end though, South Africa was "allowed" just over two years to indulge in this illusion of economic exceptionalism. Bigger pressures were beginning to exert themselves: the World Bank, IMF and South African and multinational corporations were increasingly visible at government events. Even in the heyday of the RDP, World Bank staffers routinely attended national RDP workshops, officially as observers, but often giving presentations and certainly mingling with the crowds.[15] The heads of the World Bank and IMF started paying official courtesy visits, but the official government response to criticism and concern raised in this regard remained dismissive: we are doing our own thing!

By mid-1996 the illusion of exceptionalism was finally over, when the government announced their contentious new Growth, Employment and Redistribution (GEAR) policy.[16] Referred to by Patrick Bond (1997) as 'home-grown structural adjustment', this economic plan was formulated by the Department of Finance, drawing on technical advice from economists from the World Bank, the Universities of Cape Town and Stellenbosch, as well as other public institutions and research agencies. Although ongoing commitment to the RDP was stated, critics have commented that GEAR's "emphasis on containing government expenditure, lower fiscal deficits, lower inflation, deregulation, privatisation, the priority accorded to attracting foreign investment, and minimalist state intervention are in fundamental opposition to the basic policies and developmental thrust of MERG and the RDP" (Habib, 1997, in Habib & Padayachee 2000:14).

In practice, the RDP Office was closed, and the country and ordinary people who pinned their hopes on this programme lost all sense of a coherent developmental vision. Carter and May (2001:1992) state that:

> during Mandela's presidency, the South African government's orientation towards addressing the problems of poverty and inequality underwent some marked shifts, in language and emphasis, if not in substance. The 1996 closure of the Office of the RDP signalled to some an at least symbolic reduction in the priority given to improving the access of the majority of South Africans to adequate shelter, sanitation and education.

The "no alternative" mantra had arrived on our shores and, like elsewhere, was wielded like a weapon by its adherents, dismissing alternative discussion. Thus, in a few short years, South Africa had been brought on a par with the rest of the world, the end of our illusion of economic exceptionalism. Michael Blake (in Barberton, Blake & Kotzé (eds), 1998:47) commented at the time, "now it seems that South Africa was not a pioneer after all but was just catching up". The grand experiment was over and we joined the new world economic order, on its own standardised terms.

Reaping the benefits or counting the cost?

In retrospect, it is clear that the classic neo-liberal scenario had already fully unfolded in South Africa, not only in terms of the standard set of policies adopted, but, more importantly, in terms of the typical social and economic effects of these policies. The irony is that, with few exceptions, GEAR has not done well even by its own objectives and targets. It has, for example, not come near its projected economic and export growth rates, and "sustained inflows of direct foreign investment, which many predicted or hoped would follow democratic change, have not materialised" (Habib & Padayachee, 2000:20). Moreover, prospects for increased flows of foreign investment have been further eroded by factors like the rampant tide of violent crime and the exceptionally high HIV/Aids infection rates, not to mention the government's atrocious handling of the HIV/Aids and Zimbabwe crises in recent years.

Indeed, the relaxation of exchange controls and special concessions to South African companies have actually led to substantial capital outflows from the country. The national currency has been in a downward spiral for a number of years and interest rates, already high by international standards, have recently again been upwardly adjusted, the fourth time since the beginning of 2002. There has not been a lot of progress in realising GEAR's targets for privatisation of state assets and, most importantly, instead of the projected employment creation targets, there have been massive job losses in almost all sectors of the economy.

Tighter fiscal constraints have generally led to slower delivery of social and physical infrastructure to disadvantaged communities (Habib & Padayachee, 2000:20,21). Although considerable gains were initially made in the fields of electricity, water and housing provision, this record has been steadily eroded in recent years by the crises around cost recovery and affordability of services. David MacDonald (2002:3) estimates that:

> close to 10 million people have had their water cut off for non-payment of service bills, with the same number having experienced an electricity cut-off. More than two million people have been evicted from their homes for the same reason. [And although] it is low-income African households that bear the brunt of these service cut-offs, lower middle income families are also being affected.

Apart from the few who have benefited from economic liberalisation – mainly the upper classes of all racial groups, and in particular, the Black political, economic and professional élite who are the primary beneficiaries of affirmative action policies and Black economic empowerment deals – GEAR has had a devastating effect on the lives of millions of poor and low-income families. Habib and Padayachee (2000:24) state unambiguously that:

> the ANC's implementation of neo-liberal economic policies has meant disaster for the vast majority of South Africa's poor. Increasing unemployment and economic inequalities associated with neo-liberal policies have also pushed even more of South Africa's population into the poverty trap.

They refer to the "near barbaric" existence that a part of the population has been confined to and predict that this terrible condition of economic marginalisation is likely to undermine future political stability and the consolidation of democracy.

Other recent studies have supported Habib and Padayachee's analysis by demonstrating that poverty and inequality have increased in real and measurable ways. Carter and May (2001), using a follow-up study of approximately 1 200 Black households in KwaZulu-Natal, over the period 1993–1998 found that:

> poverty rates have increased from 27% to 43% among this cohort, and that the distribution of scaled per capita expenditure (or well-being) has become less equal. Underlying these

findings is a skewed or class-based pattern of income mobility in which initially better-off households have shown more upward mobility than initially poorer households.

Although a regional study, one can probably quite safely surmise that there would be similar trends in other parts of the country.

A shocking scenario is thus unfolding, one of the most terrible deprivation experienced by ever growing numbers of South Africans. Ironically, these are the same South Africans who lined up jubilantly to cast their votes for the ANC in 1994 and 1999, in the hope of "a better life for all". The reality is that, as long as the government doggedly adheres to its present economic policies, there is very little hope that this dismal picture will change in the foreseeable future. As a result, one can probably also expect to see crime levels rising, as an almost unavoidable expression of economic want and increasing frustration and desperation, particularly among the youth. Couple this with the terrible devastation that HIV/Aids is wreaking on this same marginalised and vulnerable population, and it is hard to believe that the government can be so blindly stuck to its self-delusional course.

Apart from the natural environment, maybe, there is not a great sense of specialness left in South Africa. Our national self-esteem is being constantly eroded by the dehumanising spectre of desperate poverty, unemployment, violent crime, Aids and the rising cost of living, existing alongside the most spectacular affluence. The growing inequality is also no longer confined to the classic racial divide, as there is widespread evidence of growing inequality within the Black community (Carter & May, 2001:1995). On a cynical note then, it seems that South Africa has indeed been "normalised", certainly by neo-liberal standards, with the new political élite having formed and entrenched relationships and alliances with the old (and new) business élites. The early exploratory relationships have now largely been established and solidified. The rich are getting richer, and the poor, poorer. This is the harsh world we are now (re)inhabiting in South Africa.

Civil society in South Africa: Understanding the new choices and challenges

The situation in South Africa has changed vastly in recent years. There have been a great many complex and multi-layered societal changes, resulting from both the political and the economic transitions of the 1990s. During the last decade, we have witnessed the most spectacular political and economic realignments and shifting alliances, many of which were to be expected in a society undergoing rapid change. With racial discrimination removed from the statute books, and thus no more formal barriers to economic advancement, new social hierarchies and trajectories have rapidly taken shape. The speed of upward and downward social mobility and the rapid assimilation of new class attributes by a section of the historically disadvantaged have been most astonishing. All part of the "normalisation" of post-apartheid society, of course, but some of it sad and disappointing, given the high hopes and moral principles the South African transition started out with.

In many ways South African society is still lingering in the exciting, but difficult space created by the transition to democracy, where remnants of the old society coexist uncomfortably with the new. Although, attitudes and mindsets have generally shifted significantly, the issue of race, for example, is still present. This scourge appears not only in its old manifestations, but also in new forms. For instance, it is undeniable that the new political élite deliberately politicise race in the current environment, either to advance their own interests or to defend themselves against criticism. Similarly, the "poor" are still with us and if a radical reconsideration of economic policy is not undertaken soon, it is a problem that is likely to grow even bigger. Interestingly enough, a new book by Ashwin Desai (2002) chronicles clearly how the issue of race has seemingly become quite secondary in poor people's struggles for basic needs and rights. And, finally, there is the scourge of HIV/Aids, which has brought many new issues and challenges to the fore.

The big question, then, is how and where South Africa's famously vibrant CSOs feature in this changed and complex new political and socio-economic landscape. How has the Third Sector, that essential, independent voice and critical conscience of society, responded to the new developments and challenges, including the worsening poverty and inequality and the HIV/Aids crisis? Are organisations within this sector adhering to their old loyalties and traditional activities or have they, in their turn, adjusted to the new social and political hierarchies and demands of the new dispensation? Most importantly, now that South Africa is in the full throes of neo-liberalism, have their responses and choices echoed those of CSOs in other countries? Are they even consciously aware of the choices and dilemmas confronting them?

The remoulding of civil society

The subject of South Africa's vibrant civil society, and its exceptional role in the anti-apartheid struggle and the transition to democracy, has been lauded and well documented; the same applies to the subsequent "collapse" of civil society (as it was then understood), as a result of changes in donor funding and political priorities (see, for example: Marais, 1997 and 1998; Murray, 1994; Taylor *et al.*, 1999; Kotzé, 1998 and 1999; Adler & Webster, 1995; Swilling & Russell, 2002). What was often lost in these discussions and debates was the realisation that civil society in South Africa is more than just the "progressive forces" that participated in the anti-apartheid struggle. In effect, like the society within which they were located, these CSOs were fundamentally divided along lines of race, class and ideology.[17] Each one served its chosen interests and/or beneficiary groups in a specific sector and area of activity. This is an important point, often overlooked in the "rhetorical consensus" around civil society.

In the harsh climate of apartheid, there were not a great many political sides to choose from and, as a result, CSOs tended to fall into two main categories – those that broadly supported the liberation movement and those that tacitly or actively supported the apartheid status quo.[18] In these extreme circumstances, both camps generally adhered quite closely to their chosen orthodoxies, and did not encourage much internal dissent or debate. Shubane (1999:12) states that, "as with all orthodoxies, debate on these ideas among adherents is limited to showing enthusiastic support or, at best, discussing the most effective means of implementation". This, of course, raises interesting questions as to how independent a voice CSOs really represent, then and now.

Some of these political divisions, mistrust, diversity and conflicting and competing interests were carried over into the new era and, like elsewhere, often got lost in the new blurred discourse about civil society. But the collapse of apartheid did bring an end to the binary divide (apartheid versus anti-apartheid) within civil society. Moreover, the transition to democracy delegitimised segregatory forms of organisation. And although the full package of neo-liberal policies, and its implications, came to South Africa relatively late, it was unrolled rapidly and the full consequences materialised very quickly. As a result, CSOs were forced to change while simultaneously being confronted with similar choices and dilemmas faced by their counterparts elsewhere in the developing world. The post-1994 existential crisis, then, caused many CSOs to turn their focus and organisational energies inward, in a search for survival and new direction. With apartheid removed, the subsequent internal transformation processes within civil society were often characterised by terrible conflict and near organisational paralysis. In the end, and which is only discernable now, civil society was significantly remoulded in South Africa

Three distinct blocs now comprise contemporary civil society. The first is the formal NGOs, which went into their well-documented crisis in the mid-1990s and, a few years later, re-emerged more streamlined and in much reduced numbers. Although it is widely acknowledged that streamlining was necessary, there were clear winners and losers in the process. The winners were essentially those bigger, more sophisticated and well-resourced NGOs that developed collaborative relationships with the state and became involved in policy development and service delivery. Evidence of this emerged in the Idasa/Core study, which demonstrated a notable rise in self-generated income among the more formalised NGOs that have come to rely substantially on government and other contracts.

Indeed, the Johns Hopkins study categorically indicated that government is by far the largest financial donor to civil society, accounting for 42% of the contribution to the sector (Swilling & Russell, 2002:34). This, as Adam Habib and Rupert Taylor (2001:224) argue, inevitably has to impact negatively on the lines of accountability between the formal NGOs and the poor and marginalised communities they claim to service.

Nowhere is this more evident than in the seeming ease with which many NGOs adopted the language of neo-liberalism. The process appeared to have taken place so naturally that few people actually seem to have noticed that it involved a massive paradigm shift. The essentially technical nature of this jargon,[19] which tends to lend itself to an easy pretence of "neutrality", probably helped to effect this smooth transition. The fact that the government adopted this essentially technicist terminology quite early on, probably also facilitated its transmission to this section of civil society, in particular because of the ANC's historical alliance with some of those NGOs and/or the latter's desire or need to partner the post-apartheid government. As a result, very few NGOs have attempted even a peek at the ideology behind the technical jargon. So it has become entrenched, now part of a kind of hybrid terminology, still speckled with some of the older notions and values that refuse to make way.

The second bloc within South African civil society is the group of informal, community-based associations, which appear to have emerged within marginalised communities to enable their residents to simply survive the ravages of poverty brought on by neo-liberalism. The survivalist structures, which, according to Swilling and Russell (2002:20), constitute 53% of an estimated total of 98 920 CSOs, are on the rise particularly as a result of the government's failure to address the HIV/Aids and unemployment crises. There are obviously various ways to interpret this finding, one of which is to regard it, as the authors of this study do, as reflecting positive new forms and manifestations of the old vibrant energies of South African civil society. It may well be that, but it is hard to dispute the darker interpretation of this finding, which stresses the survivalist character of these organisations and networks. Is it not true that, as a result of the government's policy choices, poor people have had no alternative but to return to small survivalist self-help networks? Are these organisations not a sad indictment of the retreat of the state, and people's consequent realisation that they are on their own again, with little or no immediate help to be expected from the government?

Moreover, serious questions need to be raised about the importance the authors of the Johns Hopkins study attach to their finding regarding the growth of voluntarism in civil society in South Africa (Swilling & Russell, 2002:27). Although the authors acknowledge that their sample and methodology had been weighted in favour of CBOs, they nevertheless make much of the finding that a high number of volunteers are engaged in the sector, even calculating the monetary value of this contribution to the economy.[20] This is without doubt a complex area, and does require a more in-depth follow-up study, but the unqualified positive interpretation given to this finding by Swilling and Russell must at the very least be questioned.

Voluntary work has traditionally been the preserve of middle- and upper-class women, who usually have the financial freedom and a significant amount of leisure time at their disposal. Does volunteering in poor, resource-starved communities therefore not, of necessity, mean something different? Although agrarian societies in the past had various forms of voluntary work, for example, around the harvests, the question is how one can understand voluntarism in the here and now of fragmented and poor communities in this country. Is it not tied to the unemployment and HIV/Aids crisis in South African society? Is it not just another manifestation of the failure of the state to meet its obligations to the citizenry?

It needs to be noted that the use of volunteers in development projects is not always the most satisfactory situation, as people tend to do this kind of work as a substitute for paid employment that is not available to them. They often receive training, which in some cases enables them to obtain paid employment, a gain for them, but a loss for the organisation that invested in them. Volunteers tend to be highly mobile and understandably lack the commitment and perseverance of full-time staff. In practice, they are therefore mostly utilised in smaller organisations and networks that cannot afford to employ full-time staff. In these cases, they are most often motivated by religion or personal identification with the problem at hand.

The third and final bloc within civil society is a group of more formal organisations and networks (some use the term social movements) that are starting to engage more critically with neo-liberal policies and their effects on the lives of ordinary people. These critical voices are coming primarily from the one extreme of an increasingly clear ideological and class divide that has recently become more apparent in civil society. Although the trade unions and some churches have traditionally formed the core of this critical space, it is interesting to note that they no longer exclusively inhabit this arena and that new forms of organisation and mobilisation are taking shape around the marginalisation of the poor and vulnerable.

Much of this organisation and mobilisation revolves around the politics of consumption. Located within communities, these organisations are largely preoccupied with protesting against the impact of neo-liberal social and economic policies and preventing their further implementation in South Africa. In Chatsworth, Durban, community organisations are challenging the local state and preventing it from evicting poor residents who are unable to pay their rates (Desai, 2001). In Soweto, local structures have emerged to protest against and prevent official and private agencies from cutting residents' access to electricity. Similar examples abound across the county. Issues like land, rates and rent, water and electricity are areas around which CBOs are beginning to mobilise.[21] As a result, they implicitly launch a fundamental challenge to the neo-liberal framework that conditions the behaviour and policies of the South African state.

In many ways, the civil society that emerged from the crisis of the mid-1990s is characterised by the same patterns and divisions observed in the rest of the developing world, namely, a clear and growing divide between the bigger, professionalised NGOs involved in service delivery, and smaller grassroots groupings and social movements generally opposed to the neo-liberal agenda. The former have generally managed to maintain high levels of funding and appear to have moved smoothly into the service delivery domain, while the latter tend to organise around specific and localised issues relating to increasing levels of poverty, unemployment, inequality and HIV/Aids – "bread-and-butter" or, maybe a more appropriate description in the new South African environment, "life-and-death" issues.

State and donor influences

One further question that needs to be addressed is how the repositioning and reconstitution of civil society occurred so fast, literally in the span of a few years. At one level, the answer is quite simple. The reconstitution and repositioning of civil society was largely the product of two factors – its transformed relationship with the state as a result of the transition to democracy, and the changing funding priorities of the donor community. The broad relationship between civil society and the state has undergone several transformations in the last two decades. In the 1980s progressive civil society made its debut as a result of the state's reform programme and the dramatic increase of funds made available in particular by the foreign donor community. But its relationship with the state remained tense, especially since the latter continually placed obstacles in the path of CSOs, and even actively repressed them.

The post-apartheid era was supposed to have been civil society's "wonder years", the period in which it was to have flourished and thrived. However, the relationship with the state was not entirely positive. In fact, for a short period during the RDP, the relationship between the state and civil society became quite acrimonious. After that, there was a kind of selective return on the part of the state to some NGOs, sometimes for advice on policy matters, but more often for assistance in implementing selected projects and programmes. As soon as NGOs got the general hang of it, they started to tender for government contracts to deliver various services, thereby moving into the difficult terrain of trade-offs, choices and compromises described earlier.

After the crisis and chaos of the initial period, NGOs across the country gradually became organised under the umbrella of the South African National NGO Coalition (Sangoco). Although the formation of Sangoco was initially in response to the minister responsible for the RDP, Jay Naidoo's challenge to CSOs that they "speak with one voice",[22] it did gradually develop an identity and began taking up important issues and initiatives on behalf of its members. One of its more important undertakings was its and the Non-Profit Sector Partnership's (NPP) engagement with government, which ultimately carved out a new legal and fiscal space for CSOs to operate in. This included issues of registration of CSOs, tax exemptions, as well as the establishment of the National Development Agency (NDA) that would act as a conduit for development funding to CSOs.

This process has not been entirely without problems or delays, but these initiatives did eventually culminate in a new political-legal environment that is best described by Swilling and Russell (2002:79):

> In conclusion, the state and the non-profit sector have negotiated an impressive and sophisticated public space that serves their respective interests: the state is able to harness resources (financial and institutional) to realise its development goals, and NPOs are able to access financial resources and shape delivery processes in a way that helps sustain them in the new democratic order. We must emphasize, however, that like so much else at the policy and legislative level in South Africa since 1994, it is only really the potential that has been created. There are already complications with the implementation of the framework, most of which have to do with a dearth of managerial and institutional capacity in the NDA, the Department of Welfare, and the South African Revenue Services. Much will depend on how the new mechanisms are put to use. And, more importantly, whether they are sustainable in a neo-liberal macro-economic environment. Will they simply become mechanisms for co-opting NPOs?

Clearly, the where government's funds and contracts are concerned, the playing field is likely to remain highly unequal, and the winners in this game will be those with the capacity to engage and access resources. Swilling and Russell (2002:79) argue that "if these continue to be the large, formalised NPOs in the social services and health sectors, and if the terms of the funding do not force them to serve the poorer segments of society, then state funds may not end up eliminating poverty". Indeed, they express concern about the future of the many CBOs that are unlikely to develop the capacity to access the resources available through this framework and pose the following pertinent questions:

> Will their exclusion make any difference to them? Or will they become the intermediaries between the NPOs who take delivery of the funds and the communities who are the targets of the funds? And will some community-based CBOs become the organisational facilitators of new social movements that mobilise those who stand to benefit least from a conservative

macro-economic regime and from social spending priorities that will take time to meet all needs? (Swilling & Russell, 2002:80)

The schism between service-oriented NGOs and mobilisational CBOs, fostered in large part by the post-apartheid regime's socio-economic policies and its initiatives to engage civil society, was also reinforced by the changing funding priorities of the donor community. This process was set in motion by foreign donors who, at short notice in 1994, changed their funding priorities and redirected the bulk of their funding to the new democratically elected government. Although this new direction was understandable, given that the "special status" conferred on South Africa by donors during the apartheid years no longer applied, it nevertheless had an enormous effect on civil society.

The reality is that donors wield enormous power over the political and economic development and direction of recipient organisations and countries. They also regularly change their funding priorities and, in many instances, these decisions are made by wealthy and influential board members in faraway boardrooms in rich countries. Donors can, in essence, decide which CSOs are to live and which are to die, and, in the process, consciously or unconsciously, transplant their own values and worldviews on the recipients of aid. Given that neo-liberal policies have been in place in the rich industrialised countries for over two decades, it is probably safe to surmise that donors from these countries tend to regard neo-liberalism and globalisation as little more than everyday realities. It goes without saying, then, that their decisions about which organisations to support will be heavily influenced by these beliefs.

Given CSOs general dependency on external funding, donors tend to have undue influence on the shape of civil society in a country. For example, by supporting big professionalised NGOs, with the capacity to meet complicated funding requirements and to ably deliver services, donors make a value-laden choice in favour of one section of civil society to the direct detriment of others. There is no doubt at all that many NGOs in South Africa, for the sake of survival, tailor their funding proposals to the known priority areas of particular funders. Compromises and trade-offs thus become the order of the day and development becomes unavoidably donor-driven. The primary line of accountability is most often to donors. Generally, on this unequal playing field, it is the more organised, more articulate, urban-based players that walk away with the prize.

Despite all the rhetoric, small groups and organisations that are desperately trying to make a difference to the lives of poor and vulnerable people inevitably end up as the losers in this "game". Organisations involved in the prevention of violence against women, victim support, the needs of the disabled in poor communities, and community-based Aids support groups, often continue their work with little more than sheer determination.

In the present political and economic climate, the issues and interests of the rural poor have also seemingly fallen off the bandwagon altogether. The classic "rural biases", developed by Robert Chambers in the seventies,[23] still prevent most government officials, donors and even researchers[24] from paying serious attention to the everyday struggles for survival of millions of rural people. But even this can be taken as a sign of the "normalisation" of our society in the era of globalisation.

The state's reform of the political and legal environment and the changing funding priorities and requirements of donors, both of which took effect in the post-1994 era, have had the net effect of fostering or, at the very least, reinforcing the growing schism within civil society between formal professionalised NGOs and their CBO counterparts. Like elsewhere in the world, those NGOs that have moved into the service delivery domain have largely maintained co-operative or amicable relations with government. To a large extent, these agencies operate within the parameters of the existing status quo. On the other side of the divide are informal and formal grassroots CBOs that are increasingly witnessing the further marginalisation of the communities they organise within and represent. Their struggle against this marginalisation has propelled them into an adversarial stance *vis-à-vis* the government. Increasingly, these organisations question and want to transform the status quo. A schism has thus emerged between the politics of opposition and the politics of engagement.

Of course, there have been attempts to transcend this divide. Perhaps the most successful example of this has been the work of the Treatment Action Campaign (TAC) to provide anti-retroviral therapy to prevent mother-to-child transmission of HIV/Aids. Combining opposition and engagement, mobilisation and advocacy, court injunctions and lobbying, the TAC forced the government to transcend its unscientific paranoia about anti-retroviral therapy, and compelled it to roll out a universal programme to prevent mother-to-child transmissions. Is this example replicable to other sectors and issue areas? Is the success of the TAC not confined to the peculiar circumstances of Aids activism in South Africa? Whatever the answers to these questions, what is without doubt required is the need to transcend the false divide that has emerged between opposition and engagement in South Africa. For without this transcendence, civil society is going to remain divided, and perhaps incapable of developing the sophistication to deal with advancing the interests of marginalised communities in today's neo-liberal global environment.

Conclusion

In sum then: the post-apartheid era has witnessed the "normalisation" of South African society in a neo-liberal global environment. Poverty, inequality and the attendant problems of marginalisation and governance that the Washington Consensus model of globalisation has wreaked on other parts of the world are now the hallmarks of South African society. The legacy bequeathed by apartheid has not only not been addressed, but in fact, has in many ways been reinforced and even aggravated. How to respond to and address this is the primary challenge confronting South African civil society.

Civil society's response in South Africa to these developments has been similar to that of the Third Sector in other parts of the world. Its reconstitution, informed partly by state reform and donor pressures, to differentially address the challenges spawned by globalisation has reinforced the schism within it, between those NGOs that operate within the system and those CBOs that challenge it. Increasingly, the two agencies are being propelled onto different sides of the political divide, not realising that each requires the other for its own success. In a lot of ways, service-related NGOs within the system need to recognise that reform cannot be achieved within the parameters of the status quo. Fundamental changes are required and, so long as they are oblivious to or oppose this, their engagement merely constitutes one cog in a broader systemic exploitation of South Africa's poor and disadvantaged. Similarly, mobilisational CBOs need to recognise that shouting from the sidelines and even actively opposing the state and its agencies in their day-to-day operations is not sustainable in the long term, unless reforms are consistently forthcoming through their actions.

Each thus needs the other. NGOs need to recognise that they only have a seat at the systemic table because rulers and élites fear the CBOs that threaten or have the potential to ultimately undermine the system. CBOs need the NGOs seat at the systemic table to facilitate the reforms that they require to sustain their mobilisation in the long term. A lesson needs to be drawn from the practice of social activism at the dawn of the last century, and in particular from that great German social revolutionary, Rosa Luxemburg, whose pamphlet on the *problematique* of reform and revolution inspired not only philosophical reflection but also practical engagement for decades thereafter. Its primary lesson can perhaps be summarised in the simple paragraph that opens the preface to the pamphlet:

> Can the social democracy be against reforms? Can we counter-pose the social revolution, the transformation of the existing social order, our final goal, to social reforms? Certainly not. The daily struggle for reforms, for the amelioration of the condition of the workers within the framework of the existing social order, and for democratic institutions, offers to the social democracy the only means of … working in the direction of the final goal … Between social reforms and revolution there exists for the social democracy an indissoluble tie. The struggle for reforms is its means; the social revolution, its aim. (Luxemburg, 1989:21)

Or for those at the systemic table who would prefer a more mainstream voice, there can be no better one than that of Joseph Stiglitz (2002:20), Nobel laureate for economics and former vice-president of the World Bank:

Left with no alternatives, no way to express their concern, to press for change, people riot. The streets, of course, are not the place where issues are discussed, policies formulated, or compromises forged. But the protests have made government officials and economists around the world think about alternatives to these Washington Consensus policies as the one and true way for growth and development.

Endnotes

1   In practice, Non-Governmental Organisations (NGOs) are the bigger, more formalised organisations. These have to be distinguished from Community Based Organisations (CBOs), usually smaller, less formalised groupings or associations operating at community level. At times, we also use the more all-encompassing term Civil Society Organisations (CSOs), to refer to the broad range of associations and groupings that fall under the term civil society (see our working definition on p.253).

2   The IDASA/CORE study is the most recent example of this.

3   Salamon and Anheier's analysis is based on Barrington Moore Jnr's pioneering 1966 study, *Social Origins of Dictatorship and Democracy*. Hammondsworth: Penguin.

4   For a comprehensive history of the concept and its evolution, see Cohen, J. & Arato, A. (1992).

5   For a review of various definitions of civil society, see Swilling & Russell (2002).

6   The term was coined by Samuel Huntington in *The Third Wave: Democratization in the Late Twentieth Century*.

7   In this context, civil society is equated mainly with medium to large professionalised NGOs.

8   Mahmood Mamdani (1996:27–32) also refers to the notion of South African exceptionalism.

9   Used here as an all-inclusive terms for Black, Indian and so-called Coloured people, i.e. all those who were discriminated against under apartheid.

10 Although Nedlac established a fourth chamber, the Development Chamber, there were inherent problems regarding representation, not to mention definition; for example, how the criteria to select organisations/structures to this chamber would be developed, and by whom. How could the multitude and variety of (non-governmental) organisations involved in development programmes/activities at the time possibly have been represented adequately? In practice, therefore, the fourth chamber was always a rather weak add-on, with enormous problems of representivity.

11 This assertion is primarily based on a series of wide-ranging, in-depth interviews with senior provincial RDP officials and a range of prominent civil society leaders, conducted by H. Kotzé in all nine provinces of South Africa in the course of 1995/96.

12 Ibid.

13 For example, then Minister of Public Works, responsible for the RDP in the Eastern Cape, Mr Mhlahlo, in an interview with H. Kotze, 1996.

14 As a result "development consultancy" became an extremely lucrative field and suddenly just about everybody was a development expert/consultant, quite independent of prior development experience. The local branches of major international accounting firms, almost overnight, had development/rural development divisions in place.

15 Authors' participant observations during 1995/96.

16 For a more detailed discussion of the policy processes, choices, trade-offs, as well as policy prescriptions of GEAR, see Habib & Padayachee (2000).

17 For a more detailed discussion of these divides, see Habib & Taylor (2001) and Shubane (1999:12).

18 One could add a third category, the liberal establishment and the CSOs faithful to it, but these tended to implicitly fall into one of the other two camps.

19 Often derived directly from World Bank and IMF "speak" and characterised by a preoccupation with quantitative assessments/studies, planning frameworks, targets, modelling, business plans, etc.

20 The authors of the report give a figure of R5.1 billion in this regard (Swilling & Russell, 2002:27).

21 For a review of these struggles, see Bond (2001), McDonald & Pape (2002) and Desai (2002).

22 A clearly impossible demand, and based on a complete misreading of the basic nature of civil society.

23 Chambers, Robert, "Rural Development, Putting the Last First", circa 1976.

24 In both the Johns Hopkins and the Core/Idasa studies, money and time constraints prevented the inclusion of anything much beyond peri-urban areas in the research samples.

References

Adler, G. & Webster, E. (1995) "The Labour Movement, Radical Reform, & Transition to Democracy in South Africa", *Politics and Society*, Vol. 23, No. 1.

African National Congress (1994) *The Reconstruction and Development Programme: A Policy Framework*. Johannesburg: Umanyano Media.

Bond, P. (1997) "Home-grown Structural Adjustment: Implications for Social Policy and Social Movements." Paper presented to the Initiative for Participatory Democracy, April.

Bond, P. (2001) *Against Global Apartheid*. Cape Town: University of Cape Town Press.

Byers, M. (2000) "Woken Up in Seattle", *London Review of Books*, Vol. 22, No.1.

Carter, M. R. & May, J. (2001) "One Kind of Freedom: Poverty Dynamics in Post-Apartheid South Africa", *World Development*, Vol. 29, No 12.

Cohen, J. & Arato, A. (1992) *Civil Society and Political Theory*. Boston: MIT Press.

Desai, A. (2001) *The Poors of Chatsworth*. Institute for Black Research/Madiba Publishers, University of Natal.

Desai, A. (2002) *The Poors of South Africa: Class, Race, and Social Movements*. New York: Monthly Review Press.

Habib, A. & Taylor, R. (2001) "South Africa: Anti-Apartheid Non-Governmental Organisations (NGO's) in Transition." In Anheier, H. & Kendall, J. (eds) *The Non-Profit Sector at the Crossroads*. London: Routledge.

Habib, A. & Padayachee (2000) "Economic Policy and Power Relations in South Africa's Transition to Democracy", *World Development*, Vol. 28, No. 2.

Hertz, N. (2001) *The Silent Takeover: Global Capitalism and the Death of Democracy*. London: William Heinemann.

Huntington, S. (1991) *The Third Wave: Democratisation in the Late Twentieth Century*. Oklahoma: University of Oklahoma Press.

Idasa/Core (2001) *Two Commas and a Full Stop, Civicus Index on Civil Society, South African Country Report*.

Kihato, C. (2001) "Shifting Sands: The Relationship between Foreign Donors and South African Civil Society During and After Apartheid." Research Report No. 86. Centre for Policy Studies, Johannesburg.

Kihato, C. & Rapoo, T. (1999). "An Independent Voice? A Survey of Civil Society Organisations in South Africa, Their Funding, and Their Influence Over the Policy Process." Research Report No. 67. Centre for Policy Studies, Johannesburg.

Kotzé, H. (1998) "Civil Society, Setting the Record Straight." In Barberton, C., Blake, M. & Kotzé, H. *Creating Action Space: the Challenge for Poverty and Democracy In South Africa*. Cape Town: Idasa/David Philip.

Kotzé, H. (1999) "Swimming in a Wild Sea: The New challenges Facing Civil Society." In Maharaj, G (ed.) *Between Unity and Diversity, Essays on Nation-building in Post-Apartheid South Africa*. Cape Town: Idasa/David Philip.

Leys, C. (2001) *Market Driven Politics: Neo-Liberal Democracy and the Public Interest*. London, New York: Verso.

Luxemburg, R. (1989) *Reform or Revolution*. London: Bookmarks.

MacDonald, D. (2002) "The Bell Tolls for Thee: Cost Recovery, Cut-offs, and the Affordability of Municipal Services in South Africa." Unpublished mimeo.

MacDonald, D. & Pape, J. (2002) *Cost Recovery and the Crisis of Service Delivery in South Africa*. Pretoria/London: HSRC Press/Zed Books.

Mamdani, M. (1996) *Citizen and Subject – Contemporary Africa and the Legacy of Late Colonialism*. Kampala/London: Fountain Publishers/James Curry.

Marais, H. (1997) "Annual Review: The Voluntary Sector and Development in South Africa, 1996/97", *Development Update*, Vol.1, No. 3.

Marais, H. (1998) *South Africa – Limits to Change: The Political Economy of Transformation*. Cape Town: University of Cape Town Press.

Moore, B, Jr. (1966) *Social Origins of Dictatorship and Democracy*. Hammondsworth: Penguin.

Murray, M. (1994) *The Revolution Deferred: The Painful Birth of Post-Apartheid South Africa*. London: Verso.

Pearce, J. (2000) "Development, NGO's, and Civil Society. Selected essays from Development in Practice." In *Development, NGOs, and Civil Society: The Debate and its Future*. (Series editor D. Eade). United Kingdom: Oxfam.

Reitzes, M. & Friedman, S. (2001) "Funding Freedom?: Synthesis Report on the Impact of Foreign Political Aid to Civil Society Organisations in South Africa." Research Report No. 85. Centre for Policy Studies, Johannesburg.

Salamon, L. & Anheier, H. (1998) "Social Origins of Civil Society: Explaining the Non-Profit Sector Cross-Nationally", *Voluntas*, Vol. 9, No. 3.

Shubane, K. (1999) "No Easy Walk to Civility: Civil Society Organisation and the South African Context", *Policy: Issues and Actors*, Vol. 12, No. 4. Centre for Policy Studies.

Stiglitz, J. (1998) "More Instruments and Broader Goals: Moving Towards a Post-Washington Consensus." Wicker Annual Lecture, Helsinki, 7 January.

Stiglitz, J. (2002) *Globalization and its Discontents*. London: The Penguin Press.

Swilling, M. & Russell, B. (2002) *The Size and Scope of the Non-Profit Sector in South Africa*. The Centre for Civil Society, University of Natal and the School of Public and Development Management, University of the Witwatersrand.

Taylor, R., Cock, J. & Habib, A., (1999) "Projecting Peace in Apartheid South Africa", *Peace and Change*, Vol. 24, No.1.

Tvedt, T. (1998) *Angels of Mercy or Development Diplomats: NGOs and Foreign Aid*. Trenton: Africa World Press.

9 Unfinished Business: Gender Equality in Post-apartheid South Africa

Nomboniso Gasa

Introduction

> The implementation of the economic policies of the current architects of globalisation has a devastating impact on the economic and social plight of women, in at least three areas. Cutbacks in state expenditure, mean firstly job losses for women in the public sector, and secondly, the cutback in critical social services which women depend on to reproduce their families. This simply transfers the costs of social services that ought to be borne by the state to the household, and to women in particular. (Cosatu, 1999)[1]

Serious engagement with globalisation requires an understanding of the historical, economic and cultural processes that have underpinned certain interpretations of human behaviour through the lens of a particular race, class and gender. Although the tendency in many studies is to look at globalisation from an economic perspective, it is important to develop a more complex understanding of the current conjuncture and its many-faceted implications for society, especially the poorer strata, amongst whom women are highly represented.

In the context of South Africa, history remains a take-off point and it is in understanding its texture and its impact on the present that it is possible to fully grasp some of the unfolding developments in South Africa today. For example, poverty and its impact on urban women are somewhat different from those of their rural counterparts, who are beginning to have access to land and are benefiting from land programmes that are aggressive in increasing production, and who for the first time are acquiring title deeds to their ancestral lands. However, even though these initiatives have developed in rural South Africa, poverty remains the most disempowering and alienating experience for the majority of people.

The chapter weaves between the past and the present, and also examines the extent to which the legal framework, the macroeconomic policies and the national machinery for gender equality have empowered or disempowered decision makers and ordinary people to defend and address their interests. From the outset, the chapter attempts to historicise, as a way not only of looking back but also of locating the choices, mistakes and advances within the legacy of South Africa. This is to avoid a static geography (especially because one of the elements of globalisation is the fluidity of location) in assessing the choices, decisions and options within the context of the country and its history.

The world over, the impact of economic globalisation on female dominated industries such as footwear, textiles and social services has marginalised women from the economy (Cosatu, 1999). It has been argued that globalisation de-links the state from its social responsibility and also de-links citizens from their communities.

Across Africa, the images of mass migration offer useful insights into disloca-tion, not only because of violence but also because of migration resulting from poverty. This erodes social relations and affects women differently from men. In this context, even traditional coping mechanisms are undermined, as the socially dislo-cated and often home-based industries make it difficult for workers to be unionised (Cosatu, 2000). So, whatever industrial rights and legal protection they may have, the vulnerability of their position makes it difficult for women to make choices.

Unemployment is not the preserve of women, but the burden, socially and otherwise, on women is different from that of men because of the social construction of their gen-der roles. Furthermore, in situations of distress, economic or otherwise, it is often women who experience violence (Gasa, 2002). The concern in this chapter is to provide a con-textual understanding of the impact of globalisation in South Africa and to examine its gendered implications.

In his poem *The Children of This Land*, on the impact of economic marginalisation and other forms of social exclusion, Soyinka (2000) looks at the generations of Nigerian soci-ety and the extent to which disempowerment and alienation are reproduced, with impli-cations beyond the economic sphere.

> The children of this land grow the largest eyes
> Within head sockets. Their head are crowns
> On neat fish spines, whose meat has passed
> Through swing doors to the chill of conversation
> And chilled wine. But the eyes are dead.
> They pierce beyond the present through dim passages

Across the world of living.
These are children of the dispossessed
The hope and land deprived. Contempt replaces
Filial bonds. The children of this land
Are castaways in holed crafts, all tortoise skin
And scales – the callus of their afterbirth.
Their hands are clawed for rooting, their tongues
Propagate new social codes, and laws.
A new race will supersede the present
Where love is a banished stranger, lonely
Wanderer in forests prowled by lust
On feral pads of power,
Where love is a hidden, ancient ruin, crushed
By memory, in this present
Robbed of presence.

The poem speaks of dislocation resulting from years of "militocracy" and structural adjustment programmes (SAPs) in Nigeria; and it serves as a constant reminder and warning of the impact of economic marginalisation. Its relevance far exceeds the borders of Nigeria and requires that we examine trends and choices and their impact on many other societies.

This chapter revisits the earlier history of the political women's and gender equality struggle in South Africa, to provide a historical context for the issues of today. It also considers the extent to which South Africa's post-apartheid policies have tried to establish a common citizenship for all and to "propagate new social codes, and laws". An examination of past struggles and the emergent legal, economic, political and constitutional framework demands that the choices be examined in the context of a quest to build a present that is not "robbed of presence".

One of the questions posed by the new conditions in South Africa, is to what extent earlier struggles of women and their organisations have facilitated or impeded their capacity to adapt and contest, where necessary, the demands of globalisation. It is not only the context that must be examined but also what that context teaches in terms of capacity to deal with the new.

The South African transition saw South African women and men unleash concentrated energy to develop and enshrine a constitution, which created a common citizenship and used gender equality as a basic premise. This deepened women's status as citizens at the political and legal levels. The Equality Clause in the Constitution presents a critical starting point. Furthermore, Section 6 of the Constitution provides for a Commission for Gender Equality as one of the key statutory institutions for entrenching constitutional democracy and equality.

Later in this chapter, the section on the national machinery will deal in detail with its components and examine some issues that have emerged in the national debate. Amongst the questions to be considered is the present state of the national machinery and the implications of this for entrenching gender equality in South Africa. A caveat must be noted. In assessing the strength and weakness of the national machinery, it is critical that a comparative framework be kept in mind, which will locate these structures in relation to other statutory bodies (e.g. the Human Rights Commission, the Office of the Public Protector and the Land Claims Court) that are not specifically dedicated to gender equality. The point being that, although the national machinery has faced serious setbacks, some of these are not restricted to gender equality alone.

Questions that arise out of such an assessment relate to the dislocation and position of women and gender equality activists in the current period in South Africa. What have been the implications and hidden costs of the advances made? How do these affect the place of women who were at the forefront of the campaigns for gender equality and women's representation in the 1990s? To what extent has it been possible for the links to be maintained? What are the implications of this in the face of new challenges and rising levels of poverty affecting women in lower income groups? What are the voices in the current conjuncture? Whose voices? What are their locations? How have the current macroeconomic policies and strategies affected women's economic status? How do the economic choices and decisions of the government impact on women and their ability to be self-sustaining and independent, or, for the majority, at least to care for their children?

The South African constitution provides for socio-economic rights and in a direct manner. Paradoxically, the gains made at the level of constitutional and other legal provisions, which have deepened women's equality, are in danger of being undermined by the burden of poverty on the majority of women in South Africa. However, the Constitutional Court has set legal precedents in the area of second-generation rights with some of its landmark judgements. Of relevance here, are the *Grootboom* judgement on the provision of housing, and also the decisions on the provision of anti-retroviral drugs. In these judgements, the state's responsibility in the provision of socio-economic benefits for its citizens has been established.

Located within the context of Africa, the role of the state is significant not only because of "economic governance" but because the crisis of postcolonial Africa is partly related to the weakness or absence of the state (Abdul-Raheem, 2002). The character of the state will have to be defined in terms of its democratic, developmental nature, social delivery, human rights and gender equality (Gasa, 2002).

The strength and character of the state is critical in the context of post-apartheid South Africa. It is the primary mechanism through which redistribution and redress can occur.

Although there are other critical mechanisms and institutions, including the market, the state has to play a pivotal and regulatory role. Given the constitutional commitments to socio-economic rights, how has the South African state met these in the light of the feminisation of poverty?

The women's movement: Some definitions

In later sections, this chapter touches on the complexity of the women's movement in South Africa. Perhaps, a classical definition of the women's movement along the lines of the following is needed so as to locate South African women's history and political choices within an international history:

> Evoking a collectivity of women who mobilise to protest or to pursue shared goals, the description is often used co-terminously with feminist movement, but women's movements pre-date and may be distinct from feminism. They are social movements, which display heterogeneity of goals, and associational or organisational forms … It is in the nineteenth century that women in many regions of the world began to organise against inequalities based on sex and to demand legal reforms aimed at removing patriarchal controls over women in the family and in society at large. (Molyneaux, 1993:715)

> The movement to promote the emancipation, liberation, rights and interests of women, as there are defined by women, which has existed as a political force in modern times since the early nineteenth century. (Scruton, 1982:582)

> To disarm patriarchy, to resist and transform relations of male and female subordination, must be the ultimate goal of feminism. (Roseneil, 1995:1)

From the above definitions, it is clear that the core meaning of the women's movement is the struggle against women's oppression. Although many scholars and activists will differ on whether that should entail feminism, the essential element of the women's movement is its definition of gender oppression as the central focus.

The idea of a movement is evocative of large numbers of women with different backgrounds and ideological perspectives but whose primary agenda in coming together is to challenge patriarchy. There is usually an understanding that women who come together in the form of a movement have multiple identities and interests and may be linked to other broader social and political movements. In such a context, the women's movement, although it may be linked to or in alliance with other political and social organisations and trade unions, is understood as a political vehicle on its own.

However, the notion of gender oppression as a primary oppression has always been controversial in feminist scholarship and political thought. Whereas there is no denying the fundamental nature of gender oppression and its impact on women's lives, many women, especially of colour, have argued that the women's movement cannot tackle gender-based oppression without looking at other forms of oppression, such as race, class, caste, ethnic prejudice and discrimination on the grounds of sexuality. A classical definition of the concept of the women's movement is elusive and nebulous, because, in many ways, there is no "one size fits all". The context in which such movements are built determines the nature of the movement and the issues it will advance as its primary concerns.

This is where the historical tension comes in. From the anti-slavery period, the suffrage movements and national liberation struggles, the issue of women's identity and location has been critical in the development of their agency. Some of these concerns are dealt with later. Suffice it to say, in the history of South Africa, the linkages of racism, class and gender as a continuum of marginalisation meant that the women's struggle took a form that is not consistent with the classical definitions and preoccupations of suffrage movements elsewhere.

In fact, from the very first act of public protest in 1913, when women marched against passes in Bloemfontein, their agenda has tried to address women's citizenship and equality in political, economic and other terms. In subsequent periods, women tried to build organisations that linked gender oppression with other forms of oppression. There have been struggles on many fronts, including those with compatriots in the political organisations who had difficulty in understanding the fundamental nature of women's oppression.

This chapter is premised on the understanding that in South Africa, gender, race and class and other forms of exclusion are linked. Therefore, in devising policies and assessing governance in post-apartheid South Africa, this understanding must be kept in mind.

The women's struggle in South Africa: A recent history

[J]ust as for the ancients there was an absolute vertical with reference to which the oblique was defined, so there is an absolute human type, the masculine ... Thus humanity is male and man defines woman not in herself but as relative to him; she is not regarded as an autonomous being ... She is defined and differentiated with reference to man and he with reference to her; she is the incidental as opposed to the essential. He is the Subject; he is the Absolute – she is the Other. (De Beauvoir, 1949)

What do women know about political negotiations? Ha! Which South African man knows anything about this process? And where did they acquire such expertise? The demand for 50% representation at the negotiations table is not based on simplistic notions of "sisterhood". We do not believe that women are inherently progressive. Obviously there are problems with this demand, for one thing, it is mechanistic ... There are contradictions amongst women – this is South Africa. But we want women there. These are negotiations about the future of South Africa; women's exclusion gives us worrying signals. (Mbete, 1992)

The cartography of women's contribution to national liberation and independence struggles all over the world reveals the complexity of women's status once freedom has been attained.

As the South African transition unfolded, one of the central issues was to ensure that women were not left solely "with the scars of memory" but that post-apartheid South Africa embedded gender equality as one of its foundations.

> We must remember we are not the first. In many countries, combatants like myself, returned after having fought for their countries and they were relegated to the kitchen. Their comrades now wanted "proper" African women. Whatever the future brings, we must use this moment to the maximum. (Zulu, 1993)

In many ways, the first African National Congress (ANC) conference after its unbanning set the context for the struggles and contestations that unfolded in the mid-1990s. To buttress the demand for a 30% representation on the ANC National Executive Committee, feminists and gender activists marched out of the ANC 1991 National Conference. The stance sent a shockwave through the ANC and, although the women lost and the action was seen as divisive, the action itself signified a change of strategy by feminists and activists within the ANC.

It is instructive that the ANC Women's League (ANCWL) began to articulate positions and undertook campaigns on issues that may have been seen as "no-go areas" from the cultural and political standpoints. For its Women's Day celebrations on 9 August 1993, the ANCWL printed t-shirts and produced posters with slogans such as "women demand: abolish *lobola*", and also mounted a public campaign on reproductive rights, at a time when the ANC had not quite resolved its position on the issue.

The urgency with which the League undertook these public campaigns and "awareness raising on women's demands for the new South Africa" (Zulu, 1993) was in actual fact a result of brooding militancy on these issues within sections of the ANCWL and the ANC. Some may view campaigns such as the anti-*lobola* t-shirts as insufficiently nuanced, but in the context of the mid-1990s, many women in the ANC argued that it was best to put these issues "out there in the public domain and to make these things right there, *phakathi*, in the centre, of the national debate" (Zulu, 1993).

Shireen Hassim (2002) argues that women's mobilisation in the transition process was a struggle against marginalisation. At the beginning of the Kempton Park process, the ANCWL was forced to take one of its most autonomous and public stances in challenging ANC and other political party leadership.

Threatening to boycott elections if women's representation was not taken seriously, the ANCWL organised a protest outside the negotiations and demanded 50% women's participation at the table. It was finally decided that every political party had to bring one man and one woman as representatives at the negotiations. Those who could not find a woman were to lose 50% of their representation. Threatened with the possibility of public embarrassment and obvious alienation of women at a time of heightened political activity, most political parties brought women delegates to the negotiations table.

As Mbete and other activists inside and outside of ANC had anticipated, the demand for representation was not without its problems. There were those who argued that an emphasis on the issue could divide the movement and create an awkward situation where the ANC had to establish a working relationship with other structures, such as Congress of Traditional Leaders (Contralesa). Later, the issue of representation and participation and the resultant shortcomings are examined in detail.

One of the key issues that underpins the debate is the need to distinguish between representation and participation. Representation, on the one hand, often implies an awareness of the responsibility beyond oneself, in order to serve others. In the context of women's representation, this would mean a consciousness of the need to advance policies and practices that will promote women's equality. The implication is that of opening the doors, making it possible for others to come in, speaking together with those who are left behind, outside of processes. The one who "represents" might have access to power and thus become part of decision-making, but often there is a part outside, some kind of subaltern voice that is retained. Participation, on the other hand, may encompass much of the above and may be premised on an understanding that one is part of the process and decision-making. It may also mean that those who are included see their participation on their own terms and in their own right. There may be no external movement to which they have to be accountable, not in the sense that is outside of the establishment and its institutional structures. They may want to participate and may even be effective as politicians, business executives, academics or whatever the realm of engagement.

At times, it might be the experience of women who are part of decision-making, that they are not really allowed to participate in the process and that they are given the responsibility without the authority. This is neither bad nor good as such. Often, within the limited mandate, women politicians who adopt this approach tend to be effective, focussed and professional. They master the game of doing politics. They may even have effective constituency offices, accountable to their political parties, and may carve out a niche for themselves.

The debate on women's representation and participation tends to conflate these two issues. Often expectations and assumptions are made on the basis that women are there to change the nature of institutions. The tension lies in working out what to do once women (or those often excluded, such as the poor) "get there". Representation and participation are often dialectically linked and there is an intangible area of connection between them. Perhaps, in South Africa, it is not so much a question of using "the master's tools to demolish the master's house" (Lorde, 1984) but of finding ways of working with the tools in order to construct a new house.

This is an area that is not sufficiently developed in either gender studies or feminist discourse. In much capacity-building training, which tends to be undertaken by "gender support groups", where women have entered into the realm of politics, there tends to be an emphasis on working with the rules and making the rules work for women (considered outsiders or subordinate), who are assumed to be in need of skills and development.

It has become necessary to examine these difficult issues and to assess the implications of power and of women being a part of the process. It is not an option to be outside of it, because that too has its own sets of dynamics and problems. A critical area that needs careful examination is the impact of location on the psyche of those who have gone into the structures of governance and on their relationship with organisations outside. The view from inside is much more complex, and to engage it is even more challenging. One of the resulting questions is whether such representation has ensured that the post-apartheid state has integrated gender equality in its policies and political process.

In looking at the context of globalisation, it is important to assess the "nation-building project" and the extent to which it provides space for women to participate in governance. How is democratic governance working for gender equality? The earlier period of transition is relevant because it provides a backdrop to some of the policies, approaches and complexities of the current conjuncture and to decisions that have a bearing on the present capacity of women.

In assessing gender equality advances in post-apartheid South Africa, it is necessary to contextualise South Africa's particularities and history. It is important to review and critique the extent to which national liberation has integrated women's equality. What consequences has this had for women's organisations? Have they been domesticated or contained or have they acquired new power? Have they been marginalised out of the decision-making processes?

Mobilisation of women in the national liberation struggle presented a possibility for women (and men) to challenge patriarchal relations of domination by the state and by all other forces in society, including the national liberation struggle itself. Women's political identity and positionality have been important factors in the history of the women's movement and broader political movements in South Africa. This does not mean that the liberation struggle guaranteed gender equality, but it is arguable that one cannot conceive of women's emancipation in South Africa outside the national liberation struggle itself. Writing on a similar subject in the American context, Bell Hooks (1988) has argued:

> Concurrently, they know that many males in their social groups are exploited and oppressed. Knowing that men in their groups do not have social, political and economic power, they would not deem it liberatory to share their social status.

Women (and some men) have had to contest and widen the scope within the national liberation movement's framework, at times with great success, and often with frustrations and setbacks. There are different interpretations of the above statements and their meanings in relation to the complexity of the heterogeneous feminist discourse, which confronts the complexity of women's subordination and the resultant feminism.

In the 1980s, a debate developed within the Mass Democratic Movement, which sought to address the issue of separate women's organisations. Many of the organisations that existed were autonomous and affiliated to the United Democratic Front and other bodies. These organisations were not necessarily feminist. The main argument developed along lines that women had to organise under an unapologetic feminist banner. Much of the argument was based on a comparison with trade unions. If workers could be organised in trade unions, it was argued, women could be organised under the feminist banner. However, there were those who argued in the 1980s that mobilising women for national liberation undermined feminist interests.

The issue of the political identity of women is at the heart of South Africa's political history. The problem with arguing for "pure" feminist struggles is that it seemed to propose that it was possible for women, especially black women, to actualise their gender identities and liberation in the context of apartheid. For many feminists in the national liberation movement, there was no alternative to political participation; it was part of a complex journey of gender, race and class struggle.

The struggle against apartheid was critical as a first step towards self-liberation. It was not a question of this or that first, but of finding ways of dealing with all manifestations of oppression in their complexity and without prejudicing or privileging one or the other. Whether this was always adhered to or not is another matter. In fact, some of the difficult issues manifested in the split between the United Women's Organisation and United Women's Congress in Cape Town speak to this complexity. The articulation of the split reluctantly acknowledged some of the issues, even though the main problem was put across as "women's divisions and political orientation" (Gasa, 1994).

Women's political identity and choice is informed by their experience and location. The identities imposed by race, gender and class have shaped the kind of feminist response (or at least activism) that has emerged from women in this context. The tension lies not only in the disarticulation of these identities but also in understanding that in their different forms they are fundamental and, as such, the post-apartheid project had to be informed by the nature of this relationship.

The Malibongwe Conference[2] in 1990 provides a useful frame of reference. The conference, which brought together activists from inside the country and exile, solidarity groups from Cuba, Philippines, Palestine, southern Africa and others, provided women (of the ANC and Mass Democratic Movement) with a space to deliberate on the status of women in post-apartheid South Africa. The Malibongwe Conference resolved that: "The ANC and MDM must develop policies and forms of organisation that facilitate the participation of women in decision-making processes in the struggle that lies ahead and in the post apartheid South Africa". It also concluded that women "must deliberate on the forms and processes of developing a women's movement in South Africa" (Malibongwe, 1990).

The conference was a threshold in the political history of South Africa in that, for the first time, gender oppression and women's status was legitimated as one of the key political problems in South African society. However, the majority of conference papers and positions did not fully address the complexity of women's status within the family and in broader society.

The debates and subsequent deliberations laid a basis for some of the policy considerations during the constitutional negotiations. Amongst these was the ANC statement in May 1992 referred to as "the May document", which declared that: "Gender oppression is everywhere. It is embedded in our cultural and religious practices" (ANC, 1992). The statement was the first ANC document to acknowledge gender oppression in such direct terms.

It is this attempt to bring to the foreground the private as political and the political as gendered that made the 1990s such an exciting period in the feminist history of South Africa.

The Malibongwe Conference did not resolve women's identity. Much of the debate and the papers tended to position women within the context of patriarchy. Women were defined in terms of their relationship to men, as daughters, mothers and sisters. Even in the context of the liberation struggle, and women's position in society as "women comrades" or "our women", there was a suggestion of these identities and relationships.

In many ways, the ANC was much more advanced than other political formations in South Africa. Although women in the Inkatha Freedom Party (IFP) had a women's brigade, they were very much viewed in the context of their relationship to men; and most of the statements or political expressions relating to women in the IFP were located within this framework and their role was seen in welfarist terms. The Pan Africanist Congress (PAC) did not depart from this approach. It tended to see the very notion of women's liberation as part of Western feminist discourse, with which they were uncomfortable, as others had been in earlier stages of the South African struggle.

The ANC and its allies had much more developed policy proposals and principles in terms of advancing women's emancipation and equality in South Africa. Women in the

ANC and its allies had been engaged in battles to change the political orientation since the inception of the ANCWL and the Federation of South African Women, amongst others. To a large extent, they had been able to win the recognition of women's oppression as a legitimate concern affecting society as a whole. The "triple oppression" thesis, referring to the intersection of class, race and gender in South Africa, was based on these debates and shifts (Baard, 1985).

With steps towards negotiations at the end of the 1980s, in the Harare Declaration and the Constitutional Guidelines, the ANC began to consider the need to enshrine gender equality as a founding principle for the future society (ANC, 1990). As the negotiations began, differences amongst women became obvious. The basis on which women could build solidarity amongst themselves was not altogether obvious. Historically, there had been problems between Black and White women in general. This could be traced to the suffrage movement in the 1920s, as a result of which White women received the vote in 1930. In the eyes of many, this was at the expense of universal enfranchisement. Some of these questions have arisen in other struggles and feminist movements, such as the civil rights and universal suffrage movements in the United States of America (Davis, 1981). However, within the anti-apartheid and democratic movement there had been a history of political solidarity and engagement against the apartheid state and its implications for women. Dating back to the anti-pass campaigns of 1913 in Bloemfontein, there developed in South Africa a contingent of women who recognised the need to build solidarity across colour lines (Wells, 1993).

In the 1950s, despite their auxiliary status in the ANC, women at times developed an autonomous political stance and took initiatives to build alliances outside the ANC. The mobilisation of women in the 1950s and the birth of the Federation of South African Women, and their position on the impact of apartheid laws on African women, in particular, represented a significant development in the articulation of the political stance of women. The alliance between women of the Congress of Democrats, the Coloured People's Congress, and the Natal and Transvaal Indian Congress, presents an interesting framework in understanding alliance formation amongst women and the expression of gender-specific issues in the decades that followed. The women's march to Pretoria in 1956 was organised almost independently of the women's "political organisations".

In the period between the 1960s and 1990s, there emerged a plethora of women's organisations, such as the Federation of South African Women, ANC Women's League, United Women's Congress, United Women's Organisation, Port Elizabeth Women's Congress and Natal Women's Organisation, to name but a few. Women's activism in South Africa grew progressively. However, it was also in the turbulent 1980s that a number of formations and counter-formations emerged.

Amongst Black women, there were (and still are) political and ideological contradictions. The complex relationship between Inkatha and UDF women in the 1980s is one such case of a problematic relationship. There were also serious areas of disagreement between UDF and Azanian People's Organisation (Azapo) women, between ANC and PAC women and so on. These were probably the most obvious contradictions and much easier to distinguish as they dealt with ideological differences. The result was often violence, although many will hasten to argue that women were not direct participants in the violent conflict, and were victims; there are, however, indications and evidence of women's participation, including at the level of political decision-making in many of these organisations.

At a subtle but complex level, there have always been complex differences in the interpretation of women's position in African cultures. Were these of political concern? Could these be tabled as political considerations or problems? To what extent could African women problematise African cultures in the context of ongoing emasculation of Black manhood by the apartheid state? What are the implications of studies that have over-concentrated on the patriarchal aspects of African cultures while being silent on others? What about Judaism and Islam (for a large part of the 1980s), amongst others? Part of the difficulty in the women's organisations in the 1980s related to these issues. There was a sense that it was important for women to speak of all the different forms of patriarchy, and to see how the religious and customary laws could be integrated in a new constitutional dispensation in a manner that accorded the right to practice by their members but acknowledged that the constitution was the supreme law of the land.

In the Cape, African women often made remarks under their breaths whenever those from the suburbs came to join as new members and attended meetings in the townships (*"mhm, bazobhal'incwadi ngathi aba"* – "they have come to write books about us," they would say). There were organisations and communities that had gone beyond this point and built across racial lines, but the resentment and weight of South African history was also there. Organisations and individuals struggled on both sides to counter the impact of apartheid and to learn to trust each other. The complexity has remained and in the current period it takes different forms.

What then, were the legitimate concerns to bring to the open debate? How necessary was it to politicise the personal? What saliency do such questions have in the struggles of today? Do they have any bearing in dealing with globalisation? To what extent does the current economic climate undermine or consolidate the earlier struggles? What alliances should be formed, and in terms of which issues? Against whom and for whom will such alliances be built? What are the faces of the poor? What is the texture of their lives? Where do these overlap with the advances that have been made? The post-1990 political period presented an opportunity to deal with some of these concerns, and in the laws passed and the institutional mechanisms and structures that have been built since the democratic elections, some of these questions are beginning to be addressed. However, the dialogue continues and, while this chapter tries to cover some aspects, these issues are intricate and cannot be dealt with singly.

The Malibongwe Conference presented an opportunity for women in the liberation movement to articulate these concerns. There was also a tendency to romanticise family and community, and these units were not adequately problematised. Albie Sachs pointed out that "in post-apartheid South Africa there would be the daunting task of resuscitation of those families torn apart by apartheid legislation and the productive demands of capitalist accumulation". Sachs did identify a caveat, which recognised that the family can be the site of production of patriarchal relations. However, in not examining how this could be undone, the conference fell short of conceptualising gender oppression as something that occurs both within the family and outside, as constructed by state policies and capitalist exploitation. One of the main challenges of post-apartheid governance is the extent to which it is possible to restore some of the dignity of family life and community, while at the same time acknowledging that often these too can become sites of exploitation.

Bridgett Mabandla argued at the conference that: "The academics regard customary practices as central to women's oppression. This argument is inaccurate as factors contributing to the oppression of African women are much more complex than presented by these academics". Mabandla's point about customary practices requires some attention. It is true that not all within customary practice is necessarily oppressive; the codification of customary law often misrepresented familial relations and ownership. It is the codification of customary law that provided for the male family head having sole ownership of land, consistent with Western societies' interpretations based on their own value systems. By all accounts, the codification process was based on rather crude notions and distortions of African customs, and impacted negatively on the rights of women (Simon, 1968). The notion of ownership by a single head of the family in these terms is foreign to many African communities. Men hold title to land in custody for their families and that is a very specific arrangement, which does not mean they "own" the land. As such, in times when they have been found to abuse their authority and the trust of their families, they could be displaced and removed from their position as head of the household. In many communities, this practice still holds. But, this does not mean that there is not a patriarchal character to the society nor does it guarantee women's independence as such.

> So, the one on the other side of the mountain writes and says, I am the head. I say, very well then. The head is the law. Secretly, I wonder, and what about the neck? Of what value, is the head without the neck? Which is more important? Who is more important, the dead or the

living? These are children's riddles. But I am woman, I say nothing. Go on then, be the head all you want. This neck will just do nothing, not carry the head, not provide a link with the body. I say, chop the neck and let's see what the head will do. Who is the head? Who is asking? Who came first, the living or the dead? (*Ntab'ezikude ziza nemihlola*, part of a traditional song of Xhosa "migrant workers widows")

In the constitutional debates and in looking at gender equality measures, it is critical that the cultural experiences of women be documented and understood in their context. There is a need to develop a way of understanding what forms of expression and strategies women and men develop to deal with their own challenges.

South Africa is not a uni-cultural society and although the constitution makes this clear, the tendency is to want to take a Eurocentric view to explain how South Africa functions. Gender equality movements are directly challenged by these issues. There are those who provide a cultural apologist's view and use culture and tradition to justify women's oppression. That is not what is argued here.

The central question of empowerment lies in the ability of women and men to access their rights and make choices that do not denigrate themselves. Often, the extent to which ordinary men and women have integrated these in their consciousness is missed, because assumptions are made about forms of expression. This has implications for governance, because without taking these factors into consideration, many of the programmes will not really change the quality of women's lives. A democratic form of governance will also teach that there are these voices, which are often in the margins of society, and they need to be part of the debate on policies.

The Women's National Coalition (WNC)

The object of the coalition is to co-ordinate a national campaign for the development and education of women, which will acquire and disseminate information about women's needs and aspirations; unify women in adopting a charter or other document and entrench gender equality in the constitution of South Africa. (WNC, 1992)

The constitutional negotiations provided an opportunity for South Africans to articulate the legal framework that would underpin the future South African society.

In addition to demands for representation, women and gender equality activists pushed for the "mainstreaming of gender equality considerations into the negotiations and constitutional talks" (Zulu, 1993). This was done by women through their political parties and organisations and through the formation of the WNC, and other strategies.

ANC women pursued one of the resolutions of the Malibongwe Conference on the "formation of a women's movement in South Africa for furthering Gender Equality and

Women's emancipation" (Shope, 1992). However, the idea of a women's movement, as noble as it was, presented a number of difficulties. The challenge, as indicated in the section on the women's movement above, had been the need to discover a common platform despite the history of division amongst women, and to find appropriate organisational expressions that could be utilised effectively.

Was it possible for women to build such a movement within so short a space of time? How effective could such a movement be in the constitutional talks? Who would take responsibility for the formation of the women's movement? It was clear that there was insufficient time to fully consider these complex questions and, as Ginwala (1992) put it, "the strength of the initiative will be in seizing the moment and putting women into the centre of the political agenda".

The WNC was launched in 1992. It was a coalition of political parties, religious organisations, cultural organisations, trade unions, professional bodies, welfare organisations and the rural women's movement, amongst others. In its founding document, the WNC acknowledged that South African women comprise heterogeneous groupings (WNC, 1992) and as such could not all come together as sisters. This recognition and acceptance of the complexity of South African women's different histories and political identities was the strength of the WNC.

Its single mandate was to develop the Charter for Effective Equality, which was seen as a participatory and nationwide campaign. Dubbed "operation big ears" by the coalition's first national convenor, Frene Ginwala, the campaign was seen as a process of listening to women and providing space for them to express their concerns, demands and proposals for the future of South Africa. The campaign was seen as a dialectical process, which collected demands and codified them and, at the same time, fed these into the constitutional process.

The key element of the campaign was massive participatory research, which aimed to bring together academics, politicians, women activists and ordinary women in focus groups and other public platforms. Of course, the method of research was subjected to debate in search of consensus and an empowering process. An extensive media campaign was mounted. The coalition set up regional offices and there developed a network of women's organisations in the regions and in local areas, connected to each other through their affiliation to the WNC. The potential of its power was immense. Likewise, the challenge of bringing together women from such diverse backgrounds was daunting.

As the political pressure increased during the constitutional negotiations, so did the need of political parties to control women. As could be expected, the contradictions amongst women emerged from time to time. Sometimes it was possible for women to work them out within the coalition and to arrive at a compromise. On other occasions, that was impossible and contradictions were played out in public. Some political parties were not comfortable with the growing autonomy of the "women's sections" and this also created complications in decision-making. It slowed decision-making and often, when difficult issues arose, women were not able to take their own decisions – they needed to consult with the mother body. For example, the National Party's women's section was once recalled by their political party and told that the coalition was interfering with their political loyalty. Once, when the issues of disagreement became strong, the NP women walked out of the WNC.

If any of this sounds rather melodramatic now, in the context of South Africa's transition it was very normal. It was a time of intense political calculation and commitment to a process, but without certainty as to its outcomes. The drama played out in the coalition was nothing compared with the melodrama of high politics at the negotiations table. Trust is after all a political product in processes like these and there was not much to base that on in the history of the country. There was little more than some vague idea that "this was necessary for the future" (Gasa, 2002).

The tensions in the coalition were not always across racial lines. Most of the disagreement was on the definition of "equality". What were its meanings and implications for South African women? Was it substantive equality women wanted? What was the framework in which gender equality could best be addressed in South Africa? Many of the tensions were within the left, as represented in particular by the ANC and its allies. ANC women had to confront their areas of difference even though they came from the same movement. At times this reflected different organisational cultures within the liberation movement.

The complexity of the decision-making process in the coalition also somewhat complicated the extent to which the charter campaign could feed into the negotiations process. At the World Trade Centre, discussions were moving quickly and there were not always opportunities for women to consult and reach consensus.

Women developed flexibility and different levels of planning and strategy within their political organisations and at the negotiations. It was easier for some parties to develop a working relationship at the negotiations and, where possible, women collaborated there. However, on substantial issues, such cross-party alliances were not always achievable as these dealt with division in society in general. On such issues, women had to rely on their constituencies and the mandate given by their parties.

As open and transparent as the negotiations were, it was evident that some decisions were taken without consultation of constituencies. It became important for the gender activists to be part of the working groups and organisational machinery that took decisions at the negotiations. Women in the ANC and its allies won some measure of openness and participation and, through the representatives in the negotiations, a system of report-back was devised. The ANC Commission on Emancipation of Women, for example, created a reference group on negotiations within the ANC. This became a group that discussed ideas and anticipated some of the issues that would emerge at the negotiations table. If women wanted to make an impact during the talks, they needed to develop a nuanced process of engagement and an ability to respond to issues as they unfolded.

The Charter for Effective Equality was finally launched in February 1994, towards the end of the Interim Constitutional Negotiations process at the National Conference in Johannesburg. It could not be fed into the talks, because by then most of the decisions had been taken and the Interim Constitution had been developed. However, it would be a mistake to assume that the issues that came from the charter were marginalised. There was a symbiotic process, particularly because some of the women who were part of the coalition's research desk were also part of the technical committees during the talks. Political activists were also exerting their pressure and influence through their political parties.

One of the issues of major contestation in the coalition was the status of the charter. Was it conceived as a political or a legal document? Once adopted, what legal standing could it have? This affected issues of language and framework as well as the articulation of some issues dealt with in the charter. To avoid political problems, many of the clauses were couched in oblique and imprecise language.

A most instructive debate during the launch conference was the disagreement on "women's reproductive rights", and the issue of customary law and women's status within this. Almost all the feminists and politicians avoided direct expression on customary law and the discussion from the floor was couched in such a way that custodians of power under customary law would not be offended. That was so until one of the delegates from the Transvaal Rural Women's Movement took the microphone and presented the experience of polygamy of the women in her community. Her speech evoked images of humiliation and oppression of women in this context. In no uncertain terms, she voiced their rejection of the practice and urged the coalition to accommodate their position in the charter.

The preamble of the Charter for Effective Equality finally declared:

> We hereby set out a programme for equality in all spheres of public and private life, including the law and administration of justice; the economy; education and training; development infrastructure and the environment; social services; political and civic life; family life and partnerships; custom, culture and religion; violence against women; health and media.

The charter's concerns were not new but its strength lay in the public campaign and the education that accompanied the campaign. In fact, there was not a radical difference between the issues articulated in the charter and those in other documents adopted by

South African women, notably, the Women's Charter adopted by the Federation of South African women in the 1950s. The language may be different from the charter of the 1950s but the core issues remained the same. Some analysts saw this as an indication of the conservatism of the WNC, but it would be more accurate to see it confirming the continuity of women's oppression in South Africa and the desire to redress this. The WNC charter campaign sought to legitimise the concerns and demands of women.

However, the very strength of the coalition was also its area of vulnerability and ultimately weakness. The decision-making process was slow, cumbersome and not always democratic, and affected the timing of the charter campaign. There had to be a great deal of balancing, accommodation and compromise.

Interestingly, there is much consistency with the struggles of women's movements in other countries. Some of the struggles around the definitional and conceptual issues had been experienced, for instance, in the second wave feminist movement in the United States. In the American feminist movement, Susan Sherman confronts the contradictions of power and unequal power relations amongst women in the movement. She calls for the need to accept and work with the notion of women's difference as a starting point; women are differentiated because of poverty, race, sexual orientation, political history and other issues that "affect products of the location and identity of women" (Sherman, 1990).

The period of the mid-1990s provides a useful reference for the future of the women's movement in South Africa. It was an ambitious project and a courageous act for women of such diverse political backgrounds to come together in such a highly politicised environment.

To the extent that the coalition met its goal and developed and achieved the charter, it was successful. To the extent that it provided a platform and frame of reference for debate on gender equality and women in political processes, it exceeded the expectations of the women of this country. It was possible for women to come together, despite a complex history and unequal power relations resulting from that historical baggage.

Those who championed the WNC as a platform never underestimated the complexity of that process. The strategic advantage was in understanding that women would have areas of discontinuity and that for many women, particularly on the left, what could be expected of the coalition was seen in very real terms. There were issues to be presented to the coalition on which to build consensus, and there were issues that women took to their political parties.

It was in this space that many women engaged in the most intricate battles. Here, in their own parties, they came to stake their claim and argued that women should not be left only with scars of memory but that substantive equality and an enabling environment had to be created for the future of South Africa. ANC women articulated much of the controversial debates and anger inside the ANC. They confronted the ANC and the South African Communist Party's (SACP) main negotiators. This was not based on devaluing the coalition and its potential but on the need for women to claim their due. They could speak in uncompromising terms with the negotiations committee at the ANC head office; they were part of that movement.

There was fragility to the platform offered by the WNC. It was a potentially powerful platform but could easily break down. It was a new kind of sisterhood, and was delicate and extremely limited. By its nature, the WNC brought women together from different sections of South Africa and, in order to achieve the minimum goals, there had to be a lot of compromise. There were also areas of discomfort, such as when Cosatu women felt that the WNC was not emphasising the issues of working women sufficiently. There was a need to balance these concerns with the vision of the WNC and, as a result, a number of matters were not dealt with directly. In simple terms, the WNC attempted to cross a historical divide and while all those involved were committed to this, there was a feeling, at times, that the "cost was too much for small returns" (Mokgalo, 1992). It was much easier, generally, to concentrate on the battles inside political parties and to conserve women's energies for the debates with their "own" political comrades, with whom they shared a history of struggle and a wider vision for the future South Africa.

The ANC needed to commit itself to certain arrangements and certain provisions and, in many ways, it did. In cases where the ANC had to accommodate other players in the process, the women devised a plan to cushion the potential impact on the status of women, if it was deemed to have potentially adverse results. One such issue was the status of women in customary law.

The departure of women from the WNC into parliament and formal politics weakened the coalition. Although, at the WNC conference in 1994, many women politicians saw their work in parliament as continuing to work inside the new government structures to further equality, there were clear indications of the problems to come. In her farewell speech as the convenor of the WNC, on the eve of the inauguration of the new parliament, Ginwala (1994) addressed the conference on her multiple identities as a woman, an MP and an ANC member. Using herself as a metaphor, she argued that all these identities meant that, wherever they are located, women who are committed to equality could work together with women elsewhere. If Ginwala's metaphor addressed the identity of an individual like herself and that of her counterparts in parliament, it fell short of addressing power relations between women left outside and those inside the corridors of power. The metaphor was also silent on the WNC itself and the direction it had to take.

There was an optimistic view of these relationships amongst many feminist activists in the mid-1990s. There was a sense of continuity and an assumption that having been in the same trenches, literally and figuratively, meant that women could continue as equals in post-apartheid South Africa.

Despite its earlier success, the WNC is but a shadow of its former self. Not surprisingly, some of the issues are a direct result of the political conjuncture and women's representation in decision-making. Although the departure of women to parliament in 1994 dented the coalition, the reasons are much more fundamental than that.

Firstly, what had brought the WNC together was the mandate of drafting the charter, and also the climate of the 1990s. Its composition made it possible for women to come together and, although there were problems, there was a sense of common purpose. There are a number of issues that could provide such a basis today, such as "gender-based violence", but in the context of post-apartheid South Africa women's political identities have been reshaped in a manner that makes it difficult to unite in a similar fashion.

In the post-1994 period, the WNC has struggled to find its balance and to recapture the earlier magic. It has been seriously affected by the demands made by the opening of other avenues and the brain drain of women from the coalition to the new levels. But most importantly, the WNC faces a crisis of identity and legitimacy. Its founding documents made it possible to exist within a particular framework and with a specific mandate. To take itself beyond the campaign for the charter has also meant that it would have to redefine itself. This is where its major weakness is today. It no longer brings together politically diverse groups as it did in the mid 1990s. This is beyond the WNC; it speaks to the political paradigm of present-day South Africa.

Legal provisions and framework

Following the United Nations Decade for Women in the 1980s, a number of countries launched special women's ministries and programmes to "improve women's status".

Faced with the possibility of democratic elections and a new constitution, South Africans began to consider the best options for effective equality and women's participation. They looked at other countries and reviewed what could be learnt from comparative international experience. However, the picture was somewhat fuzzy; there were no simple answers, and no solutions that could be easily adapted to South Africa.

The experience of the Women's Decade and women's ministries left a somewhat problematic legacy, as women's ministries tended to be marginalised and became a dumping ground for whatever governments did not want to address. There are a handful of women's ministries and initiatives that have been successful. Australia is one of those countries where women utilised the Women's Decade effectively, and the result was the putting into place of a number of legislative frameworks and institutions. During the Women's Decade, the labour government passed the anti-discrimination laws and created public committees and other institutions where qualitative gender equality gains were made. Of course, there were other sections of the society who probably did not feel included, especially the aboriginal communities and Asian minorities.

In other countries, women's ministries have tended to have no presence in the cabinet, and often derive access through the office of the president or prime minister. In France, the women's ministry can veto legislation. However, the success of French women in gaining access to political decision-making and direct representation in parliament and the cabinet has been limited. France ranks as one of the countries with the lowest representation of women in parliament and the cabinet. Uganda has a Ministry for Gender and Community Development and Ugandan women argue that it has had some success in entrenching gender equality. The former Minister of Women's Affairs became the Deputy President in the mid-1990s, and this was seen by gender activists in Uganda as a positive development given her commitment to gender equality.

In South Africa, the advent of democracy brought about the following provisions that had direct implications for gender equality.

The Equality Clause in the Constitution

The starting pointing for entrenching a legal framework for gender equality was seen to be ensuring that the Constitution contained an Equality Clause, which would be fundamental and overriding should such issues as customary law, personal law and others be in conflict with it. The aim was to ensure that the Equality Clause provided women with legal recourse should they want to invoke it in the face of other laws and practices that might infringe their rights and freedoms.

The Bill of Rights

It was also considered important to ensure that the Bill of Rights incorporated women's human rights and enshrined gender equality as a fundamental principle in society.

The South African Constitution is considered one of the most gender-sensitive constitutions, since gender equality is expressed in unambiguous terms in the Equality Clause and the Bill of Rights. Although the Constitution confers all these rights other sections can undermine them. For example, some of the issues on local government and the delineation of powers between the local government and traditional institutions also have gender implications. In cases where tradition may impinge on the status of a woman, it is difficult to delineate where custom begins and how it stands in relation to equality. Most complex is the issue of access to legal instruments that may be of assistance to a woman in a given situation.

The national machinery: A caveat

The idea of a national machinery was first tabled in the earlier debates on the "structures and package of representation" in the early 1990s. After the adoption of the Platform of Action, South Africans began to use the term "national machinery".

While it is important to respect international trends and the need to link with other powerful conventions and documents, there is something alienating about the concept of national machinery and its masculine associations. Language usage aside, the emphasis is on creating institutions and establishing mechanisms. The approach limits the scope and the flexibility of the structures. True to its identity, the national machinery tends to be mechanistic and, once it is physically there, it appears that the minimum has been done. The problems that emerge are much more difficult to conceptualise outside of the "fixation" with structures.

There is the danger of bureaucratisation of the structures and also femocratisation[3] of the women's movement and gender equality. In South Africa today, the national machinery is experiencing a number of these problem in different ways. Although the government, parliament, the Commission for Gender Equality (CGE) and other bodies make commitments to a dynamic interaction with civil society and women's organisations, there is a lack of such interaction between civil society and government structures, including the CGE, not only from the side of government and official political structures, but also from the weakened women's movement.

The phenomenon is not unique to South Africa. Globally, in feminist literature there is a preoccupation with the nature of relationships between women inside and outside political structures. The "inside and outside dichotomy" brings its own set of dynamics and problematics (International IDEA, 1998). It also magnifies contradictions amongst women, gender activists and feminists. Issues of accountability arise in relation to women inside political structures and the national machinery. All these signify the crisis of representation and accountability that is presented by democratisation. The section on representation below deals with some of these questions and concerns.

Additional to this, the governance angle as it unfolds in the current political discourse gives rise to a whole range of complications. Governance itself as a system of institutions and as a framework tends to be seen as overemphasising benchmarks and mechanisms that are measurable. There is nothing inherently wrong with either benchmarks or mechanisms but there is a need to develop a nuanced and holistic system of analysis, which looks at the issues with different lenses. An overemphasis on structures may obscure other ways of assessing the meaning of equality and also the extent to which women's lives have changed.

For example, one of the unintended impacts of electricity provision is the lifting of a burden on women's lives. It has also provided a space for other new forms of relationship to emerge inside and beyond the household. As one of the women interviewed for a project, "South Africa: What does change mean in our lives"[4] reported:

> Since the 'lectric came, things are easier. Now, my husband takes the iron and presses his pants. I might sneak my blouse in and he will iron it. I say to him, "ah, if the old man, Mandela made his own bed and he is an old man, nothing wrong with men making their beds." My husband laughs and he says, "ah, but he was a jailbird. In the jail they did not have women to do these things. Now it is habit." I say, "yes, but he still is a man isn't he ... ah these are the things we are learning, here."

On the face of it, these issues may seem unlinked to governance and the benchmarks we want to establish to measure progress. But that analysis has to learn to capture the texture, the quality and experience of life at all different levels. To do this, there is a need to develop an unawareness that is less static and rigid, while emphasising measurable pointers. Benchmarks, mechanisms, instruments, multi-partyism, all these are useful but the problem is in the detail of the way in which the new principles and policies are integrated into everyday existence.

The national machinery for effective gender equality

All the structures in Chapter 6 of the Constitution, dedicated to promote democracy, can be argued to be part of the national machinery for effective equality. These include, the Human Rights Commission (HRC), the Office of the Public Protector (OPP) and the CGE. The main reason for this assumption is that the HRC is mandated by law to take up all cases of discrimination on whatever grounds, be it race, gender, disability – all aspects of discrimination that may limit a citizen's access to his or her enjoyment of full status and rights.

Canada provides an interesting example of a human rights commission structured in such a way that discrimination on the grounds of gender can be dealt with as a human rights violation. However, literature from Canada does hint at the fact that gender equality becomes lost.

The Commission for Gender Equality

As the debate on the "package for effective equality" ensued and before the various gender equality lobbies, including the WNC, could achieve consensus on the contents and status of such machinery, events unfolded quickly at the World Trade Centre. One such instance was the decision to include the Council for Traditional Leaders in the constitution. Gender equality activists and women negotiators wanted to ensure that there would be an independent structure dedicated to gender equality that would be part of the statutory provisions; they also sought to ensure that women's human rights and equality would be protected under all circumstances and that equality would be an overriding principle.

According to the Gender Equality Act of 1996, the CGE is a statutory body that should not be subject to any pressure from government or elsewhere. Its aims are to:

- monitor and review all policies and practices of publicly funded bodies, including the business sector;
- review new and existing legislation to ensure that it promotes equality, and, where necessary, to recommend new legislation;
- investigate complaints on any gender-related issues (if need be, it may refer matters to the HRC or the Constitutional Court);
- monitor and report on compliance with international conventions, such as the Convention on the Elimination of All Forms of Discrimination Against Women (Cedaw) or the Beijing Platform of Action and other documents to which the South African government is a signatory;
- conduct research and recommend that research be undertaken to further the objectives of the commission; and
- investigate matters that are brought to it's attention – in so doing, the CGE may search any premises on which anything connected with the investigation is or is supposed to be violating the constitutional provisions for gender equality, may call people or institutions to appear before it in order to pursue any investigations brought to the attention of the CGE and may hold public hearings on any issue relevant to its work.

The Office on the Status of Women

The Office on the Status of Women (OSW) was established in 1995 as a unit within the Presidency. The idea was to have the structure co-ordinate at the level of the government and assess the extent to which cabinet ministers were "mainstreaming gender equality" into their work and policies. As part of the national machinery, its mandate was to provide a locus of influence within government and to liase with various ministries and gender desks at departmental level.

Gender desks and focal points

Gender desks are located in line departments to provide gender focal points. They are set up as part of ministers' briefs. The debate on gender desks consumed the women's movement in the mid-1990s. Experience from other countries revealed that gender desks could be marginalised easily and were often given little scope of influence or power (CGE, 1998). In some departments they are established at senior levels and enjoy the support of senior administrators. The Departments of Land Affairs, Agriculture, and Minerals and Energy have made major advances in this regard. However, in most cases the gender desks have not been successful.

The question of the location of gender desks or focal points is a complex one. Are they co-ordinating units in terms of the gender implications of a particular line ministry? Are they administrative units to provide back-up on issues that may have gender implications? Are they a policing unit to check performance and compliance of the department, ministry or line function in terms of gender? What is their relationship with other structures outside of their departments? How do they link up with the OSW? Is it through ministers being accountable to the minister in charge of gender in the President's Office? Is it through the OSW itself, which in turn reports to the cabinet through the minister?

The OSW was seen as a structure that would co-ordinate the gender desks and ministries and also provide back-up at the level of the cabinet. However, there are indications that the OSW is battling with these responsibilities and that there are not sufficient mechanisms to ensure that line ministries and departments comply with set targets. This largely touches on the political will and commitment of particular ministers and heads of department; for example, the Department of Minerals and Energy has led the way in implementing policies that empower women in the energy sector. Again, these questions and issues are raised in this chapter not to provide answers *per se*, but to flag them as challenges that continue to confront gender equality efforts the world over. To deal with the issues in any detail requires a different brief and space of engagement.

Through the national machinery and the elaborate structures that are in place, the South African government has complied with its own laws and policies and international conventions such as Cedaw and the Platform of Action.

The earlier debate on the nature of structures in the mid-1990s could never really be resolved and, as such, some package had to emerge. The package included a form of representation at the cabinet level, through a committee or an office in the cabinet, a standing committee on gender equality in parliament, legal provisions and laws that prohibited discrimination, gender focal points in departments and a structure outside of government with statutory powers. Part of the difficulty with the debate is that, in comparative terms, the national machinery is fraught with problems. It seems that in whatever package the structures may come, there is always the danger of marginalisation and under-resourcing.

From its inception, the CGE has been under-resourced. Much of the action on gender equality in post-apartheid South Africa has not been initiated by the CGE. It has not been able to be the nerve-centre of women's activism for a number of reasons, including its structural weaknesses, capacity and its location and approaches. Amongst other issues, the CGE has struggled to secure sufficient funds in order to deal with its mandate competently. The nature of its structure and its size have also been seen as inadequate, given the enormous challenges it faces. An aspect of this deals with the concept of gender equality itself, at both definitional and conceptual levels. Technically, the CGE is established to look at all issues of discrimination on the grounds of gender, including male experiences. However, the brief is at once broad and limiting.

In the first instance, if gender were truly mainstreamed, it would be assumed that all structures and institutions that receive public funds would take this as a critical issue to address within their own framework. The GCE is seen as advocating and playing the role of watchdog. It is a nebulous role; so are its powers. As powerful as it may seem in its legal instrument, the success of the CGE relies on its ability to balance the use of its legal powers with persuasive and educative methods. Most importantly, it relies on the strength of its relationship with the "organs of the women's movement", institutions of governance and the private sector.

The relationship issues between the CGE and the government, on the one hand, and civil society, on the other, have been complex. As a statutory body, it is independent of the government and parliament, but in reality the relationship is fragile because statutory bodies are dependent on public funding. Secondly, while the CGE's legal instrument provides powers to monitor the government's implementation of gender equality measures, the government has taken much of the responsibility to develop policies.

Independence of the statutory bodies cannot be fully achieved, simply because the law says so. It is an ongoing relationship and definition. In some cases, there may be a need to push the independence to challenge government, the private sector and other institutions. However, the success and ultimately the impact of the CGE depend on its tenacity and ability to approach different situations. There is a need to be flexible without compromising the CGE's independence and integrity. The critical aspect of this will be the extent to which all the partners and stakeholders can work out collaborative relationships. There is a dynamic here, which is a worldwide phenomenon. A large body of feminist work tries to grasp the issues and problematise the "institutionalisation strategies". Some of these will be explored later in the section evaluating the post-1994 process in its totality.

In the years of its existence, the CGE has not been able to yield the level of relevance and limelight it needs to be seen as a reference point on issues of gender equality. This partly relates to its internal problems, including inadequate funding. But there are far more fundamental reasons, including issues of perception and strategic location as a statutory body that is independent and has powers to monitor, review and also make the government, the private sector and society at large account for measures to effect gender equality. The meaning of this location needs to be examined in order to fully grasp the challenges; this falls beyond the scope of the chapter but it is a critical area of enquiry.

Women in parliament: The challenges of representation

It can be said that women's presence in formal politics will not bring about a qualitative change by putting social issues on the national agenda. It can be argued that women, because of their gender alone, will not place gender issues on the national agenda. Women in the upper echelons of politics are more likely to become an élite group among women and develop their own vested interests (Bahari, in Karam (ed.), 1998).

The energy and commitment of the WNC and other women's organisations was palpable during the transition. Indeed, the women's movement was at its most visible in that period. The result was that many political parties recognised the need to adopt "gender sensitive approaches" in their manifestos and electoral campaigns (ANC, 1992).

The women's movement considered it important for women to develop electoral strategies and to gain access to political platforms and representation. Since the 1980s there has been debate about the quota system and a discomfort with the notion that "numbers will guarantee power and influence" (Gasa, 2000). In some ways, quotas are a remedy to a disease, but in some cases they lead to another disease. As we have seen in Central and Eastern European countries, quotas have created a ceiling. They have led countries to not develop a political culture whereby women are integrated into the political system. But rules are not enough (Pintat, 1997). At its July 1991 conference, the ANC saw an unprecedented action by women who pressed for representation and a discussion of the quota system. These earlier struggles within the ANC resulted in women entering the higher echelons of decision-making in the organisation. In its election manifesto, the ANC stressed its commitment to women's emancipation and gender equality.

Women concentrated on intra-party politics to ensure that gender equality was integrated in the manifesto and the election lists of the ANC. The result was the adoption of a 30% quota by the ANC, and also the alternating of women and men on the list to ensure that women were not left at the bottom of the list. This placed a large number of women in parliament in 1994 and 1999.

The responses of other political parties were as follows.[5] The Democratic Party (DP) did not adopt a quota. The argument was that the quota system is tokenism. The DP argued that women's participation must result from gradual development within the party. The social and economic impediments on women's participation must be addressed and it is through such means that women can have access to representation. Consistent with its liberalism, the DP has argued that the quota system undermines civil liberties and it is reverse discrimination. However, the DP does not carry this argument to its fullest conclusion by rejecting the proportional representation system, which others argue may interfere with the right to choose candidates based on public selection.

The New National Party (NNP) has also argued that the quota system obscures the fundamental problems in society, the real issue being training, experience and ability. The NNP has kept its eye on the developments within the ANC and, despite its position on the quota, some inroads have been made by women in the party and women have influenced the NNP leadership. The party has the second highest representation of women in parliament.

The Inkatha Freedom Party (IFP) shares these reservations with the quota system. Along the same lines, it argues that society must address social impediments and women's access to education (Gasa, F., 1994).

There are various problems with quotas that have been expressed by feminists and organisations such as Azapo and the PAC, albeit for different reasons. The PAC and Azapo have tended to see quotas as élitist and have defined the issue as being the need to empower grassroots' women.

The approach of the parties against the quota system is based on assumptions about women's political immaturity and lack of capacity to handle political challenges. There is also an assumption that once women reach levels acceptable to and defined by men, they will automatically move into the upper echelons of power within the party.

Representation and its limitations

Gender activists and feminists in South Africa agree that the high levels of women in parliament have had a positive impact on public policy and perceptions of women. The proportional representation system made this possible, because once party leadership committed itself to representation, it became possible for women to be included in decision-making structures.

There is plethora of feminist literature and voices of women within the movement, which argue that the quota system has serious limitations and often can work against women. There are questions of both representation and accountability. Formal participation does not automatically guarantee a critical mass that will engage with issues in a manner that is always consistent with gender equality and the issues affecting women.

In March 1994, during its preparations for the first democratic elections, the ANC Commission on the Emancipation of Women organised a workshop with all the women on the list. The later workshop, "Towards the Women's Agenda"[6] was an attempt to confront the questions of representation and the expectations and pressure on women.

> But, what is the women's agenda? How do we define our constituency in a way that makes it possible for us to continue gender activism inside parliament and the corridors of power? How do we continue the link with the women's movement outside, while recognising that we have shifted – we are in parliament. (Mlambo-Ngcuka, 1994)

> There is also the question of the institutions themselves. They impose certain constraints. Rules of procedure of parliament. The very culture of parliament. We might say here, these are priorities and we endeavour to push these. How will the institution enable us? What should we do to the institution to make it work for us and for those we represent. I am talking about transformation of parliament itself, its rules and its procedures. (Marcus, 1994)

The increase in women's participation in parliament has had a dramatic impact in South Africa, at the level of representation and also in the relationship between the Parliamentary Women's Group (PWG) and other women's organisations and organs of the women's movement.

Comparative literature and experience suggests that in cases where women are incorporated in parliament and other structures of decision-making, they are often at the bottom of the hierarchy (Shvedova & Skjete, 1998). The ministries allocated to women tend to be "the traditional women's ministries", such as health, welfare and education. South Africa's experience departs from this trend radically. Women are represented at high levels of government and in the cabinet.

Although the "traditional ministries" were allocated to women in 1994, health and social welfare were the bedrock of the ANC's electoral manifesto and the Reconstruction and Development Programme. These were central to the policies of the government. The 1999 election brought women into "hard" ministries, such as foreign affairs, minerals and energy and land affairs. The current cabinet has eight women ministers out of 29 and 8 women deputy ministers out of 13. In parliament itself, women are present in the leadership, notably the Speaker, Deputy Speaker and the Head of the Council of Provinces. There is also representation at the level of chairs of portfolio committees such as finance. The upper echelons of the civil service have also been radically changing, with more women coming to senior levels of administration and policy development. South Africa's experience in this regard is in line with international trends (Hassim, 2002). In both elections, the ANC responded positively to calls for gender representation, and has integrated this into many of its policies and practices.

Notably, parliament has passed acts that deal with women's status in direct terms. These include, the Termination of Pregnancy Act of 1996, the Domestic Violence Act of 1998 and the Employment Equity Act of 1998, which provides women with the scope to challenge unfair labour practices and discrimination on the grounds of gender. Inside parliament, there has been a consistent, leading contingent of women's voices on some of these issues.

Deepening alliances amongst women in parliament

There are differences amongst women MPs of different parties over what needs to be transformed. Party whips keep women accountable to the party and not the Parliamentary Women's Group (PWG). What is the status of the PWG? There are only a limited number of areas in which women are able to stand united (Manzini, 1997).

Once women arrived in parliament there was a concerted effort to build bridges and for women of different political parties to come together. But soon it became clear that the agenda could not sustain an ongoing structure. The political parties themselves were nervous of the implications of this alliance, and issues of accountability to the party and its mandate were put on the table.

The status of the PWG was also an area of serious contention in relation to the rules of parliament. It operated without a budget and had to raise funds from donor agencies. The PWG had no legal recognition in parliament and this affected its ability to influence legislative debates.

Although women agreed on broad terms such as "gender equality", they disagreed on what that equality entailed and how it could be achieved in parliament and in society in general.

Women are not a homogeneous group and the parliamentary system heightens the differences. Some women from the opposition parties found it difficult to develop a commitment to the PWG because of the "ANC dominance". They questioned ANC leadership, despite the track record of these MPs in women's organisations and their co-operative approach (Manzini, 1997). In fact, even such issues as the celebration of National Women's Day became contested, and opposition MPs did not like the ANC's overt recognition of and identification with the day. However, it has been the custom of parliament to celebrate the day in the chambers, with different parties making their speeches. In the beginning, the PWG wanted to use the day in a much more significant and creative manner and create platforms of interaction with women from outside parliament. Nozizwe Madlala-Routlegde, the first Convenor of the PWG and now Deputy Minister of Defence, observed that:

> An inter-party alliance between women MPs is important. Knowing the difficulties and differences – we agreed on a minimum agenda. The will to work together was there but there were obstacles in parliament. Their caucuses dictated on them and questioned their loyalty. Women felt pressure and they were uncomfortable. Even the ANC Women's Caucus was questioned. But the party had to observe its own principles and political obligations. (Madlala-Routledge, 1998)

Gender activists and individual feminists in other political parties have not been able to overcome their ideological and party-political interests in pursuit of legislative reform. The ANC Women's Caucus has been the main force in this process.

Under the leadership of Pregs Govender, parliament set up a Standing Committee on the Quality of Life and Status of Women to identify areas of legislative reform, such as the Domestic Violence Act of 1998 and the Maintenance Act of 1998. The committee has not only provided an institutional framework for parliament to examine these issues, it has also provided a critical link with civil society. It held hearings on a number of policy issues including the "poverty hearings", which were aimed at examining the feminisation of poverty and its impact on women. The Women's Budget initiative was another innovative programme of this committee; it was aimed at ensuring that the process of drawing up the national budget took cognisance of its implications for women.

Accountability: Areas of difficulty

The preceding sections have already hinted at some of the complexities of the relationship between women in parliament and the movement outside. To whom are the women MPs accountable? How is such accountability fulfilled and addressed?

Comparative literature and experience demonstrates that the problem is not unique to South Africa. Australian women in the labour government have documented some of their experiences on the question of accountability and loyalty. Although critiques of the proportional representation system argue that party control makes it difficult for women, the literature reveals that this is not necessarily the case (Karam, 1998). Although the party whips and structures may put direct pressure on women, this does not mean that in open-slate systems women are not faced with this dilemma, especially in the case of feminists who enter politics. Indeed, how do they define and limit their constituencies? Increasingly, women are uncomfortable with the lack of accountability of women MPs. In the electoral debate, there was strong emphasis on how women in parliament had not changed the institutions of power, and had not shown sufficient accountability to the women of South Africa.

An interesting dimension to this debate is the evident silence in questioning men in parliament about their accountability to women, particularly on gender-specific issues such as domestic violence. These questions do get directed at the parties, in general, but not at male candidates *per se*. The whole approach tends to overburden women and lets the parties off the hook. By emphasising the lack of accountability of women MPs, gender and feminist activists collude in the scapegoating of women MPs, and do not question the environment in which all MPs work or measure the performance of individuals, rather than a gender group.

At a subtle but highly problematic level, there is a sense that "you do not belong there – justify your presence to us women". This is not problematic in and of itself, especially if it is directed at all MPs, male and female, and other public officials. However, because society has been socialised to see women play specific roles, there is the residual feeling across sections of society that women's presence in parliament is simply tokenism. So, in judging and evaluating their performance, accountability and governance, there is a tendency to project them as incompetent and inefficient. There have been numerous public debates and images, which reinforce these stereotypes. Some of the problems of the quota system and proportional representation speak to these issues. Are seats allocated to women as a gender? Are they therefore expected to serve this constituency? While demanding high levels of accountability by public officials is a good practice in democratic governance, there is a danger of women becoming soft targets.

The maturation of the women's movement and gender equality movement will be indicated by the quality of women's participation in politics. It will also be measured by the sophistication of the movement in foregrounding patriarchy in all its assessments. While demanding high levels of competence and accountability from women, the women's movement also needs to question power relations and patriarchies within government, political parties and the social movements themselves, including the gender equality movement.

In the evaluation of governance and the mechanisms that have been established in South Africa, it is necessary to understand the many ways in which power is gendered. There is a need to develop an understanding of the complexities that arise. This is not to say that all women in parliament are committed to gender equality. Some are not willing to take political chances and the risks associated with them. Some, of course, do not agree on the very issue of gender equality.

Globalisation and its gender implications

[U]nder the guise of "labour market flexibility" women are disproportionately the victims of retrenchments, underemployment, and casualisation. This means that women are increasingly concentrated, where they are employed, in low paying, part time jobs, with little or no job security. Both the quality and quantity of jobs occupied by women are under attack. (Cosatu, 1999)

On the eve of the democratic elections, in April 1994, South Africa signed the General Agreement on Tariffs and Trade (GATT), in an attempt to achieve smooth entry by the textile and footwear industry into the global market. Already, those observing global trends warned that the agreement would have dire consequences for the industry. This was the beginning of South Africa's liberalisation of trade.

By 1999, the consequences of GATT for the textile industry were clear. Between 1990 and 1999, there had been 80 000 job losses. A similar process was unfolding within the footwear industry. According to a submission by the South African Congress of Textile Workers Union (Sactwu) to the Department of Trade and Industry, there was a 40% decrease in the labour force between 1992 and 1999 (Sactwu, 2002). Sactwu's submission linked the job losses to GATT and the restructuring that took place within the footwear industry to meet "global requirements". This is a feminised industry and the impact on women has been tremendous.

At the same time, there has been a growing restructuring towards casual labour. The growing casualisation and the redeployment of workers to home-based work (sweatshops) have meant not only that women work in difficult conditions but also that levels of unionisation have dropped. So, those who have jobs in home-based industry are vulnerable, with little or no possibility of recourse. Their rights remain unattainable for the majority of South African women. The Employment Equity Act has by and large benefited middle-class and especially upper-middle-class White women, because of their location and the positions they already occupy in the various industries. Cosatu has stressed that job losses have resulted in a massive economic depression amongst working-class families. The burden on women and on girl children in particular has increased (Cosatu, 2000). The feminisation of poverty is unrelenting and so is its impact on women's lives. It is not a gender-neutral process and it goes beyond the socio-economic. It touches on the increasing vulnerability of women.

There has been a wide-ranging debate on the economic policy of the post-apartheid government. The defendants of the Growth, Employment and Redistribution programme (GEAR) have argued that in prioritising the reduction of internal debt, the government sends positive signals to the markets. According to Minister of Finance Trevor Manuel (1999), this has paid off because the deficit has been reduced and there is economic growth. Perhaps these are sound economic arguments on one level. The central issue, however, is how economic growth relates to promoting development and creating employment opportunities. What is the meaning of economic growth without growth in employment?

In a market economy it would be unreasonable to expect the government and the private sector not to want to be globally competitive. In many ways, competitiveness is in the interest of the South African economy, in order to secure its place in a global environment. However, there is no safety net for the poor. There is no respite for the majority of women in this country. This deepens inequalities and undermines the rights enshrined in laws and in the constitution. It deepens the marginalisation of women as they work in sectors that are much more vulnerable to cutbacks or changes in work environment. Many companies have introduced flexitime to cut labour costs, and have also used workers beyond the stipulated hours of work. Casual workers work late and on Sundays or public holidays.

The argument put forward by companies is that this creates jobs, but in reality it preys on people who are already vulnerable. Working hours have always been a contentious and political issue in South Africa but the structuring of the work environment undercuts gains made by the labour movement. In Black townships in the Cape, there was even a socialised identity of young people who worked during school vacations, earnest and obviously teased by their peers – *amacasuala*. That has changed. These are the main bread-winners. The Basic Conditions of Employment Act and the Labour Relations Act do not protect these large numbers of workers. Their economic vulnerability is palpable.

There have been several dimensions to the problem in many communities. Women tra-ditionally worked in the textile industry and men in the footwear industry. Men see women who have moved into the footwear industry as outsiders. The employers are aware of this and take women on as casuals. A whole range of issues arises from this exploita-tion, and sometimes women take on work for their male colleagues "to make things easy" in the work place. In some situations, casual workers are victimised not only by the employers but also by their fellow workers, who may see them as threatening their jobs. So, the levels of victimisation are multiple.

Women are not listened to or seen by the movements on the left, which are fighting against globalisation, and are obviously ignored by the state and global capital.

Challenging the negative impact of globalisation: Rethinking the strategies

Alongside deepening inequalities globally, has been the recognition by international financial institutions, states and other international instruments that there must be an engagement with civil society. A number of civil society organisations have taken the opportunity and forced governments and international capital to recognise civil society and engage with it in the decision-making process.

The impact of "Seattleisation" has been an acknowledgement of the need to engage in dialogue. However, the danger is that the basis for participation does not provide space to fully explore the impact of poverty in its fullest implications (Webster, 2002). In the images beamed across the world, there has been a decidedly cultural and gendered inter-pretation of the faces of poverty and its meanings. There are areas of silence and missing faces and voices in that process; and, in many ways, the new social movements reproduce patterns of silence.

Gender equality represents one of those areas where the contradictions have come to the fore. The experiences of women at Beijing and also at Beijing plus 5 increased the sense of alienation that women from powerless communities feel on such platforms. The system of accreditation and representation at the "NGO Steering Committees" at the United Nations International Conference has tended to privilege organisations from the North or those from the South that seem very close in definition to their northern counterparts. Super NGOs and super social movements have developed. Of course, the language of discourse and engagement is often masculine, but in the gender discourse there has been a tendency to represent and speak "on behalf of".

The debate on social movements provides a useful reference point. The reality is that women have been forming social movements and linkages for decades; one of the oldest social movements in Africa is the organisation of market women in Nigeria. It emerged during the mercantile period as a women's coping mechanism and support network as they travelled as far as Europe to trade. Its history provides an interesting frame of reference as a movement that emerged out of a particular need and as an issue-based initiative. In times of political strife and crisis in that country, market women have the ability to mobilise, network and mount an effective political campaign (Onoge, 2000). The strategies and the lessons from this period might be instructive.

In terms of building gender equality, the new social movements are not necessarily the answer. A number of initiatives to build women's movements have had some of the characteristics of the new social movements, and often their successes were limited. From the Zapatistas to other movements, those that are able to endure and campaign effectively are the movements rooted in a particular social and historical reality, shaped by their experience, as a starting point.

The potential to build bridges and solidarity lies in the connections made beyond mobilisation against global conferences, and satellite television. It lies in understanding the spaces available and in taking advantage of these. It comes in redefining these spaces and reclaiming them so that the issues are part of the public voice.

The potential to engage in a meaningful way lies in asking, listening and absorbing answers. How do women survive? How do they deal with the fact that even traditional survivalist attempts in the informal economy are severely eroded? What, in fact, does having water supply mean for rural women in the Eastern Cape? How does HIV/Aids affect women? How can the campaign for treatment also take into consideration the gendered aspects of HIV? What about unequal power relations amongst working class communities? And other classes? How can these be brought to the fore as part of our understanding of globalisation and its impact on women?

Mainstreaming gender

Let us briefly return to governance and the location of gender within that. After the Decade of Women and post-Beijing, it has been argued that, to avoid marginalisation, gender must be mainstreamed.

Many gender activist and gender-planning experts developed models and arguments to integrate gender into the mainstream of policy development and implementation. From a gender development perspective, it has been argued that the integration of gender is part of the efficiency of the state and governance. Many departments in South Africa have tried this approach and report to the cabinet minister responsible for gender equality. The OSW is considered to be the co-ordinating structure in the Presidency. Parliament has also tried to integrate gender through a whole range of mechanisms, including the transformation process driven by the Speaker's office. From the point of view of governance, these benchmarks and indicators will require careful assessment. The issue is the nature of the mainstream itself. How do we assess impact there?

Labour's document for a developmental macroeconomic framework raises a number of proposals. Effective implementation of developmental programmes to address women's concerns is not possible in the context of inappropriate macroeconomic policies. For example, low interest rates are needed to facilitate the entry of women into small enterprises, re-regulation of capital markets and tariffs are required to stem job loss, and more expansionary fiscal policies are necessary to allow the broadening of social services, social security and public sector employment (Cosatu, 1999).

What options are available to the South African state, even in the context of a constraining global environment? What considerations go into the choices of the economic framework? How does this relate to some of the bills and laws currently being debated, including the Minerals Act and the proposed bill dealing with the finance industry?

Reports from the gender desks in line ministries reveal a complex picture of what mainstreaming means. Some have set targets, depending on political will and leadership, and they have stuck to these targets. The Minerals Act is one example of where ownership is likely to benefit men and women. The Department of Land Affairs is an area where there is a developing linkage between the policy, the law and actual gender equity in access, acquisition and benefit, especially, for poor women.

In many ways, this leaves us with the problem of defining the South African state as "neo-liberal". In terms of women, there has not been a withdrawal of the state; in fact, the opposite is true. As this chapter was being written, vast tracts of land, which had been lying uncultivated in the Eastern Cape, were being ploughed in a partnership scheme between the government and the citizenry. About 40% of the direct beneficiaries of this scheme will be women. This is a first in this much-neglected region. To what extent will it be sustainable? This is their first planting season so it is difficult to tell.

Conclusion: The women's movement, what future?

This chapter has tried to illustrate that the notion of a "women's movement" is a deeply contested one in South Africa. This is so, from a historical perspective and also from contemporary politics.

Some scholars and activists assert that the brain drain of women moving from civil society to parliament, the private sector and the government created a leadership crisis for the women's movement. The proponents of this view tend to argue that this accounts for the weakness of the women's movement in South Africa today. Women did not strategise for the demands of leadership carefully. Women did not plan for the new structures that were to emerge, or anticipate the impact on the women's movement of women getting into these positions. A lot of organisations were left without proper leadership, and these need to be examined and strengthened (Mtintso, 1997).

This is certainly an important angle to the problem, but it may be suggested that the women's movement was never strong outside of its political identity in South Africa. Historically, the strength of the women's movement has been attached to that of the congress movement, even in times when the women were autonomous from it. Their political identity is what drove them and linked their demands to the national liberation struggle.

In the early 1990s, the United Democratic Front and other ANC-aligned organisations decided to close many grass roots organisations, such as the United Women's Congress and the South African Youth Congress, with the aim of joining forces under the banner of the ANC. The strategic objective was to unite the congress movement and to speak with one voice in the campaign for the first democratic elections in South Africa. "We had always been ANC and we wanted to be so now, in public and as one voice" (Mokaba 1993). It is not the purpose of this chapter to examine the implications of these decisions in the long term. Suffice it to say, some women activists did not make an easy transition from their women's organisations to the ANCWL. There had been a sense of relative autonomy for many activists, even though they fully identified with the ANC. The collapse of the organisations created a kind of identity crisis for the women who were not fully ANC in their political outlook, even though they broadly supported its objectives.

The nature of the transition presented new dynamics of location and identity. By the mid-1990s some of these women had already begun to withdraw from active gender struggles. In the few years leading up to the first democratic elections, feminists and gender activists were presented with new dynamics, which impacted on their strategies and approaches. In the heat of the political transition, these organisations did not really have time to work out what the implications of a changing South Africa would be. What would it mean to their location, identity and the role they would play as individuals and as a collective? In the few instances where this question was tabled, there was an overwhelming sense of continued solidarity.

However, the structural and organisational meanings were not fully explored. Women who are inside the structures of governance and those who remained outside have had to work through a number of constraints, opportunities and political issues. On some levels, there are areas of continuity, whereas at other levels the "sisters" sit on opposite sides of the table. This is a phenomenon that requires a deeper understanding, because of women's shared history. Being on different sides of the table does not always mean being oppositional, but sometimes it does mean exactly that.

Countries that have gone through transitions to democracy recently have seen the weakening of civil society and women's movements in particular. This has been said to be due to a number of problems, including the withdrawal of funding that supported the pro-democracy movement and a changing political environment. The south-eastern European transitions tend to be used as an example in this regard (International IDEA, 1998).

In the case of South Africa, one of the critical issues facing women's organisations is that of political identity and location in post-apartheid South Africa. South Africa has never had a "women's movement" as such, at least not in the sense of an all-encompassing organisation under whose banner all women activists march. Indeed, this is not only unrealistic but also undesirable. There is a rich history of alliance forming among federations and networks of organisations that came together for particular causes. At times, these networks have been weak, absent or struggling, depending on the issues and the political mood of the country.

This chapter takes the view that currently there is an increased emergence of new forms of organisation. Amongst these are the various coalitions and networks of organisations and trade unions that work in the areas of gender-based violence, Aids, policy advocacy and feminisation of poverty. There has also been an increase in the number of branches of the ANCWL across the country. What these developments indicate needs careful study. Some of these initiatives constitute a critical component of what can be called a "women's movement".

The extent to which women will be able to build or strengthen existing alliances and take up issues is what will determine their ability to constitute a force with the potential to impact on the South African political, economic and socio-cultural landscape.

Endnotes

1 All the citations on Cosatu have been taken from a cd-rom recently compiled by Cosatu. It is a collection of all of Cosatu's Policy Submissions, 1994–2001.

2 The Malibongwe Conference was organised by the ANC and the anti-apartheid movement in Amsterdam. It brought together women from inside the country and those who were in exile for the first time since the banning of political organisations in 1960. The Malibongwe Conference papers cited here can be found in the University of Cape Town library, ANC archives. Sachs' comments and those of Bridget Mabandla were made in the course of the conference and are from notes taken by the author; however, they are verifiable in the collections at the UCT library.

3 Femocratisation is a concept that has been coined to refer to a system where government bureaucracy simply brings in women without ensuring that they have the authority or competence to implement their responsibilities.

4 This was a collaboration between Gasa and a Swedish film-maker, Maj Westerman. The project was aimed at documenting the history of women's struggle and the extent to which women were integrated in the new South Africa. In the end, funds were limited and Maj went ahead with the film on the history, but the contemporary documentary was not developed. Literature and films were collected and these are part of the collection of the author. Some of these have been used for the purposes of this chapter.

5 In March 1994, the WNC held a national conference at which all political parties had to present their views on gender equality and state their positions and manifestos on women. These references are based on the proceedings of that conference. The WNC never issued a formal report but the papers are available for reference in the WNC office. The references here are from the author's notes of that conference.

6 "Towards the Women's Agenda" was held in May 1994 after the first democratic elections. The aim of the workshop was to familiarise ANC future parliamentarians with the parliamentary system. This was also an opportunity to discuss the issue of women's agenda and participation. The citations of Phumzile Ngcuka and Gill Marcus are from their contributions from the floor during the workshop discussions. There is no formal report of the workshop. The ANC has the collection of papers and documents of the workshop. The references are from the author's collection of papers.

References

Abdul-Raheem, T. (2002) "From OAU to AU – The Challenges and Only Questions. August Postcard. Pan African Movement." E-mail correspondence.

African National Congress (1992) "May Statement: Launching the Commission on the Emancipation of Women."

African National Congress (1995) "Towards a Women's Agenda in Parliament." Workshop, May.

Baard, F. (1985) "A Mother Will Hold the Knife on The Sharp End." In Barret, J., Dawber, A., Klugman, B. & Yawitch, J. (eds) *South African Women Speak*. Birmingham: Third World Publications.

Commission on Gender Equality (CGE) (1997) *Report of the Commission on Gender Equality*. Information and Evaluation Workshops.

Cosatu (1999) "Submissions to the Portfolio Committee on Labour." National Parliament, Cape Town.

Davis, A. (1981) *Women, Race and Politics*. New York: Women's Press.

De Beauvoir, S. (1967) *The Second Sex*. Harmondsworth: Penguin Books.

Gasa F. (1994) "Women in the Negotiations, the IFP Persepective." Women's National Coalition. Unpublished paper.

Gasa, N. (1993) "How Far Have They Come?", *New Nation*, August.

Gasa N. (2000) "Understanding Gender Equality in the Constitution." Unpublished paper.

Gasa, N. (2002) "Nkrumah's Political Kingdom Was Built With Women", *Sunday Independent*, August.

Ginwala, F. (1989) "Women and Race in South Africa." Unpublished paper. ANC Archives. Mayibuye Centre, University of the Western Cape.

Ginwala, F. (1992) "Women in the ANC." Papers of the ANC Commission on the Emancipation of Women. Unpublished.

Ginwala, F. (1994) "Farewell Speech to the WNC." Unpublished paper.

Govender, P. (1994) "Making Parliament Work for Women", Parliamentary Debate on Gender Equality. Unpublished speech.

Hassim, S. (2002) "Identities, Interests and Constituencies: The Politics of the Women's Movement in South Africa. 1980–1999." PhD thesis, York University.

Hooks, B. (1988) *Aint I a woman*. Boston: South End Press.

Hooks, B. (2000) *Feminist Theory. From Margin to Center*. Boston: South End Press.

International IDEA (1998) *Democracy and Deep-rooted Conflict: Options for Negotiators*. Stockholm.

Karam, A. (1998) "Women in Parliament: Making a difference." In Karam, A. (ed.) *Women in Parliament: Beyond Numbers*. Stockholm: International IDEA.

Lorde, A. (1984) *Sister Outsider. The Master's Tools Will Never Dismantle The Master's House*. California: The Crossing Press/Freedom.

Madlala-Routledge, N. (1998) "Challenges of Representation." National Parliament, Cape Town.

Malibongwe Conference Papers (1989) Unpublished.

Manuel, T. (1999) Addressing Portfolio Committee on Finance in Parliament. Unpublished.

Manzini, M. (1998) "Women Empowered: Women in Parliament in South Africa." In Karam, A. (ed.) *Women in Parliament: Beyond Numbers*. Stockholm: International IDEA.

Mbete, B. (1992) "Women's Participation in the Negotiations." Papers of the ANC Commission on the Emanicapation of Women. Unpublished.

Mfeketho, N. (1991) Interview by Nomboniso Gasa.

Mogkalo, D. (1992) "Cosatu's Dilemmas with the WNC." Papers of the ANC Commission on the Emancipation of Women. Unpublished.

Mokaba, P. (1993) "The Future Role of the ANC Youth League", *Umrabulo*, ANC.

Molyneux, M. (1993) "Women's Movement." In Outhwaite, W. & Bottomore, T. (eds) *The Blackwell Dictionary of Twentieth-Century Social Thought*. Oxford: Blackwell.

Mtinsto, T. (1997) "Gender and Race Issues. Challenges for the Commission for Gender Equality." Unpublished paper. CGE workshop.

Onoge, O. (2000) "Market Women and the New Social Movements, the Nigerian Experience." International IDEA Workshop on Gender, Democracy and Governance, Lagos. Unpublished.

Pintat, C. (1998) "Inter-Parliamentary Union." In Karam, A. (ed.) *Women in Parliament: Beyond Numbers*. Stockholm: International IDEA. Switzerland.

Roseneil, S. (1995) *Disarming Patriarchy*. Philadephia: Open University Press.

Sactwu (2002) "Submissions to the Ad Hoc Committee on the Quality of Life and Status of Women". National Parliament, Cape Town.

Scruton, R. (1982) "Women's Movement." In Scruton, R. *Dictionary of Political Thought*. Kent: Macmillan Press.

Simons, H. J. (1968) *African Women: Their Legal Status in South Africa*. London: Charles Hurst.

Sherman, S. (1990) *Down the Rabbit Hole. The Colour of the Heart*. Willimantic, TC: Curbstone Press.

Shope, G. (1992) Interviewed in *Malibongwe*. ANCWL.

Shvedova, N. & Skjete, H. (1998). "Obstacles to Women's Participation in Parliament." In Karam, A. (ed.)*Women in Parliament: Beyond Numbers.* Stockholm: International IDEA.

Smuts, D. (1994) Parliamentary Debate on Effective Representative System. May, Hansard.

Soyinka, W. (2000) "The Children Of This Land." Unpublished poem.

Vaid, U. (1995) "Beyond Rights and Mainstreaming." In *Virtual Equality.* New York: Doubleday.

Volbrecht, G. & Gasa, N. (1996) "Shouldn't We Change the Subject: Gender and Poverty." Unpublished paper.

Webster, E. (2002) Notes taken by the author in conversation on the impact of globalisation.

Wells, J. C. (1993) *We Now Demand. The History of Women's Resistance to Pass Laws in South Africa.* Johannesburg: Witwatersrand University Press.

WNC (1992) "Preamble of the Women's National Coalition Constitution."

Zulu, L. (1993) "Towards a Non-sexist South Africa", *Malibongwe*, ANCWL.

10 Contesting "Sustainable Development": South African Civil Society Critiques and Advocacy

Patrick Bond and Thulani Guliwe

Introduction[1]

One of the world's momentous events linking globalisation and governance – the World Summit on Sustainable Development (WSSD) in Johannesburg, in August and September 2002 – also served as a site of intense conflict between elements of South African civil society, in relation to each other and also to the state. The most ambitious modern plan for Africa's further integration into the world economy – the New Partnership for Africa's Development (Nepad) – was not only a chapter of the WSSD document, but served as a lightning rod for complaints about the South African government's philosophical and practical approach to development.

Looking at this approach through the lens of progressive civil society activist groups, this chapter argues that a renewed set of divisions in South African society – class, gender, environment, as well as residual racial divisions – are being exacerbated, notwithstanding political liberation and a degree of deracialisation since 1994. Many of the divisions are apparent in relation to environment and development issues associated with the WSSD. Eight years after the first democratic election, many of the same social forces that worked hand-in-hand with the African National Congress (ANC) were found working vigorously on the opposite side; although, as will become obvious, such civil society conflicts with state officials had been brewing since 1994. The main argument we will consider and provide documentation to uphold, is that tense relationships between state and civil society, as well as within civil society, stem from excessively neo-liberal policies, based on the logic of the market.[2] Ironically, these are not dissimilar processes to those occurring in many settings around the contemporary world, notwithstanding the claim by Pretoria that South Africa's rulers are intent on fighting what President Thabo Mbeki has termed "global apartheid".

Following a brief consideration of semantics and of discursive strategies that have come to be associated with the notion of sustainability, we then assert the core theses associated with our reading of state-society relations, drawing upon our grounding in Frantz Fanon's work (especially his considerations of the "pitfalls of national consciousness").

Semantic and discursive problems

Some terminological issues should be addressed immediately. The idea of "civil society" – which ranges from small community-based organisations, to development agencies and charities, to large-scale social movements, many of which are typically serviced by Non-Governmental Organisations (NGOs) – has an extremely controversial pedigree in transitional South Africa, based on contestation from various ideological positions, class orientations and political allegiances.[3] These controversies also reflect global trends, through which criticism has emerged of what Petras and Veltmayer (2001) term "NGOs in the service of imperialism".[4] Some NGOs, generously funded by foreign foundations and governments, have often done the bidding of neo-liberal policy-makers: promoting liberalisation and deregulation; buying into the idea of smaller states; and co-opting grassroots organisations into dead-end strategies that transfer the burden of household reproduction from society as a whole to low-income people, especially women. Likewise, NGOs in post-apartheid South Africa and across the world have been captured through state patronage, and play less of a role than in previous years (especially the late apartheid period) in promoting pro-poor policy advocacy.

Hence, when we consider the role of South African civil society in issues related to the WSSD, local complexities and divergent strategies are highly significant. It is also appropriate to turn to international ideological debates over even the term "sustainable development". The main point behind the sustainable development thesis is a technicist and reformist one, namely that environmental externalities such as pollution should, in the classical example, be brought into the marketplace. By doing so through taxes or the trading of pollution rights, for example, regulators assure that these costs are adequately accounted for in "polluter-pays" profit-loss calculations. The idea of "sustainability" was redefined in lowest-common-denominator intergenerational terms by Gro Harlem Brundtland's World Commission on Environment and Development in 1987: "development that meets the needs of the present without compromising the ability of future generations to meet their own needs".

In contrast, ecological economist Herman Daly takes the notion of sustainability further:[5] "We should strive for sufficient per capita wealth – efficiently maintained and allocated, and equitably distributed – for the maximum number of people that can be sustained over time under these conditions".[6] Daly offers a tougher definition than

Brundtland, in order to highlight the difference between "growth" and "development" in a context in which there do exist physical ecosystem limits – the earth's capacity to act as a "sink"– to the absolute size of the global economy. Daly's definition of sustainable development is: "development without growth beyond environmental carrying capacity, where development means qualitative improvement and growth means quantitative increase".[7]

These views are reflected in different positions taken in South African policy debates; for example, the environment's carrying capacity for resource utilisation in cross-catchment water transfers to Johannesburg, and greenhouse gas emissions, became issues in campaigns over differential human versus corporate access to water and electricity.

While some NGOs might be comfortable with the less threatening Brundtland formulation, many South African social movements support the latter interpretation as part of a broadly redistributive "red-green" political fusion. In relation to major debates over water, energy and the like, these movements have begun linking the global and local in ways that address both national resource management issues and human-scale environmental issues, *stressing qualitative improvements in the lives of the poor, ahead of economic growth*. One rationale for the hostility now arising against South Africa's contemporary natural resource distribution is that the benefits of massive water use by corporate (or White-dominated) agriculture and timber plantations, or of energy use in mining houses and smelters, disproportionately accrue to foreign-headquartered corporations.

In Pretoria, however, far less challenging notions of sustainable development are used in official South African discourse. Some of these are potentially progressive, for instance when the 1998 National Water Pricing Policy insists that water users be taxed for two reasons: firstly, because of scarcity – often a social construct but in the case of water in southern Africa, also a physical constraint; and, secondly, because many (wealthier) South Africans' consumption patterns are terribly inefficient. But as we will see, the crucial criteria for whether development practices become genuinely sustainable are *tests of power and need*.

Most South African civil society organisations have alleged that in the highest-profile examples since 1994 expediency prevailed, the interests of the wealthy and of large corporations were rewarded because of prevailing power relations, and the needs of the environment and society were denigrated. As an alternative to the co-option of sustainable development by capital and states (including the United Nations), most of the South African groups whose efforts we will consider below have attempted to infuse the definition of "sustainable" with values of "environmental justice".

This strategic discursive approach situates ecological problems and possibilities within a socio-political context, first and foremost, and poses firm moral and distributional questions about that context. Sometimes, invoking the notion of justice requires resort to cultural defences and symbolic critique, which brings its own dangers. But mainly, the use of the rights-based arguments by social, labour, women's and environmental movements in post-apartheid South Africa has been rational, progressive and capable of the nuance required to transcend "Not In My Back Yard" (the "Nimby" defence) with "Not in Anyone's Back Yard". Indeed, the environmental justice discourse is grounded in values so well-recognised that they were included in the South African Constitution's Bill of Rights in 1996: "everyone has the right to an environment that is not harmful to their health or well-being ... everyone has the right to have access to healthcare services, including reproductive healthcare; sufficient food and water; and social security" (Republic of South Africa, 1996: s 24(a), s 27(1)).[8]

Distinctions in these definitions are important, given how far some civil society groups can be drawn into subservient relations with capital. For Andrew Jamison (2001), one mode of ecological thinking and practice, "green business", has co-opted environmentalism into the nexus of capital accumulation, using concepts of sustainable development. The interaction of academic and industrial research has generated a politics devoted to flexible or soft regulation regimes. The philosophical basis includes faith in science and technology, a methodology founded upon instrumental rationality, and an ideological commitment to market democracy. This is the "economising" of ecology.

In contrast, what Jamison calls "critical ecology movements" have practiced resistance to green business, drawing upon concepts of environmental justice. Their repertoire includes critical research, demands for stronger legal enforcement, and active campaigns against corporate enemies of the environment. They remain sceptical of science and technology at a deeper philosophical level, they promote a communicative rationality, and they are committed to deliberative democracy. This "politicising" of ecology runs counter to green business in virtually all issues and processes.[9] While diverse, the green business perspective *is* coherent and, to the extent that there is any genuine effort to address environmental issues by global élites, the green business strategy is dominant in settings like the WSSD.

Critical ecology movements in civil society have suffered a fragmentation of what Jamison terms "cognitive praxis", resulting in four broad and often competing types of environmentalism, "knowledge forms" and "knowledge interests". Firstly, "civic" environmentalism includes local campaigns and social ecology; its knowledge is based on both factual and traditional forms, and its core objective is empowerment. Secondly, "professional" environmentalism flows from mainstream organisations and an ethos of green expertise, grounded in scientific and legal knowledge, aiming at enlightenment. Thirdly, a "militant" environmentalism is based upon radical splinters, especially direct action groups, whose knowledge is often rhetorical and symbolic, which ground and expand their knowledge through political protest. Fourthly, a "personal" environmentalism is growing, based upon new-age practitioners and green consumers, fostering spiritual and emotive knowledge, and seeking authenticity.

Below, in our conclusion, we consider Jamison's ideas for a synthesis in the critical ecology movements. To do so with confidence requires that we first review praxis-oriented campaigning against the dominant green business logic in South Africa, and that we test local environmentalisms for fragmentation and incoherence. This requires that we not shy away from the logical implications of red-green politics, even when these are disarmingly radical.

Theoretical and practical problems of postcolonial African politics

Ultimately, this is no mere academic exercise in discourse analysis. It follows a legacy of powerful African critiques of postcolonial state degradation and rising grievances expressed in civil society, as captured in the analyses of Ake, Amin, First, Mkandawire, Nabudere, Nyerere, Odinga, Onimode, Rodney and Shivji, to name a few. To illustrate, consider the theory of state bureaucracy and party politics developed in the works of Mahmood Mamdani and Frantz Fanon. Mamdani (1996:111) argues that much of Africa's state administration, especially in rural settings, amounts to "decentralised despotism". Virtually all attempts to reform colonial-era Native Authorities (and equivalent ethnic-based systems) failed, leaving a bifurcated duality of power: between a centrally located modern state (sometimes directly responsible for urban order in capital cities) and a "tribal authority which dispensed customary law to those living within the territory of the tribe". With this observation, Mamdani (1996:287) addresses global-national-local processes:

> In the absence of democratisation, development became a top-down agenda enforced on the peasantry. Without thorough-going democratisation, there could be no development of a home market. The latter failure opened wide what was a crevice at Independence. With every downturn in the international economy, the crevice turned into an opportunity for an externally defined structural adjustment that combined a narrowly defined programme of privatisation with a broadly defined programme of globalisation.

The top-down agenda enforced on ordinary people corresponded to the adverse material conditions associated with systemic underdevelopment. Agency has also been crucial, as Fanon (1963:181,182) reminds us:

> Very often simple souls, who moreover belong to the newly born bourgeoisie, never stop repeating that in an underdeveloped country the direction of affairs by a strong authority, in other words a dictatorship, is a necessity. With this in view the party is given the task of supervising the masses. The party plays understudy to the administration and the police, and

controls the masses, not in order to make sure that they really participate in the business of governing the nation, but in order to remind them constantly that the government expects from them obedience and discipline.

Political parties, hence, are doomed to internalise the contradictions that Africa faces in its relations with international finance and national private capital. Under such conditions, Fanon (1963:204) noted that "bourgeois leaders of underdeveloped countries imprison national consciousness in sterile formalism". Fanon (1963:152,153) posited that leaders would turn both inward in internecine battle, and outward for inspiration:

The national middle class discovers its historic mission: that of intermediary. Seen through its eyes, its mission has nothing to do with transforming the nation; it consists, prosaically, of being the transmission line between the nation and a capitalism, rampant though camouflaged, which today puts on the mask of neocolonialism. The national bourgeoisie will be quite content with the role of the Western bourgeoisie's business agent, and it will play its part without any complexes in a most dignified manner. But this same lucrative role, this cheap-Jack's function, this meanness of outlook and this absence of all ambition symbolise the incapability of the middle class to fulfill its historic role of bourgeoisie. Here, the dynamic, pioneer aspect, the characteristics of the inventor and of the discoverer of new worlds which are found in all national bourgeoisies are lamentably absent. In the colonial countries, the spirit of indulgence is dominant at the core of the bourgeoisie; and this is because the national bourgeoisie identifies itself with the Western bourgeoisie, from whom it has learnt its lessons.

The turn inward includes a sometimes vicious state backlash against its former constituents. The turn outward is more fickle, reflecting the need above all to hold power at home. As in the cases of Zambia and Zimbabwe, this can lead to a "zig-zag" approach to the politics of structural adjustment. Indeed, it is not impossible to posit a five-stage trajectory that follows directly from these experiences:

- a liberation movement that won repeated elections against a terribly weak opposition, but under circumstances of worsening abstentionism by, and depoliticisation of, the masses;
- concomitantly, that movement's undeniable failure to deliver a better life for most of the country's low-income people, while material inequality soared;
- rising popular alienation from, and cynicism about, nationalist politicians, as the gulf between rulers and the ruled widened inexorably, and as more numerous cases of corruption and malgovernance were brought to public attention;
- growing economic misery as neo-liberal policies were tried and failed; and
- the sudden rise of an opposition movement based in the trade unions, quickly backed by most of civil society, the liberal petit-bourgeoisie and the independent media – potentially leading to the election of a new, post-nationalist government.

All such bullets were fired in Zambia, culminating in the 1991 election of a new government led by the Movement for Multiparty Democracy (MMD) – but without changing external conditions (the country's debt burden and export dependence upon copper), the new-found political freedom did not translate into economic gains and indeed corruption, malgovernance and a stolen election were the inevitable results. In Zimbabwe, the election of a post-nationalist Movement for Democratic Change (MDC) was foiled by two unfree, unfair elections from 2000–02. In South Africa, all but the last bullet were also loaded. Even during the ANC's first term in office, strong critiques of the state were offered by way of advocacy. Subsequently, coherence began to emerge in the critiques of the WSSD and Nepad, notwithstanding important "splits". Finally, the way forward for social and political movements appeared to include the need to revisit ideological orientations, so as to better fuse environment and development demands. Each of these will be dealt with in turn.

Advocacy on WSSD issues, 1994–1999[10]

Prior to discussing detailed aspects of civil society's response to the WSSD and Nepad, we begin with a survey of critical policy advocacy during 1994–99 by unions, community-based organisations, women's and youth groups, NGOs, think-tanks, networks, progressive churches, political groups and independent leftists (see Bond, 2000:Chapters 3 and 4). The issue areas established in the first round of advocacy work – water, energy, health, agriculture, environment, economics, welfare, education, and foreign and military policy – are all relevant both to the WSSD/Nepad, in terms of content, and to the nature of state-society relations.

Such relations could have taken a co-operative form, had the advocacy movements and state bureaucrats heeded the view of ANC intellectual Joel Netshitenzhe, in an African National Congress (1998:12) paper entitled "The State, Property Relations and Social Transformation". There, he insisted, in view of "counter-action by those opposed to change":

> Mass involvement is therefore both a spear of rapid advance and a shield against resistance. Such involvement should be planned to serve the strategic purpose, proceeding from the premise that revolutionaries deployed in various areas of activity at least try to pull in the same direction. When "pressure from below" is exerted, it should aim at complementing the work of those who are exerting "pressure" against the old order "from above".

As we will see, pressure from below was actively guided against the ANC, in a manner consistent with the trajectory Mamdani and Fanon predicted. To make the ordering of these issue areas as simple and consistent as possible, consider the five "Wehab" topics: water, energy, health, agriculture and biodiversity. Biodiversity saw very little civil society advocacy during the late 1990s, while "agriculture" can be taken more broadly to include land, eviction and housing issues. A few other topics follow logically: environment, economics, welfare and education, and foreign and military policy.

Water

The national water ministry – the Department of Water Affairs – earned the wrath of the SA Municipal Workers Union (Samwu) for the privatised/corporatised rural water programme and the promotion of public-private partnerships in municipal water delivery. Some representative community organisations, social movements and NGOs – mainly affiliated to the National Land Committee and Rural Development Services Network – complained that the majority of the new taps installed after 1994 quickly broke, and that hence millions of South Africans remained without water, notwithstanding the Reconstruction and Development Programme's (RDP) commitment to provide all with at least emergency supplies. There were, in contrast, a few NGOs or state agencies (e.g. Mvula Trust and Independent Development Trust), which welcomed the water ministry's 100% cost-recovery mandate (in a 1994 white paper), and which engaged in water cut-offs without regard to constitutional issues. Moreover, environmentalists in the Group for Environmental Monitoring, the Environmental Monitoring Group, Earthlife and the Soweto and Alexandra civic associations complained that the ministry stubbornly championed the unneeded expansion of the Lesotho Highlands Water Project.

When it came to advocacy on municipal-scale water services, the national ministry of Constitutional Development was condemned by Samwu and community organisations (including the South African National Civic Organisation, Sanco), which remained unhappy about the local government fiscal squeeze. Many also protested against intensifying municipal water cut-offs that ultimately affected an estimated ten million people. Protests were fierce, especially in the townships of Gauteng (Soweto, Alexandra, Thembisa and KwaThema), Durban (Chatsworth and Mpumalanga), Cape Town (Khayelitsha and Tafelsig) and several smaller towns. A national network of anti-eviction and anti-privatisation organisations subsequently emerged from 2001. Criticism also continued against low infrastructure standards, such as mass pit latrines in urban areas, and against the central government's closure of two-thirds of South Africa's 843 local municipalities through amalgamation, hence putting local government geographically out of reach of many people too poor to travel long distances.

Energy

The Department of Minerals and Energy came under criticism from civil society forces, initially for malgovernance issues: a corrupt nexus that involved local and Liberian con artists, and a baseless, unsuccessful attack on the auditor general's bona fides regarding a departmental fund. But the National Union of Mineworkers (NUM) also complained vigorously about the ministry's liberalisation of nuclear energy, and, via a state bureaucrat, a scandalous deal that exempted mining houses from radiation regulation. The most angry civil society activists, mainly in local civic associations, complained about the high tariff rates for Eskom connections, which followed a 1998 white paper mandate for "cost-reflectiveness" from the ministry. Electricity tariffs were five to ten times as much as those paid, per kilowatt hour, by large smelters and mining houses and, when payment became impossible, Eskom and municipalities cut off supplies to ten million people. In response, civic groups in some townships helped to destroy prepaid meters and to reconnect electricity illegally.

Critics of energy policy in the community groups, social movements and trade unions, especially the National Union of Metalworkers of South Africa (Numsa) and NUM, attributed many of the problems to privatisation. Tens of thousands of jobs were eliminated by Eskom. The Department of Public Enterprises was criticised for its shallow, foreign-influenced approach to privatising parastatals.

Health

The Department of Health was extremely active in transforming several sectors. However, the ministry was attacked by progressive health workers for lethargy on HIV/Aids, such as the refusal to provide cheap anti-retroviral medicines to pregnant women, and for deep pedagogical confusion, as witnessed in the Sarafina 2 episode. Other critiques included the ministry's deep cuts into hospital budgets, including closures, prior to the construction of promised primary healthcare clinics. Community health worker advocacy groups criticised the de-emphasis on innovative primary healthcare strategies.

Interestingly, where the Department of Health and civil society organisations were potentially allied, the government disappointed many groups – the anti-tobacco lobby, the health-worker unions and health-sector NGOs – for failing to mobilise allies in civil society before going into battle against tobacco companies, international pharmaceutical corporations (and with them the US government), urban doctors, medical aid firms and insurance companies.

Agriculture/land/housing

The Department of Land Affairs and the Department of Agriculture were condemned by emergent farmers' associations and rural social movements for failing to redirect agricultural subsidies; for allowing privatisation of marketing boards; for redistributing a tiny amount of land (in part, because of the adoption of a World Bank-designed policy); for failing to give sufficient backup support to large communal farming projects; and for not fighting for constitutional property rights more vigorously.

The Department of Housing was criticised by the civics movement for lack of consultation; for insufficient housing subsidies; for "toilets-in-the-veld" developments far from urban opportunities; for a near-complete lack of provision of rural housing; for gender design insensitivity; for violating numerous detailed RDP housing provisions; and for relying upon bank-driven processes – via behind-closed-doors agreements that the banks immediately violated with impunity – which were extremely hostile to community organisations.

Environment

Overall, the Department of Environmental Affairs was seen by its civil society critics – the Environmental Justice Networking Forum, GroundWork and others – to be ineffectual at enforcing environmental regulations, particularly when it came to mining houses. The department, while paying lip-service to "consultations" with environmentalists, was considered an inactive, untransformed bureaucracy that failed to conduct rudimentary monitoring and inspection and, instead, passed the buck to ill-equipped provinces.

Economics

The finance ministry was condemned by left critics not only for sticking so firmly to the Growth, Employment and Redistribution (GEAR) strategy when all targets (except inflation) were missed, but also for sometimes draconian fiscal conservatism; for leaving VAT intact on basic goods, while providing corporate tax cuts (from 48% in 1994 to 30% in 1999); for real cuts in social spending, while repaying apartheid-era debt; for restructuring the state pension funds to benefit old-guard civil servants; for letting the country's largest corporations shift financial headquarters to London; for liberalising foreign exchange and turning a blind eye to capital flight; for granting permission to "demutualise" two big insurance companies; for failing to more aggressively regulate financial institutions (especially in terms of racial and gender bias); for not putting discernable pressure on the Reserve Bank to bring down interest rates; and for putting forth legislation that would have transferred massive pension fund surpluses from joint-worker/employer control directly to employers.

Likewise, the Department of Trade and Industry was criticised by civil society activists for the post-1994 deep cuts in protective tariffs, leading to massive job losses; for weakness in presiding over the UN Conference on Trade and Development, such that the neoliberal agenda prevailed on issues like the Multilateral Agreement on Investments and structural adjustment; for giving out billions of rands in "supply-side" subsidies (redirected RDP funds) for Spatial Development Initiatives (SDIs), considered to be "corporate welfare"; for cutting decentralisation grants, which led to the devastation of ex-bantustan production sites; for inserting huge loopholes in what was once a tough liquor policy; for failing to promote small businesses; for lifting the Usury Act exemption (i.e. deregulating the 32% interest rate ceiling on loans); and for failing to impose a meaningful anti-monopoly and corporate regulatory regime.

Notwithstanding some major improvements in worker security through labour legislation, the Department of Labour was attacked by trade union experts for a Labour Relations Act that disempowered unions by overemphasising what were seen as co-optive workplace forums.

The Department of Public Works was criticised, especially by trade unions – both Cosatu and the Construction and Allied Workers Union – for its dramatic reduction in national staff capacity (retrenching civil servants and outsourcing many functions); for tending to favour old-guard consulting firms and to leave communities out of local "community-based" projects (which, in any case, received a surprisingly low priority and meagre funding); for the high level of provincial public works incompetence and corruption; and for extremely low pay for contract workers on rural public works projects.

Welfare and education

The Department of Welfare and Social Development was bitterly criticised by the church, NGOs and the welfare advocacy movement for attempting to cut the child maintenance grant by 40%, and for failing to empower local community organisations and social workers.

The Department of Education was censured by teachers' unions, the student movement and education experts for often incompetent (and typically not sufficiently far-reaching) restructuring policies; for failure to redistribute resources fairly; and for a narrow, instrumentalist approach to higher education.

Foreign and military policy

Relations between civil society NGOs and the first ANC government's Departments of Defence and Foreign Affairs were also controversial. The defence ministry's R60 billion arms purchase sustained longstanding criticism from groups like Economists Allied for Arms Reduction and the Ceasefire Campaign, not least for the confusing "spin-offs" justification and for the failure to reverse South Africa's record of arms sales to repressive regimes in and beyond Africa. The foreign ministry was ridiculed by solidarity organisations for chaotic and generally conservative foreign policy, including flip-flops on Nigerian generals (first hostile, then friendly) and Laurent Kabila's Democratic Republic of the Congo (once friendly, then hostile); for cozying up to Indonesian dictator Suharto (Cape of Good Hope medalist a few months before popular revulsion sent him packing); for the 1998 Lesotho invasion fiasco; for often playing a role as US lackey; for prioritising arms sales over human rights; and for the failure of South

African leadership to put forward or sustain more transformative positions in the Non-Aligned Movement (NAM), the Southern African Development Community (SADC), the Organisation of African Unity (OAU) and the Commonwealth.

Civil society's responses

Much of what occurred during this period was slow, careful development of issues, in the spirit of creating (not seizing) power bases in civil society. However, most memorably, civil society mobilisations included the national "stay-away" strikes of millions of workers, which were called annually against neo-liberal policies, beginning in 1995. Sometimes Cosatu rallies in major urban centres included mass marches that stretched for kilometres.

Allied with Cosatu, the Treatment Action Campaign (TAC) did exceptionally powerful advocacy work to gain access to Aids medicines beginning in 1999, resulting in formidable pressure against government policies that had begun to be labelled "genocidal" by responsible health practitioners such as the heads of the Medical Research Council and the SA Medical Association. Other notable allies included the other trade union federations and especially the National Education, Health and Allied Workers Union (Nehawu), Sangoco, the South African Communist Party (SACP), the SA Council of Churches (SACC), the Aids Law Project, the Aids Consortium and various orphanages and hospices.

Effective alliances have emerged around other issues, and although they have a lower profile than economic justice and Aids medicines, several key areas of activism deserve mention:

- The Jubilee movement put the apartheid debt on the agenda, and progressive church groups helped form advocacy coalitions for reparations from apartheid profiteering. A 2002 lawsuit against US and European companies and banks was only one of the many activities underway to raise consciousness about the historical legacy of injustice. The Archbishop of Cape Town, Njongonkulu Ndungane, did particularly high-profile advocacy.

- A Basic Income Grant coalition included churches, Cosatu and the Cape Town-based South African New Economics Foundation.

- Prohibitions on Genetically Modified (GM) food have been sought by local and international groups, including BioWatch, Earthlife Africa, the Environmental Justice Networking Forum, Friends of the Earth/groundWork, Greenpeace, Safe Age and Sangoco.

- Supported by the National Land Committee and rural-oriented NGOs, the Landless People's Movement marched and occupied land periodically.

- The Environmental Justice Networking Forum included strong community-based campaigns, as well as national issue development ranging from leaded petrol to global warming. Important players here included the Sustainable Energy and Climate Change Partnership, South African Climate Action Network, the Minerals and Energy Policy Centre, the Greenhouse Project, the Group for Environmental Monitoring and the Environmental Monitoring Group.
- Students regularly fought expulsions from universities on grounds of affordability, and in 2002 joined eight organisations – including NGOs and education-sector trade unions – which mobilised to demand free education for all, including expanded Adult Basic Education.
- Women's rights were pushed strongly by leading individuals, although without a sense of a broader feminist movement emerging. However, the journal *Agenda* continued to provide extremely valuable analytical material about the racial and economic justice intersections with women's empowerment.

Overall, tough "progressive movement" politics prevailed in gatherings of labour, communities, HIV-positive people and a few other sectors. In the background, however, was the threat of co-option by government, especially as mediated by NGOs.

Conflict-ridden civil society advocacy in the run-up to the WSSD

The division of civil society along especially class (but also gender and ethnic) grounds had become an international dilemma by the early 2000s. It was particularly evident in Latin America and Asia, according to James Petras and Henry Veltmayer (2001:231,232), because of the mediating role of NGOs:

> When millions lose their jobs and poverty spreads to significant portions of the population, NGOs engage in preventative action focusing on survival strategies, not general strikes, and they organise soup kitchens not mass demonstrations against food hoarders, neoliberal regimes or US imperialism. NGOs demobilised the populace and fragmented the movements. In the 1980s and 1990s, from Chile, Philippines to South Korea, and beyond, NGOs have played an important role in rounding up votes for regimes which continued or even deepened the socio-economic status quo. In exchange, many NGOers ended up running government agencies or even becoming government ministers in portfolios with popular sounding titles (women's rights, citizen participation, popular power, etc.).

Civil society splits

Do these criticisms apply in South Africa? Some do, but there are, in addition, people's NGOs and more accountable service organisations and training/research agencies that work with and through the militant grassroots and labour movements. For example, three high-profile left-wing think-tanks and popular education centres are Khanya College, the International Labour Resource and Information Group and the Alternative Information and Development Centre, but there are many others that qualify as being organically connected to social movements. However, those movements do not have a united voice, and the din of political contestation of the WSSD civil society organising process reached unprecedented levels during 2001–2002.

In the complicated positioning, the more radical groups formed a Social Movements Indaba, which was formerly known as the Civil Society Indaba until July 2002. In contrast, what became known as the Global Civil Society Forum was dominated by mass-based organisations closer to the mainstream, and serviced by a UN secretariat comprising talented technocrats.

In managing the politics associated with the split, lessons were learned from the Durban World Conference Against Racism (WCAS) in August 2001. At that point, frustration had built up in the trade union movement to the point that Cosatu's national leadership called a two-day national strike against ANC privatisation policies. More than four million workers heeded the call. The timing was important, for the strike humiliated the ANC on the eve of the WCAS, attended by more than 10 000 delegates who wanted to believe that South Africa was genuinely liberated.

Still, demonstrating how fickle the politics of alliances remained, Cosatu agreed to hold a joint mass march against racism in Durban alongside the ANC and the SACP, the day after a much more militant demonstration by anti-neoliberal movements that marched under the banner of the Durban Social Forum. The Social Forum pulled together an estimated 20 000 protesters on behalf of Palestinian freedom, land rights, debt cancellation, community housing and services, and the need for an alternative to neo-liberalism. The mood was extremely hostile to the ANC, and neither President Mbeki nor UN Secretary-General Kofi Annan deigned to personally accept the memoranda presented at the Durban convention centre.

As tensions simmered and then cooled within the ANC-SACP-Cosatu alliance in the subsequent weeks, leaders of Cosatu joined Sangoco, the SACC and Sanco to take over the Civil Society Secretariat in early 2002. The Civil Society Indaba was booted out unceremoniously, according to Cosatu and its allies (2002), on the dual grounds that:

> The structures of the Indaba give disproportionate power to small and unrepresentative NGOs. This occurs by giving NGOs three-fold representation: through the so-called provincial representatives, the NGO constituency, and the votes given NGOs under the heading of "rural and urban communities". In contrast, key groups of civil society – notably the disabled and civics – have no seats at all.

> The financial management of the Secretariat to the Indaba remains open to question. Remuneration is extraordinarily high for non-profit civil society – initially topping out at over R40 000 a month, including car allowance, although this figure was reduced somewhat this January, following our protests. In addition, we have some evidence of alleged misappropriation of funds, which we can provide on request. The audit commissioned by the Civil Society Secretariat has proven to be superficial and inadequate.[11]

The "First Nations" of indigenous South Africans were repelled by the Cosatu-led purge, and resisted subsequent attempts to draw them back. Another angle also emerged, as reported in the *Mail & Guardian*:

> The New Partnership for Africa's Development appears to be key to the divisions in this sector … The Civil Society Indaba has a leftist, anti-globalisation focus. It has claimed there is big brother interference from the government in the new, mainstream South African Civil Society Forum set up by Cosatu and its allies.[12]

Potential civil society unity on Nepad?

Nepad would continue to cause controversy, not least because in October 2002, Mbeki dismissed the idea of a political peer review process to promote good governance. But well before then, both South African and African progressive social movements would unify on the following points:

- Progressive civil society organisations have traditionally demanded that all policies, programmes and projects of government be conducted in a transparent, participatory and respectful manner. Nepad's formulation failed on all accounts.

- Progressive civil society organisations have also traditionally provided rights-based advocacy that takes basic needs as human rights. At a philosophical foundational level, Nepad fails here and, instead, promotes market-related strategies and privatised infrastructure even with respect to basic infrastructural services.

- Moreover, progressive civil society organisations have opposed the international neo-liberal agenda of free markets, trans-national corporate dominance of the South, lower government budgetary spending (under the rubric of alleged macroeconomic stability) and the lowering of standards for the sake of foreign investors. In terms of content, Nepad fails on these points.

- Finally, progressive civil society organisations have most forcefully promoted good governance and democracy. While Nepad gives lip-service to these ideals, it fails to take them sufficiently seriously to publicly criticise and punish obvious violations (e.g. of recent elections in Congo-Brazzaville, Madagascar, Zambia and Zimbabwe). As one of Nepad's own co-authors, Senegalese President Wade put it, the leaders of Africa, including Nepad co-authors in South Africa and Nigeria, appear to have a "trade union" approach that gives mutual support and solidarity to dictators and tyrants.

While the first six months of 2002 led virtually all African civil society groups to reject Nepad, later it became apparent that once Mbeki began to intervene, it was possible to criticise Nepad's form, content and process, yet still agree to "engage" the Nepad leadership. To illustrate, in April 2002, the Central Executive Committee of Cosatu added its view on the problems intrinsic to Nepad:

> The CEC believe that the transformation of Africa can only happen if it is driven by its people. There was a strong feeling that the Nepad plan has been developed only through discussions between governments and business organisations, leaving the people far behind ... The CEC raised concerns about the economic proposals in the Nepad. In particular, we need to ensure that macroeconomic governance does not stray too far towards stabilisation, at the cost of growth and employment creation. Moreover, the emphasis on privatisation in the section on infrastructure ignores the reality: that privatised services will not serve the poor on our continent.[13]

Thus, by no means did the Cosatu-led takeover of the UN side of the WSSD require a formal ideological retreat. Even the ANC (2002:1), as a political party, spoke in the same anti-neoliberal language when drawing out support for a protest march "against world poverty" on 31 August 2002:

> The Johannesburg Summit convenes against the backdrop of a city visibly scarred by the profound contradictions of its history. Wealth and poverty lie cheek by jowl, a stone's throw from the central venue of the intergovernmental conference. And Jo'burg's landscape is strewn with the waste of one hundred years of resource extraction; in the service of which South Africa's racial hierarchy was constructed with violent determination. The city's contemporary social and environmental panorama is an ever-present reminder of our country's painful past. This divided geography also reflects the state of the world as we enter the twenty-first century: a globalised world built on the foundation of imperial conquest and colonial domination, which continues to define the contours of privilege and underdevelopment.

The battle to "take" Sandton

Ridiculing the ANC alliance discourse as "talk left, act right", the international landless people and the Social Movements Indaba attempted, as at Durban the previous year, to draw larger and more militant crowds to their march, with a strongly anti-Mbeki message. The National Land Committee and Landless People's Movement (LPM, 2002) made clear their desire to distance themselves in a July press statement:

> The March of the Landless on 31 August 2002 will not include organisations which are part of the Tripartite Alliance whose record of governance has ensured the failure of land reform in South Africa. The March of the Landless will be led by the LPM on the same day in alliance

with other civil society organisations. The march will be the culmination of an alternative Week of the Landless that will take place decisively outside of the formal UN processes of the WSSD.

The purpose of the March of the Landless will not be to support the World Summit on Sustainable Development, or to make vague calls for "sustainable development" through unsustainable policies like Nepad or GEAR. Instead, the purpose of the March of the Landless will be to denounce the unsustainable policies being fortified by the world's elite in the Sandton Convention Centre; to focus world attention on the failure of South Africa's World Bank-style land reform programme; and to forward the demands of the 19-million poor and landless rural South Africans and 7-million poor and landless urban South Africans. That demand is: "End Poverty: Land! Food! Jobs!"

The march of the landless and other protesters in the Social Movements United alliance – including the Anti-Privatisation Forum, Jubilee, the Environmental Justice Networking Forum, via Campesino and others – was indeed principled and radical. For 90 years, the combined geographical and political implications of locating an urban Bantustan, called Alexandra Township, on a small block of land in northeast Johannesburg were unexplored. On 31 August 2002, South Africa's most militantly anti-government march since 1994 drew at least 20 000 activists (according to even the BBC) in and out of Alexandra. They marched ten kilometres on a sunny, hot spring day to the site of the WSSD, condemning global élites and the regime in Pretoria for unending neo-liberalism. Class/community struggle had finally breached the highway separating the country's richest suburb, Sandton, from one of the poorest.

As the marchers assembled, they looked west. Looming on the horizon across a valley was the glistening Sandton skyline, mainly constructed during the 1990s flight of white capital from the Central Business District (CBD). The Convention Centre where 6 000 WSSD delegates were working sat next to Citibank's Africa headquarters, in the shadow of the Michaelangelo Hotel and the opulent Sandton City skyscraper and shopping mall. Sandton's financial firms, hotels and exclusive retail outlets draw in Alexandra's workers for long, low-paid shifts in the security, cleaning and clerical trades. Once they clock out, Alexandrans are quickly repelled from consumption due to high prices, blatant class hostility and intensive surveillance. They return to shacks, broken sewage systems and, for many tens of thousands, a single yard water tap sometimes serving 40 families in overcrowded filth. Materially, nothing much here had changed since democracy arrived 1994, aside from new but tiny houses on the township's eastern hill, and a vicious slum-clearance and displacement programme along the filthy stream coursing through the slum.

Just as important as the symbolic route of the march were the battles of numbers and of passion: the independent left surprised itself by conclusively trumping the mass-based organisations. The Global Civil Society Forum supported by trade unions, churches and the ANC itself attracted fewer than 5 000 to the Alexandra soccer stadium to hear Mbeki two hours later. At stake in this contest were both prestige in South African politics and the ability of Pretoria politicians to disguise deep dissent from world leaders. Mbeki's attempts to manage South Africa's – and the world's – socio-economic contradictions were for naught that day. The SA NGO Coalition of 3 000 member organisations had pulled out the day before, claiming the ANC was manipulating the gathering. Just 1 000 Civil Society Forum marchers left the stadium for the long trek to Sandton, and many of these had been locked in earlier when they tried to exit, as the larger march passed nearby. It was a crucial battle for the ANC's (and the government's) legitimacy, so that Mbeki's own "ANC Today" letter the day before carried this challenge:

> So great is the divide that even as many are battling in the WSSD negotiations for a meaningful outcome that will benefit the billions of poor people in our country, Africa and the rest of the world, there are others, who claim to represent the same masses, who say they have taken it upon themselves to act in a manner that will ensure the collapse of the Summit. These do not want any discussion and negotiations. For this reason, they have decided to oppose and defeat the UN, all the governments of the world, the inter-governmental organisations, the major organisations of civil society participating in the Summit and the world of business, all of which are engaged in processes not different from those that take place regularly in our statutory four-chamber Nedlac, which includes government, business, labour and non-governmental organisations. Those who hold these views, which they regularly express freely in our country, without any hindrance, also have their own economic views. As with all other ideas and views about the central question of the future of human society, we have to consider and respond to them rationally, whatever is happening in the streets of Johannesburg, for the benefit of the global mass media.[14]

However, with more than 20 times as many people on the United Social Movement's march, and with a mostly empty stadium as his audience, it was impossible to co-opt the social movements through class-compromise gambits such as Nedlac. British author George Monbiot had, a few weeks earlier, described the global movements associated with Social Movements United as beneficiaries of a reality check caused by the terrorist attacks:

> Look, it's like the Peasants' Revolt. The peasants revolt, they meet the king, the king promises them the earth and they all go home. Whereupon their leaders are hanged and nothing happens. If we follow that model, we're doomed, so you could say that 11 September, by putting a roadblock in the way of that model, did us a favour.[15]

The favour was evident in Johannesburg, because the greatest risk was of co-option into the UN process before the movement had come together strategically. In the event, there was an insufficient power-bloc of international NGOs to endorse the weak compromises on offer from post-Washington Consensus managers like Kofi Annan (e.g. working fruitlessly on agricultural subsidy and tariff barrier reductions, or forming "Type 2" public-private partnerships with multinational corporations). While some opportunistic NGOs did pursue reformism along these lines, the Social Movements United protest focused on non-reformist matters, namely the elements of a radical socio-economic programme that is feasible within the confines of global capitalist finance, technology and administration, but which will not be granted because it upsets capitalist/patriarchal/racial power relationships.

By October 2002, the ANC's Political Education Unit made clear how deeply the militancy of August 31 had impressed the ruling party:

> The charge of neo-liberalism constitutes the most consistent platform presented by the "left" opposition in its fight against the ANC and our government ... In our country, it is represented by important factions in the SA Communist Party and Cosatu, as well as the Anti-Privatisation Forum, the local chapter of Jubilee 2000, and other groups and individuals. All of these maintain links with their like-minded counterparts internationally and work to mobilise these to act in solidarity with them in support of the anti-neoliberal campaign in our country ... These specific anti-neoliberal formations define our efforts to contribute to the victory of the African Renaissance as an expression of sub-imperialism. They assert that the ANC and our government are acting as the representative and instrument of the South African bourgeoisie, which they say seeks to dominate the African continent. They go further to say that the soul of the ANC has been captured by a pro-capitalist, and therefore neoliberal faction ... The anti-neoliberal coalition hopes that it will trample over the fallen colossus, the ANC, and march on to a victorious socialist revolution, however defined. Better still, it hopes that by engaging in all manner of manoeuvre, including conspiring about who its leaders should be, it can capture control of the ANC and use it for its purposes. To achieve these objectives, the anti-neoliberal coalition is ready to treat the forces of neoliberalism as its ally. Therefore it joins forces with them, together to open fire on the ANC and our government.[16]

The preposterous claim that the independent left was working with the neo-liberal right needed no serious consideration. However, of importance was the perception that international solidarity had become a meaningful political variable. That, in turn, would strengthen the independent social movements, as they prepared for a future, inevitable split of great magnitude, not within civil society, but between the ANC and its alliance partners. In short, the logic of fighting back against neo-liberalism, patriarchy, racism, ecological degradation and many other ills could unite progressive South Africans *one day* – even though the manoeuvres associated with long-held ANC-alliance loyalties, and the bitter left-wing anger at multiple betrayals, meant that the WSSD was hotly contested.

Rights discourses and practical politics

This chapter has demonstrated that many extreme forms of human indignity and environmental degradation had become mundane, and that confusion in South African civil society had resulted, nearly becoming debilitating at the time of the WSSD in 2002. As a more hopeful way forward, an alternative current in civil society – the demand for decommodification – warrants exploration.

Decommodification, life and liberation

The demand for "lifeline" supplies of water and electricity is being made from the urban ghettos like Soweto to the many rural areas that have still not received piped water. The need for free access to anti-retroviral medicines, for five million HIV-positive South Africans, is also acute. A campaign for a Basic Income Grant has also been taken up by churches and trade unions. The Landless People's Movement objects to the failure of a commodified land reform policy designed by the World Bank, and insists upon access to land as a human right. Such demands, based upon the political principle of decommodification, are central to campaigns ranging from basic survival through access to health services, to resistance to municipal services' privatisation.

The verb "decommodify" has become popular amongst progressive strategists, in part through studies of social policy conducted by Gosta Esping-Andersen, a Swedish academic. In his book *The Three Worlds of Welfare Capitalism*, Esping-Andersen (1990) points out that during the first half of the twentieth century, the Scandinavian welfare state grew because of urban-rural, worker-farmer, "red-green" alliances that made universalist demands on the ruling élites.

Those demands typically aimed to give the working class and small farmers social protection from the vagaries of employment, especially during periodic recessions. They therefore allowed people to escape the prison of wage labour, by weaving a thick, state-supplied safety net as a fall-back position. To decommodify their constituents' labour in this manner required, in short, that the alliance defend a level of social protection adequate to meet basic needs. Over a period of decades, this took the form of generous pensions, healthcare, education and other free state services, like childcare and eldercare, which disproportionately support and liberate women.

The electoral weight and grassroots political power of the red-green alliance was sufficient to win these demands, which were paid for through taxing wealthy households and large corporations at high rates. These were defended until recently, as corporate power and the ideology of competitiveness have forced some cutbacks across Scandinavia. A similar, although much less far-reaching, construction of welfare-state policies occurred elsewhere across the world, in the context of a Cold War that required western capitalism to put on a more humane face against the East Bloc and to maintain state spending, in the spirit of John Maynard Keynes, so as to boost macroeconomic growth.

In the post-war US, in contrast, corporations lobbied more effectively against state entitlements such as healthcare and pensions, preferring to hold control over workers through company health and pension plans, which would then deter workers from going on strike. (The failure to decommodify labour power helps to explain the durability of the US trade union movement's pro-corporate – and often pro-imperialist – position, until it began shifting leftward in the mid-1990s.)

As the 1950s–1960s virtuous cycle of economic growth and expanding social policy came to an end, it was replaced not by a strengthened socialist struggle, as the limits of such reforms were reached, but rather by an era of neo-liberalism, which began during the late 1970s. Because the balance of forces has been inauspicious, for a variety of reasons, this recent period of class war by ruling élites continues to be characterised by austerity-oriented economic policies, shrinkage of social programmes, privatisation, trade and financial liberalisation, corporate deregulation and what is often termed "the commodification of everything".

In a setting as unequal as South Africa – with 45% unemployment and, alongside Brazil and Guatemala, the world's highest income disparities – the neo-liberal policies adopted during the 1990s pushed even essential state services such as water and electricity beyond most households' ability to pay. Some of these policies were adopted before political liberation from apartheid in 1994, but many were the result of influence on Nelson Mandela's ANC by the World Bank, US AID and other global and local neo-liberals during the late 1990s.

It is not difficult to draw out various problems associated with the neo-liberal approach to basic services. They often relate to the dismissive regard with which positive eco-social externalities associated with water/sanitation, energy and other services are understood by neo-liberals, for whom, Lawrence Summers (1991) informs us, "the economic logic of dumping a load of toxic waste in the lowest-wage country is impeccable". The failure to fully cost in the social and environmental benefits of state services is typical of commodification, because when state services undergo commercialisation, the state fragments itself as water, electricity, health and other agencies adopt "arms-length" (non-integrated) relationships that reduce them to mere "profit-centres".

A company that takes a privatisation or outsourcing contract has no qualms about cutting off the service to those who cannot afford to pay the full "cost-recovery" market price plus a profit mark-up. It has no responsibility for the social and personal costs incurred by health clinics and the patients themselves as a result of diseases. It feels no guilt when women and children suffer most. It does not repair environmental damage when women are forced to cut down trees to heat their families' food. It pays none of the local economic costs when electricity cut-offs prevent small businesses from operating, or when workers are less productive because they have lost access to even their water and sanitation.

This ability to avoid the social implications of public/merit goods allows huge multinational corporations to make enormous profits by expanding infrastructure systems just to the point where low-income people live. Usually this is a geographic decision, so that areas served by privatised services are noticeably "cherry-picked": wealthy consumers get the services but poor people are denied access. Most of the pilot water privatisation projects in South Africa have recreated the old apartheid boundaries of Black townships.

The first stage of resistance to the commodification of water and electricity often takes the form of a popular demand for a short-term, inexpensive flat rate applicable to all consumers. In Durban, community groups are, at the time of writing, mobilising for a R10 monthly fee for all municipal services, alongside an insistence that no one's supply be cut off.

More compellingly for medium-range policy, a redistributive demand for decommodification is advanced by groups like the SA Municipal Workers Union, Rural Development Services Network, Johannesburg Anti-Privatisation Forum and Soweto Electricity Crisis Committee (SECC): a specific minimum daily amount of water (50 litres) and electricity (one kilowatt hour) to be supplied to each person *free*. The free services should be financed not only by subsidies from central government, but also by a "rising block tariff" in which the water and electricity bills for high-volume consumers and corporations rise at a more rapid rate when their usage soars to hedonistic levels.

When charged at ever-higher rates, the consumption of services by hedonistic users should decline, which would be welcome. South Africa is a water-scarce country, especially in the Johannesburg area, which depends upon socio-ecologically destructive Lesotho dams. The WSSD host is also one of the world's worst sites of greenhouse gas emissions, when corrected for population and relative income. Hence, conservation through higher rates for large consumers makes eco-socio-economic sense on merely technical grounds.

Resistance to South African decommodification

These demands, grounded in decades of social struggles to make basic services a human right were originally given political credibility with the promise of lifeline services and rising block tariffs in the Reconstruction and Development Programme of 1994, the ANC's campaign platform in the first democratic election. They were partially incorporated in the 1996 Constitution, as discussed earlier.

The World Bank immediately became the most effective opponent of this philosophical principle and political strategy, arguing (incorrectly) that South Africa does not have sufficient resources to make good on the RDP or the Constitution. To reiterate a key point, the main criticism of a free lifeline and rising block tariff offered by World Bank water official John Roome was that water privatisation contracts "would be much harder to establish" if poor consumers had the expectation of getting something for nothing. If consumers did not pay, Roome continued, South Africa required a "credible threat of cutting service".[17] In short, a private supplier logically objects to serving low-income people with even a small lifeline consumption amount. Hence, the demand for such a rising block tariff is, as Roome pointed out, indeed a serious deterrent to privatisation.

Demands to reverse the government's full cost-recovery policy were made by labour and social movements during the late 1990s, and Minister Kader Asmal's mid-1999 replacement, Ronnie Kasrils, began hinting at a policy change in February 2000, after rural water projects broke down at a dramatic rate – mainly because impoverished residents could not keep the vital service maintained by themselves without a subsidy. When cholera broke out, with about 70 473 reported cases and 149 deaths between 15 August 2000 and early 2001, less than four months before nationwide municipal elections, the ANC government reacted by promising a free services lifeline. It was progress, although for poor households the promise was half the amount of water needed, and for electricity was undefined but in practice amounted to only a tenth of essential needs.

As might have been predicted, Roome and his colleagues saw Kasrils' and the ANC's free-services promise as potentially dangerous. In March 2000, the World Bank's *Sourcebook on Community Driven Development in the Africa Region* laid out the policy on pricing water:

> Work is still needed with political leaders in some national governments to move away from the concept of free water for all … Promote increased capital cost recovery from users. An upfront cash contribution based on their willingness-to-pay is required from users to demonstrate demand and develop community capacity to administer funds and tariffs. Ensure 100% recovery of operation and maintenance costs.

Social disasters from such rigid neo-liberal policy were strewn across Africa, especially when low-income people simply could not afford any state services, or cut back on girls' schooling or healthcare when cost recovery became too burdensome. In October 2000, the Bank was instructed by the US Congress never to impose these user-fee provisions on education and healthcare, and in 2002 a campaign by progressive NGOs in the US expanded to decommodify water as well.

In South Africa, since free water came into effect in July 2001 as official policy – notwithstanding widespread sabotage by municipal and national bureaucrats responsible for administering the policy – there have been no new water privatisations, in large part due to the fear that cherry-picking and supply cuts will be deemed unconstitutional. Moreover, some of the major pilot cases have resulted in disaster. For example, the French water private corporation, Saur had to renegotiate its Dolphin Coast contract in mid-2001 due to lack of profits, with research showing that it regularly denies services to poor people. For similar reasons, Saur also pulled out of its Maputo, Mozambique contract in late 2001. An even larger Paris water privatiser, Suez was thrown out of Fort Beaufort (also known as Nkonkobe) for failure to perform for low-income township people. The Johannesburg Water Company, also managed by Suez, is controversially introducing pit latrines, in spite of porous soil and the spread of the E.Coli bacteria, to prevent poor people flushing their toilets. If these are unacceptable, Johannesburg Water offers a low-flush "shallow sewage" system to residents of "condominium" (single-storey) houses arranged in rows, connected to each other by sanitation pipes much closer to the surface. Given the limited role of gravity in the gradient and the mere trickle of water that flows through, community residents are required to negotiate with each other over who will physically unblock sewers every three months. With this sort of attitude, public health problems, including mass out-breaks of diarrhoea and even cholera, will continue to embarrass officials in the WSSD host city.

Electricity privatisation also remains an acute source of conflict. The SECC continues to hold protests against politicians who insist that the privatisation of the state electricity utility, Eskom, requires cut-offs of power to those who cannot pay. At one point in 2001, when Eskom was cutting the supplies of 20 000 Soweto households each month, activists went door-to-door like Robin Hood, illegally reconnecting people for free. The SECC achieved folk-hero status as a result.

The other acute embarrassment for the South African government remains its fear of alienating international pharmaceutical companies. Hence, Mbeki maintains an Aids-denialist posture, claiming that anti-retroviral medicines are either too toxic or that they do not work. But the same spirit of decommodification has emerged from the TAC and its international allies like the Aids Coalition to Unleash Power (ACT UP), Medicins sans Frontieres and Oxfam. Like activists demanding free water and electricity, the campaign has also hit the barrier of trans-national (and local) corporate power.

The same conflicts were imported into the broader WSSD process, beginning at the Rio Earth Summit in 1992. Privatisation of basic services is moving ahead at great speed globally, under the rubric of public-private partnerships. Nepad, drafted by a team under Mbeki's direction, also calls for a massive dose of foreign investment in privatised infrastructure. If African leaders genuinely embrace the neo-liberal plan, which would simply extend the economic policies that have ravaged the continent for the past two decades, the most powerful water privatisers and Eskom would be the main beneficiaries. Mbeki won official endorsements of the plan at both the June 2002 summit of the G8 leaders in Alberta, Canada and the July launch of the African Union in Durban. Demonstrations by anti-capitalists from African and Canadian social movements embarrassed Mbeki at each event, leading him to brand their criticisms "easy, routine, uninformed and cynical".[18]

Merging red and green

The green and red critiques reviewed above come together in Johannesburg. What the South African experience these last few years shows is that full cost-recovery does not work and will be resisted, especially if combined with cut-offs of services. Those services create additional social welfare in the form of public/merit goods, but only if they are not privatised, because only the state – if it genuinely represents society – has an inbuilt incentive to use services like water and electricity to promote public health, gender equity, environmental protection and economic spin-offs.

Not only do privatisers ignore public goods, they are also inevitably opposed to free lifeline supplies and redistributive pricing. Hence, as so many South Africans have learned recently, the fight against privatisation is also a fight to decommodify the basic services we all need simply to stay alive. By succeeding in that fight, there is a chance that the state can be won over to its logical role: serving the democratically determined needs and aspirations of the huge majority for whom the power of capital has become a profound threat to social and environmental well-being.

The socialist strategy has always entailed making profound demands – in some discourses, "transitional" and in others, "non-reformist reforms" – upon the capitalist state. When invariably the *class power* of capital is challenged in the process, no matter how "feasible" the demands are in fiscal/administrative respects, the question of socialist revolution inexorably emerges. The demands for decommodification are popular, sane, logical and backed by solid democratic organisation.

Where does that leave those arguing for traditions of human rights, decommodification and socialism-from-below? Four sorts of task present themselves:

- link up the demands and campaigns for free services, medicines and universal-entitlement income grants;

- translate these from the spheres of consumption into production, beginning with creative re-nationalisation of privatised services, restructured municipal work, expansion of the nascent co-operative sector and the establishment of state-driven local generic drug manufacturing;

- strengthen the basis for longer-term alliances between poor and working people, which are in the first instance rooted in civil society and which probably within the next decade will also be taken up by a mass workers' party; and
- regionalise and internationalise these principles, strategies and tactics, just as Pretoria politicians and Johannesburg capital intensify their sub-imperialist ambitions across Africa, using concepts of deglobalisation and the formula of internationalism plus the nation-state.

One very hopeful sign is the rise of anti-privatisation forums in several South African cities (including Nelspruit) and in Harare, where mass-democratic groups are at the core, supported by explicitly socialist activists. Third World debt and campaigns to kick out the World Bank and the International Monetary Fund (IMF) are common starting points. The more that South African sub-imperialism emerges as a key problem, the more unity these movements will find in common opponents. The Southern African People's Solidarity Network is one of the main vehicles for ideological development, and the African Social Forum will also continue expanding through debt, trade, environment and other sectoral networks.[19]

The terrain is, therefore, being prepared for a deep-rooted challenge to capitalism. Aside from short-term splits over divided loyalties to exhausted political parties, which can be expected not only in South Africa but in many sites of African struggle, the prospects for unity between radical communities, labour, women, environmentalists and health activists have never been greater. The kinds of internationalist, anti-capitalist sentiments that rocked Europe during 2002 and scared so many "globo-élites" at their summits and conferences in prior years are becoming rooted in at least some southern African soil. Through growing direct links to similar grassroots campaigns in places as diverse as Accra, Cochabamba, Narmada Valley and Porto Alegre, the struggle to decommodify life has enormous potential to grow from autonomous sites of struggle like Soweto into a full-fledged socialist movement.

Uneven politics of scale

Notwithstanding the pessimistic tone adopted, this chapter has sought to transmit the great hope that has been sewn through the seeds of some recent social justice struggles occurring at various levels:[20]

- the living *body* of the HIV+ individual (e.g. one of millions of South African rape victims) facing a fatal disease, but through intense struggle against even President Mbeki, winning anti-retroviral medicines to hold Aids at bay;
- the *household*, where the woman celebrates a preliminary victory in the campaign for free lifeline water and electricity;

- the Soweto *neighbourhood* that successfully resists service cuts through anti-discon-nection activism;
- policy debates that typically occur at the *nation-state* level, which progressives can win not through technicist inputs but rather through mass mobilisation, direct action and humiliation of the neo-liberal state;
- *regional* African cross-border grassroots alliances, such as those prefigured by the critiques of Nepad; and
- *global-scale* protests against an international élite that, faced with eco-social crises such as water scarcity and global warming, attempts to revitalise capitalism by making profits out of resource trading.

However, it would be unfair to conclude without noting some of the philosophical and practical pitfalls of green-red consciousness. Some pitfalls are removed when we take the limits of the eco-social justice movement and consider their relevance to particular scales, instead of invoking full-fledged universalism. That strategy gets us beyond the constraints of localism and the utopianism of global-reformism.

The challenge is to establish dialectical-strategic work, so that the periodic conceptual barriers that keep the "critical ecology movements" of various types apart can in future be removed. Andrew Jamison's typology is of assistance here, and is adapted for use in Table 10.1.

Jamison concedes that green business can sometimes, perhaps often, co-opt environmentalism into the nexus of capital accumulation, using concepts of sustainable development. The critical ecology movements resist green business, drawing upon concepts of environmental justice. But the battle of environmentalists and green NGOs against TNCs, states and global agencies will not succeed without a dialectical advance to the next stage: hybrid red-green networks.

Table 10.1: Dialectics of environmentalisms and eco-socialism

Terrain	Critical ecologies	Green business	Eco-socialism
type of agency	environmentalists and green NGOs	TNCs, states and global agencies	hybrid red-green networks
forms of action	popularisation, resistance	commercial, brokerage	exemplary mobilisation
ideal of "science"	factual, lay	theoretical, expert	situated, contextual
knowledge sources	traditions	disciplines	experiences
competencies	personal	professional	synthetic

Source: adapted from Jamison (2001)

As for emblematic forms of action, the repertoire of popularisation and resistance tactics utilised by the eco-social justice activists comes into direct conflict with the commercial, brokerage functions of green business. The eco-socialist project, in contrast, has to advance to the stage of what Jamison terms "exemplary mobilisation", in which the ideas that "another world is possible" and "socialism is the future, build it today" become more than the slogans of Porto Alegre and the SACP, and take on real meaning.

Intellectual buttressing remains crucial, and hence the ideal articulation of "science" is also worth dwelling upon briefly. This chapter has considered discourses, including the factual and lay languages of activists, and the theoretical, expert inputs (no matter how flawed in reality) of promoters working from a green business standpoint. What we seek is to build upon the first by confronting the second, and achieving a situated, contextual science. The knowledge sources that undergird such efforts are typically divided into the political traditions of eco-social justice, the technical disciplines of green business, and the transcendental experiences of the eco-socialist project. As for the terrain of competencies, the critical ecologists invoke personal commitment; the green-business-suits claim professionalism; and eco-socialists strive for a synthetic understanding of the personal, professional and, above all, political.

With a similar grasp of the dialectical challenge, one of the leading contemporary historical materialists, David Harvey (1996:400,401) insists that eco-socialist programmes must be explicitly forward-looking, and hence must:

> deal in the material and institutional issues of how to organise production and distribution in general, how to confront the realities of global power politics and how to displace the hegemonic powers of capitalism not simply with dispersed, autonomous, localised, and essentially communitarian solutions (apologists for which can be found on both right and left ends of the political spectrum), but with a rather more complex politics that recognises how environmental and social justice must be sought by a rational ordering of activities at different scales.

Thus, it is vital to transcend both technical and political critiques of environment and development problems, and to think more broadly about how society should manage its inherited environment.

Conclusion

The world has witnessed, since the early 1970s, three broad discourses emerging around environmental management: neo-liberalism, sustainable development and eco-social justice. The area between these is sometimes grey, and partisans often move fitfully – often largely rhetorically – between the camps. But the material discussed above gives us a sense of how these discourses have played out in a country characterised by a dramatic political power shift in 1994, but also by residual economic domination by corporate interests and a surprising degree of ideological adherence to the Washington Consensus world-view.

What underlies the discourses, however, is not only material interest but also political power to transform a particular discourse into a hegemonic discourse. What this means, concretely, is that South Africa is replete with radical intentions, based on a highly-politicised history and the obvious legacies of apartheid-capitalism, on the one hand, but centrist bargaining forums and severely compromised legislative processes, on the other; and in their most concrete manifestations, in actual cases of environmental management, extremely conservative policies and practices reflecting, above all, the dominance of major economic actors.

This is all widely understood, and does not go unchallenged. One expression of the implications of uneven political power relations for moral discourses about environmental management was provided by Constitutional Court judge Albie Sachs (1990):

> People who have washing machines have no right to condemn others who dirty streams with their laundry. Those who summon up energy with the click of a switch should hesitate before denouncing persons who denude forests in search of firewood. It is undeniably distasteful to spend huge sums on saving the white rhino when millions of black children are starving.

Yet, the privileges and prejudices of élites and of companies that still wish society to carry the overall burden of externalised environmental costs remain in place. It is in this sense that the generation of socio-ecological inequality and the failure of South Africa to achieve even a modicum of "sustainable development" can be traced not just to existing power relations but, further, to the capitalist mode of production. The structural relationship between the capitalist mode of production and environmental crisis, and the need to articulate such a relationship in policy, legislation and concrete practice, is explained by Paul Burkett (1995:92):

> Mainstream environmentalism bypasses the connections between capitalism's social relations of production and the system's tendency to devour, dispose of, and degrade nature to the point of threatening the basic conditions of human-material reproduction. Sustainable development, we are told, can be achieved via state policies (so-called "green" tax/subsidy schemes and other technical fixes) and changes in individual behavior (recycling, marketing and consumption of more ecologically correct products, etc.) without changing the class relations between people and necessary conditions of their material reproduction. The assumption here is that eco-destruction is an inessential "externality" of capitalism, which does not fundamentally implicate the system's essential relations of class-exploitation and competition.

Notwithstanding South Africa's rights-based rhetoric and various attempts to tinker with environmental management problems through technical, market-oriented solutions, the imperatives of ecological exploitation and the impossibility of more fundamental reversals of environmental degradation are obvious. In contrast, an eco-socialist perspective starts with the very ingredient missing from virtually all post-apartheid government initiatives: popular mobilisation. In this sense, virtually all issues associated with the survival of society's oppressed communities are environmental management problems that can only be understood and tackled through an increasing convergence of green, brown, feminist, racial/ethnic justice, and class politics ("militant particularisms", as David Harvey describes them).

This kind of serious environmentalism, Harvey (1996:401) insists, must claim the broadest appropriate terrain as its mandate, and seek to rationally reorder the economy in a way that directly confronts capitalism's various neo-liberal discourses:

> The reinsertion of "rational ordering" indicates that such a movement will have no option, as it broadens out from its militant particularist base, but to reclaim for itself a noncoopted and nonperverted version of the theses of ecological modernisation. On the one hand that means subsuming the highly geographically differentiated desire for cultural autonomy and dispersion, for the proliferation of tradition and difference within a more global politics, but on the other hand making the quest for environmental and social justice central rather than peripheral concerns. For that to happen, the environmental justice movement has to radicalise the ecological modernisation discourse.

As neo-liberal economic orthodoxy continues to prevail in so many areas of South African and international environment and development, and as sustainable-development discourses, policies and legislation fall far short of resolving the growing crisis, it is to more radical confrontations with powerful forces that South Africa's eco-social justice movements will be inexorably drawn. To their credit, the South African civil society movements have continued to call forth local citizens and generous international solidarity with a simple appeal: "Another World is Possible!"

Endnotes

1 For their valuable inputs, the authors thank Omano Edigheji, the participants at a seminar on "Globalisation and the Challenges of Governance in Post-Apartheid South Africa", and an anonymous reviewer. The financial support of the Ford Foundation and logistical support from Wits P&DM is much appreciated.

2 In the macroeconomic sphere, neo-liberal policies include trade liberalisation, financial liberalisation, deregulation of business, flexibilised labour markets, privatisation (or corporatisation and commercialisation) of state-owned enterprises, export-oriented industrial policy, austere fiscal policy (especially aimed at cutting social spending) and monetarism in central banking (with high real interest rates). In microdevelopmental terms, neo-liberalism implies the elimination of subsidies, promotion of cost-recovery and user fees, disconnection of services to those who do not pay, means-testing for social programmes, and reliance upon market signals as the basis for local development strategies. To some extent, these kinds of policies characterise post-apartheid South Africa, although obviously social and labour struggles have prevented their full-fledged introduction and implementation.

3 Readings of Gramsci were diverse. See Gramsci (1971 edn), and early 1990s South African interpretations, including Bernstein & McCarthy (1994), Botha (1992), Carter (1991), Cross (1992), Friedman (1991, 1992), Jacobs (1992), Mayekiso (1996), Murray (1995), Nzimande & Sikhosana (1991, 1992), Seekings (1992), Shubane (1992), Shubane & Madiba (1992), South African National Civic Organisation (1994), Stadler (1992) and Swilling (1991, 1992). A renewed set of debates is likely to follow a durable dispute: whether civil society is most importantly a site of discipline so as to enforce co-operation with the state — as implicitly argued in various papers from thinktanks such as the Centre for Development and Enterprise, Centre for Policy Studies, Core and Case (see, e.g., the "Civil Society and Governance: South Africa" series at http://www.sussex.ac.uk/). In contrast, others point out its role as a terrain of quite ferocious class struggle, often aimed at reversing neo-liberal state policies: Alexander (2002), Bond (2002), Cock (2002), Desai (2002), Hart (2002), and McDonald & Pape (2002).

4 See also the helpful discussion of this issue by Omano Edigheji in Chapter 3 of this volume.

5 Daly, author of the seminal *Steady State Economics* (1991), worked with Robert Costanza to found the sub-discipline and journal *Ecological Economics*, and co-authored (with John Cobb) *For the Common Good* (1994). The quotes that follow are drawn from Daly (1996:220,9,88–93).

6 Trying to operationalise this philosophy, Daly grew frustrated and quit his backroom job at the World Bank in 1995, because: "Although the World Bank was on record as officially favouring sustainable development, the near vacuity of the phrase made this a meaningless affirmation … The party line [from Larry Summers] was that sustainable development was like pornography — we'll know it when we see it, but it's too difficult to define."

7 Daly proposed at least four operative policy recommendations for both the World Bank and governments:
   - stop counting natural capital as income;
   - tax labour and income less, and tax resource throughput more;
   - maximise the productivity of natural capital in the short run, and invest in increasing its supply in the long run; and
   - move away from the ideology of global economic integration by free trade, free capital mobility, and export-led growth — and toward a more nationalist orientation that seeks to develop domestic production for internal markets as the first option, having recourse to international trade only when clearly much more efficient.

   The last recommendation is a radical break from the sustainability discourses of ecological modernisation, and would present the South African government with the challenge of rethinking global economic integration. But all four are sufficiently radical that they have been rejected, in practice, not only by the World Bank but also by the South African government. If, for example, Pretoria's GDP figures were adjusted to exclude the non-renewable resources that mining houses strip from the ground, South Africa would have a long-standing net negative GDP. In turn, that might compel the ruling élites and bureaucrats to begin scrambling for a means of accumulating capital that is not so explicitly unsustainable.

8 Tellingly, however, the Constitution also provided a caveat in mandating "reasonable legislative and other measures that prevent pollution and ecological degradation, promote conservation, and secure ecologically sustainable development and use of natural resources while promoting justifiable economic and social development", consistent with sustainable-development rhetoric (s 24(b)). Moreover, "No one may be deprived of property except in terms of law of general application, and no law may permit arbitrary deprivation of property" (s 25(1)).

9 To dig deeper, using Jamison's typology, green business relies upon arguments such as eco-efficiency, natural capitalism and ecological modernisation. The premier green business networks are the Business Council on

Sustainable Development, Greening of Industry, Cleaner Production Roundtable, and Natural Step. New technology practices in this spirit include cleaner production, green products and environmental management systems.

10 The socio-economic situation is discussed in Chapter 2 of this book, and therefore does not warrant repetition in this chapter.

11 It should be noted that the director of the Indaba, Jacqui Brown, was cleared of charges and in a July 2002 labour arbitration hearing, won the right to reclaim her job.

12 *Mail & Guardian*, 24 May 2002. For more on the Social Movement Indaba critique of Cosatu's action, see http://southafrica.indymedia.org

13 This and a larger set of critiques can be found at http://www.aidc.org.za, and in Bond (ed., 2002).

14 *ANC Today*, http://www.anc.org.za, 30 August 2002.

15 *The Observer*, 14 July 2002.

16 *Mail and Guardian*, 18 October 2002.

17 Cited and analysed in Bond (2002:Chapters 3–5).

18 *Business Report*, 4 July 2002.

19 http://www.aidc.org.za

20 The examples here are drawn from the core chapters of Bond (2002).

References

Alexander, N. (2002) *An Ordinary Country*. Pietermaritzburg: University of Natal Press.

African National Congress (1998) "The State, Property Relations and Social Transformation." ANC discussion document (mimeo). Johannesburg, October.

African National Congress (2002) "Statement to the Global Civil Society Forum on the World Summit on Sustainable Development." Johannesburg, July.

Bernstein, A. & McCarthy, J. (1994) "'High Time for Some Soul Searching by Civic Organisations", *Business Day*, 4 November.

Bond P. (2000) *Elite Transition: From Apartheid to Neoliberalism in South Africa*. London/Pietermaritzburg: Pluto/University of Natal Press.

Bond, P. (2002) *Unsustainable South Africa*. London/ Pietermaritzburg: Merlin Press/University of Natal Press.

Bond, P. (ed.) (2002) *Fanon's Warning: A Civil Society Reader on the New Partnership for Africa's Development*. Cape Town/ Trenton: AIDC/Africa World Press.

Botha, T. (1992) "Civic Associations as Autonomous Organs of Grassroots' Participation", *Theoria* #79, May.

Burkett, P. (1995) "Capitalization Versus Socialization of Nature", *Capitalism, Nature, Socialism*, 6, 4.

Carter, C. (1991) "Comrades and Community: Politics and the Construction of Hegemony in Alexandra Township, South Africa, 1984–1987." DPhil thesis, University of Oxford.

Cock, J. (2002) "Local Social Movements and Global Civil Society: Some Cases from the Back Alleys of South Africa." Paper presented to the Sociology of Work Programme, University of the Witwatersrand, Department of Sociology, Johannesburg, 27 September.

Congress of SA Trade Unions, SA Council of Churches, South African Youth Council, Disability Sector and Sanco (2002) "Statement on Civil Society Participation in the WSSD." Johannesburg, 17 January.

Cross, S. (1992) "From Anomie to Civil Society in South Africa: Reflections on Development Planning." African Studies Seminar paper, St. Antony's College, Oxford.

Daly, H. (1991) *Steady State Economics.* Washington: Island Press.

Daly, H. (1996) *Beyond Growth: The Economics of Sustainable Development.* Boston: Beacon Press.

Daly, H. & Cobb, J. (1994) *For the Common Good.* Boston: Beacon Press.

Desai, A. (2002) *We are the Poors.* New York: Monthly Review Press.

Esping-Andersen, G. (1990) *The Three Worlds of Welfare Capitalism.* Princeton: Princeton University Press.

Fanon, F. (1963)[1961] *The Wretched of the Earth.* New York: Grove Press.

Friedman, S. (1991) "An Unlikely Utopia: State and Civil Society in South Africa", *Politikon,* December.

Friedman, S. (1992) "Bonaparte at the Barricades: The Colonisation of Civil Society", *Theoria* #79, May.

Gramsci, A. (1971 edn) *Selections from the Prison Notebooks.* London: Lawrence and Wishart.

Hart, G. (2002) *Disabling Globalisation.* Berkeley: University of California Press.

Harvey, D. (1996) *Justice, Nature and the Geography of Difference.* Oxford: Basil Blackwell.

Jacobs, B. (1992) "Heading for Disaster?", *Work in Progress* #86, December.

Jamison, A. (2001) *The Making of Green Knowledge: Environmental Politics and Environmental Transformation.* Cambridge: Cambridge University Press.

Mamdani, M. (1996) *Citizen and Subject: Contemporary Africa and the Legacy of Late Colonialism.* Princeton: Princeton University Press.

Mayekiso, M. (1996) *Township Politics: Civic Struggles for a New South Africa.* New York: Monthly Review Press.

McDonald, D. & Pape, J. (2002) *Cost Recovery and the Crisis of Service Delivery in South Africa.* London/ Pretoria: Zed Press/HSRC Publications.

Murray, M. (1995) *The Revolution Deferred.* London: Verso.

National Land Committee and Landless People's Movement (2002) "Joint Press Statement: SA Landless will not March with Cosatu", 23 July.

Nzimande, B. & Sikhosana, M. (1991) "Civics are Part of the National Democratic Revolution", *Mayibuye,* June.

Nzimande, B. & Sikhosana, M. (1992) "Civil Society and Democracy", *African Communist* #128, First Quarter.

Nzimande, B. & Sikhosana, M. (1992) "'Civil Society' does not Equal Democracy", *Work in Progress,* September.

Petras, J. & Veltmayer, H. (2001) *Globalisation Unmasked: Imperialism in the Twenty-first Century.* London: Zed Press.

Republic of South Africa (1996) *The Constitution of the Republic of South Africa,* Act 108 of 1996, Cape Town.

Sachs, A. (1990) *Protecting Human Rights in a New South Africa.* Cape Town: Oxford University Press.

Seekings, J. (1992) "Civic Organisation in South African Townships." In Moss, G. & Obery, I. (eds) *South African Review 6.* Johannesburg: Ravan Press.

Shubane, K. (1992) "Civil Society in Apartheid and Post-Apartheid South Africa", *Theoria* #79, May.

Shubane, K. & Madiba, P. (1992) "The Struggle Continues? Civic Associations in the Transition", *CPS Transition Series,* Research Report #25. Johannesburg: University of the Witwatersrand Centre for Policy Studies.

South African National Civic Organisation. (1994) *Making People-Driven Development Work.* Johannesburg, April.

Stadler, A. (1992) "A Strong State Civilises Society: A Response to Louw", *Work in Progress,* December.

Summers, L. (1991) "Memo", Office of the World Bank Chief Economist, Washington, December 12, http://www.whirledbank.org

Swilling, M. (1991) "Socialism, Democracy and Civil Society: The Case for Associational Socialism", *Work in Progress,* July/August.

Swilling, M. (1992) "Quixote at the Windmills: Another Conspiracy Thesis from Steven Friedman", *Theoria* #79, May.

World Bank (2000) *Sourcebook on Community Driven Development in the Africa Region: Community Action Programs.* Africa Region, Washington, DC, 17 March.

Part Four
Emerging Trends and Challenges of Governance

11 Towards Developmentalism and Democratic Governance in South Africa

Guy Mhone and Omano Edigheji

Introduction

This book has addressed a number of themes related to the grand *problematique* of how democracy and governance may be consolidated, and sustainable human development promoted in the context of global imperatives calling for economic liberalisation and formal political liberalisation. The contributions in this book range from those with the view that current trends appear to suggest that in the long term the goals of consolidating democracy, effecting good governance, and promoting sustainable human development are being compromised, to those contending that current outcomes are generating a fluid situation with various contradictory outcomes with respect to the goals of democratisation and sustainable human development, which need to be addressed explicitly and resolved satisfactorily. The contributions are relatively unanimous that South Africa currently faces tremendous difficulties in attempting to realise the three goals of moving toward substantive democracy, good governance and equitable growth, as implied by the goal of sustainable human development.

Recent developments in Africa suggest that South Africa is not unique in finding itself in this predicament. A number of African countries have made the transition to formal democracy and have over the past decade and a half embraced neo-liberal economic policies aimed at liberalising and stabilising their economies in accordance with global imperatives. However, current developments suggest that almost all of the countries are finding it difficult to reap the rewards of economic and political liberalisation in the current global environment. For almost all African countries, except Mauritius, poverty levels are increasing, exacerbated by the scourge of HIV/Aids, natural disasters and political conflict.

In some, political conflict has become endemic, while in many others struggles to assert democratic gains won in recent years continue. The evidence from many African countries suggests that the current gains made in the transition to democracy and economic liberalisation are not enough to address the fundamental political and economic problems confronting them. This is the conclusion arrived at in this book with respect to South Africa. The contributors to this book do not believe that all that is needed is a longer time-period within which the anticipated gains can be realised. Rather, the contributors contend that more creative and bolder policies, which are related to democratisation, governance and economic policy, are needed in order to proactively promote substantive democracy and good governance as well as sustainable human development.

Emerging trends in governance and development in South Africa

The struggle by South Africans against apartheid and for democratic governance was undertaken against the background that, in its wake, democratic governance would usher in socio-economic justice by providing access to basic needs such as food, shelter, medical care, housing and education. It was also hoped that democracy would lead to the equitable distribution of income and wealth. Sadly, as we have shown in this volume, while the post-1994 period has led to the promotion and protection of civil and political rights of all South Africans, irrespective of race and gender, governance in the context of economic liberalisation has not translated into development and socio-economic justice. In spite of some of the gains made by the post-apartheid government in terms of increasing access to basic services to all South Africans, those achievements remain limited, given the context in which such policies are being undertaken. Although we do not expect the government to wipe out poverty in the space of ten years, it has been argued that had the government undertaken a different course of action, being a more activist state, South Africa could have maximised the space created by democratic governance. The location of policies within the global orthodoxy of economic liberalisation has resulted in increased poverty and unemployment, coupled with a widening gap within the Black community. Even as this book goes to press, statistics released by Statistics South Africa show that the rate of unemployment is growing. From the existing evidence, we can conclude that the transition to democratic governance has not necessarily lead to development, especially as socio-economic policy is predicated on neo-liberal economic reforms. Therefore, after almost a decade of non-racial multi-party democracy, the horrendous legacy of apartheid continues to exist. As lamented by the president of the South African National NGO Coalition, Lucas Mafumadi (2002):

> Since the introduction of the macro-economic policy GEAR in 1996 the poverty level has grown from bad to worse. Where there is some delivery of basic services such as water and electricity they are no longer affordable to many poor families. This is attributable to the privatisation of basic services by the government, which deepens poverty. The privatisation ... has also resulted in increased retrenchment and high rate of unemployment.

These are not just the words of a die-hard ultra-leftist; as the various chapters in this book have shown, this is the lived reality of the post-1994 period for large segments of the population. In the face of overwhelming evidence to the contrary, the government continues to stress that the "fundamentals are sound". The fundamentals cannot be sound while a great number of South Africans continue to live in abject poverty, stay in hostels and informal settlements, remain unemployed and have no access to the basic social and physical services and infrastructure that are necessary for the protection of their human dignity. Such proclamations tend to predicate the objective of governance in the democratic dispensation on macroeconomic stabilisation, along the lines of the Bretton Woods institutions – the World Bank and the International Monetary Fund. In the view of the contributors to this volume, the soundness of fundamentals must be based on, among other things, the social sustainability of policies.

The adoption of a conventional approach to economic management by the South African government has also brought about an end to "South African exceptionalism", with the consequent normalisation of South Africa as part of the global market orthodoxy (Chapter 8). South Africa is now experiencing similar socio-economic trends to those obtaining in other parts of the African continent. Noting this trend in the rest of the continent, Abrahamsen (2000:133,134) has observed that:

> Although democracy may, at least initially, have expanded the room for political expression, particularly in terms of a more critical press and opportunities for social and industrial protest, the political influence of Africa's newly enfranchised citizens has been highly limited. In particular, demands for socio-economic improvements by the poorer sections of the population have been effectively ruled out a priori ... In this sense, these are exclusionary democracies: they allow for political parties and elections but cannot respond to the demands of the majority or incorporate the masses in any meaningful way.

Economic liberalisation, marked by fiscal restraint, privatisation and commodification, has constrained the capacity of the post-apartheid state to respond to the needs of the majority of the people, while at the same time expanding the rights of private capital as the greatest beneficiary of the post-apartheid period. This has major implications for governance. In the absence of equal opportunities for all to basic essentials for human existence, the equality stressed in liberal democracy is compromised. As African scholars such

as Awa (1991) and Ake (1996) have argued, democracy must be able to deliver some economic empowerment and a higher standard of living for the people. A democracy that
cannot deliver on the basic needs of the people will be short-lived, due to factors to be
highlighted shortly. As in other African countries and most of the developing world, what
is occurring in South Africa is what Abrahamsen calls "exclusionary democracy" or what
may also be referred to as "exclusionary governance". By this is meant that although the
post-1994 period has seen the mushrooming of structures and processes for citizens' participation, the nature of governance is such that it has not been able to respond to and
incorporate the needs and demands of the majority of the poor, who are mostly Blacks
and predominantly Africans. It is our contention that democratic governance and development must go hand in hand, and must be mutually reinforcing.

The importance of socio-economic justice to the sustenance of democratic governance
cannot be overemphasised. Citizens are able to exercise real choice and participate meaningfully and equally only after they have gone beyond poverty, squalor and ignorance.
These problems constitute constraints on freedom and equality. But where inequalities
exist, and where economic reforms are premised on marketisation and commodification
of basic services, consultative and participatory processes and structures can indeed lead
to tensions and can exacerbate conflicts between groups from different socio-economic
strata, as we have seen in the Nedlac case (Chapter 3) and with school governing bodies
(Chapter 6). Such tensions and conflicts threaten the new democracy in South Africa.
Economic liberalisation and formal democracy tend to unravel the incipient contradictions in South African society, which had previously been suppressed under apartheid;
yet, democracy also provides the enabling environment for resolving these very same contradictions. This is the dilemma that South Africa faces.

Despite all the proclamations in favour of democratic governance emanating from the
government, the integration of South Africa into the global economy, based on market
fundamentalism, in both policy terms and intellectual discourse, is such that globalisation
is helping to reproduce a society that is essentially undemocratic. A society in which the
scope for civil society actors, especially civic organisations, trade unions and NGOs to
make an input and to influence the policy agenda and outcomes in favour of the poor and
workers is considerably constrained. This is not to say that citizens watch helplessly as
marketisation erodes the quality of their life through the "privatisation of everything". To
the contrary, as shown in Chapter 10 by Bond and Guliwe, social movements have risen
to challenge the race to the bottom brought about by corporate globalisation. Citizens are
continuously organising and mobilising against the negative effects of globalisation,
although the successes have been modest, in part due to the fragmented nature of civil

society organisations and incipient conflicts among some of them, and in part due to the narrow, single-issue agendas of some. Thus, civil society activism has yet to transform protest into an effective "voice" that can begin to influence a shift toward a developmental stance and outcome in the country. But more importantly, civil society in the post-apartheid period lacks political direction, hence the need to transcend the divide between civil society and political society becomes crucial. As Edigheji (Chapter 3) argues, the current global conjuncture calls for "a different kind of politics", a politics that is based on alliances. Whether this will mean civil society consolidating its alliances with the ruling party, or exploring an alternative route for political mobilisation and assertion, is an issue that may have to be resolved if that part of civil society that "represents" the poor and marginalised seeks to effectively change the direction of policy in South Africa toward developmental outcomes. Civil society must go beyond "protesting on the sideline" to either engaging the government more effectively or to constituting itself into a political force to contest for power.

One other noticeable trend is that the post-1994 period has been marked by the consolidation, in practice, of the hegemony of the interests of the dominant class in South Africa, which, given the history of the country, happens to be predominantly the White business class. Current counsultative structures and processes have further entrenched the interests of this class, while those of the previously disadvantaged communities continue to be marginalised, as highlighted by Edigheji (Chapter 3) and by Habib and Kotzé (Chapter 8). And as shown by Mhone (Chapter 2), there has been no significant reduction in income and wealth inequality along racial lines. In fact, the poor are being further disempowered by the policies emanating from such structures and the resort to "new managerialist" and technocratic policy making. Participatory structures and technocracy have become a means to legitimatise the interests of the dominant groups in society. Ironically, technocracy undermines democratic control over public policy, thereby also reducing its legitimacy, as public participation, parliamentary debates or other consultative mechanisms are sidestepped. In this respect, Mkandawire (1999:123) has observed that:

> in current practice, the formulation and implementation of policies is carried out completely oblivious of the demands of good governance and long-term economic development. Indeed policies are often introduced in isolation from the considerations of political stability or the legitimacy of the authority of elected bodies.

Thus, a major conclusion that can be derived from the various chapters in this book is that democratic governance and economic reforms predicated on market fundamentalism as the dominant logic of globalisation are incompatible and irreconcilable.

It has been contended in this book that, in the face of gross inequalities and relative underdevelopment, economic liberalism has tended to compromise substantive democracy in post-1994 South Africa. This is amply demonstrated by the manner in which the government embarked upon GEAR unilaterally, circumventing democratic processes, because of the likely opposition such measures would generate from the majority of the populace. Thus, consultation, co-operation, consensus seeking and compromise, which are essential elements of governance, are being replaced by nominal consultation, unilateralism and conflict. And even when consultations take place, they serve primarily as information-sharing mechanisms rather than for social partners to make a meaningful input and influence the policy agenda and outcomes. Thus, important policies to integrate the domestic economy into the global economy are being ruled out of the purview and ambit of consultative and consensus-seeking structures. Where consultation takes place around microeconomic issues, the macro environment of economic stabilisation is taken as given and not subject to discussion or consultation. By foreclosing debates on such important political economy issues, the government is undermining a key tenet of governance. As Mkandawire (1999) has rightly argued, "[i]n democracy the outcome of debates cannot be fixed a priori. They are themselves part of democratic contestation". Governance is about debate, contestation of ideas and policies, and about compromises.

As noted in Chapter 3, the recourse to unilateralism has not been limited to the government. In the post-1994 period, all the major social partners, including civil society, trade unions and the business community, have at one point or another resorted to unilateralism without recourse to democratic process. These types of action threaten social and political stability and impede the consolidation of democracy, especially as strikes and other mass protests intensify. Elsewhere in the developing world, in the face of overwhelming mass rejection of the policy of marketisation and commodification, governments have felt compelled to resort to authoritarian measures to suppress the demands of the populace. Abrahamsen (2000:136) has succinctly captured this tendency among exclusionary democracies in Africa, as follows:

> Such exclusionary democracies seem almost doomed to persistent unrest and instability, which in turn may induce authoritarian responses by the beleaguered governments ... the demand for economic liberalization has at the same time impeded the consolidation of democracy. Instead of consolidation, the result has been fragile democracy, often little more than a façade, and this seems an almost inevitable outcome of the pursuit of simultaneous economic liberalization and political liberalism in conditions of poverty and underdevelopment.

The issue is not so much about the sequencing of economic liberalisation and political liberalisation, but rather that democratic governance must be predicated on an overall strategy and accompanying policy aimed at improving the welfare of all citizens, especially the poorest, and not entrenching existing patterns of inequality. For this to occur, the formulation of strategies and polices aimed at promoting sustainable human development needs to be premised on popular participation, that is the participation of citizens in all structures of governance, at all levels, from agenda setting, through policy formulation, to implementation and to evaluation. At the moment, in South Africa, Nedlac has remained the pre-eminent structure of interaction between the social partners, although the Mbeki presidency has established presidential working groups, and there are also the integrated development programmes at the local government level. One weakness of these structures and processes is that there is very little co-ordination between them. Popular participation must be premised on a greater degree of co-ordination in consultation and consensus seeking.

Conclusion

The key issues raised in the book concern: first, the grand *problematique* of the tensions, if not the contradictions, generated by the attempt to pursue formal democracy and liberalise the economy in the context of gross inequalities, pervasive poverty and unemployment in South Africa; second, those pertaining to social partnership and social dialogue; third, those pertaining to the tensions arising from the quest for devolution and decentralisation; fourth, those pertaining to the quest for managerial efficiency in the public sector; fifth, those pertaining to the divisions being precipitated among civil society organisations as they take positions in support of, or against, the current political and economic policy stances of the government; sixth, those pertaining to service delivery and the commodification of services in the quest for cost recovery; seventh those pertaining to gender and governance, democratisation and equitable development; and eighth those pertaining to the uneasy balance between local-level attempts at planning and the overall macroeconomic stance taken by government at the national level. The contributors contend that fundamental problems still remain to be addressed and resolved in all of the foregoing areas if democracy is to be consolidated, good governance promoted and sustainable human development attained in the long term.

Whatever the merits of the arguments made by the various contributors and the conclusions arrived at, there are at least two issues that may not have been adequately addressed in the book, which deserve additional comment. The first issue concerns whether there are any other options apart from those currently being pursued, given the current global order; and the second concerns what alternative policies might consist of at the national and global levels.

With respect to the first issue, the contributors in this book would not support the contention that "there is no alternative" (TINA). The conclusion arrived at by Gasa (Chapter 9) in her comment on mainstreaming gender is apposite in this respect, in that it can be contended that there is a need to deconstruct and reconstruct both the national and global environment in order to create an enabling environment for a developmental agenda to be pursued. The global environment is characterised by various structural patterns that militate against equitable gains between developed and developing countries, and that continue to marginalise the majority of the population in developing countries. These patterns relate to an unequal division of labour or specialisation, unequal capital flows, unequal trade patterns and unequal capacities to exploit the global environment. In the current global environment, developed countries stand in a much better position to take advantage of the opportunities offered than developing economies such as South Africa. In addition, global regulatory, governance and policy regimes are dominated by the interests of developed economies and multinational companies in a manner that severely restricts the ability of developing countries to extract the presumed benefits of the global order.

As noted by Bond and Guliwe (Chapter 10), all of the above constraints are currently being challenged, and it is increasingly recognised, by developed and developing countries alike, that the global environment needs to be readjusted in terms of the structural patterns that underpin unequal gains and that restrict the ability of developing countries to pursue their development agendas to the full. Indeed, the pressure for change in the global environment is being driven by social movements across the globe whose strength and voice continue to expand, while in multilateral forums, governments from the South and sympathetic governments from the North continue to lobby for a more equitable order. Thus, the TINA syndrome in discourses on globalisation needs to be tempered by the potential of social movements from across the globe and national governments from the South to change the global order. A conclusion that arises from this book is that the issue is not so much how a country like South Africa accommodates itself in the global order, nor how it challenges this global order, but rather how South Africa co-operates with other forces at the multilateral level and how social forces within South Africa coalesce with international movements to call for a restructured global order. Indeed, the president of the country has been quite vociferous and vigilant in leading this particular challenge in multilateral forums, while the number of social movements within South Africa that are linking up with international social movements in lobbying for a more just global order is also increasing.

There is a need to challenge the tyranny of neo-liberalism, as reflected in the insistence (through conditionalities tied to loans, foreign direct investment and trade preferences) on economic liberalisation and stabilisation measures by organisations such as the World Bank, International Monetary Fund and the various international groupings dominated by the leading industrial countries. There is a need to challenge the protectionism of developed countries in trade and intellectual property rights. There is need to challenge the restrictions on the mobility of labour internationally, especially from the South to the North. There is a need to convince developed economies to be supportive of developmental initiatives that are aimed at the broadening of the economic base and redefining the position of countries like South Africa in the international division of labour by using heterodox economic policies, other than those advocated by supporters of economic liberalism, such that global outcomes result in positive sum gains for all parties. More generally, there is a need to make global and multilateral institutions more inclusive, democratic and equitable in terms of representation and voice, especially with respect to facilitating the interests of developing countries. Essentially, there is a need for globalisation to be managed and regulated in an equitable and representative manner, in order to promote and support democracy, good governance and sustainable human development. The claim that nothing can be done about de facto global trends and so-called imperatives is a mere succumbing to the whims of monopolistic and oligopolistic elements, which stand to benefit the most from the current order while the interests of the majority are compromised.

The second issue concerns whether alternative policies are possible at the national level and also feasible globally. The contributions in this book suggest that while this issue is a theoretical or policy one, requiring that one propose a coherent and defensible set of alternative theories and associated policies or strategies to the current neo-liberal stance, the issue is also a political one, which simply says that there is not only a need, but there is also an impetus and an imperative to formulate and implement policies that address the needs of the majority globally and within nations such as South Africa if stable societies are to be attained globally and nationally. Thus, just as global restructuring and reordering should reflect the interests of the majority worldwide, so is a restructuring needed at the national level to accommodate the interests of the marginalised and excluded if democracy is to be consolidated, good governance promoted and sustainable human development attained in the long term. For this to occur, a number of issues need to be addressed, as noted in the various contributions in the book.

In this respect, there are at least three issues at stake. The first concerns clarifying the development agenda so that it strengthens the move toward sustainable human development and substantive democracy. The second concerns the need to ensure, through good governance and substantive democracy, that the developmental agenda not only reflects the interests of the majority (most of whom are poor, underemployed and unemployed), but that it is also substantively driven by the majority. The third issue concerns the necessity that a developmental agenda at the national level is complemented by continuous lobbying for a restructured global order.

The developmental agenda has to be premised on the understanding that the current economic environment is biased in favour of a narrow formal sector linked to the global economy. By predicating growth on this sector, a built-in bias against inclusive growth and development is perpetuated. The biases in favour of the formal economy, which militate against the efficacy of anticipated "trickle-down" effects and "boot-straps" approaches to growth and redistribution of neo-liberal policy advocates, encompass fiscal policies, monetary policies, trade policies, the operation for financial and foreign exchange markets, regulatory policies, incentive structures, infrastructure provision, promotion of research and development and so on. These policies are outcomes of past policies and to a large extent are built into the economy and taken for granted, yet they yield the following distortions:

- large-scale bias in enterprise structure, which also militates against SMME growth and development;
- capital intensive bias, which militates against labour-intensive growth;
- a bias toward excess capacity, due to inadequate aggregate demand, given the low effective demand of a significant part of the population;
- a bias toward external dependency regarding markets, savings, investment, skills and technology, due to the lack of an internal momentum to propel growth;
- high import elasticities and low export elasticities of demand; and
- low employment elasticities with respect to output and investment.

The bias is further reinforced by the following outcomes in the non-formal sector, in which most of vulnerable groups reside and work:
- inadequate assets;
- missing or absent value chains;
- underdeveloped value channels;
- high transaction costs;
- unrecognised resource utilisation regimes (indigenous) due to inadequate commodification;
- missing or low levels of social and economic infrastructure;
- demographic pressures; and
- land and environmental pressures.

As a consequence, large segments of the population in the non-formal sector and in low-paying formal sector employment are socially and economically vulnerable, marginalised and prone to poverty.

Regarding the aspect of clarifying the development agenda, a number of contributions in the book have called for the state to reverse the current economic stance by first postulating a developmental or transformation agenda as the primary grand strategy, within which considerations related to stabilisation can be considered as secondary issues. Such a strategy should be aimed at precipitating an inclusive growth path that begins to define endogenously driven development. For South Africa, redistribution of key assets and opportunities of productive employment and income generation has to be a precondition for defining a broadly based growth path as the basis for moving toward sustainable human development. Redistribution cannot be seen simply as an outcome of growth, which can be exclusionary in the absence of exogenous interventions by the state, rather it can be used to redefine the growth path so as to make it more inclusive. One aspect of the development strategy has to be aimed at a conscious desire to develop value channels and value chains that would result in South Africa redefining its status in the international division of labour by moving up the global value chain, but in a manner that supports and is compatible with a broad-based and inclusive growth path. Another aspect concerns the need to formulate and implement proactive policies aimed at broadening the economic base by restructuring the economy in such a way that it becomes more inclusive of the majority.

Proactive measures are needed to address distributive, allocative, microeconomic and dynamic distortions and inefficiencies inherited from the past, which underlie the marginalisation and vulnerability of large segments of the population (Mhone, 2000). Additional measures are needed to decommodify essential services and to ensure a social safety net for all. The government needs to utilise incentives, disincentives and subsidies to steer the economy toward particular developmental outcomes, and to do this in a way that achieves the critical mass of interventions needed to precipitate a virtuous cycle of interaction to lift the economy out of its low-income and low-growth equilibrium trap, in a manner that does not unduly destabilise the economy. The current policy stance is far from achieving the foregoing requirements, since developmental policies stand marginal to stabilisation requirements, which indeed preclude bolder measures to kick-start a dynamic, inclusive growth path that would begin to reduce unemployment, underemployment and poverty. As we are reminded by Gills (2000:10):

> Neither the market nor capital logic ever create equality or social justice automatically. The creation of a just and prosperous society always requires conscious normatively committed human action recognising our moral duty to fellow humanity. Wealth and prosperity are socially determined outcomes and are achieved through fair distribution of resources and social product. Human progress is measured by the achievement of social justice and the elimination of poverty and oppression, not by the unbridled accumulation of private wealth or the naked exercise of power. (Gills, 2000: 10)

In order to ensure that a developmental agenda is driven and underpinned by the people, there is a need for what Edigheji has called a "different kind of politics", through institutionalised participatory and consultative processes. The contributions in this book suggest that while the stipulations built into the Constitution and the various government policies that have been formulated and implemented to date are well meant, a number of weaknesses still remain to be addressed. These are related to the role and status of the executive arm of the state and its bureaucracy, decentralisation and devolution, social partnerships, the capacity of civil society and the role and status of women. In general, state-centric approaches to governance (such as *Batho Pele* and periodic country-wide consultations, *Imbizos*) tend to be narrow in their conceptualisation, and tend to overwhelm society-centric approaches rooted in and driven by civil society. State-centric approaches do not provide an adequate basis for promoting good governance and consolidating democracy in the long term. In this respect, the need for a "hand-in-glove" relationship between the state and civil society is needed, as called for by the notion of embededness. Such embededness needs to entail structures of participation and consultation in an appropriate bottom-up and top-down synergy. Such structures should not necessarily entail co-option of civil society, nor should they mean some artificial harmony of interests among various inherently antagonistic groups within civil society. It merely provides a structured environment for contestation and lobbying, in the hope that through numbers and organisation the majority can assert its interests against those of narrow élites by pushing for a developmental agenda. Thus, this aspect of governance and democratisation is needed to underpin the quest for a developmental agenda and its implementation at national and global levels. In this way, the need for a developmental agenda and its execution are not left to the discretion of an élite, which may decide otherwise based on its own narrow interests, as is currently the case in South Africa.

A final aspect concerns the need to lobby for an appropriately restructured global environment. There are examples of countries (China and Malaysia, for instance) pursuing developmental agendas in spite of global imperatives, indeed against such imperatives. However, there is a need to ensure that (through regional, continental and international forums) the South African government and internal social movements continue to lobby for a restructuring of the global order in a manner that would facilitate the developmental project at the national level, while at the same time proactively exploiting every opportunity at the global level to promote the development agenda. This can be done by undertaking the promotion of productive income generating and employment promoting opportunities, in order to exploit global markets to the degree possible, especially in niche products and services for SMMEs.

The import of the contributions in this book is that it is appreciated that South Africa has embarked upon a promising path through its transition to democracy, and its commitment to good governance and developmentalism, albeit in a fragmented and diffused manner; however, by predicating its main policy stance on the so-called global imperative of economic liberalisation and a narrow preoccupation with formal democracy rather than substantive democracy, the country is compromising the potential for consolidating democracy, promoting good governance and attaining sustainable human development. The contributors call for more proactive policies to challenge the global order, promote inclusive and broad-based growth, and institutionalised participatory and consultative co-operative forms of governance. The contributors contend that in the absence of such a drastic shift, the very goals the government seeks to pursue will remain elusive, and the current policy stance is most likely to threaten the stability and sustainability of the hard-won democratic gains the country now enjoys and cherishes.

References

Abrahamsen, R. (2000) *Disciplining Democracy: Development and Good Governance in Africa.* London: Zed Books.

Ake, C. (1996) *Democracy and Development in Africa.* Ibadan: Spectrum Books Limited.

Awa, E. (1991) "Democracy and Governance in Africa: Preliminary Statement." In Aderinwale, A. & Mosha, F. G. N. (eds) *Democracy and Governance in Africa: Conclusions and Papers Presented at a Conference of the Africa Leadership Forum.* Ota: Africa Leadership Forum.

Gills, B. K. (2000) "Introduction: Globalisation and the Politics of Resistence." In Gills, B. K. *Globalisation and the Politics of Resistance.* New York: Palgrave.

Mafumadi, L. (2002) "President's Overview: Implementation of Grassroots Action for Poverty Eradication", *NGO Matters.* Newsletter of the South African National NGO Coalition. Vol. 7 No. 5. Braamfontein.

Mhone, G. C. Z. (2000) "Enclavity and Constrained Labour Absorptive Capacity in Southern African Economies." ILO/SAMAT Discussion Paper No. 12, Harare.

Mkandawire, T. (1999) "Crisis Management and the Making of 'Choiceless Democracies'." In Joseph, R. *State, Conflict and Democracy in Africa.* Colorado and London: Lynne Rienner Publishers, Inc.

Index

Note: Page numbers in italics refer to Figures and Tables